D1431345

LOEB CLASSICAL LIBRARY

FOUNDED BY JAMES LOEB 1911

EDITED BY
JEFFREY HENDERSON

CALLIMACHUS
I

LCL 421

CALLIMACHUS

AETIA · IAMBI
LYRIC POEMS

EDITED AND TRANSLATED BY

DEE L. CLAYMAN

HARVARD UNIVERSITY PRESS

CAMBRIDGE, MASSACHUSETTS
LONDON, ENGLAND
2022

Library of Congress Control Number 2022904856
CIP data available from the Library of Congress

ISBN 978-0-674-99734-9

*Composed in ZephGreek and ZephText by
Technologies 'N Typography, Merrimac, Massachusetts.
Printed on acid-free paper and bound by
Maple Press, York, Pennsylvania*

CONTENTS

CONTENTS

LYRIC POEMS

These volumes are dedicated with love and gratitude
to my dear husband, Charles Clayman.

PREFACE

It is now just over one hundred years since the first publication of LCL 129 (1921), containing 6 hymns, 64 epigrams, and 272 fragments of Callimachus, along with Lycophron's *Alexandra*, edited and translated by Alexander William Mair, and Aratus' *Phaenomena*, edited and translated by Gilbert Robinson Mair. The texts of the *Hymns* and *Epigrams* benefitted from the third edition (1907) of Wilamowitz's *Callimachi hymni et epigrammata*, but not apparently from Smiley's re-collation and analysis of the manuscripts published in a later series of articles (1920–1921). Mair's edition presents a selection from Schneider's *Callimachea* (1870–1873), augmented by a few papyri recently published at that time, with fragments from the *Aetia* and *Iambi*.[1] With the addition of these papyri, Mair's 1921 text of Callimachus was a great step forward.[2] Though additional papyri continued to appear, no plans were made for an update, until the arrival of the first volume of Pfeiffer's *Callimachus* in 1949. Pfeiffer collected, re-edited, and re-ordered every fragment of the poet's work then

---

[1] *P.Oxy.* 7.1011 (1910), *P.Ryl.* 13 (1911), and *P.Oxy.* 11.1362 (1915), not to mention *P.Rain.* VI published originally in 1893. No papyri with fragments of the *Hymns* had come to light yet.

[2] Unfortunately, Mair was not able to make use of Pfeiffer's *Callimachi fragmenta nuper reperta*, published in the same year.

known, including papyri that had not yet been published. The second volume (1953) contains Pfeiffer's own edition of the *Hymns* and *Epigrams* with a ninety-four page introduction in Latin describing all the sources in detail, as well as the editor's views on various issues, such as dates, attributions, the poet's life, and more. To improve the text of the *Hymns*, he was able to rely on Wilamowitz's fourth edition (1925) and on Smiley (1920–1921). He also recollated most of the manuscripts himself and integrated readings from additional papyri.

After Pfeiffer the need for a new Loeb that could bring the treasures of his edition to a wider audience was clear. By 1953 Mair was long deceased[3] and the project was entrusted to Constantine Trypanis. Since all of Callimachus could no longer fit between one set of covers, the decision was made to publish the fragments in a new volume (LCL 421), but to republish the *Hymns*, *Epigrams*, *Phaenomena*, and *Alexandra* exactly as they appeared in 1921 with a table of variant readings from a few papyri.

Since then, additional important papyri have come to light and a number of modern editions and commentaries have appeared. Among these are the comprehensive editions of D'Alessio (4th ed., 2007) and Asper (2004), as well as texts, translations, and commentaries on the poetic fragments (Durbec 2006), the *Aetia* (Harder 2012; Massimilla 1996 and 2010), the *Hecale* (Hollis 2nd ed., 2009), the *Iambi* (Kerkhecker 1999; Lelli 2005), the *Epigrams* (Gow-Page 1965), the *Hymns* (Stephens 2015), and individual hymns (Bornmann 1968; McLennan 1977; Williams 1978; Hopkinson 1984; Mineur 1984; Bulloch 1985;

---

[3] He died in a fire in 1928 (*The Scotsman*, Nov. 14, 1928).

Manakidou 2013). Additionally, fragments from newly published papyri were collected and edited by Lloyd-Jones and Parsons in the *Supplementum Hellenisticum* (1983).

This new, three-volume Loeb edition offers an up-to-date text incorporating all the improvements and additions since 1921, and a fresh translation, along with notes and introductory materials that reflect the development of scholarship on Hellenistic literature over the past century. It also includes Callimachus' prose fragments, which are absent from Trypanis' edition, and all of the unplaced fragments and fragments of uncertain authorship, which were likewise passed over.

The arrangement of the texts across three volumes was guided by Pfeiffer's choice to follow the order of Callimachus' works in *P.Oxy.* 1011 and the *Diegeseis*, with modifications required by the practicalities of Loeb volume size and page counts. Volume 1 contains the *Aetia*, *Iambi*, and *Lyrics*; volume 2, the *Hecale*, *Hymns*, and *Epigrams*; and volume 3, miscellaneous epics and elegies, other fragments, and testimonia.

Special thanks are due to the Institute for Advanced Study in Princeton, the Advanced Research Collaborative at the Graduate Center of the City University of New York, and the Fondation Hardt for making available to me time, space, and bibliographical support during critical periods in the development of this project. I am also grateful to Annette Harder, Antonios Rengakos, and their colleagues for hosting stimulating conferences in Grongingen and Thessaloniki, where I was able to present some of the ideas and approaches to the text that are found in these

PREFACE

volumes. Especially valuable have been discussions with Peter Bing, Kathryn Gutzwiller, Nita Krevans, and Ludwig Koenen, along with many others too numerous to name.

I also wish to thank my students Keren Freidenreich, Victoria Hsu, Kiran Mansukhani, and Melissa Marturano for their expert proofreading, and Artemida Tesho and Marcia Tucker for their invaluable bibliographical assistance. Jeffrey Henderson, Richard Thomas, and Michael B. Sullivan offered their unflagging support throughout and made many welcome suggestions for improvements.

GENERAL INTRODUCTION

LIFE OF CALLIMACHUS

The outlines of Callimachus' life are clear, but details are lacking and precise dates for his birth and death are controversial. His family originated in Cyrene, an important Greek city on the coast of Libya, but he lived his long, productive life in Alexandria, where he wrote under the patronage of the second and third Ptolemies (T 1 = *Suda* κ 227).

Some of the works that he produced for his royal patrons suggest dates, for example, a poem on the marriage of Ptolemy II to his sister Arsinoe II (*Var.* 392), which took place sometime between 276 and 273/2 BC, and a poem on her death and apotheosis (*Mel.* 228) in 270 or 268 BC.[1] The poet's activity in this decade is also corroborated by references to Philadelphus' victory over Gaulish mercenaries (279/8 BC) in the *Hymn to Delos* (*Hymn* 4.171–89). At a later date his famous "Lock of Berenice" (*Aet.* 110–110f) presupposes the safe return of Ptolemy III from the Third Syrian War in 245 BC, and the "Victoria Berenices" (*Aet.* 54–60) celebrates the Queen's victory at the Nemean games of 245 or 243 BC. Later dates are suggested by

---

[1] On these dates, see Elizabeth Carney, *Arsinoe of Egypt and Macedon* (Oxford: Oxford University Press, 2013), 70, 104.

Callimachus' note in his *Pinakes* that Lysimachus wrote about the education of Attalus (Ath. 6.252c), who became king at Pergamum as early as 241 or as late as 236 BC. And, finally, the Sosibius who is honored by the poet in *Var.* 384 and 384a was probably the notorious minister of Ptolemy IV who was active during the reign of Ptolemy III beginning in the 230s.[2] A range of dates for the poet's life might then be 303 to 235 BC, though some put his birth a decade earlier.[3]

CYRENE

Callimachus demonstrates his pride in his Cyrenean heritage directly in his poetry. For example, he asserts his ancestral connection to Apollo Carneius, the Doric Apollo who had cults at Cyrene's mother cities, Sparta and Thera, while narrating the city's foundation story (*Hymn* 2.65–96). Its founder was Battus, who followed an oracle of Apollo and overcame daunting challenges to bring his party of colonists to North Africa in the middle of the seventh century BC.[4] It is this Battus whom Callimachus

---

[2] If the poem was for the elder Sosibius, who was a minister of Ptolemy I, Callimachus would have started his career before the king's death in 282 BC.

[3] This range of dates was proposed by Luigi Lehnus, "Riflessioni cronologiche sull'ultimo Callimaco," *ZPE* 105 (1995): 6–12. Evidence for an earlier birthdate has been found in some enigmatic lines in the *Hymn to Zeus* (*Hymn* 1.57–66). On this, see the discussion of the hymn in volume 2.

[4] The story is also told by Herodotus, who reports both a Theran (Hdt. 4.150–53) and a Cyrenean version (Hdt. 4.154–58), and by Pindar (*Pyth.* 4.17–63, 9.1–75).

claims as an ancestor when he says in his own mock-epitaph (*Epig.* 35 = *Anth. Pal.* 7.415),

> You are walking beside the tomb of a son of Battus
> who knew song well, and over wine how to laugh at
> the right moments.

Since the Battiad line disappeared in the middle of the fifth century, it is unlikely that this is literally true, but rather a way to suggest common cause with Berenice II, the wife of Ptolemy III, who was also born in Cyrene and whose father had declared himself king, i.e., a new Battus.

Even if Callimachus was not strictly speaking a Battiad, there is evidence that he was a scion of the Cyrenean aristocracy. Another of his mock-epitaphs claims that the poet's father is the son of another Callimachus who "commanded the arms of his country" (*Epig.* 21 = *Anth. Pal.* 7.525). The grandfather's name, as well as those of his two sons and a brother, appear on inscriptions found in Cyrene that attest to their high civil and military status.[5] Callimachus' social standing, then, explains how he came to the household of the Ptolemies as a "young man of the court,"[6] that is, a page, and stayed to write poetry for the royal family. An alternative version in the *Suda* says that he

---

[5] SEG IX 1.84, 87. The evidence is evaluated in A. Cameron, *Callimachus and His Critics* (Princeton: Princeton University Press, 1995), 7–9, and in André Laronda, *Cyrène et la Libye hellénistique* (Paris: Éditions CNRS, 1987), 95–128.

[6] Tzetzes, *De comoedia. Gr. Prooem.* II (W. Koster, *Scholia in Aristophanem*, pars 1[Groningen & Amsterdam, 1975], p. 32) = Call. T 14c.

began his career as a schoolteacher, but this is an often repeated insult here misread as biography.[7]

ALEXANDRIA AND ATHENS

Callimachus spent his professional life in Alexandria, and it used to be said that he never left the city,[8] but an Athenian inscription dated about 247 BC lists a certain Callimachus among contributors to a fund in support of the latter polity.[9] If this is the poet he would have been at Athens just before the accession of Ptolemy III and would have found his countryman Eratosthenes there. Eratosthenes of Cyrene, the mathematician, poet, and polymath, who is called Callimachus' student, came to Alexandria the subsequent year to take his place as head librarian.[10] Whether

---

[7] *Suda* K 227 Adler. Other examples of insulting rivals by calling them schoolteachers are Demosthenes against Aeschines (Dem. *De cor.* 129, 258), Nausiphanes against Epicurus (Diog. Laert. 10.8), Epicurus against Protagoras (Diog. Laert. 10.8), Timon of Philus against Epicurus (825 *SH* = 51 Diels), and Callimachus himself in *Iamb* 5 (*Ia.* 195), where his unnamed target is characterized as a lascivious schoolteacher.

[8] Trypanis, viii, n. c. This "fact" is based on an overreading of *Aet.* 178.32, where a merchant from Icos congratulates the narrator on a life untroubled by the dangers of seafaring. The risk of traveling by sea is a common literary trope that can be found elsewhere, including in Callimachus' own epigrams (*Epig.* 17, 18). On earlier literary precedents and metaphorical meanings of the trope, see Harder vol. 2, 985–86.

[9] G. J. Oliver, "Callimachus the Poet and the Benefactor of the Athenians," *ZPE* 140 (2002): 6–8.

[10] *Suda* ε 2898; *P.Oxy.* 1241. In ancient biographies, a student/teacher relationship often indicates only relative ages.

or not Callimachus ever traveled to Athens, his enduring interest in the city is clear from the detailed knowledge of Attic myth and cult that informs his *Hecale*.

THE LIBRARY

Under the patronage of the Ptolemies, Alexandria became a center for research and writing that attracted intellectual talent from far and wide. There the famous Library and Museum provided an infrastructure and probably support for the work of collecting, organizing, and editing texts, systematizing knowledge, and pursuing scientific discoveries. Though little is known about how these institutions operated, Callimachus was at home in them, and much of his voluminous writing—the *Suda* estimates an incredible eight hundred volumes—were works of nonfiction in prose. Judging from their titles, which is all that is left of them, they covered a wide variety of topics, such as *On Winds* (*Fr. Doct.* 404), *Barbarian Customs* (405), *On Nymphs* (413), *On Birds* (414–28), *Foundations of Islands and Cities and Their Changes of Name* (412a), not to mention collections of paradoxes, glosses, and more.[11] The fruits of Callimachus' research are evident in the *Aetia*, the *Hecale*, and his other poetry, which is enriched with specialized knowledge of all kinds.

The most important of Callimachus' scholarly works were the *Pinakes*, or *Index of All Those Preeminent in Literature and of Their Writings in 120 Books* (*Fr. Doct.*

---

[11] Nita Krevans, "Callimachus' Philology," in *Brill's Companion to Callimachus*, ed. Benjamin Acosta-Hughes, Luigi Lehnus, and Susan Stephens (Leiden: Brill, 2011), 118–33.

429–53). These, too, have been lost, but references in later literature indicate that they were organized by genre and in each category the authors' names were arranged alphabetically. Their works were listed by title and grouped by subcategories where relevant, like the *Odes* of Pindar, which were organized as they still are today by the location of the contest. Callimachus also added biographical details about the authors, the opening verses, and line counts. The *Pinakes* have been described as a catalog for the great Library, but Callimachus never held the post of head librarian (*P.Oxy.* 1241), and it is better to think of them as a kind of "national bibliography."[12] Nothing of this sort and this scale had ever been attempted before, and it is proof of Callimachus' breadth of learning and attention to detail, as well as his encyclopedic knowledge of Greek literature. His learning is apparent in almost every line of his verse, which incorporates and reworks the language of his predecessors in inventive and expressive ways.

STYLISTIC AND LITERARY CRITICISM

Callimachus' interest in literary language extended to issues of style as well, and he is unique among Greek poets for the spirited defense of his stylistic values directly in the body of his poetry. The most well-known example is the prologue to his elegiac *Aetia*, where he defends

---

[12] Blum 1991, 239. The *Suda* also attributes to Callimachus a separate *Index of the Glosses and Writings of Democritus* (*Fr. Doct.* 456; cf. T 1 on the list of Works), and an *Index and Register of the Dramatic Poets in Order from the Beginning* (*Fr. Doct.* 454–56).

the principles of brevity, clarity, lightness, sweetness, and creativity against the mythical Telchines, wizards and iron workers whose art produced cacophony. He also treats the subject in the first and the thirteenth *Iambi* (*Ia.* 191 and 203), at the conclusion of his *Hymn to Apollo*, and in some of the epigrams as well (*Epig.* 27, 28).[13] By creating vivid dramatic settings for his pronouncements on style, Callimachus invites his readers, both ancient and modern, to understand his artful straw men as contemporary poets and critics, and so they have. The epic poet Apollonius of Rhodes has been most frequently named as his literary rival, but Apollonius' stylistic goals seem close if not identical to Callimachus', and it is hard to credit the stories of their conflict found in Apollonius' ancient *Lives* and in the scholia.[14] Other evidence has been cited from passages of poetry where Apollonius, Aratus, and Theocritus seem to rework Callimachus' verses in their own compositions. In these instances, it is difficult for modern readers to be certain who is borrowing from whom, and whether this practice is intended as criticism or homage.[15]

[13] Also there is critical intent in a few unassigned comments, such as "a big book is the same as a big evil" (*Fr. Doct.* 465), and a complaint that Antimachus' *Lyde* is "a thick book and unclear" (*Epig.* 6).

[14] On the unreliable evidence, Mary Lefkowitz, *The Lives of the Greek Poets*, 2nd ed. (Baltimore: The Johns Hopkins University Press, 2012), 113–21.

[15] Adolf Köhnken, "Hellenistic Chronology: Theocritus, Callimachus, and Apollonius Rhodius," in *A Companion to Apollonius Rhodius*, ed. T. Papanghelis and A. Rengakos (Leiden: Brill, 2001), 73–92.

WORKS

In addition to Callimachus' prose treatises, the *Suda* lists poetic works that have left no trace. These include genres such as tragedies, comedies, and satyr plays, as well as specific titles such as *Ibis*, *Io*, *Semele*, and so on. Conversely, it is silent on works from which we have substantial fragments, including the *Aetia* (a "catalogue elegy" in four books); the *Iambi*; lyric poems;[16] and his epic *Hecale*, as well as others extant in one or only a few fragments. Papyrus evidence suggests that an edition of his collected works, or more likely a selection of them, was assembled by the poet himself, but it also appears that some of its components circulated independently, such as "The Lock of Berenice" (*Aet.* 110–110f)."[17] Only the *Hymns* and sixty-three epigrams have come down for the most part intact through the medieval manuscript tradition. The rest are fragments gathered from papyri and citations in the work of ancient scholars. These have been painstakingly assembled by generations of scholars beginning in 1489, when Ianus Politianus published the first fragments and testimonia of the *Hecale* in his *Miscellanea*. The history of the constitution of the text is told in Pfeiffer vol. 2, xliii–l, and in the introductions to individual works.

16 Pfeiffer used the title *Melē* for the four lyric poems that come between the *Iambi* and the *Hecale* in the *Diegeseis* (*Mel.* 226–29), but they may be poems 14 through 17 of the *Iambi*. See, for example, Lelli 2005, 1–80.

17 Evidence for "The Lock's" circulation as an occasional poem is provided by *P.Oxy.* 2258. The case for a collected edition was first made by Pfeiffer vol. 2, xxxvi–xxxviii, and revised by P. Parsons, "Callimachus' *Victoria Berenices*," *ZPE* 25 (1977): 1–50.

THE *DIEGESEIS* AND SCHOLIA

The work of modern scholars in reconstituting and interpreting Callimachus' *oeuvre* is indebted to ancient scholarship, particularly to the *Diegeseis*. These are summaries of a collection of Callimachus' works on a papyrus produced between the second half of the first century and the first half of the second century AD and found in Tebtynis in 1934.[18] They include summaries of various lengths and the first lines of individual *aitia* from the last part of Book 3, all of Book 4, the thirteen *Iambi*, four "lyric" poems, the *Hecale*, and the *Hymns to Zeus* and *Apollo*. They were apparently intended as an aid to ancient readers and have been essential in determining the order of many fragments. In addition, scholia of various levels of sophistication were copied into the margins of some of the manuscripts and papyri. These are included as text and fully translated in what follows.

THIS EDITION

The Greek text of this edition is based on Pfeiffer's, enriched by papyri published since 1953 and the judgment of later editors. The notes on the text do not constitute a full apparatus, but give the reader additional information about textual difficulties and variants that affect the interpretation of the text. The English translation has no literary pretensions, but is intended to help readers make their way through the Greek and to give a sense of Callimachus' art without attempting to reproduce it. The notes to the

[18] *P.Mil.Vogl.* See Vogliano 1937.

translation explain the often recherché names and place-names in which the poet delights and offer other useful information about his sources. For the most part, the references in the notes are to other ancient texts, many of which are available in the Loeb Classical Library.

THE CITATION OF CALLIMACHUS

The texts of the *Hymns* and *Epigrams* in this edition follow Pfeiffer's numbering system, as do all of the fragments except those of the *Hecale*, which follow Hollis' second edition (2009), and the *Aetia*, which follow Harder (2012). In adding new fragments, I follow Harder's system of preserving Pfeiffer's numbers by designating the new fragments with letters. As for the rest, I divide the fragments into sections following Pfeiffer, but with some minor changes of title and arrangement. *Melē* (*Mel.* 226–29) remains the same, but *Epica et elegiaca minora* has become *Carmina epica et elegiaca varia* (*Var.* 378–92); *Fragmenta epigrammatum* (393–402 Pf.) are now printed directly after the *Epigrams* and renumbered (*Fr. Epig.* 1–10); *Fragmenta grammatica* have been rechristened *Fragmenta docta* (*Fr. Doct.* 403–66). *Fragmenta incertae sedis* (*Fr. Inc. Sed.* 467–725) and *Fragmenta incerti auctoris*[19] (*Fr. Inc. Auct.* 726–814) are unchanged. The fragments are designated by the title of the poem for the *Aetia* and *Iambi* or the section name followed by the fragment number, for example, *Aet.* 10; *Fr. Doct.* 450; and so on. "Fr." does not precede these numbers, because except for

[19] Including the *Dubia*.

the *Hymns* and *Epigrams*, nothing of Callimachus remains except fragments.

A concordance to the fragments of the *Aetia* along with concordances linking the fragment numbers of the *Hecale* in this edition to Pfeiffer's and the numbers of the *Epigrams* to Gow-Page (1965) is provided at the end of volume 3.

ABBREVIATIONS

PAPYRI

BKT   *Berliner Klassikertexte*. Hermann Diels,
                 Wilhelm Schubart, et al., eds. Berlin,
                 1904–.

P.Amh.   *The Amherst Papyri*. Edited by Bernard
                 P. Grenfell and Arthur S. Hunt. 2 vols.
                 London, 1900–1901.

P.Ant.   *The Antinoopolis Papyri*. Colin H. Rob-
                 erts et. al., eds. 3 vols. London, 1950–
                 1966.

P.Bodl.   *Papyri at the Bodleian Library, Oxford*.
                 Ms. Gr. class. f. 109 (P)^r. Readings in
                 Pf.

P.Cair.   *Greek Papyri, Catalogue général des an-
                 tiquités égyptiennes du Musée du
                 Caire*: N°s 10,001–10,869. Edited by
                 Bernard P. Grenfell and Arthur S.
                 Hunt. Oxford, 1903.

P.Fay.Coles   Coles, Revel. "New Literary and Sub-
                 Literary Fragments from the Fayum."
                 *Zeitschrift für Papyrologie und
                 Epigraphik* 6 (1970): 247–66.

ABBREVIATIONS

P.Gen.	*Les Papyrus de Genève.* Edited by Paul Schubert et al. Vol. 3. Bibliothèque de Genève, 1996.
P.Mich.	*Papyri in the University of Michigan Collection.* Edited by Campbell C. Edgar et al. Ann Arbor, MI, 1931–.
P.Mil.Vogl.	*Papiri della R. Università di Milano.* Edited by Achille Vogliano. Milan, 1937.
P.Montserrat	*Greek Papyri from Montserrat (P.Monts. Roca IV).* Edited by Sofia T. Tovar and Klaas A. Worp. Barcelona, 2014.
P.Oxy.	*The Oxyrhynchus Papyri.* Edited by Bernard P. Grenfell, Arthur S. Hunt, et al. 80 vols. London: Egypt Exploration Society, 1898–.
P.Rain.	Papyri in the "Papyrus Erzherzog Rainer" Collection of the Nationalbibliothek, Vienna.
P.Ryl.	*Catalogue of the Greek and Latin Papyri in the John Rylands Library, Manchester.* Edited by Arthur S. Hunt et al. Manchester, 1911–.
PSI	*Papiri greci e latini* (Pubblicazioni della Società Italiana per la ricerca dei papiri greci e latini in Egitto). Edited by Girolamo Vitelli, Medea Norsa, et al. Florence, 1912–.

LEXICA

Epim. Hom.	Dyck, Andrew, ed. *Epimerismi Homerici.* Berlin, 1983–1995.

ABBREVIATIONS

Et. Gud.	*Etymologicum Gudianum.* A-ζειαί. In *Etymologicum Gudianum*, edited by Eduardo L. De Stefani. 2 vols. Leipzig, 1909–1920; repr., Amsterdam, 1965. Also, Sturz, Freidrich, ed. *Etymologicum Graecae linguae Gudianum et alia grammaticorum scripta*. Leipzig, 1818; repr., Hildersheim, 1973.
Et. Mag.	*Etymologicum Magnum.* α-β. In *Etymologicon magnum: seu verius lexicon* . . . , edited by L.-L. and Thomas Gaisford. Oxford, 1948.
L.-L.	François Lasserre, and Nikolaos Livadaras, eds. *Etymologicum magnum genuinum: Symeonis etymologicum una cum Magna grammatica; Etymologicum magnum auctum*. Rome, 1976–.
Suda	Adler, Ada, ed. *Suidae Lexicon*. 5 vols. Leipzig, 1928–1938.

SCHOLIA

Eust.	Van der Valk, Marchinus. *Eustathii archiepiscopi Thessalonicensis commentarii ad Homeri Iliadem perinentes*. Leiden, 1971–1987.
Schol. ad Ap. Rhod.	Wendel, Karl. *Scholia in Apollonium Rhodium Vetera*. Berlin, 1935.
Schol. ad Dion. Thrax	Pecorella, Giovan. *Dionisio Trace: Techne Grammaike*. Bologna, 1962.

ABBREVIATIONS

Schol. ad Dionys. Per.	Bernhardy, Gottfried. *Dionysius Periegetes Graece et Latine*. Leipzig, 1828.
Schol. ad Eur.	Schwartz, Eduard. *Scholia in Euripidem*. Berlin, 1887–1891.
Schol. ad Hom. *Il*.	Erbse, Hartmut. *Scholia graeca in Homeri Iliadem*. Berlin, 1969–1988.
	Van Thiel, Helmut. *Scholia D in Iliadem*. Online only, 2000.
Schol. ad Lyc. *Alex*.	Scheer, Eduard. *Lycophronis Alexandra*. Vol. 2. Berlin, 1908.
Schol. ad Ov. *Ib*.	Ellis, Robinson P. *Ovidii Nasonis Ibis: Ex novis codicibus edidit scolia vetera*. Cambridge, 2013.
Schol. ad Paus.	Spiro, Friedrich. *Pausaniae Graeciae Descriptio*. Vol. 3. Lepizig, 1903.
Schol. ad Pind.	Drachmann, Anders. *Scholia vetera in Pindari carmina*. Leipzig, 1903.
Schol. ad Thuc.	Hude, Karl. *Scholia in Thucydidem ad optimos codices collata*. Leipzig, 1927.

TEXTS

AB	Austin, Colin, and Guido Bastianini, eds. *Posidippi Pellaei quae supersunt omnia*. Milan, 2002.
Anth. Pal.	*Anthologia Palatina*. Edited by Hermann Beckby. 4 vols. Munich, 1957.

ABBREVIATIONS

AO	Cramer, John A. *Anecdota Graeca e codd. manuscriptis bibliothecarum Oxoniensis* II. Oxford, 1835; repr., Amsterdam, 1963.
BNJ	*Brill's New Jacoby*. Edited by Ian Worthington. Online edition of Felix Jacoby, *Die Fragmente der griechischen Historiker* (FGH). Berlin, 1923–1958.
Dieg.	Norsa, Medea, and Girolamo Vitelli, eds. *Diegeseis di poemi di Callimacho: in un papiro di Tebtynis*. Florence, 1934.
DK	Diels, Hermann, and Walther Kranz, eds. *Die Fragmente der Vorsokratiker*. Rev. 6th ed. Berlin, 1951–1952.
FGrH	Jacoby, Felix. *Die Fragmente der griechischen Historiker*. See *BNJ*.
FHG	Müller, Karl. *Fragmenta Historicorum Graecorum*. Paris, 1841–1870.
FRL	*Fragmentary Republican Latin: Ennius*. Edited by Sander M. Goldberg and Gesine Manuwald. Cambridge, MA, 2018.
G.-P.	Gow, Andrew S. F., and Denys Page, eds. *The Greek Anthology: Hellenistic Epigrams*. 2 vols. Cambridge, 1965.
Gramm. Gr.	*Grammatici Graeci*. Lepzig, 1867–1910; repr., Hildersheim, 1965.

iii.i: *Herodiani technici reliquae.* August Lentz, ed., 1868–1870. iv.i and iv.ii: *Theodosii Georgii Choerobosci scholia, Sophronii Patriarchae Alexandrini excerpta.* Alfred Hilgard, ed., 1889 and 1894.

K.-A.   Kassel, Rudolf, and Colin Austin. *Poetae Comici Graeci.* Berlin, 1983–.

L.-L.   Lasserre, François, and Nikolaos Livadaras, eds. *Etymologicum magnum genuinum: Symeonis etymologicum una cum Magna grammatica; Etymologicum magnum auctum.* Rome, 1976–.

M.-W.   Merkelbach, Reinhold, and Martin L. West, eds. *Fragmenta Hesiodea.* 3rd ed. Oxford, 1990.

OGIS   Dittenberger, Wilhelm. *Orientis Graeci Inscriptiones Selectae.* Leipzig: Georg Olms, 1903.

Powell   Powell, John U., ed. *Collectanea Alexandrina.* Oxford, 1915.

RE   Pauly, August F. von, Georg Wissowa, and Wilhelm Kroll, eds. *Paulys Realencyclopädie der classischen Altertumswissenschaft.* 34 vols. in 68 with index and 15 suppl. Stuttgart, 1894–1978.

SH   Lloyd-Jones, Hugh, and Peter Parsons, eds. *Supplementum Hellenisticum.* Berlin, 1983.

ABBREVIATIONS

S.-M.	Snell, Bruno, and Herwig Maehler. *Pindari carmina*, Pars II: Fragmenta. Leipzig, 1975.
Steph. Byz.	Billerbeck, Margarethe, et al. *Stephani Byzantii Ethnica*. Berlin, 2006–2017.
TrGF	Snell, Bruno, Richard Kannicht, and Stefan Radt. *Tragicorum Graecorum Fragmenta*. Göttingen, 1971–ca. 2004.

REFERENCES

SIGNIFICANT EARLY EDITIONS
OF CALLIMACHUS

Pol.
: Politian (Angelo Ambrogini). *Miscellanea centuriae primae ad Laurentium Medicem*, ch. LXXX. Florence, 1489. Editio princeps of *Hymn 5* with a Latin translation.

La.
: Ianos Lascaris. Καλλιμάχου Κυρηναίου ὕμνοι. Florence, 1494–1498. Editio princeps of text and scholia.

Ald.
: Aldus Manutius. *Pindari Olympia, Pythia, Nemea, Isthmia. Callimachi hymni qui inveniuntur. Dionysii de situ orbis. Lycophronis Alexandra.* Venice, 1513.

Vasc.
: Michel de Vascosan. *Callimachi hymni cum scholiis.* Paris, 1549.

Steph. 1566
: Henricus Stephanus (Henri Estienne). *In Corpus Poetarum Graecorum Principium Heroici Carminis et Alii Nonnulli.* Paris, 1566.

REFERENCES

Steph. 1577   Henricus Stephanus (Henri Estienne).
               *Callimachi Cyrenaei hymni (cum
               suis scholiis graecis et epigram-
               mata)*. Geneva, 1577. With Nicode-
               mus Frischlin's translation. About
               one hundred years later, Thomas
               Stanley wrote his own notes into the
               margins of a copy now in the British
               Museum.

Vulcanius   Bonaventura Vulcanius. *Callimachi
               Cyrenaei hymni, epigrammata et
               fragmenta quae exstant*. Antwerp,
               1584. With notes.

Fabri   Anne Lefebvre (Mme. Dacier). *Calli-
               machi Cyrenaei hymni, epigram-
               mata et fragmenta*. Paris, 1675. With
               notes.

Graevius   Theodore J. G. F. Graevius. *Callimachi
               hymni, epigrammata et fragmenta ex
               recensione Theodori J.G.F. Graeuii
               cum eiusdem animauersionibus*.
               Utrecht, 1697. With contributions
               from Frischlin, Stephanus, Vulca-
               nius, Voetius, Fabri, Richard Bent-
               ley, and Spanheim.

Bentley   Bentley, Thomas . *Callimachi hymni et
               epigrammata: quibus accesserunt
               Theognidis carmina: nec non epi-
               grammata centum septuaginta sex ex
               Anthologia Græca: quorum magna
               pars non ante separatim excusa est.*

REFERENCES

	His adjuncta est Galeni suasoria ad artes. London, 1741.
Ernesti	Ernesti, Johann A. *Callimachi hymni, epigrammata et fragmenta, cum notis integris H. Stephani, B. Vulcanii, Annae Fabri, Th. Graevii, R. Bentleji; quibus accedunt Ezechielis Spanhemii commentarii, et notae nunc primum editae Tiberii Hemsterhusii et Davidis Ruhnkenii.* Leiden, 1761. With Latin translation and his own notes.
Brunck	Brunck, Richard F. Ph. *Analecta uetera poetarum graecorum.* Strasbourg, 1772–1776.
van Santen	van Santen, Laurens. *Callimachi Hymnus in Apollinem, cum emendationibus ineditis Lud. Casp. Valckenaerii et interpretatione Laur. Santenii.* Leiden, 1787.
Ruhnken	Ruhnken, David. *David. Ruhnkenii, Lud. Casp. Valckenaerii, et aliorum ad Joh. Aug. Ernesti epistolae. Accedunt Dav. Ruhnkenii Observationes in Callimachum.* Leipzig, 1812.
Blom.	Blomfield, Charles J., ed. *Callimachi quae supersunt.* London, 1815.
Boiss.	Boissonade, Jean-François, ed. *Callimachus, Cleanthes, Proclus.* Paris, 1824.
Hecker	Hecker, Alphons. *Commentationum*

REFERENCES

	Callimachearum capita duo. PhD diss. Groningen, 1842.
Naeke	Naekii, Augustii Ferdinandi. *Opuscula philologica collegit et disposuit Augustus Ferdinandus Naeke*. Bonn, 1845.
Meineke	Meineke, Augustus, ed. *Callimachi Cyrenensis: Hymni et epigrammata*. Berlin, 1861.
Schneider	Schneider, Otto, ed. *Callimachea*. 2 vols. Leipzig, 1870–1873.

MODERN EDITIONS AND COMMENTARIES

Asper	Asper, Marcus, ed. and trans. *Kallimachos Werke*. Darmstadt: Wissenschaftliche Buchgesellschaft, 2004.
Bornmann	Bornmann, Fritz, ed. and comm. *Hymnus in Dianam*. Florence: "La nuova Italia," 1968.
Bulloch	Bulloch, Anthony W., ed., comm., trans. *Callimachus: The Fifth Hymn*. Cambridge: Cambridge University Press, 1985.
Cahen	Cahen, Émile, ed. and trans. *Callimaque*: *Épigrammes, Hymnes*. 3rd ed. Paris: Les Belles Lettres, 1953.
D'Alessio 1996	D'Alessio, Giovan Battista, ed. and trans. Vol. 1, *Callimaco: Inni, Epigrammi, Ecale*. Vol. 2, *Callimaco:*

REFERENCES

Aitia, Giambi e altri frammenti. Milan: BUR, 1996.

D'Alessio 2007 ———, ed. and trans. Vol. 1, *Callimaco: Inni, Epigrammi, Ecale*. Vol. 2, *Callimaco: Aitia, Giambi e altri frammenti*. 4th ed. Milan: BUR, 2007.

Durbec Durbec, Yannick. *Callimaque, Fragments poétique*. Origins, Iambes, Hécalè, fragments de poèmes élégiaques, fragments de place incertaine. Paris: Les Belles Lettres, 2006.

Gigante Lanzara Gigante Lanzara, Valeria. *Callimaco: Inno a Delos*. Pisa: Giardini, 1984.

Harder Harder, M. Annette, ed., trans., comm. *Callimachus: Aetia*. 2 vols. Oxford: Oxford University Press, 2012.

Hollis Hollis, Adrian S., ed., trans., comm. *Callimachus: Hecale*. 2nd ed. Oxford: Oxford University Press, 2009.

Hopkinson Hopkinson, Neil, ed., comm., trans. *Callimachus: Hymn to Demeter*. Cambridge: Cambridge University Press, 1984.

Kapp Kapp, Ida, ed. *Callimachi Hecalae Fragmenta*. Phd diss. Berlin, 1915.

Kerkhecker Kerkhecker, Arnd, comm. *Callimachus' Book of Iambi*. Oxford: Oxford University Press, 1999.

Lelli Lelli, Immanuel, ed., comm., trans.

Callimachi: Iambi XIV–XVII. Rome: In aedibus Athenaei, 2005.

Mair   Mair, Alexander W., ed. and trans. *Callimachus: Hymns and Epigrams, Lycophron. Aratus*, ed. and trans. by Gilbert R. Mair. Loeb Classical Library. Cambridge, MA: Harvard University Press, 1921.

Manakidou   Manakidou, Flora P. (Μανακίδου, Φλώρα Π.), ed., comm., trans. Καλλίμαχος: Εἰς λουτρὰ τῆς Παλλάδος. Athens: Daidalos, 2013.

Massimilla 1996   Massimilla, Giulio, ed., comm., trans. *Aitia: Libri primo e secondo*. Pisa: Giardini, 1996.

Massimilla 2010   ———, ed., comm., trans. *Aitia: Libro terzo e quarto*. Pisa: Serra, 2010.

McLennan   McLennan, George R. *Callimachus: Hymn to Zeus: Introduction and Commentary*. Rome: Ateneo & Bizzarri, 1977.

Mineur   Mineur, Wilhelmus H. *Callimachus: Hymn to Delos: Introduction and Commentary*. Leiden: Brill, 1984.

Pfeiffer 1921   Pfeiffer, Rudolf, ed. *Callimachi fragmenta nuper reperta*. Bonn: Marcus & Weber, 1921.

Pf.   ———, ed. *Callimachus*. 2 vols. Oxford: Clarendon Press, 1949–1953.

Stephens   Stephens, Susan A., ed., trans., comm. *Callimachus: The Hymns*. Oxford: Oxford University Press, 2015.

REFERENCES

Trypanis — Trypanis, Constantine. *Callimachus: Aetia, Iambi, Hecale, and Other Fragments. Musaeus: Hero and Leander*, edited by Thomas Gelzer and translated by Cedric Whitman. Loeb Classical Library. Cambridge, MA: Harvard University Press, 1958.

Wilamowitz — Wilamowitz-Moellendorff, Ulrich von, ed. *Callimachi hymni et epigrammata*. 4th ed. Berlin: Weidmann, 1925.

Williams — Williams, Frederick, ed. and comm. *Callimachus: Hymn to Apollo, a Commentary*. Oxford: Clarendon Press, 1978.

OTHER TEXTUAL STUDIES AND USEFUL REFERENCES

Editions of scholia are listed in Eleanor Dickey, *Ancient Greek Scholarship* (Oxford: Oxford University Press, 2007).

Barber — Barber, Eric A. "Review: *The Hymns and Epigrams of Callimachus*." *Classical Review* N.S. 4 (1954): 227–30.

Boissonade — Boissonade, Jean-François, ed. *Callimachus, Cleanthes, Proclus*. Paris: Lefevre, 1824.

Buttmann — Buttmann, Philipp. "Über die Fabel der Kydippe." *Mémoir. Acad. Munich* 9 (1823–24): 199–216.

REFERENCES

De Jan   De Jan, Friedrich. *De Callimacho Ho-*
                meri interprete. PhD diss. Strass-
                burg: Argentorati, 1893.
Dilthey   Dilthey, Carolus. *De Callimachi Cy-*
                dippa. Leipzig: Teubner, 1863.
Hermann   Hermann, Gottfried. *Dissertatio de*
                loco Callimachi Hymni in Delum et
                quibusdam epigrammatis. Leipzig,
                1847.
Kuiper   Kuiper, Koenraad. *Studia Callimachea*.
                Vol. I. Leiden: Sijhoff, 1896.
Lehnus 2000   Lehnus, Luigi. *Nuova bibliografia cal-*
                limachea (1489–1998). Alessandria:
                Edizioni dell'Orso, 2000.
Lehnus 2011   ———. "Callimachus Rediscovered in
                Papyri." In *Brill's Companion to*
                Callimachus, edited by Benjamin
                Acosta-Hughes and Susan Stephens,
                23–38. Leiden: Brill, 2011.
Livrea   Livrea, Enrico. "Callimaco et la Beozia
                (*Suppl. Hell.* Fr. 257, 1–8: Lav. Pall.
                61)." *ZPE* 67 (1987): 31–36.
Lobel   Lobel, Edgar, et. al., eds. *The Oxy-*
                rhynchus Papyri. Part XIX (2208–
                2244). London: Egypt Exploration
                Society, 1948.
Maas   Maas, Paul. *Textual Criticism*. Oxford:
                Clarendon Press, 1958.
Meineke 1823   Meineke, Augustus. *Menandri et Phile-*
                monis reliquiae. Berlin: Mylius,
                1823.

REFERENCES

Meineke 1843   ——. *Analecta Alexandrina* . . . Berlin: Mylius, 1843.

Meineke 1847   ——. *Fragmenta comicorum Graecorum: Fragmenta poetarum comoediae antiquae.* Berlin: Reimeri, 1847.

Reitzenstein   Reitzenstein, Richard. "Inedita Poetarum Graecorum Fragmenta." *Index Lectionum in Academia Rostochiensi* (1890/1): 1–18.

Smiley 1920a   Smiley, M. Thomas. "The Manuscripts of Callimachus' *Hymns*." *CQ* 14 (1920): 1–15.

Smiley 1920b   ——. "The Manuscripts of Callimachus' *Hymns* (Continued)." *CQ* 14 (1920): 57–77.

Smiley 1920c   ——. "The Manuscripts of Callimachus' *Hymns* (Continued)." *CQ* 14 (1920):105–122.

Smiley 1921a   ——. "The Manuscripts of Callimachus' *Hymns* (Continued)." *CQ* 15 (1921): 57–74.

Smiley 1921b   ——. "The Manuscripts of Callimachus' *Hymns* (Continued)." *CQ* 15 (1921): 113–25.

GENERAL BIBLIOGRAPHY

Editions of the texts and their abbreviations are listed under "References," and bibliography specific to individual texts is listed in their Introductions.

Acosta-Hughes, Benjamin. *Arion's Lyre: Archaic Lyric into Hellenistic Poetry*. Princeton: Princeton University Press, 2010.

Acosta-Hughes, Benjamin, Luigi Lehnus, and Susan Stephens, eds. *Brill's Companion to Callimachus*. Leiden: Brill, 2011.

Acosta-Hughes, Benjamin, and Susan A. Stephens. *Callimachus in Context*. Cambridge: University of Cambridge Press, 2012.

Bastianini, Guido, and Angelo Casanova, eds. *Callimaco, cent'anni di papyri: atti del convegno internazionale di studi*, Firenze, 9–10 Giugno, 2005. Studi e testi di papirologia NS 8. Florence: Istituto papirologico G. Vitelli, 2006.

Bing, Peter. *The Well-Read Muse*. Rev. ed. Ann Arbor: Michigan Classical Press, 2008.

Blum, Rudolf. *Kallimachos: The Alexandrian Library and the Origins of Bibliography*. Translated by Hans H. Wellisch. Madison, WI: University of Wisconsin Press, 1991.

Cameron, Alan. *Callimachus and His Critics*. Princeton: Princeton University Press, 1995.

Carney, Elizabeth D. *Arsinoë of Egypt and Macedon: A Royal Life*. Oxford: Oxford University Press, 2013.

Clauss, James, and Martine Cuypers, eds. *A Companion to Hellenistic Literature*. Malden, MA: Wiley-Blackwell, 2010.

Clayman, Dee L. *Callimachus' Iambi*. Leiden: Brill, 1980.

———. "Callimachus' *Iambi* and *Aetia*." *ZPE* 74 (1988): 277–86.

———. *Timon of Phlius: Pyrrhonism into Poetry*. Berlin and New York: De Gruyter, 2009.

———. "Did Any Berenike Attend the Isthmian Games? A Literary Perspective on Posidippus 82 AB," *ZPE* 182 (2012): 121–30.

———. *Berenice II and the Golden Age of Ptolemaic Egypt*. Oxford: Oxford University Press, 2014.

Dalby, Andrew. "Lynceus and the Anecdotists." In *Athenaeus and His World: Reading Greek Culture in the Roman Empire*, edited by David Braund and John Wilkins, 372–94. Exeter: University of Exeter Press, 2000.

Fantuzzi, Marco, and Richard Hunter. *Tradition and Innovation in Hellenistic Poetry*. Cambridge: Cambridge University Press, 2004. Originally published as *Muse e modelli: la poesia ellenistica da Alessandro Magno ad Augusto*. Rome: Laterza, 2002.

Fraser, Peter M. *Ptolemaic Alexandria*. 3 vols. Oxford: Oxford University Press, 1972.

Gallavotti, Carlo. *Il libro dei Giambi. Testo critico e versione*. Naples: Macchiarolli, 1946.

Harder, Annette, Remco Regtuit, and Gerrigje Wakker, eds. *Callimachus*. Groningen: Forsten, 1993.

———, eds. *Callimachus II*. Leuven: Peeters, 2004.

Hölbl, Günther. *A History of the Ptolemaic Empire*. Translated by Tina Saavedra. Oxford: Routledge, 2001.

Hunter, Richard. *The Shadow of Callimachus*. Cambridge: University of Cambridge Press, 2006.

Hunter, Richard, Antonios Rengakos, and Evian Sistakou, eds. *Hellenistic Studies at a Crossroads: Exploring Texts, Contexts and Metatexts*. Berlin: De Gruyter, 2014.

Huss, Werner. *Ägypten in hellenistischer Zeit 332–30 v. Chr.* Munich: Beck, 2001.

Hutchinson, Gregory O. *Hellenistic Poetry*. Oxford: Clarendon Press, 1988.

Klooster, J., M. A. Harder, R. F. Regtuit, and G. C. Wakker, eds. *Callimachus Revisited: New Perspectives in Callimachean Scholarship*. Leuven: Peeters, 2019.

Koenen, Ludwig. "The Ptolemaic King as a Religious Figure." In *Images and Ideologies: Self-Definition in the Hellenistic World*, edited by Anthony Bulloch et al., 25–115. Berkeley: University of California Press, 1993.

Köhnken, Adolf. "Hellenistic Chronology: Theocritus, Callimachus, and Apollonius Rhodius." In *A Companion to Apollonius Rhodius*, edited by Theodore D. Papanghelis and Antonios Rengakos, 73–92. Leiden: Brill, 2001.

Lapp, Friedrich. *De Callimachi Cyrenaei tropis et figures*. PhD diss. Bonn, 1965.

Laronde, André. *Cyrène et la Libye hellénistique: Libykai Historiai*. Paris: Ed. CNRS, 1987.

Lasserre, François. *Die Fragmente des Eudoxos von Knidos*. Berlin and New York: De Gruyter, 1966.

Lefkowitz, Mary R. *The Lives of the Greek Poets*. 2nd ed. Baltimore, MD: The Johns Hopkins University Press, 2012.

Lehnus, Luigi. "Riflessioni cronologiche sull'ultimo Callimaco." *ZPE* 105 (1995): 6–12.

———. *Nuova bibliografia callimachea (1489–1998)*. Alessandria: Edizioni dell'Orso, 2000.

Lehnus, Luigi, and Franco Montanari, eds. *Callimaque: sept exposés suivis de discussions*. Entretiens sur l'antiquité classique 48. Geneva: Fondation Hardt, 2002.

Lenfant, Dominique. *Ctésias de Cnide. La Perse: l'Inde; autres fragments*. Collection des universités de France. Série grecque, v. 435. Paris: Les Belles Lettres, 2004.

Maas, Paul. "ΔΙΗΗΣΕΙΣ di poemi di Callimaco. Exkurz I–III." *Papyri della Università di Milano*. Milan, 1937.

Martin, Jean. *Scholia in Aratum vetera*. Leipzig: Teubner, 1974.

Morrison, Andrew D. *The Narrator in Archaic Greek and Hellenistic Poetry*. Cambridge: Cambridge University Press, 2007.

Nisetich, Frank, trans. *The Poems of Callimachus*. Oxford: Oxford University Press, 2001.

Norsa, Medea, and Girolamo Vitelli. *Διηγήσεις di poemi di Callimaco in un papiro di Tebtynis*. Florence: Tipografia Enrico Ariani, 1934.

Oliver, Graham J. "Callimachus the Poet and the Benefactor of the Athenians." *ZPE* 140 (2002): 6–8.

Rawles, Richard. *Callimachus*. London: Bloomsbury, 2019.

Reinsch-Werner, Hannelore. *Callimachus Hesiodicus: Die Rezeption der hesiodischen Dichtung durch Kallimachos von Kyrene*. Berlin: Mielke, 1976.

Rose, Valentin. *Aristotelis qui ferebantur librorum fragmenta*. Leipzig: Teubner, 1886[2].

Selden, David. "Alibis." *Classical Antiquity* 17 (1998): 299–412.

Sharples, Robert W. *Theophrastus of Eresus: Sources for His Life, Writings, Thought and Influence. Commentary vol. 3.1, Sources on Physics*. Leiden: Brill, 1998.

Slings, S. R. "Poet's Call and Poet's Status in Archaic Greece and Other Oral Cultures." *Listy Filologické* 112 (1989): 72–80.

Stephens, Susan A. *Seeing Double: Intercultural Poetics in Ptolemaic Alexandria*. Berkeley: University of California Press, 2003.

Weber, Gregor. *Dichtung und höfische Gesellschaft: die Rezeption von Zeitgeschichte am Hof der ersten drei Ptolemäer*. Stuttgart: Steiner, 1993.

Wehrli, Fritz. *Herakleides Pontikos. Die Schule des Aristoteles*. Vol. 7. Basel: Schwabe, 1969[2].

West, Martin L. *Greek Metre*. Oxford: Oxford University Press, 1982.

Wilamowitz-Moellendorf, Ulrich von. *Hellenistische Dichtung in der Zeit des Kallimachos*. 2 vols. Berlin: Weidmann, 1924.

AETIA

INTRODUCTION

The *Aetia* is a collection of narratives in four books that explain the origins (*aitia*) of cults, customs, place-names, historical and religious artifacts, and more throughout the Greek world. Today it is extant only in fragments, but in light of their number and the quantity of scholia and other aids for readers, as well as references and adaptations in later literature, both Greek and Latin, it must have been Callimachus' most influential poem in antiquity.

GENRE

Based on its structure, the *Aetia* can be considered an example of "catalogue poetry." Catalogues are a feature of Greek poetry from earliest times and include such well-known passages as the Homeric catalogue of ships (*Il.* 2.494–759) and catalogue of women (*Od.* 11.225–330). Catalogues also structure long sections of Hesiod's *Theogony*, *Works and Days*, and especially the pseudo-Hesiodic *Catalogue of Women*. This latter poem is a series of genealogies that trace the origins of certain mythic Greek families to sexual encounters between a woman and a deity. Some of these are introduced with the words ἠ᾽ οἵη, "or such as," which link the diverse narratives and give the work its Greek title, the *Ēhoiai*. Later catalogue poems in the Hesiodic tradition include didactic works, such as Aratus' *Phaenomena*, which lists constellations and weather signs, while others are elegies with erotic contents, such as the *Lyde* of Antimachus of Colophon, a catalogue of tragic love affairs.[1] In a similar vein, Callimachus' older contemporaries Hermesianax and Phanocles composed their elegiac lists of mythological lovers, male and female, with an occasional use of *ēhoiē* to mark their generic affinity with the Hesiodic tradition.[2]

Callimachus acknowledges his own debt to Hesiod early in the *Aetia*'s first book, in which he imagines himself transported in a dream to Mt. Helicon, where Hesiod claims he first met the Muses who gave him his staff and commanded him to become a poet (*Theog.* 22–34; *Aet.* 2–2j). Although the details of Callimachus' dream are lost, it is clear that his own encounter with the Muses was the beginning of a conversation that becomes an organizing device for the first two books of the *Aetia*. Though Books 3 and 4 unfold without a frame, the dream is reprised at

[1] This characterization of the *Lyde* in [Plut.] *Cons. ad Apoll.* 106b seems influenced by Hermesianax fr. 3.41–46 Lightfoot and is not consistent with the few extant fragments. See Helen Asquith, "From Genealogy to Catalogue: The Hellenistic Adaption of the Hesiodic Catalogue Form," in *The Hesiodic Catalogue of Women. Constructions and Reconstructions*, ed. Richard Hunter (Cambridge: Cambridge University Press, 2005), 282–83.

[2] Mimnermus' *Nanno* and Philitas' *Bittis* have also been put forward as similar poems (Posid. 140.1–2 AB = *Anth. Pal.* 12.168.1–2; Hermesianax fr. 3.75–78), but fragments of the *Nanno* do not support this and nothing is known about the *Bittis*.

the end of the poem to fulfill the Muses' command to Hesiod that he sing of them first and last.[3]

Genealogies are a subcategory of *aitia*, that is, accounts of "origins" or "causes," but rather than limit his work to family histories, as in the Hesiodic *Catalogue*, Callimachus fills his *Aetia* with stories about the beginnings of all kinds of constructions, human and divine, natural and cultural, historical and fantastical. The variety of subjects also accommodates a mix of generic forms, with some of the *aitia* exhibiting characteristics of epigrams (*Aet.* 64), hymns (*Aet.* 7.13–14), epinicia (*Aet.* 54–60), and epithalamia (*Aet.* 67–75e). Many allusions to Homer and an elaborate treatment of the legend of the Argonauts (*Aet.* 7c–21d, 108–9a)[4] subsume epic, as well. Overall, the didactic predominates, and the *Aetia's* narratives are filled with diverse information gleaned from various sources, including local histories in prose that the poet occasionally cites by the author's name.[5] Like the Hesiodic *Catalogue*, Callimachus' stories vary widely in length, with some seeming to grow out of the collection altogether to take on lives of their own.[6] And also as in the *Ēhoiai*, Callimachus chooses

[3] Hesiod himself does not return to the Muses at the end of his poem.

[4] For bibliography on the long scholarly discussion on whether the Argonaut episodes in the *Aetia* preceded Apollonius' *Argonautica*, see Harder vol. 1, 32n102.

[5] An example is Xenomedes of Ceos on Acontius and Cydippe (*Aet.* 75.53–55). See also his comment on the historian Leandrius (*Aet.* 92.2–3).

[6] "Acontius and Cydippe" from Book 3 and the "Lock of Berenice" that concludes Book 4 apparently circulated independently. An example of a long, independent narrative in He-

subjects, or promotes and explores details, that are distinctly unheroic.

COMPOSITION, ORGANIZATION, AND DATE

Though the diverse narratives of the *Aetia* are loosely linked, they are contained in a larger framework. This begins with an elaborate Prologue, discussed below, in which the poet defends his artistic choices, followed by a second Prologue, recounting his dream of the Muses. Four books of *aitia* follow, the first two structured as a conversation with the Muses and the last two bracketed by longer *aitia* honoring Queen Berenice II, wife of Ptolemy III Euergetes: the "Victoria Berenices" (54–60j) that begins Book 3 and the "Coma Berenices" (110–110f) that concludes Book 4. An Epilogue (112) follows that reprises the dream and links the *Aetia* to the *Iambi*, which follow it in the principal papyrus (*P.Oxy.* 1011) and in the *Diegeseis*.

This complex structure and the likelihood that at least two of the *Aetia*'s longer episodes circulated independently in antiquity[7] have given rise to theories about its composition and date. An important model was proposed by Pfeiffer, who suggested that the whole of the *Aetia* was first composed before 270 BC, relatively early in Callimachus' career, then revised after 246 BC, when the Pro-

---

siod's *Catalogue* is the account of Mestra and her descendants (43a M.-W.).

[7] "Acontius and Cydippe" (*P.Oxy.* 2211) and the "Coma Berenices" (*P.Oxy.* 2258).

logue, Epilogue, and "Lock of Berenice" were added.[8]
This model was modified by Parsons after the discovery
of the "Victoria Berenices" and its placement at the be-
ginning of Book 3, which now had to be dated after the
queen's arrival in Alexandria in 246 BC. To accommodate
the new text, Parsons proposed that Callimachus wrote
Books 1–2 early in his career, then collected various etio-
logical poems that he had continued to write over the
years into his third and fourth books, which he framed
with the two poems honoring Berenice.[9] A new Prologue
and Epilogue for the whole composition were also added
at this time. Though this scenario has not been universally
accepted,[10] it has become the standard view, with a mod-
ification by Harder, who demonstrates that certain inter-
nal structural devices across all four books suggest that
Callimachus made revisions within Books 1 and 2 at the
time of the final editing.[11]

THE PROLOGUE

The Prologue, one of the most influential passages in the
Callimachean corpus, is extant in forty fragmentary verses
(*Aet*. 1.1–40) augmented by two fragmentary commentar-
ies, the Florentine Scholia (*Aet*.1b) and the London Scho-

---

[8] R. Pfeiffer, "Ein neues Altersgedicht des Kallimachos'"
Hermes 63 (1928): 339–41, and Pf. vol. 2, xxxvi–xxxviii. The date
of the revision is determined by the date of the "Lock," which is
set after the first year of the Third Syrian War.

[9] Parsons and Kassel 1977, 50.

[10] See the dissent of Cameron 1995, 104–32.

[11] Harder vol. 1, 2–8.

lia (*Aet.* 1d). It functions both as an introduction to the *Aetia* and a defense of stylistic principles that the poet promulgates elsewhere (*Hymn* 2.105–13; *Ia.* 13; *Epig.* 27, 28). It is framed as an attack against the Telchines, mythical wizards and primitive artists,[12] whom Callimachus uses as proxies for his critics. These are not named in the Prologue itself, which has encouraged readers, both ancient and modern, to identify them with historical individuals.[13] However this may be, the poet's own reticence is a first indication of the playfulness that characterizes his style here and elsewhere.

As the Prologue begins, the poet, speaking in the first-person, claims that the Telchines grumble at his song because it is not a continuous composition of many-thousands of lines on kings and heroes but written in small increments like the work of a child, although the decades of his years are not few (*Aet.* 1.1–6). In response to this self-formulated charge, Callimachus cites precedents from earlier poems characterized here as large women (*Aet.* 1.9–12), and if the Florentine Scholia (*Aet.* 1b.12–15) are correct, he is comparing the long poems of earlier elegists, Philitas and Mimnermus, with their own short poems. His criteria for judgment, which include weight, length, and sound quality, are amplified with negative images (e.g., the "Massageti shoot from afar," the long "Persian chain," "thundering" at *Aet.* 1.13–20) and contrasted with advice

---

[12] They were associated with Rhodes (Diod. Sic. 5.55.1–3) and Ceos (*Aet.* 75.64–69), where their destruction is described.

[13] The Florentine Scholia suggest, among others, the epigrammatists Asclepiades and Posidippus as well as Praxiphanes of Mytilene (*Aet.* 1b.4–9).

he received from Apollo in his youth to keep his Muse "slender" and travel on "narrow," "untrodden ways" (*Aet.* 1.21–30). Finally, he imagines himself as a tiny, winged thing, a cicada dining on dew, and prays that he can slough off old age, which weighs him down like Sicily presses on the deadly giant Enceladus (*Aet.* 1.31–36). With these images, which include references to more than ten different literary figures and texts,[14] the poet restates his aesthetic values and concludes by asserting the continued support of the Muses, who "do not reject the grey-beard friends whom they looked on with a favoring eye as children" (*Aet.* 1.37–40).

STYLE, LENGTH, AND CONTENTS

The *Aetia* itself conforms closely to the stylistic preferences set out by Callimachus in the Prologue. Though he characterizes himself as childlike, his work is learned, literate, elegant, self-confident, self-conscious, humorous, and modern. The breadth of his subject matter is impressive, and it includes kings and heroes, but for the most part not those featured in epic, and not in long, epic-like compositions with continuous narrative. Individual *aitia* range in length from just a few lines to several hundred, with some of the longer pieces able to stand as independent compositions. More difficult is the question of the overall length of the work. Harder, who reexamined all the evidence, estimates that the four books together had five thousand lines, give or take a few hundred, or close to the

---

14 Acosta-Hughes and Stephens 2002, 246–53.

length of Apollonius' *Argonautica*.[15] About 25 percent of these are preserved or otherwise accounted for.

Harder has produced a survey of the contents, which lists all of the known subjects of the *Aetia* in the order in which they appear based on the papyri and the *Diegeseis* (Harder vol. 2, Appendix I). Below is a partial list of the best-preserved *aitia* and a few others of interest:

"Against the Telchines" (1–1e)—the polemical Prologue.

"The Dream" or "Somnium" (2–2j)—a second Prologue that begins the *Aetia* proper, and an homage to Hesiod. It is reprised in the Epilogue, which concludes Book 4 to form a frame for the entire work.

"The Return of the Argonauts" (7c–21d) in Book 1 and "The Anchor of the Ship Argo Left at Cyzicus" (108–9a) in Book 4—both episodes are included in Apollonius' *Argonautica* and raise issues about priority of composition. They form an inner ring within the frame defined by "The Dream."

"The Victory of Berenice" (54–60j)—an epinician in the manner of Pindar celebrating the Nemean victory of Queen Berenice II, wife of Ptolemy III Euergetes. The contest's foundation myth features Heracles, whom the Ptolemies claimed as an ancestor.

"The Tomb of Simonides" (64)—an epigram type, well-preserved, that features an important predecessor in the composition of elegy.

"Acontius and Cydippe" (67–75e)—including, after the

---

[15] Harder vol. 1, 12–15.

Hymns, the longest stretch of Callimachean verse still extant. A charming love story that the poet says he found in a local history by Xenomedes of Ceos, whose work he also summarizes (75.53–77).

"Phrygius and Pieria" (80–83b)—another love story with parallels to Acontius and Cydippe.

"A Roman Gaius" (106–107a)—shows Callimachus' awareness of the growing importance of Rome and the Western Mediterranean.

"Of the Lock of Berenice" (110–110f)—the concluding and best known episode preserved in a Latin translation by Catullus (Catull. 66). It is a fantasy told in the voice of Berenice's lock of hair that becomes the constellation Coma Berenices.

"The Epilogue" (112)—The conclusion of the *Aetia* and link to the *Iambi*, which follows in *P.Oxy.* 1011 and the *Diegeseis*.

THE *AETIA* AS COURT POETRY

Callimachus lived and worked at the court of Ptolemy II Philadelphus and Ptolemy III Euergetes. Philadelphus married his second wife, Arsinoe II, who was also his sister, sometime between 276 and 273 BC, and Callimachus wrote poems on the occasion of their marriage (*Var.* 392), her death (*Mel.* 228), and an epigram commemorating a young girl's gift to her (*Epig.* 5). Although the composition of Books 1 and 2 of the *Aetia* is dated to the 270s, the fragments contain no formal dedication to her.[16] It has

---

[16] Unless she is a "tenth Muse" in "The Dream," as conjectured by the London Scholia (*Aet.* 2e.1–6).

been suggested that she was addressed in the farewell that formed the transition between "The Lock" and the Epilogue (*Aet.* 110.94a), where a female is saluted and characterized as "dear to children," but the addressee is more likely Berenice II.[17]

It is Berenice II who is named and honored in the "Victoria Berenices" (54–60j) that introduces Book 3 and "The Lock" (110–110f) that concludes Book 4. The former celebrates her victory in a four-horse chariot race at Nemea, though the greater part of the poem is taken up by an account of Heracles' visit to the farmer Molorcus on his way to slay the Nemean Lion and found the contest.[18] Its detailed rendering of Molorcus' hardscrabble life along with the short shrift the poem gives to Heracles' heroic deed recalls the *Hecale*.

"The Lock of Berenice," the concluding section, tells how a lock of her hair ascended to the heavens to become a constellation after she dedicated it in the temple of Arsinoe-Aphrodite at Zephyrium to fulfill a vow following her husband's safe return from the Third Syrian War. Here Callimachus mixes palace life with fantasy, teases his queen like a doting uncle, and brings the *Aetia* to a grand finale.

AFTERLIFE OF THE *AETIA*

The popularity of the *Aetia* is attested by the large number of papyrus copies that have survived, albeit in fragments,

---

[17] See discussion in Harder vol. 2, 852–53.

[18] The Ptolemies claimed Heracles as an ancestor (*OGIS*, 54). See Clayman 2014, 131.

dating from the late third or early second century BC (*P.Lille* inv. 76d, 78a–c, 79, 82, 84), soon after Callimachus' lifetime, to the early sixth century AD (*P.Oxy.* 2258).[19] These have been discovered not only in Alexandria but also in provincial towns, where they would have found less sophisticated readers. They include text and sometimes commentary intended to clarify Callimachus' recherché diction and obscure allusions. Summaries, including the *Diegeseis*, which were found on a papyrus of the first to second century AD (*P.Mil.Vogl.* 1.18), were aids for general readers, while learned commentaries, such as those of Theon (1st c. BC/AD) and Epaphroditus (1st c. AD), served a more scholarly readership. Such commentaries may have fueled the enthusiasm of the Augustan poets for Callimachus that is briefly sketched below. In late antiquity, Gregory of Nazianzus (4th c. AD) and Nonnus of Panopolis (4th/5th c. AD) both knew and used the *Aetia* in their own work, while Marianus rewrote it in iambic trimeters in the fifth or sixth century AD. In the twelfth century, the Homeric scholar Eustathius was still referring to it, as was his pupil, Michael Choniates (*Epist.* 2.350), who is the last person known to have in his possession a complete copy of the *Hecale*. After Michael, the *Aetia* disappears from view until Politian (1454–1494) launched the modern reconstruction of the text.

Although Callimachus' works as a whole were of fundamental importance to Roman poetry, it would not be an exaggeration to say that the *Aetia* was the most influential.[20] Dramatic evidence of this is Catullus 66, a close

19 Harder vol. 1, 65–67. Also Lehnus 2011, 30–34.
20 Important studies include Wimmel 1960; Thomas 1983; and Hunter 2006.

translation of "The Lock of Berenice" (110–110f), and Catullus 65, its versified letter of transmission to the poet's friend.[21]

Although the Augustan poets clearly knew the *Aetia* as a whole, the poetic program that Callimachus sets out in his Prologue became a touchstone by which they authorized their own artistic values. An early example is found in Virgil's *Eclogues* (*Ecl*. 6.1–12), in which the Roman poet announces he will not sing of kings and battles, then reworks Apollo's instructions to Callimachus (*Aet*. 1.21–24) as he recounts to his dedicatee, Varus, how the god told him to feed fat sheep, but sing a slender song.[22] Virgil later complicates his relationship with Callimachus in the proem to the third book of his *Georgics*, where he presents his poetic program in the context of an *epinicion* for Octavian with references to Callimachus' "Victoria Berenices," which similarly introduces the third book of the *Aetia*.[23] A central component of that episode (*Aet*. 54–60j) is the foundation of the Nemean games by Heracles, who

[21] Catullus translated ninety-nine verses of the Greek text, of which we have about one-third of the original. The translation is not literal at every point, but where the Greek is missing altogether, Catullus is an indispensable though not always perfect guide. See Bing 1997. Ten additional lines in Catullus' rendition (Catull. 66.79–88) absent from the fragmentary original (*P.Oxy.* 2258) have been used as evidence that Callimachus' poem circulated in two versions, an earlier one represented by *P.Oxy.* 2258 and a later one with the ten additional verses known to Catullus.

[22] Other examples of Augustan poets echoing Callimachus' *recusatio* are Hor. *Carm.* 1.6.5–12; Prop. 2.1.1–4, 17–26, 39–42; Ov. *Am.* 1.1.1–4.

[23] See Thomas 1983, which argues that Prop. 3.1.1–4 is another example of this receptional thread.

enjoys the modest hospitality of the rustic Molorcus,[24] whom he frees from the ravages of the Nemean Lion. So too in Virgil's *Aeneid* the Arcadian king Evander receives Hercules, who will rid him of the marauding Cacus (*Aen.* 8.184–369).[25] This is the last of a series of thirteen *aetia* (*Aen.* 8.1–369) that the River Tiber recounts to Aeneas as he dreams by its banks in a scene inspired by Callimachus' own dream of conversing with the Muses by the Hippocrene (*Aet.* 2–2j).[26]

Propertius also has the *Aetia* in mind in the first poem of his fourth book, where he asserts in so many words that he is a Roman Callimachus (Prop. 4.1.64). It is not only Callimachean style that Propertius appropriates but also the subject matter of the *Aetia*: "Sacred days I will sing and the ancient names of places" (Prop. 4.1.69). An even more thoroughgoing reimagining of the *Aetia* was produced by Ovid in his *Fasti*. In that poem's first line Ovid announces as his subject "the order of the calendar throughout the Latin year and its causes" (i.e., *causae*, a literal translation of *aitia*).[27] Like Callimachus' interviewing the Muses in *Aetia* 1–2, Ovid begins by questioning the god Janus, whom he asks about the reason for his two faces (Ov. *Fast.* 1.89). More questions follow, and later,

[24] For the spelling ("Molorcus" is traditional), see J. D. Morgan, "The Origin of Molorc[h]us," *CQ* (1992): 533–38.

[25] Michael A. Tueller, "Well-read Heroes Quoting the *Aetia* in *Aeneid* 8," *HSCP* 100 (2000): 371–75.

[26] E. V. George, *Aeneid VIII and the Aitia of Callimachus* (Leiden: Brill, 1974), 88–92.

[27] "Let others sing of Caesar's wars, our subject will be his altars and the sacred days he added" (Ov. *Fast.* 1.13–14).

14

like Callimachus, he introduces human informants and other sources. Also like Callimachus, Ovid mixes his anti-quarian lore with panegyric to the royal family. With Ovid, then, Callimachus' reputation among Roman poets and their admiration for the *Aetia* reaches its apogee. Though Statius writes short pieces of an etiological character in his elegiac *Silvae* and includes Callimachus in a list of Greek and Roman predecessors (Stat. *Silv.* 1.2.253), by the end of the first century AD, Callimacheanism is no longer the fashion among Roman poets.

CONSTITUTION OF THE TEXT

Unlike Callimachus' *Hymns* and *Epigrams*, the *Aetia* was not preserved in the medieval manuscript tradition. Our text is a collection of quotations gleaned from Byzantine scholia, grammars, and lexica, and augmented by frag-mentary papyri excavated in Egypt since the end of the nineteenth century.

Early Editions of the Aetia

The text of the *Aetia* was lost in the thirteenth century, and the difficult work of recovery began three hundred years later, when Politian included some verses of Catul-lus' Latin translation of "The Lock of Berenice" (Catull. 66) in his *Miscellanea* of 1489 (chs. 68 and 69). The first to gather some Greek text and *testimonia* to the *Aetia* was Ianus Parrhasius (ca. 1500), but no more was added until the second edition of Stephanus in 1577, which included twelve fragments collected by Henricus Stephanus and Nicodemus Frischlin.

15

Vulcanius (1584) added more, as did others, including
Anna Fabri (1675) and Richard Bentley, who collected
417 fragments of Callimachus, the majority from the *Aetia*, published in Graevius' edition of 1697. It was not until the nineteenth century that efforts began to identify some of the *Aetia*'s major episodes. Both Philipp Buttmann (1823–24) and Karl Dilthey (1863) attempted reconstructions of "Acontius and Cydippe," while Alphons Hecker (1842) argued for the existence of a polemical prologue, which he mistakenly attached to the *Hecale*. Schneider's effort in 1873 to organize the *Aetia* into four "*agōnes*" was greeted skeptically at the time and then decisively disproved by papyri.

Papyri of the Aetia

The text of the *Aetia* has been greatly enlarged by additions from papyri beginning in 1910 with the publication of *P.Oxy.* 1011, edited by A. S. Hunt with the collaboration of U. von Wilamowitz and Gilbert Murray. Its seven mutilated folios and five fragments contain parts of *Aetia* Books 3 and 4, including substantial parts of the story of Acontius and Cydippe (*Aet.* 75) and the Epilogue that concludes Book 4 (*Aet.* 112). In 1911, *P.Ryl.* 13 appeared, with a substantial fragment from Book 1 of the *Aetia*, "Linus and Coroebus" (*Aet.* 26); and in 1913, fragments of "Molorcus" (*Aet.* 54h) from Book 3 and fragments of the "Sacrifice at Lindos" (*Aet.* 23) were published as *P.Berol.* 11629 A and B. In 1915, *P.Oxy.* 1362 supplied the text of "The Man from Icus" (*Aet.* 178), which established a sympotic context for some of the *aitia*.

Other important additions to the *Aetia* from papyri followed the First World War. The 1920s saw the publication of the "Prologue against the Telchines" (*Aet.* 1), in *P.Oxy.* 2079, and a substantial fragment of "The Lock of Berenice" (*Aet.* 110.44–66), in *PSI* 1092; and in 1934, Vitelli published the text of the Milan *Diegeseis* (*P.Mil.Vogl.* 1.18). It offers invaluable guidance for identifying the contents and the order of the *aitia* in Books 3 and 4 and for establishing its relationship with the *Iambi*. A number of other fragments of the *Aetia* appeared both before and after the Second World War, the most important of which is *P.Lille* 76, with the "Victoria Berenices," published by Meillier in 1976 and in 1977 by Parsons, which introduces Book 3 and balances "The Lock of Berenice" at the end of Book 4. These are just a few of the highlights. A complete list of all papyri of the *Aetia* follows below.

Modern Editions of the Aetia

The foundation of all modern texts of the *Aetia* is Rudolph Pfeiffer's *Callimachus* (1949–1953). Not only did he reevaluate every fragment available at the time but he also included papyri that were not yet published, as well as scholia, the relevant *Diegeseis*, and other testimonia, all illuminated by copious Latin notes. For the *Aetia*, he ignored the numbering of previous editors and imposed his own based on a reconstruction of the four books following the order of *aitia* in the *Diegeseis*. He also proposed the influential theory of composition described above. Pfeiffer's edition is still authoritative, but papyri continued to be published, and in 1983 Lloyd-Jones and Parsons added thirty-nine new fragments in their *Supplementum Helle-nisticum*, including the text of the "Victoria Berenices," the dedicatory first *aition* of Book 3 (*SH* 254–69).

Pfeiffer's edition inspired others to bring the fragments to a wider audience, beginning with Trypanis' Loeb edition of 1958 with an English translation, D'Alessio (in four editions beginning in 1996) with an Italian translation, and Asper in 2004 with a German translation. The *Aetia* received its first edition apart from the other fragments in 1996, when the first volume of Massimilla's *Aetia* appeared containing Books 1 and 2 in a critical edition with copious notes, a full commentary, and an Italian translation. The second volume (Books 3 and 4) followed in 2010. Two years later Harder's *Aetia* appeared, also a critical edition, with notes, detailed commentary, and an English translation. Both stand squarely on the shoulders of Pfeiffer and Lloyd-Jones/Parsons, enriched by additional papyrus fragments and almost thirty years of scholarship. Among the new fragments they were able to add is 54a Harder = 144 Massimilla, incorporating *PSI* inv. 1923 and inv. 2002, which were combined by Bastianini in 2008 as inv. 1500. This is a fragment of twenty-four partial lines from the first part of the "Victoria Berenices" that develop the theme of mythical interactions between Argos and Egypt introduced in the opening lines of the poem. It corrects an impression made by previously published fragments that the poem did not offer much beyond a lengthy rendition of the founding myth of the Nemean festival where Berenice II won her victory. Additionally, new fragments of the Milan *Diegeseis* (*PSI* inv. 1006 and 28b) were added demonstrating that three previously unknown *aitia* follow "Acontius and Cydippe," a discovery

that raises new questions about the order of the *aitia* in
Book 3.

The text of the *Aetia* below is built on the work of
Massimilla and Harder. To accommodate the new texts
since Pfeiffer, Massimilla renumbered all of the frag-
ments, while Harder maintained Pfeiffer's original num-
bering and designated new additions with letters.[28] This
edition follows Harder's numbering, which simplifies con-
nections between the text and the wealth of scholarship
published since Pfeiffer.

CATALOG OF PAPYRI

The list of relevant papyri below follows the number-
ing and order of Mertens-Pack[3], the online database of
the Centre de documentation de papyrologie littéraire
(CEDOPAL) at the Université de Liège, which provides
additional information and bibliography.[29] Each entry be-
gins with the inventory number assigned by Mertens-
Pack[3], followed by the series name in standard abbrevia-
tions, the numbers in the *Supplementum Hellenisticum*,
Pfeiffer and Harder where applicable, its estimated date,
and the verses in the *Aetia* that it supplies.

> 00186.000: *P.Oxy.* 2258 (+ *P.Oxy.* 30, pp. 91–92; *SH*
> 290–91). Pap. 27 Harder, 37 Pf. 6th–7th c. AD. *Aet.*

[28] See Harder vol. 1, 73, for an explanation of the methodol-
ogy she followed in determining the order and numbering of the
fragments.

[29] Additional information about the papyri can also be found
in Pf. vol. 2, ix–xxvi; *SH*, pp. 89–122; Harder vol. 1, 63–67; Lehnus
2011, 23–38; Asper, 537–39.

CALLIMACHUS

54c.4–6; schol. in 60f and 60h; 74; 75.3–6; 110.43–
55, 65–78, 89–94b; schol. in 110e–f.
00195.000: *P.Oxy.* 2079 (+ *P.Oxy.* 2167 + *PSI* 1217A–
B). Pap. 15 Harder, 15 Pf. 2nd c. AD. *Aet.* 1; schol.
in 1c; 7.1–17; schol. in 7b; 7c; 11; 17; 18.1–12; 113e;
116–17.
00196.000: *PSI* 1219 (*P.Cair.* inv. JE 68909). Pap. 36
Harder, 24 Pf. 1st–2nd c. AD. Scholia Florentina in
Aet. 1b; 2d; 7a; 21a; 23a.
00197.000: *P.Lit.Lond.* 181 (*Brit.Libr.* inv. 131.2r).
Pap. 6 Harder, 5 Pf. 1st c. AD. Scholia Londinensia
in *Aet.* 1d; 2a; schol. in 2e.
00197.100: *P.Oxy.* 2262. Pap. 29 Harder, 20 Pf. 2nd c.
AD. *Aet.* 1a; 2b; 2c; schol. in 1e and 2f–2j.
00198.000: *P.Oxy.* 2208. Pap. 20 Harder, 29 Pf. 3rd c.
AD. *Aet.* 2; 113; 113f; 114.1–12.
00198.100: *P.Berol.* inv. 17057 (*SH* 249A). Pap. 4
Harder, not in Pf. 5th–6th c. AD. *Aet.* 7.9–11; 7d.
00200.000: *P.Berol.* inv. 11521. Pap. 3 Harder, 17 Pf.
2nd c. AD. Schol. in *Aet.* 21b.
00201.000: *P.Oxy.* 2168 + *P.Berol.* inv. 11629A–B.
Pap. 17 Harder, 32 Pf. 4th–5th c. AD. Aet. 12; 18.9–
15; 23–24; 54h; 54i.18–22; schol. in 60j.
00201.100: *P.Mich.* inv. 3688r (*SH* 250–51). Pap. 7
Harder, not in Pf. 2nd c. AD. *Aet.* 17.8–10; schol. in
21c.
00202.000: *P.Oxy.* 2209A–B. Pap. 21 Harder, 9 Pf. 2nd
c. AD. *Aet.* 21; 118.
00203.000: *P.Ryl.* 13. Pap. 32 Harder, 13 Pf. 2nd c. AD.
Aet. 26.
00205.000: *P.Oxy.* 2263. Pap. 30 Harder, 26 Pf. 2nd–
3rd c. AD. *Aet.* 31c; 31i; *Dieg.* in 31a; 31g; 31h.

00205.100: *P.Oxy.* 2261. Pap. 28 Harder, 14 Pf. 2nd c. AD. *Aet.* 30a.

00205.200: *P.Ant.* 113 (*SH* 238–49). Pap. 1 Harder, not in Pf. 3rd–4th c. AD. *Aet.* 137a–l.

00206.000: *P.Oxy.* 2080 (+ *P.Oxy.* 19, p. 147). Pap. 16 Harder, 18 Pf. 2nd c. AD. *Aet.* 43; 43b; schol. in 43a and 43c.

00207.000: *P.Oxy.* 2210. Pap. 22 Harder, 10 Pf. 2nd ct. AD. *Aet.* 43.8–9; 119.2–7; 120–37.

00207.100: *P.Sorb.* inv. 2248 (*SH* 252–53). Pap. 37 Harder, not in Pf. 1st c. AD. *Aet.* 46.2–11; 137m.2–16.

00207.200: *P.Oxy.* 2173 (+ *PSI* 1500). Pap. 19 Harder, 23 Pf. 2nd c. AD. *Aet.* 54; 54a.

00207.300 *P.Lille* inv. 76d + 78abc + 79 +82 + 84 (*SH* 254–58 and 260–63). Pap. 5 Harder, not in Pf. 3rd c. BC. *Aet.* 76d, etc.

00207.400: *PSI* 1218 (+ *P.Oxy.* 2170; *SH* 257, 259). Pap. 35 Harder, 6 Pf. 1st–2nd c. AD. *Aet.* 92; 93; 95; 96; 175; 54b.21–34; 54c.

00208.000: *P.Oxy.* 2212 (+ *P.Oxy.* 19, p. 144, and *P.Oxy.* 20, p. 167; *SH* 265.1–11). Pap. 24 Harder, 11 Pf. 2nd c. AD. *Aet.* 54i; 80.1–21; 83–84; 114.12–14; 138–57.

00209.000: *P.Oxy.* 2169 (*SH* 265.8–25). Pap. 18 Harder, 22 Pf. 2nd c. AD. *Aet.* 54i.8–25.

00210.000: *P.Oxy.* 2211. Pap. 23 Harder, 31 Pf. 3rd c. AD. *Aet.* 63–64; 66–67; 113e.11–21; 114.11–14; 114a.

00211.000: *P.Mil.Vogl.* 1.18 (*P.Cair.* inv. JE 67340) + *P.Mil.Vogl.* inv. 28b + *P.Mil.Vogl.* inv. 1006. Pap. 11 Harder, 8 Pf. 1st–2nd c. AD. *Diegeseis* of *Aet.* 3–4 re *Aet.* 75a; 76b; 77b; 78; 78b; 79; 79a; 84; 85a; 86; 89a;

90; 90a; 91; 92a; 93.1; 93a; 94; 95a; 96.1; 96a; 97; 97a;
98; 99a; 100a; 101; 101a; 102; 102a; 103; 103a; 104;
104a; 105; 105a; 106; 107a; 108; 109a; 110.1; 110a.

00211.100: *P.Oxy.* 1011. Pap. 13 Harder, 35 Pf. 4th c.
AD. *Aet.* 75; 76; 112.

00211.110: *P.Oxy.* 4427. Pap. 31 Harder, not in Pf. 1st–
2nd c. AD. *Aet.* 75.11–15 and schol. in 75.23; 75c.25.

00212.000: *P.Oxy.* 2213. Pap. 25 Harder, 12 Pf. 2nd c.
AD. *Aet.* 75.50–58; 77a; 78; 80.3–24; 81; 85; 158–74.

00214.000: *PSI* 1092. Pap. 33 Harder, 1 Pf. 1st c. BC.
Aet. 110.44–64.

00216.000: *P.Oxy.* 1362. Pap. 14 Harder, 3 Pf. 1st c.
AD. *Aet.* 178–83.

00217.000: *P.Oxy.* 2214. Pap. 26 Harder, 2 Pf. 1st c.
BC. *Aet.* 186.

00217.010: *P.Mich.* inv. 6235. Pap. 10 Harder, not in
Pf. 2nd–3rd c. AD. *Diegeseis* in 190b.

00217.100: *P.Ant.* 114 (*SH* 271–74). Pap. 2 Harder, not
in Pf. 3rd–4th c. AD. *Aet.* 113a–d.

00217.200: *P.Mich.* inv. 4761c (*SH* 276). Pap. 8 Harder,
not in Pf. 2nd c. AD. *Aet.* 190a.5–15.

00217.300: *P.Oxy.* 14 (*SH* 276). Pap. 12 Harder; not in
Pf. 2nd cent. AD. *Aet.* 190a.1–14 and 17–20.

Not in Mertens-Pack[3]: *P.Mich.* inv. 5475c. Pap. 9
Harder, not in Pf. *Aet.* 21.6–14.

BIBLIOGRAPHY

EDITIONS

Harder, Annette. *Callimachus: Aetia*. Introduction text, translation, and commentary. 2 vols. Oxford: Oxford University Press, 2012.

Massimilla, Giulio. *Callimaco Aitia. Libro primo e secondo*. Pisa: Giardini, 1996.

———. *Aitia: libro terzo e quarto*. Rome: F. Serra, 2010.

CRITICAL STUDIES

Acosta-Hughes, Benjamin, and Susan Stephens. "Rereading Callimachus' *Aetia* Fragment 1." *CPh* 97 (2002): 238–55.

Asper, Marcus. *Onomata allotria: Zur Genese, Struktur und Funktion poetologischer Metaphern bei Kallimachos*. Hermes Einzelschriften 75. Stuttgart: Steiner, 1997.

Barigazzi, Adelmo. "Mimnermo e Filita, Antimaco e Cherilo nel proemio degli Aitia di Callimaco." *Hermes* 84 (1956): 162–82.

Bing, Peter. "Reconstructing Berenice's Lock." In *Collecting Fragments/Fragmente sammeln*, edited by Glenn W.

Most, 78–94. Göttingen: Vandenhoeck und Ruprecht, 1997.

Bulloch, Anthony W. "The Order and Structure of Callimachus' *Aetia* 3." *CQ* 56 (2006): 496–508.

Casanova, Angelo. "Cent'anni di papiri callimachei." In *Callimaco. Cent'Anni di Papiri: Atti del Convengo internazionale di studi, Firenze 9–10 giugno 2005*, edited by Guido Bastianini and Angelo Casanova, 1–13. Florence: Istituto papirologico G. Vitelli, 2006.

Clayman, Dee. "The Origins of Greek Literary Criticism and the *Aitia* Prologue." *Weiner Studien* 11 (1977): 27–34.

———. "Berenice and Her Lock." *TAPhA* 141 (2011): 229–46.

D'Alessio, Giovan Battista. "Le Horai e le pemphiges: fr. 43, 40–41 Pf. (= 50 M.)." In *Callimaco, cent'anni di papiri*, edited by Guido Bastianini et al., 101–17. Florence: Atti del convegno internazionale di studi, 2006.

George, Edward V. *Aeneid VIII and the Aitia of Callimachus*. Brill: Leiden, 1974.

Hunter, Richard. *The Shadow of Callimachus*. Cambridge: Cambridge University Press, 2006.

Krevans, Nita. "Fighting against Antimachus: The *Lyde* and the *Aetia* Reconsidered." In *Callimachus*, edited by Annette Harder et al., 149–60. Gröningen: Forsten, 1993.

Lobel, E. "An Unnoticed Imitation of Callimachus, *Aetia* Fr. 1.1 Pf." *Hermes* 70 (1935): 31–45.

Marione, Nino. *Berenice da Callimaco a Catullo*. 2nd ed. Bologna: Pàtron, 1997.

Massimilla, Giulio. "The *Aetia* Through Papyri." In *Brill's*

Companion to Callimachus, edited by Benjamin Acosta-Hughes and Susan Stephens, 39–62. Leiden: Brill, 2011.

Parsons, Peter, and R. Kassel. "Callimachus: Victoria Berenices." *ZPE* 25 (1977): 1–50.

Pontani, Filippomaria. "The First Word of Callimachus' ΑΙΤΙΑ." *ZPE* 128 (1999): 57–59.

Storck, Karl Christian. *Die ältesten Sagen der Insel Keos.* PhD diss. Giessen, 1912.

Thomas, Richard. "Callimachus, the Victoria Berenice and Roman Poetry." *CQ* 33 (1983): 92–113.

Vogliano, Achille. "18. ΔΙΗΓΗΣΕΙΣ di poemi di Callimaco." *Papiri della R. Università di Milano 1* (1937): 66–145.

Wimmel, Walter. *Kallimachos im Rom.* Wiesbaden: Steiner, 1960.

ΑΙΤΙΩΝ Α΄

1–1e In Telchinas

1 (1.1–40 Pf.) *P.Oxy.* 2079 fr. 1; 14–21, *P.Oxy.* 2167 fr. 1

Πολλάκι‿ι[1] μοι Τελχῖνες ἐπιτρύζουσιν ἀ‿οιδῇ,
   νήιδε‿ς οἳ Μούσης οὐκ ἐγένοντο φίλοι,[2]
εἵνεκε‿ν οὐχ ἓν ἄεισμα διηνεκὲς ἢ βασιλ[η[3]
   ......]ας ἐν πολλαῖς ἤνυσα χιλιάσιν
5 ἢ .....].ους ἥρωας, ἔπος δ᾽ ἐπὶ τυτθὸν ἐλ[ίσσω
   παῖς ἅτ‿ε, τῶν δ᾽ ἐτέων ἡ δεκὰ‿ς‿ οὐκ ὀλίγη.
   ......].[.] καὶ Τε[λ]χῖσιν ἐγὼ τόδε· "φῦλον α[
   ....] τήκ[ειν] ἧπαρ ἐπιστάμενον,
   ......]‿ρεην [ὀλ]ιγόστιχος· ἀλλὰ καθέλ‿κει
10 ...πο‿λὺ τὴν μακρὴν ὄμπνια Θεσμοφόρο[ς·
   τοῖν δὲ][4] δυοῖν Μίμνερμος ὅτι γλυκύς, α‿ἱ γ᾽ ἀπαλαὶ [
   .....] ἡ μεγάλη δ᾽ οὐκ ἐδίδαξε γυνή.

[1] Schol. Marc. Gr. 613 M[a] ad Hom. *Od.* 2.50 (p. 1.80.2 Dindorf); Pontani 1999, 57–59; coni. Lobel 1935, 32

[2] Choerob. in Theod. (*Gramm. Gr.* vol. 4.1, p. 200.18 Hilgard), νήιδες—φίλοι

[3] Apoll. Dysc. *Conj.* (*Gramm. Gr.* vol. 2.1, p. 239 Hilgard), εἵνεκεν—διηνεκὲς

[4] Suppl. Housman ap. Hunt

---

[1] Legendary sorcerers, metalworkers, and arms manufactur-

AETIA I

1–1e Against the Telchines

1 (1.1–40 Pf.) Oxyrhynchus papyri

Often the Telchines[1] grumble at my song, know-nothings
who are not friends of the Muse, because I have not com-
pleted one continuous song with many thousands of lines
about kings [5] . . . or heroes, but I unwind a poem little
by little like a child, though the decades of my years are
not few. And to the Telchines I say this, "Tribe, who know
how to melt away your own hearts, . . . [10] with a few lines;
but munificent Demeter Thesmophorus[2] far outweighs
the long (lady),[3] and of the two works, his delicate (verses)
taught that Mimnermus was sweet, not the great lady.[4] Let

ers (Call. *Hymn* 4.31) associated with Rhodes (Strabo 14.2.7) and
Ceos (*Aet.* 75.64–69 below, where their destruction is described).
Here Callimachus associates his literary rivals with some of the
Telchines' characteristics: primitive, raucous, malevolent. Cal-
limachus himself does not name his critics, but *Schol. Flor.* 1–9
(*Aet.* 1b below) offers a list of possibilities.   [2] Perhaps a
reference to the *Demeter* of Philitas (4th c. BC elegist). The trope
of weighing verses is borrowed from Aristophanes (*Ran.* 1364–
410).   [3] An unidentified poem also written by Philitas.

[4] Two poems of Mimnermus (7th c. BC elegist) are compared,
perhaps the *Nanno* and the *Smyrneïs* (Cameron 1995, 310–17).
Schol. Flor. 12–15 (*Aet.* 1b below) confirms that Callimachus is
comparing the long poems of Philitas and Mimnermus with their
own short poems.

.....]ον ἐπὶ Θρήϊκας ἀπ᾽ Αἰγύπτοιο [πέτοιτο[5]
αἵματ]ι Πυγμαίων ἡδομένη [γ]έρα[νος,[6]

15 Μασσα,γέται ,κ,αὶ μακρὸν ὀϊστεύοιεν ἐπ᾽ ἄνδρα
Μῆδον]·[7] ἀ[ηδονίδες][8] δ᾽ ὧδε μελιχρ[ό]τεραι.
ἔλλετε Βασκανίη,ς[9] ὀλοὸν γένος· αὖθι δὲ τέχνῃ
κρίνετε,][10] μὴ σχοίνῳ Περσίδι τὴν σοφίην·[11]
μηδ᾽ ἀπ᾽ ἐμεῦ διφᾶ,τε μέγα ψοφέουσαν ἀοιδὴν

20 τίκτεσθαι· βρονταῶ,ν οὐκ ἐμόν, ,ἀλλά, Διός."[12]
καὶ γὰρ ὅτ,ε πρώτιστον ἐμοῖς ἐπὶ δέλτον ἔθηκα
γούνασι,ν,[13] Ἀπ[ό]λλων εἶπεν ὅ μοι Λύκιος·
".......].... ἀοιδέ, τὸ μὲν θύος ὅττι πάχιστον
θρέψαι, τὴ]ν[14] Μοῦσαν δ᾽ ὠγαθὲ λεπταλέην·

25 πρὸς δέ σε][15] καὶ τόδ᾽ ἄνωγα, τὰ μὴ πατέουσιν
ἄμαξαι
τὰ στείβε,ιν, ἑτέρων δ᾽ ἴχνια μὴ καθ᾽ ὁμὰ[16]
δίφρον ἐλ]ᾶν[17] μηδ᾽ οἶμον ἀνὰ πλατύν, ἀλλὰ
κελεύθους
ἀτρίπτο]υς,[18] εἰ καὶ στε,ι,νοτέρην ἐλάσεις."

5 Suppl. Lobel   6 Jul. Ant. Anth Pal. 11.369; Suppl. Pf.
7 Suppl. Pf.   8 Suppl. Housman ap. Hunt   9 ἔλλετε
Eust. ad Hom. Il. 9.364 (p. 756.37 Van der Valk), ἔλλετε—γένος:
ἔλλατε Schol. Lond., fr. 1d infra   10 Suppl. Housman ap.
Hunt   11 Plut. De exil. 10 (602 F), μὴ—σοφίην   12 Hephaest (p. 52.14 Consbruch), τίκτεσθαι—Διός; Plut.
De adul. et amic. 10 (54d)   13 Apoll. Dysc. Synt. (Gramm.
Gr. vol. 2.2, p. 441.1 Uhlig), καὶ-γούνασιν   14 Suppl. Pf.
15 Suppl. Hunt 1927   16 Eust. ad Hom. Il. 23.585
(1317.15–16, p. 307 Stallbaum), ἑτέρων—ὁμά

the crane, who enjoys the blood of pygmies, fly from Egypt[5] to the Thracians, [15] and let the Massagetae shoot from afar at the Median warrior.[6] In this way nightingales[7] are sweeter. Begone, you deadly race of spiteful sorcerers. Judge poetic skill by art, not by the Persian chain.[8] Do not look to me to bring forth a great noisy song. [20] Thundering belongs to Zeus, not to me." When first I put a writing tablet on my knees Lycian Apollo said to me, "Singer, raise a sacrificial beast to be as fat as possible, but, my friend, keep your Muse slender. [25] And I give this command: tread the paths where wagons do not go and do not drive your chariot along the same tracks as others or on a wide road, but on untrodden ways, even if you will drive it on a narrower path."[9]

[5] A reference to Homer (*Il.* 3.3–6). These verses emphasize the length of Homeric poems and reverse the direction of the cranes' flight, so their noisy honking leaves Egypt. [6] A reference to the long-distance battle between Tomyris, queen of the Massagetae, and the Persian Cyrus (Hdt.1.205–14). Callimachus may have in mind a treatment of the story by Choerilus (4th c. BC epic poet; see Barigazzi 1956, 162–82). [7] In *P.Oxy.* 2079 Housman supplied "nightingales" in this lacuna (cf. Call. *Epig.* 2.5). [8] The *schoenus*, a Persian land measure also used in Egypt (cf. Hdt. 2.6). [9] On the "path of song" in Greek literature and philosophy, see Asper 1997, 21–107 (cf. Pind. *Pae.* 7b.10–14).

---

[17] Suppl. Hunt, *Oxyrh. Pap. XVII* (1927)
[18] Suppl. Pf.

τῷ πιθόμη]ν·[19] ἐνὶ τοῖς γὰρ ἀείδομεν οἳ λιγὺν ἦχον
30   τέττιγος,[20] θ]όρυβον δ᾽ οὐκ ἐφίλησαν ὄνων."
θηρὶ μὲν ο,ὐατόεντι[21] πανείκελον ὀγκήσαιτο
   ἄλλος, ἐγ]ὼ δ᾽ εἴην οὑλ[α]χύς, ὁ πτερόεις,
   ἃ πάντ,ως, ἵνα γῆρας ἵνα δρόσον ἢν μὲν ἀείδω
   προίκιο,ν ἐκ δίης ἠέρος εἶδαρ ἔδων,[22]
35   αὖθι τ,ὸ δ᾽ ,ἐ,κδύοιμ,ι,, τό μοι βάρος[23] ὅσσον ἔπεστι
   τριγ,λώ,χι,ν ὀλ,οῷ, νῆσος ἐπ᾽ Ἐγκελάδῳ.[24]
. . . .   Μοῦσαι γ,ὰρ ὅσους ἴδον ὄθμα,τ,ι παῖδας
   μὴ λοξῷ, πολιοὺς, οὐκ ἀπέθεντο φίλους.[25]
. . . .]σε [, ,] πτερὸν οὐκέτι κινεῖν
40   . . . .] η τ[ῆ]μος ἐνεργότατος.

[19] Suppl. Wilamowitz ap. Maas, *DLZ* 49 (1928): 130
[20] Suppl. Lobel 1935, 33   [21] Pollian. *Anth. Pal.* 11.130.5
θηρὶ μὲν οὐατόεντι; Eust. ad Hom. *Il.* 11.633 (p. 870.6 Van der
Valk) et *Il.* 23.264 (p. 1299.37 Van der Valk)   [22] Schol. Ambr.
et Vat. ad Theoc. 4.16a (p. 139 Wendel), προίκιον—ἔδων
   [23] *Et. Gud.* (p. 232.22 de Stefani), αὖθι-ἐκδύοιμι   [24] Schol.
ad Pind. *Ol.* 4.11c (vol. 1, p. 132.7 Drachmann), τριγλώχιν—
Ἐγκελάδῳ   [25] Schol. ad Hes. *Theog.* 82 (p. 17 Di Gregorio),
Μοῦσαι—φίλους

1a (vol. 2, pp. 100–101 Pf. lemmata in fr. 1a), 11–19
P.Oxy. 2262 fr. 1 col. II, 1, 7, 8

1   .] ,ν [.]. [

2   θ[. . .]ηνη[

3   θ[

30

I obeyed him. We sing among those who love the clear sound [30] of the cicada, not the cacophony of asses.[10] Let someone else bray like the long-eared beast. May I be the tiny, winged one. Oh yes! May I sing dining on dew, a gift from the heavenly air. [35] And also, may I slough off old age, which is a weight upon me like the three-pointed island[11] on deadly Enceladus.[12] . . . the Muses do not reject the graybeard friends whom they looked on with a favoring eye as children. . . . no longer to stir its wing . . . [40] then the most vigorous.

[10] On poets as cicadas, see Acosta-Hughes and Stephens 2012, 36–39 (cf. Pl. *Phdr.* 259b5–d8).   [11] Sicily.   [12] A giant whom Athena killed by hurling the island of Sicily on top of him (cf. Apollod. *Bibl.* 1.6.2). Earthquakes and the eruptions of Mt. Etna were attributed to his anger.

1a (vol. 2, pp. 100–101 Pf.) Oxyrhynchus papyrus (lemmata)

1 . . .

2 . . .

3 . . .

1b (vol. 1, p. 3 Pf.) Schol. Flor. 1–15; *PSI* 1219 fr. 1.1–15
ad *Aet*. 1.1–12

πολλάκι μοι Τελχῖνες ἐπιτρύ̲ζουσιν ἀοιδῇ

[   ]τε̣ι̣.δ[...]..[..].
                    ].Διονυσίοις δυ[σ]ί, τῷ..
              ]νι κ(αὶ) τῷ ἴλειονι κ(αὶ) Ἀσκλη-
5 [πιάδη τῷ Σικε]λίδη κ(αὶ) Ποσειδίππῳ τῷ ονο
   [   ]υρίππῳ τῷ ῥήτορι κ(αὶ) Αν̣α̣
   [   ]β̣ῳ κ(αὶ) Πραξιφάνη τῳ Μιτυ-
   [ληναίῳ, τοῖς με]μφομ(έν) ο[ι̣]ς αὐτοῦ τὸ κάτισ̣-
   [χνον τ(ῶν) ποιη]μάτ(ων) κ(αὶ) ὅτι οὐχὶ μῆκος ηρα
10 [......]..[.............] ουμ(εν)ο.[.] οι.[..].
   ...].ων λου.[.]ο.[.].πα..[....]
   [παρα]τίθεταί τε ἐν σ(υγ)κρίσει τὰ ὀλίγων στί-
   [χ(ων) ὄν]τ(α) ποιήματα Μιμνέρμου τοῦ Κο-
   [λοφω]νίου κ(αὶ) Φιλίτα τοῦ Κῴου βελτίονα
15 [τ(ῶν) πολ]υστίχων αὐτ(ῶν) φάσκων εἶναι [....

1c *P.Oxy.* 2079 fr. 1.1 et 30 (Schol. marg. et superlin. ad
1 Pf.)

1.1   Τελχῖνες· [β]άσκανοι

1.30   ἐφίλησαν (.)· θέλουσιν[

1b (vol. 1, p. 3 Pf.) Florentine Scholia

Often the Telchines grumble at my poem

. . . two Dionysioi[1] . . . and Asclepiades (Sicelides) and Posidippus;[2] the rhetor and Ana . . . and Praxiphanes of Mytilene;[3] and those blaming the excessive thinness of his poems and because [he writes] nothing long . . . He compares the short poems of Mimnermus of Colophon and Philitas of Cos, saying that they are better than their poems of many lines.

[1] The first of the proposed Telchines. The two authors named Dionysius cannot be identified.   [2] Epigrammatists, older contemporaries of Callimachus who both wrote poems praising Antimachus' *Lyde* (Asclepiades, 32 G.-P. = *Anth. Pal.* 9.63; Posidippus, 9 G.-P. = *Anth. Pal.* 12.168 = 140 AB), which Callimachus lampooned (*Epig.* 6).   [3] Peripatetic philosopher and grammarian who wrote a treatise *Against Callimachus* (fragments in Wehrli 1969²).

1c Oxyrhynchus papyrus (marginal and superliner scholia)

1.1   Telchines: sorcerers

1.30   they loved (.): they wish

CALLIMACHUS

1d (vol. 1, pp. 3, 7 Pf.) Schol. Lond. 1–41; *P.Lit.Lond.* 181
col. I, 7–41, col. II, 1–34

1.7 .αηνεως
[[. .α.σ .]]
[3 aut 4 versus deleti]
Αἴας τ̣ι̣να
Τέκμησσαν
Ὀδυσσεύς
αι̣α̣ιν

1.8 οτ̣ι̣ (ἐστι) τὸ ἧπαρ
αιαις()

1.9–10 ἤτοι πολὺ καθέλ-
κει ἢ τ(ὴν) πολὺ μακ̣(ρήν)

1.11–12 ἐδίδαξαν αἱ ἁ̣παλ(αί),
οὐκ ἐδίδ(αξεν) ἡ μεγάλ(η)
λέγει ὅτι γλυκ(ὺς) ὁ Μίμ(νερμος)

1.16 ὧδε· οὕτω(ς) ἡδύ(τεραι) ἐν το(ῖς) μικ(ροῖς)

1.17 ἔλλατε βασκ(ανίης)· κἂν
μηδὲν γ(ὰρ) δυνη(θῶσι),
ποσῶς βλάπτουσι

1d (vol. 1, pp. 3, 7 Pf.) London Scholia

1.7   . . . Ajax, a certain Tecmessa[1] . . . Odysseus . . . Ajax

[1] Princess whom Ajax took captive during the Trojan War. Ajax, Tecmessa, and Odysseus all appear in Sophocles' *Ajax*.

1.8   that is, the liver

1.9–10   either it drags down by much or the much longer

1.11–12 The tender (verses) taught, the great lady did not teach . . . he says that Mimnermus was sweet.

1.16   In this way. Thus, they are sweeter in small [works].

1.17   Away with sorcery. Even if they avail nothing, how much harm they do!

1.19–20 οὐκ ἔχω τὰ μακρὰ
ὥσπερ οὐδ(ὲ) τὰ βρον̣τ̣(ήματα),
οἱ δ(ὲ) μέγα ψοφέο(ντες)
κραυγάνο(νται) κ(αὶ) εκλ.̣.̣
ὡς κ(αὶ) ὄνο(ς) σ(υμ)βαλλ(όμενος)
τέττιγ(ι)

1.22 Λύκ̣ιο(ς)· ἐπεὶ ξένο(ις) ἥδ(ε)ται·
(ἐστὶ) δ᾽ ἄλλ(ως) κ(αὶ) μαντ(εῖον) ἐν
Λυκ(ίαι),
ὁ δ᾽ Ἀριστο(τέλης), ἐπεὶ Λητ(ὼ)
τίκτο(υσα) εἰς λύκ̣ο̣(ν)
μετέβαλε.

1.27 οἶμον· πάτο(ν) ὁμοί(ως)
τ(ὴν) πλατεῖαν

1.33–35 ἃ πάντως κ(αὶ) τὰ ἑξ(ῆς)·
ὤφελον ἵνα τὸ̣ [γῆρας]
κ(αὶ) τ(ὴν) δρόσο(ν), πρότε̣ρ̣ο̣(ν)
πρὸς̣ τ̣ὸ̣ δεύτε̣ρ̣(ον)
ἢν μὲν ἔδ̣ω̣ν
τὸ δ᾽ ἐκδύο[ι]μι

1.36 ἀναγν.̣ ( )
δὲ σφα.̣.̣ ( ) κ(αὶ)...
χειρος π....
πελιασ̣....αισ
ἐπεὶ κερ̣νο( ).̣λεισ
κοτο( ) τὸν Ἐγκέ̣λ̣(αδον ?)

36

1.19–20 I do not make great things, like thunderclaps,
but they croak noisily like an ass compared with a cicada.

1.22   Lycius. Since he is gracious to strangers. Also
there is an oracle in Lycia. And Aristotle [says], since Leto,
when she gave birth to [Apollo] turned into a wolf (Lycus).

1.27   A road. Likewise, a wide path.

1.33–35 Oh yes! And what follows. As for old age and
dew, I wish that I could put off the former by eating the
latter.

1.36   necessary . . . slaughter . . . of a hand . . . bruised
. . . when angry Enceladus(?)

1e (vol. 2, p. 100 Pf.) 1–11, *P.Oxy.* 2262 fr. 1 col. I, 1–11;
12–19, *P.Oxy.* 2262 fr. 1 col. II, 1–8

<pre>
1.36   τριγλώχιν· τρί]γωνος λέ-
       [γει δὲ τὴν Σι]κελίαν δι-
       [ὰ τὸ ἔχειν] τρεῖς ἄκρας
       [Πάχυνον,] Λιλύβαιον,
5   [Πελωρίδ]α· δοκεῖ γὰρ
       [ἐπικεῖ]σθαι τῷ Ἐγκε-
       [λάδῳ ἐ]νὶ τῶν Γιγάν-
       [των ἡ Σι]κελία. ἔστι δὲ
       [καὶ λόφ]ος¹ τῆς Ἀττι-
10   κῆς Σικελί]α καλού-
       [μενος ....]ηθησαν( )
                  ] [ ] [
</pre>

(ca. 13–21 lineae desunt)

¹ λόφ]ος Lobel: τόπ]ος vel ὄρ]ος Pf.

<pre>
1a.1   .].ν[.].[
          ] [
          ] [ ].[
          θια[
          ψε[
          ο.[
</pre>

<pre>
1a.2   θ[...]ηνη[
</pre>

38

1e (vol. 2, p. 100 Pf.) Oxyrhynchus papyrus

1.36   Three-cornered: A triangle. He says that Sicily is a triangle because it has three promontories [Pachynus], Lilybaeum, and [Pelorus]. It seems that Sicily lies on top of Enceladus, one of the Giants. There is also an Attic hill called Sicelia.

1a.1   . . .

1a.2   . . .

1a.3   θ[υμὸν ἐπήϊεν[1]

[1] Suppl. Livrea + Schol. (2G infra)

2–2j Somnium

2 *P.Oxy.* 2208 fr. 1

Ποιμ‚ένι μῆλα νέμ‚οντι παρ᾽ ἴχνιον ὀξέος ἵππου
  Ἡσιόδ‚ῳ Μουσέων ἑσμὸ‚ς ὅτ᾽ ἠντίασεν[1]
  μ]έν οἱ Χάεος γενεσ[
  ] ἐπὶ πτέρηης[2] ὑδα[
5 τεύχω‚ν ὡς ἑτέρῳ τις ἑῷ ‚κακὸν ἥπατι τεύχει.[3]
    ]ῶ ζώειν ἄξιον α[
  ]‚εν πάντες σε· τὸ γα[
  ]‚δε πρήσσειν εὐμα[
  ] ‚‚‚ιπὰ ᾽ [‚‚] ‚[

. . . .

[1] Fronto, *Ep.* 1.4.6. hinc ad Hesiodum pastorem (sc. transeo), quem dormientem poetam ais factum. at enim ego memnini olim apud magistrum me legere: 'Ποιμένι—ἠντίασεν.᾽ τὸ ʿὅτ᾽ ἠντίασενʾ vides quale sit, scilicet ambulanti obviam venisse Musas
[2] Hapax legomenon, *Il.* 22.397   [3] Ael. *VH* 8.9

2a (1.41–45 Pf.) lemmata in Schol. Lond. 1 (vol. 1, p. 7 Pf.) et fr. 2a.5 (vol. 2, p. 102 Pf.) *P.Lit.Lond.* 181 col. II, 35

1 δεκάς

40

1a.3   It [came to his heart.]

2–2j *The Dream*

2 Oxyrhynchus papyrus

When a swarm of Muses met Hesiod, a herdsman pasturing his sheep by the footprint of the high-spirited horse[1] ... (they taught him?) the birth of Chaos[2] ... damp by the hoof ... [5] how someone doing evil to another does evil to his own heart ... to live worthy of ... all ... you ... to accomplish ...

[1] Cf. *Theog.* 22–34, where Hesiod describes his meeting with the Muse below Mt. Helicon in Boeotia, when he receives his initiation as a poet. He is at the spring Hippocrene, which was created by the foot-strike of Pegasus, the winged horse of Bellerophon (Arat. *Phaen.* 216–24).   [2] Cf. Hes. *Theog.* 116.

2a (1.41–45 Pf.) London Scholia (lemmata)

1 ten[1]

[1] Nine Muses, plus one addition. Suggestions for the tenth Muse include Zeus, Apollo, and Arsinoe II, the wife of Ptolemy Philadelphus. Cf. Pl. *Anth. Pal.* 9.506, where Sappho is the tenth Muse, and Call. *Epig.* 51, where Berenice II is the fourth Grace.

2 λίγεια

3 Ἀρκαδ( ) πεμπ( )

4 ὡς ἐνὶ δὴ πατρίο(ις)

5 ἄλλο καλό(ν)

2b (vol. 2, pp. 102–5 Pf. lemmata in fr. 2a.16–71) *P.Oxy.* 2262 fr. 2a col. I, 16

1 Ἀγανίππη

2 Περμησσ]ῷ

3 παρθένο]ς̣

4 [Ἀονίου]

5 [.....].[.]γ.[.].τ[

2 clear[1]

> [1] In this context, "clear-voiced."

3 Arcadia(n)[1] . . . send

> [1] See *Aet.* 2e below.

4 as in the ancestral

5 another lovely

2b (vol. 2, pp. 102–5 Pf.) Oxyrhynchus papyrus (lemmata)

1 Aganippe[1]

> [1] A spring on Mt. Helicon (Paus. 9.29.5).

2 Permessus[1]

> [1] River in Boeotia where the Muses wash themselves (Hes. *Theog.* 5–6).

3 daughter

4 [Aonius][1]

> [1] An ancient name for Boeotia (Call. *Hymn* 4.75; *Fr. Inc. Sed.* 572).

5 . . .

6 λέσχης

7 ἀμοιβ[

8 Ὑμησσοῖ[

9 πηγόν

10 ενκ[ο]λπ.[

11 γόνῳ

12 δαίσατε

13 πανθοιν[

14 τέων

6 conversation[1]

  [1] Cf. Call. *Aet.* 178.16, where the conversation is linked with wine and the symposium. Here it may be the poet's dialogue with the Muses.

7 verbal exchange[1]

  [1] Or, "singing contest."

8 Hymessus[1]

  [1] The Ionic spelling of Mt. Hymettus in Attica.

9 solid . . .[1]

  [1] Scholiasts argue about the meaning of this adjective in Homer. Possibilities include "strong," "solid," "black," and "white."

10 in the bosom:[1]

  [1] Or, "bay."

11 offspring

12 you could give a feast

13 [at a] festival

14 whose

2c (vol. 2, p. 101 Pf. lemmata in fr. 1a.19–30) *P.Oxy.* 2262 fr. 1 col. II, 13

1 ὑπο]κρίσι[ ]ς

2 ἀμν]ήσαιτε

3 πύ]θωνται

2d (vol. 1, p. 11 Pf.) Schol. Flor. 15–20; *PSI* 1219 fr. 1.15–20

$$[\ldots\ldots$$
ὡς κ]ατ᾿ ὄναρ σ(υμ)μείξας ταῖς Μούσ[αις ἐν Ἑ-
λι]κῶνι εἰλήφοι π(αρ᾿ α)ὐτ(ῶν) τ(ὴν) τ(ῶν) αἰτίων
[ἐξήγησιν ἀ]ρτιγένειος ὤν, ωνκ´ὑεμνησ.[
5 ....ἀ]π᾿ αὐτ(ῶν) ἀρχὴ[ν] λαβὼν ε´οσ´α[......
].λόγου>

2e (vol. 1, p. 7 Pf.) Schol. Lond. 42–62; *P.Lit.Lond* 181 col. II, 35–47 et col. III, 1–8

2a.1 δεκάς·.οξ.ελυσ
   παλον...τηρ
   παιδ( ).πα..οκ.τ.( )
   η Ἀρσιν(όη) δυω...
5 ἦν ἄνω(θεν ?) ἢ ὅτι δ(ε) κάτη(ν)
   Μοῦσαν ἐκδ(ε)....( )

2c (vol. 2, p. 101 Pf.) Oxyrhynchus papyrus (lemmata)

1 a reply

2 you might recall (or remind)[1]

[1] Probably addressed to the Muses whom the poet is asking to remind him of the "Causes" (*Aetia*), like Homer's request to the Muses at the beginning of the catalogue of ships (*Il.* 2.484–87).

3 they may learn

2d (vol. 1, p. 11 Pf.) Florentine Scholia

[. . .
How in a dream he met with the Muses on Helicon[1] and received from them the explanation of the *aetia* (causes) when he was a young man, newly bearded, and he recalled them . . . and after learning from them about the origin . . . of the tale . . .

[1] Callimachus imitates Hesiod's meeting with the Muses, but now in a dream. On poets inspired by dreams, Slings 1989.

2e (vol. 1, p. 7 Pf.) London Scholia

2a.1   ten: . . . . mud . . . a child . . . Arsinoe[1] . . . was on high or that . . . the tenth Muse . . .

[1] Arsinoe II.

2a.2   λίγεια· "τοῖον γ(ὰρ) ὑ̣ͺπ̣ͺώ-
        ρορε Μοῦσα λίγει̣α̣"
        κ(αὶ) Ἀλκ(μάν)
10   "Μῶσ' ἄγε Μ̣ῶσ' ἄγε
        λίγεια"

2a.3   Ἀρκαδ( ) πεπ( )· ἐπεὶ οἱ
        Πελοπονν(ήσιοι) ὠνο̣ύ̣μ̣(εν)ο̣ι̣
        τοὺς Ἀρκαδ(ικοὺς) ὄνους ἀνέ̣-
15   τεινον, ἵνα δύνω(νται) ταῖς
        παρ' αὐ̣τ̣ο̣ῖς τροφ(αῖς) χρᾶσθ(αι), οἱ δὲ
        ἀνάπαλ(ιν)

2a.4   ὡς ἐνὶ δὴ
        πατρίο(ις)· οὗτοι ὡς ἐν δη-
20   μοκρατίαι· ἐξουσία γ(άρ) (ἐστι)
        πολ̣λ̣ῶ(ν)

2a.5   ἄλλο καλό(ν)· ἀντ(ὶ τοῦ)
        ἀ̣λ̣λοῖον "διώκ(ειν) ὄρνεο(ν) ἄλλο"

2f (vol. 2, pp. 101–5 Pf.) 1–31, *P.Oxy.* 2262 fr. 2a col. I;
32–41, fr. 2b; 42–72, fr. 2a col. II

        ]αντ[ ]ρδ[ ]
        ]ση.[ ]ηδ.[ ]
    ].Ὅμηρος[ ]ειος
    ].ερων.[.].[ ] λος.

48

2a.2   clear: "Such was the power of the clear-voiced Muse to move (the hearts of the Argives)";[1] And Alcman, "Come Muse! Come, clear-voiced Muse."[2]

[1] Hom. *Od.* 24.62   [2] *PMG* 14 [a], 1. Two examples of *ligeia* (clear) to describe the voice of the Muse.

2a.3   Arcadia(n) . . . send: When the Peloponnesians, who had purchased some Arcadian asses, made threats, [but] they went back again so that they could have use of their own food.[1]

[1] This account of the Arcadian asses is thought to reflect on Callimachus' stubbornness in sticking to his own poetic program (E. Livrea, "Callimaco, fr. 114 Pf., il Somnium ed il Prologo degli 'Aitia,'" *Hermes* 123 [1995]: 57), or the braying of the asses is intended to contrast with Callimachus' own clear-voiced muse (A. Ambühl, "Callimachus and the Arcadian Asses: The *Aitia* Prologue and a Lemma in the London Scholion," *ZPE* 105 [1995]: 212).

2a.4   how in patriarchies: indeed not as in a democracy, for power belongs to the many.

2a.5   *allo kalon* (another lovely thing): instead of *alloion*, "to pursue another bird" (Hom. *Il.* 13.64).

2f (vol. 2, pp. 101–5 Pf.) Oxyrhynchus papyrus

. . . Homer . . .

2a.1 .....δεκ]άς· ἤ[τ]οι ε[.].του( )
...]αριθμ[.].ταῖς [Μ]ού-
σαι]ς ἢ μετὰ τῶν Μου-
σῶν] τὸν Ἀ[π]όλλωνα
ση]μαίνει· Μουσηγέ-
10 της] γὰρ ὁ θε[ό]ς· ἢ Ἀρσι-
νόη]ν προσαριθμεῖ[ ]
ὅτι] τετίμηται ταῖς
τῶν] Μουσῶν τιμαῖ[ς
καὶ] συνίδρυται αὐ-
15 ταῖς] ἐν τῷ Μουσείῳ.

2b.1 Ἀγανίππη· κρήνη ἐν Ἑλικῶ-
νι.]. αυτ..αι πηγασ[ ]
].. ται.αι Ἱπποκρή-
νη]

20 2b.2 Περμησσ]ῷ· Περμησσὸς
πο]ταμὸς τῆς Βοιω-
τία]ς, ἐξ οὗ ἔχειν τὰς
πηγ]ὰς λέγεται ἡ προ-
ειρη]μένη Ἀγανίππη.

25 2b.3 παρθένο]ς· θυγάτηρ· ὡσ[ ]
καὶ] Βακχυλίδης· [ ]
"κλ]υτοφόρμιγγες Δ[ι
ὸς ὑ]ψιμέδοντος πα[ρ-
θέ]νοι"

50

2a.1   ten: He means the Muses[1] or Apollo with the Muses. For the god is the Leader of the Muses. Or he counts Arsinoe II because she is honored together with the Muses and she receives dedications with them in the Museum.

[1] There were traditionally nine Muses, but cf. Diod. Sic. 4.7.2.

2b.1   Aganippe: A spring on Helicon . . . ice-cold . . . and Hippocrene.

2b.2   Permessus: a river in Boeotia, from which the aforementioned Aganippe has its springs.

2b.3   *parthenos* (daughter): as in Bacchylides, "the daughters, famed for their voices, of widely-ruling Zeus."

30 2b.4   Ἀονίου· Β]ρωτίου [
                                    ]ν[
               ]η[
               ]πε.[
               ].εε.[..].[
35   ] σα.. πλ[
             ].ιεπειγα[
             ]νιοισπελ[
                ]μ.[.] παρθεν[
             ].συλληπ[τ]ικῶς[
40   ].νο.[
                 ][

        2b.5   [....].[.] γ.[.]τ[
                .ε..τ[.] καὶ Οὐρανίας ὁ
                Ὑμένα[ιο]s

45 2b.6   λέσχης· [ὁ]μιλία[s]· λέγετ[αι
                 δὲ καὶ τόπος, ἐν ᾧ ἀθρ[οι-
                 ζόμεν[οι δια]λέγοντ[αι

        2b.7   ἀμοιβ[   ]ποκα[
                [ ].[ ]μενη.[

50 2b.8   Ὑμησσοῖ[· ἐν τῷ Ὑμησ]σῷ· [Ὑ-
                 μησσ[ὸς ὄρος τῆς] Ἀττι[-
                 κῆς [   ][

        52

2b.4   *Aoniou*: Boeotian . . . the maidens . . . collectively.

2b.5   . . . Hymenaeus, the son of Urania.

2b.6   *leschēs* (keeping company): the place is mentioned in which they converse together.

2b.7   *amoib* . . . (exchange):

2b.8   *Hymessoi*: on Hymessus, a mountain of Attica.

```
      2b.9    πηγόν· μ[έλαν            ἐ̓]κ[ -
                  δοχη.[                  ].υ[
55                τωγα.[                  ]..[
                  .λω[
               [ ].ου[
                  τω.[
                  νου[
60                μα.[
                  γειω[


      2b.10   ε̣νκ[ο]λπ.[


      2b.11   γόνῳ·] μ[
                  κε.[


65    2b.12   δαίσατε [


      2b.13   πανθοιν[
                  θο̣[


      2b.14   τέων [
                  μ.[
                  το[
                  [
                  ..[
                  .    .    .
```

54

2b.9   *pēgon* (solid, black): . . . interpretation.

2b.10   *enkolp* (with many vales): . . .

2b.11   *gonō* (offspring):

2b.12   *daisate* (you served a banquet):

2b.13   *panthoin* (splendid): . . .

2b.14   *teōn* (whose):

2g (vol. 2, p. 101 Pf.) *P.Oxy.* 2262 fr. 1 col. II, 1–19

       ]ε
   γράφεται κα[ὶ] "θυμὸν
   ἐπήϊεν" ἀντὶ τοῦ
   ἐπὶ τὴν ψυχὴν ἤρ-
5   χ[ε]το

2c.1 ὑπο]κρίσι[.].ς· ἀποκρίσε[ι]ς

2c.2 ἀμν]ήσαιτε· ἀναμνήσαιτέ μ[ε

2c.3 πύ]θωνται· ἀκούσωσι. Ὁμη-
   ρικῶς· "πεύθετο [γαρ
10 Κύπρονδε μέγα κλέ-
   πς" ἀντὶ τοῦ ἠκούε-
   τ[ο

2h (vol. 2, p. 106 Pf.) *P.Oxy.* 2262 fr. 3

  . . .
   ].χ..[
   ].νσ[
   ]δε[
   ]α[
5   ].[
  . . .

2g (vol. 2, p. 101 Pf.) Oxyrhynchus papyrus

He writes "it came to his heart" instead of "it went to his soul."

2c.1 *hypokrisis*: an answer

2c.2 *amnēsaite*: could you remind me

2c.3 *pythōntai*: they hear. In Homer, "He heard [all the way] from Cyprus of the great fame,"[1] instead of *ēkoueto*.

[1] *Il.* 11.21.

2h (vol. 2, p. 106 Pf.) Oxyrhynchus papyrus

. . .

2i (vol. 2, p. 106 Pf.) *P.Oxy.* 2262 fr. 4

```
          ·       ·
       ]φοβ.[
       ]μεγα[
       ] [
       ]αχ[
5      ].ιοτ[
        ]σσ[
     ·        ·
```

2j (vol. 2, p. 106 Pf.) *P.Oxy.* 2262 fr. 5

```
        ·     ·
       ]λι[
       ]ωτ[
     ].σ.[
       ]αιο[
     ·       ·
```

3–7b Gratiae

3 *PSI* 1219, 21

....].τα.............] .. κῶς ἄν[ις αὐλῶν
.ῥέζειν καὶ στεφέων εὔαδε τῷ Παρίῳ.[1]

[1] Heph. 52.19 Consbruch, τοῦ δὲ τρισκαιδεκασυλλάβου
δύο σχήματα . . . ποτὲ δὲ δεύτερος ʽῥέζειν—Παρίῳʼ

2i (vol. 2, p. 106 Pf.) Oxyrhynchus papyrus

Fear . . . great.

2j (vol. 2, p. 106 Pf.) Oxyrhynchus papyrus

. . .

3–7b The Graces

3 Papyrus fragment

How was it pleasing to the Parian[1] to sacrifice with-
out flutes and crowns?[2]

[1] The inhabitants of the island of Paros, one of the Cyclades
in the Aegean.   [2] Contrary to normal practice. For the
origin of this tradition, see *Aet.* 7a below.

4 Cyril. Alex. *Adv. Iul.* 6

Μίνως . . . οὐ τὰ Κρητῶν ἰθύνειν ἤθελε μόνον . . .
Ὅμηρος γοῦν ὀλοόφρονα γενέσθαι φησὶν αὐτόν,
Καλλίμαχος δέ,

    καὶ νήσων ἐπέτεινε βαρὺν ζυγὸν αὐχένι Μίνως

5 Schol. T ad Hom. *Il.* 9.219d

θεοῖσι δὲ θῦσαι ἀνώγει Πάτροκλον, ὃν ἑταῖρον· ὁ δ᾽
ἐν πυρὶ βάλλε θυηλάς· θῦσαι· ἀπάρξασθαι . . . Καλ-
λίμαχος δὲ κακῶς,

    τὸ μὲν θύος ἤρχετο βάλλειν

6 Schol. T ad Hom. *Il.* 18.398–99b

ἐπαναλαμβάνει, ὡς τῆς Χάριτος μητρὸς οὔσης Εὐρυ-
νόμης,

    οἱ δ᾽ ἕνεκ᾽ Εὐρυνόμη Τιτηνιὰς εἶπαν ἔτικτεν

4 Cyril of Alexandria, *Against Julian*

Minos . . . wished to rule not only the affairs of the Cretans but . . . Homer says that he had deadly intentions[1] and Callimachus,

> and Minos extended his heavy yoke over the neck of the islands[2]

[1] *Od.* 11.322.   [2] A reference to Minos' maritime empire (Hdt. 1.171; Thuc. 1.4). On his tyrannical nature, see Strabo 10.4.8. Minos was also portrayed on stage by Aeschylus (*Cretan Women*), Sophocles (*Theseus*), and Euripides (*Cretans*), and as a comic tyrant in Aristophanes' *Cocalus* and *Daedalus*.

5 Scholia to Homer, *Iliad*

He[1] ordered Patroclus, his companion, to make a sacrifice to the gods. And he cast the offerings (*thyēlas*) on the fire: to begin the sacrifice . . . Callimachus [wrote] mistakenly,

> He began to cast the offering (*thyos*)

[1] Achilles.

6 Scholia to Homer, *Iliad*

He makes a correction, that Eurynome[1] is the mother of Charis, the Grace.

> others said that Eurynome, the Titan, bore (the Graces)[2]

[1] Titan daughter of Oceanus and Tethys (Hes. *Theog.* 358, 907).   [2] For several versions of the Graces' parentage, see *Aet.* 7a.

7 (7.1–18 Pf. + *SH* 249A) 1–17, *P.Oxy.* 2167 fr. 2 col. I,
1–14; 7–16, *PSI* 1217A fr. 1.1–10; 14–18 (fin.), *PSI* 1217B
fr. 1+2, 1–5 (init.)

. . . .

>]υλ[
>]ναι
>]κατε κόλλη·
>]εγαλα.[ ]
> 5]νης.[ ]
>]θος[ ]
>] .ο. [ ].λασσαι
>]τατελε[. . . . . .]ου
>]ες ἀνείμον[ες] .ώς. ἀπὸ κόλπου
> 10 μητρὸς Ἐλειθυίη.ς ἤλθετ.ε β.ο.υλο.μένη.ς,[1]
> ἐν δὲ Πάρῳ κάλλη τ.ε καὶ αἰόλα βεύδε' ἔχουσα.ι[2]
> . . . .] ἀπ' ὀστ.λ.ί.γγων δ' αἰὲν ἄλειφα ῥέει,[3]
> ἔλλατε νῦν,. ἐ.λέ.γοισι .δ.' ἐνιψήσασθ.ε. λιπώσ.ας
> χεῖρ.ας ἐμ.οῖς, ἵνα μο.ι πουλὺ μένωσ.ι.ν ἔτος.
> 15 .]νεπὲ .[..] .[. . . .]υρος .φ[. . . .].ιδι .λει[
> . . .].έων χόν .[. . .].σατα[. . . . .]ς·
> . . .].[.].ωμο. . .[ ]εγαρα[
> ε. .κεινεπυκ[

[1] Schol. T ad Hom. *Il.* 22.80c (5.283.33 Erbse) [de κόλπος et
μαζός] τὰ γεννήσαντα καὶ θρέψαντα μέρη· ὡς—βουλομέ-
νης [2] *Et. Gen.* AB β 100 (vol. 2, 428.8 Lasserre-Livadaras)
s.v. βεύδεα· τὰ ἱμάτια· Καλλίμαχος ἐν—ἔχουσαι· σημαίνει δὲ
τὰ ποικίλα ἢ πορφυρᾶ ἱμάτια (Massimilla 1990, 183)

7 (7.1–18 Pf. + *SH* 249A) Oxyrhynchus papyrus; papyrus fragments

... stuck together ... naked as you[1] came from the womb of your mother, when Eileithyia[2] was willing, but on Paros wearing finery and shimmering cloaks. And oil always flows from your locks. Be gracious and wipe your anointed hands on my elegies, so that for me they will live on for many a year.

[1] The Graces. [2] Goddess of childbirth (Hom. *Il.* 16.187, 19.103).

---

[3] *Et. Gen.* AB . . . σημαίνει δὲ καὶ τρίχας, ὡς παρὰ Καλλιμάχῳ ἐν πρώτῳ Αἰτίων, οἷον· ἀπ'—ῥέει (Massimilla, *SIFC* 8 [1990]: 183)

7a (vol. 1, p. 13 Pf.) Schol. Flor. 21–37; *PSI* 1219 fr. 1.21–37

....].τα[...............].. κῶς ἄν[ις αὐλῶν

5 [ζητ]εῖ δ(ιὰ) τίνα [αἰτίαν ἐν Πάρ]ῳ χωρὶς αὐ[λοῦ κ(αὶ)
στεφάνου ταῖς Χ[ά]ρισι θ[ύου]σι. Μίνῳ [τ]ῷ Δ[ιὸς
κ(αὶ) Εὐρώπης θαλασσοκρατο(ῦν)τι κ(αὶ) ταῖς Χά-
ρ[ι]σιν ἐν Π[άρῳ θύοντι Ἀ[ν]δρόγεω τοῦ παιδὸς θά-
νατος ἀπηγγ[έλλετο.

10 ὁ δ(ὲ) οὔτε τ(ῶν) Χαρίτ(ων) τ(ῆς) θυσίας ἠμέλησεν,
ἀλ[λ᾽ ἔθυσεν, οὔτε τοῦ παιδὸς τὸν θάνατον παρενόμ[η-
σεν, τὸν δ᾽ αὐλητ(ὴν) ἐπέσχε κ(αὶ) τὸν στέφανον
ἀ[πέθετο· κ(αὶ) οὕτως π(αρὰ) τοῖς Παρ[ίο]ις τὸ ἔθος
ἔμεινε· τ[αὐτά τε ο(ὖν) π(αρὰ) Κλειοῦς φησιν ἀκη[κο
ένα[ι] κ(αὶ) π(ερὶ) τ(ῆς) [τ(ῶν)

15 Χαρίτ(ων) γενέσεως ὡς Διονύ[σου] εἰσὶ κ(αὶ) Κο-
ρων[ίδος νύμφης Ναξίας, αὐτὸς προ[ε]ιπὼν ὡς παρ᾽
[οἷς μ(ὲν) ἱστορο(ῦν)ται Ἥρας κ(αὶ) Διὸς [εἶ]ναι, παρ᾽
ο[ἷ]ς δ(ὲ) Ε[ὐρυν]όμης τ(ῆς) Ὠκεανοῦ κ(αὶ) Διός, παρ᾽
οἷς δ(ὲ) Ε[ὐάνθης τ(ῆς) Οὐρανοῦ κ(αὶ) Διός. τ(ὴν) δ᾽
ἱστορίαν ἔλαβεν π[(αρὰ) Ἀγίου
κ(αὶ) Δερκύλου. (ἐστὶ) κ(αὶ) π(αρὰ) Ἀριστοτέλει
ἐ[ν] τῇ Παρίω[ν πολιτεί[ᾳ.

7b (Schol. marg. dext. 7 Pf.) *P.Oxy.* 2167 fr. 2 col. I

7.11   ἱ]μάτια

7.12   Β[οστρ]ύχων

64

7a (vol. 1, p. 13 Pf.) Florentine Scholia

. . . . how without flutes (fr. 3.1)

[5] He investigates the reason (*aitia*) why on Paros they sacrifice to the Graces without a flute and a crown. Minos, the son of Zeus and Europa,[1] ruler of the sea, as he was sacrificing to the Graces on Paros, heard of the death of his son Androgeos. [10] He did not neglect the sacrifices of the Graces, but continued the ceremony. Nor did he act unlawfully with respect to the death of his son, but he held back the flute player and put aside the crown, and so the tradition has remained with the Parians. And he says that he learned these things from Clio[2] [15] about the birth of the Graces, how they are the offspring of Dionysus and the Naxian nymph Coronis, but he himself claimed earlier that a story was told by some that they were the children of Hera and Zeus; by others of Eurynome, the daughter of Oceanus, and Zeus; and still by others, the children of Euanthe the daughter of Uranus, and Zeus. He took the narrative from Agias and Dercylus[3] and it is also in Aristotle's *Constitution of the Parians*.

[1] Daughter of Agenor, king of Tyre, and Telephassa; abducted to Crete by Zeus, who assumed the form of a bull (Apollod. *Bibl.* 3.1.1). [2] One of the Muses (Hes. *Theog.* 77; Diod. Sic. 4.7.2). [3] *BNJ* 305 F 8. Dercylus (late 4th or early 3rd c. BC) is thought to have revised an earlier history of Argos by Agias.

7b Oxyrhynchus papyrus

7.11   clothes

7.12   of curls

7c–21d Argonautarum reditus
et ritus Anaphaeus

7c (7.19–34 Pf.) 1–16 (fin.), *PSI* 1217A fr. 2; 1–8, *PSI*
1217B fr. 6–13 + fr. 2; 1, *PSI* 1219 fr. 1.38; 11–16 *P.Berol.*
11521, 8–13

Κῶς δέ, θεαί, ..[...] μὲν ἀνὴρ Ἀναφαῖος ἐπ᾿
    αἰσ[χροῖς
ἡ δ᾿ ἐπὶ δυ[σφήμοις][1] Λίνδος ἄγει θυσίην,
η .[..] τηνε.[......τ]ὸν Ἡρακλῆα σεβίζῃ;
   ...επικ.[....]ως ἤρχετο Καλλιόπη·
5 "Αἴγλήτην Ἀνάφην τε, Λακωνίδι γείτονα Θήρη,[2]
    π]ρῶτ[ον ἐνὶ μ]νήμῃ κάτθεο καὶ Μινύας,
ἄ.ρχμενος ὡς. ἥρωες ἀπ᾿ Αἰήταο Κυταίου
    αὖτις ἐς ἀρχαίην. ἔπλεον Αἱμονίην
        ]εν, ὁ δ᾿ ὡς ἴδεν ἔργα θυγατρ[ός
10   ]έλεξε τάδε·
     ]κα[..].έθνος Ἰήονες αλλαμενε...[

---

[1] δυ[σφήμοις Norsa et Vitelli 1934, 132: βλ[ασφήμοις Lobel
1935, 35   [2] Strabo 1.2.39 (46C) λέγεται πολλὰ τεκμήρια
τῆς τε Ἰάσονος στρατείας καὶ τῆς Φρίξου· τῆς δ᾿ Ἰάσονος
καὶ τῶν ἐπιδιωξάντων Κόλχων καὶ μέχρι τῆς Κρήτης καὶ
τῆς Ἰταλίας καὶ τοῦ Ἀδρίου, ὧν ἔνια καὶ ὁ Καλλίμαχος
ἐπισημαίνεται τοτὲ μὲν "Αἰγλήτην Ἀνάφην τε Λακωνίδι γεί-
τονα Θήρῃ" λέγων "ἄρχμενος—Αἱμονίην."

7c–21d The Return of the Argonauts
and the Rites at Anaphe

7c (7.19–34 Pf.) Papyrus fragments; Berlin papyrus

How is it, Goddesses,[1] that a man of Anaphe[2] makes a sacrifice with obscenities, and Lindos[3] with blasphemous language . . . honoring Heracles? . . . Calliope[4] began: [5] "First keep in mind Aegletes[5] and Anaphe, the neighbor of Laconian Thera,[6] and the Minyans.[7] Beginning with how the heroes sailed back again from Cytaean Aeëtes to ancient Haemonia.[8] And when he saw the deeds of his daughter,[9] [10] he said these things, . . . Ionic people . . .

---

[1] The Muses.   [2] A small island in the Cyclades associated with Apollo. Apollonius relates the origin of the scurrilous rites there (Ap. Rhod. 4.1719–30).   [3] City on the island of Rhodes.   [4] A Muse whom Hesiod calls "the greatest of them all" (*Theog.* 79–80); mother of Orpheus (Ap. Rhod. 1.23–24).   [5] Apollo, "the radiant," who appears to the Argonauts as a gleam of light that reveals the island of Anaphe ("revelation"), saving them from all-enveloping darkness during their return voyage from Colchis (Ap. Rhod. 4.1694–718).   [6] Island near Anaphe settled by the Spartans (Hdt. 4.147–49) and the departure point for the colonists of Cyrene, Callimachus' city of birth.   [7] A Boeotian pre-Greek people, but here, the Argonauts who were said to be descendants of the daughters of Minyas (Pind. *Pyth.* 4.69).   [8] Callimachus will relate the return of the Argonauts from Colchis, where Aeëtes was king. The city of Cytaea or Cyte was on the river Phasis (Ap. Rhod. 2.399–403). Haemonia is an ancient name for Thessaly.   [9] Aeëtes, whose daughter was Medea. She had supported the Argonauts in obtaining the golden fleece and escaped from the palace with them. This may also be a reference to their killing her brother Apsyrtus, but it is not clear where the murder takes place in Callimachus' version of the events.

] πάντα δ᾽ ἀνατράπελα
σο...[ἐ,ποιήσαντό με φόρτον
σου[ ]. ν ὅ σφε φέρει
15 αὔτανδ[ρον]Ἥλιος ἴστω
καὶ Φᾶσις [ποταμῶν ἡμε]τέρων³ βασιλεύς"

³ Suppl. Schwartz ap. Pfeiffer 1921, 13

7d (*SH* 249A recto) *P.Berol.* 17057

και.[
αξε.[
πικ[
του[
αλλ[..].[
μηδειη[
εχθραπ.[

8 Schol. AB ad Eur. *Med.* 1334 Schwartz

παρὰ τὴν ἑστίαν γὰρ ἀνεῖλε τὸν Ἄψυρτον. ἢ ἐπὶ τῷ
βωμῷ τῆς Ἀρτέμιδος, ὡς [καὶ] Ἀπολλώνιός φησιν, ἢ
ἐπ᾽ οἴκου ἐν τῇ πατρίδι, ὡς Καλλίμαχος.

all things overturned . . . they sold me out . . . which carries her . . . together with the men . . . may Helios[10] be my witness and Phasis, king of our rivers."

[10] The sun, Aeëtes' father (Hom. *Od.* 10.135–39).

7d (*SH* 249A recto) Berlin papyrus

and . . . bitter . . . Medea . . . hateful

8 Scholia to Euripides, *Medea*

Beside the hearth she (Medea) killed Apsyrtus,[1] either at the altar of Artemis as Apollonius says,[2] or at home in her fatherland,[3] according to Callimachus.

[1] The brother of Medea (Ap. Rhod. 3.240–48) who was killed to distract the Colchians from pursuing her.   [2] Ap. Rhod. 4.452–81.   [3] Colchis. The murder would then take place before they set sail on the return voyage.

9

a Schol. ad Ap. Rhod. 4.282–91b Wendel

. . . οὐδεὶς δὲ ἱστορεῖ διὰ τούτου τοὺς Ἀργοναύτας
εἰσπεπλευκέναι εἰς τὴν ἡμετέραν θάλασσαν[1] ἔξω Τι-
μαγήτου, ᾧ ἠκολούθησεν Ἀπολλώνιος. ὁ μὲν γὰρ
Σκύμνος αὐτοὺς διὰ Τανάιδος πεπλευκέναι ἐπὶ τὴν
μεγάλην θάλασσαν, ἐκεῖθεν δὲ εἰς τὴν ἡμετέραν θά-
5 λασσαν ἐληλυθέναι. καὶ παρεκβολεύεται, ὡς ἄρα ἐλ-
θόντες ἐπὶ τὴν ἤπειρον οἱ Ἀργοναῦται ἐπὶ στρωτή-
ρων[2] ἐκόμισαν τὴν Ἀργώ, μέχρις οὗ ἐπὶ θάλασσαν
παρεγένοντο. Ἡσίοδος δὲ διὰ Φάσιδος αὐτοὺς εἰσπε-
πλευκέναι λέγει. Ἑκαταῖος δὲ ⟨. . . Ἀρτεμίδωρος δὲ⟩
10 ἐλέγχων αὐτὸν ἱστορεῖ μὴ ἐκδιδόναι εἰς τὴν θάλασ-
σαν τὸν Φᾶσιν. οὐδὲ διὰ Τανάιδος ἔπλευσαν, ἀλλὰ
κατὰ τὸν αὐτὸν πλοῦν, καθ᾽ ὃν καὶ πρότερον, ὡς Σο-
φοκλῆς ἐν Σκύθαις ἱστορεῖ καὶ Καλλίμαχος. ⟨. . .⟩
αὐτῶν τοὺς μὲν εἰς τὸν Ἀδρίαν πεπλευκότας μὴ εὑρεῖν
τοὺς Ἀργοναύτας, τοὺς δὲ διὰ τῶν Κυανέων πετρῶν
15 ἐπὶ τὴν Κέρκυραν, ἔνθα κἀκεῖνοι τότε ἦσαν.

[1] τὴν ἡμετέραν θάλασσαν L: τὸν Ἀδριατικὸν κόλπον P
[2] Στρωτήρων L: σαυροτήρων P

b Schol. ad Ap. Rhod. 4.301–2 Wendel

. . . διαφωνοῦσι δὲ οἱ περὶ τοῦ ἔκπλου τῶν Ἀργοναυ-
τῶν τοῦ ἐκ Κόλχων γεγραφότες. ⟨. . .⟩ ὡς καὶ Καλ-

9

a Scholia to Apollonius of Rhodes, *Argonautica*

No one reports that the Argonauts sailed to our sea[1] via this river[2] except Timagetus,[3] whom Apollonius followed. Scymnus[4] says that they sailed via the Tanais[5] to the great sea and from there came to ours. And he tells in a digression how the Argonauts, when they came to the mainland, carried the Argo on crossbeams until they reached the sea. Hesiod says that they sailed via the Phasis.[6] Hecataeus[7] . . . (but Artemidorus[8] questioning him) says that the Phasis does not connect with the sea. Nor did they sail on the Tanais, but rather along the same route as before, as Sophocles in the *Scythae*[9] says and as does Callimachus. Of the Colchians (in pursuit), the ones who sailed to the Adriatic Sea did not find the Argonauts, but the ones who sailed through the Cyanean rocks[10] to Corcyra[11] where the Argonauts were at that time, did find them.

[1] The Aegean sea.   [2] The river Ister (i.e., the Danube).
[3] Timagetus (4th c. BC), geographer and author of *On Harbors* (*FHG* vol. 4, pp. 519–20).   [4] Scymnus of Chios (2nd c. BC), geographer who wrote a *periēgēsis* of Europe and Asia.
[5] The river Don.   [6] Fr. 241 M.-W.   [7] Hecataeus of Miletus (6th–5th c. BC), historian (*BNJ* 1 F 18b).
[8] Artemidorus of Ephesus (2nd c. BC), author of a *Periplus* in eleven books.   [9] *TrGF* 547 S. Radt.   [10] Clashing rocks at the entrance to the Bosphorus (Ap. Rhod. 4.303–4, 4.1002–3).
[11] Large island in the Ionian (Adriatic) Sea, now called Corfu.

b Scholia to Apollonius of Rhodes, *Argonautica*

. . . Those who have written about the departure of the Argonauts from Colchis disagree . . . as also Callimachus.

71

λίμαχος. φησὶ δὲ Ἀπολλώνιος ὑποστρέψαι αὐτοὺς ἐναντίως Καλλιμάχῳ.

c Schol. ad Ap. Rhod. 4.303–6a Wendel

τῶν Κόλχων οἱ μὲν διὰ τῶν Κυανέων πετρῶν ἔπλευ-σαν, [ὡς καὶ Καλλίμαχος· φησὶ δὲ Ἀπολλώνιος ὑπο-στρέψαι αὐτοὺς ἐναντίως Καλλιμάχῳ], ἄλλοι δὲ μετὰ Ἀψύρτου Ἴστρον ἔσχον.

10 Schol. ad Ap. Rhod. 1.1353 Wendel

μαστεύοντες, ζητοῦντες· ἐξ οὗ καὶ μαστὺς ἡ ζήτησις. Καλλίμαχος,

μαστύος ἀλλ᾽ ὅτ᾽ ἔκαμνον ἀλητύι

11 *P.Oxy.* 2167 fr. 2 col. II, 1–7

. . . .

. [

  σ.[

οἱ ˌμὲν ἐπ᾽ Ἰλλυρικοῖο πόρου σχάσσαντες ἐρετμά

  λᾶˌα πάρα ξανθῆς Ἀρμονίης ὄφιος

5 ἄσˌτυρον ἐκτίσσαντο, τό μὲν "Φυγαδῶνά" κ᾽ ἐνίσποι

  Γρˌαικός, ἀτὰρ κείνων γλῶσσ᾽ ὀνόμηνε "Πόλας."[1]

οἱ δ[

. . . .

---

[1] Strabo 5.1.9 (215C) ἡ δὲ Πόλα ἵδρυται μὲν ἐν κόλπῳ λιμενοειδεῖ νησίδια ἔχοντι εὔορμα καὶ εὔκαρπα, κτίσμα δ᾽

Apollonius says that they returned on a different route than Callimachus.

c Scholia to Apollonius of Rhodes, *Argonautica*

Of the Colchians, some sailed through the Cyanean rocks [As in Callimachus; Apollonius says that they returned on a different route from Callimachus]. Others held to the Ister with Apsyrtus.

10 Scholia to Apollonius of Rhodes, *Argonautica*

masteuontes, *zētountes* (seeking): from which come the nouns *mastus* and *zētēsis* (search). Callimachus,

but when they had tired of their wandering search

11 Oxyrhynchus papyrus

Some, after they dropped their oars by the strait of the Illyrian Sea,[1] beside the snake of pale Harmonia,[2] they founded a city. A Greek would call it Phygadon, but in their language it is Polae. The others . . .

[1] The Adriatic. [2] After being exiled from Thebes, Cadmus and his wife, Harmonia, arrived here and were turned into snakes (Eur. *Bacch.* 1330–32, 1357–60).

ἐστὶν ἀρχαῖον Κόλχων τῶν ἐπὶ τὴν Μήδειαν ἐκπεμφθέντων, διαμαρτόντων δὲ τῆς πράξεως καὶ καταγνόντων ἑαυτῶν· φυγήν· "τὸ—Γραικὸς," ὡς Καλλίμαχος εἴρηκεν, "ἀτὰρ— Πόλας."

12 *P.Oxy.* 2168 verso, 1–7

. . . .

......β..[.] αρν[

Φαιήκων ἐγένον[τ]ο .[

  ἑσμὸν ἄγων ἑτέροις ι.[.].[.].....[

ἔκτισε Κερκ[υ]ραῖον ἐδέθλιον, ἔνθ[εν¹ ἀν᾿ αὗτις

5 στάντες Ἀμ.α.ντίνην ᾤκισ.αν Ὠρικίην.²

καὶ τὰ μὲν ὣ.ς ἤμελλε μετὰ χρόνον ἐκτελέεσθαι

  .[..] .[

. . . .

¹ ἔνθ[εν suppl. L., cett. e.g. Pf.   ² Steph. Byz. 1.176
Billerbeck s.v. Ἀμαντία

13

a Apollodorus (*BNJ* 244 F 157d) in Strabo 1.2.37

Ἀπολλόδωρος δὲ ἐπιτιμᾷ Καλλιμάχῳ, συνηγορῶν
τοῖς περὶ τὸν Ἐρατοσθένη, διότι καίπερ γραμματικὸς
ὢν παρὰ τὴν Ὁμηρικὴν ὑπόθεσιν καὶ τὸν ἐξωκεα-
νισμὸν τῶν τόπων, περὶ οὓς τὴν πλάνην φράζει, Γαῦ-
δον καὶ Κόρκυραν ὀνομάζει.

12 Oxyrhynchus papyrus

They became [neighbors] of the Phaeacians[1] . . . leading a
swarm . . . others . . . he founded a settlement on Corcyra,
and departing again from there, they settled in Amantia in
the region of Oricum.[2] And all this was to be fulfilled in
the future . . .

[1] Inhabitants of mythical Phaeacia who entertained Odysseus
when his ship was wrecked off their island (Hom. *Od*. 6.1–13.69).
Jason and Medea were also given sanctuary there on the return
voyage from Colchis (Ap. Rhod. 4.994–1222).   [2] A harbor
in Epirus (Ap. Rhod. 4.1214–15; Steph. Byz. α 253 Billerbeck s.v.
Amantia).

13

a Apollodorus in Strabo, *Geography*

Apollodorus[1] rebukes Callimachus in agreement with the
followers of Eratosthenes[2] because although he is a gram-
marian he names Gaudus[3] and Corcyra [as places where
the Argonauts stopped] in opposition to the Homeric
scheme that locates in the Ocean all the places around
which he believes the wandering took place.

[1] Apollodorus of Athens (2nd c.), philosopher and grammar-
ian.   [2] Eratosthenes of Cyrene (3rd c.), polymath and Li-
brarian of Alexandria.   [3] Small island south of Crete.

b Apollodorus (*BNJ* 244 F 157) in Strabo 7.3.6

ἐπιτιμᾷ[1] δὲ καὶ τοῖς περὶ Σικελίαν τὴν πλάνην λέ-
γουσι καθ' Ὅμηρον τὴν Ὀδυσσέως· . . . καὶ τοῖς μὲν
ἄλλοις συγγνώμην εἶναι, Καλλιμάχῳ δὲ μὴ πάνυ
μεταποιουμένῳ γε γραμματικῆς, ὃς τὴν μὲν Γαῦδον[2]
Καλυψοῦς νῆσόν φησι, τὴν δὲ Κόρκυραν Σχερίαν.

[1] ἐπιτιμᾷ Casaubon: ἐπιτεῖναι codd.   [2] Γαῦδον Casaubon:
καῦνον codd.

14 Plin. *HN* 4.52

Corcyra . . . Homero dicta Scheria et Phaeacia, Callimacho
etiam Drepane.

15 Schol. ad Dionys. Per. 493

Κέρκυραι δὲ δύο εἰσίν, ἡ μὲν λεγομένη νῦν Φαιακίς
. . . καὶ δύο λιμένας ἔχει ἡ Φαιακίς, τὸν μὲν Ἀλκινόου,
τὸν δὲ Ὕλλου· διό φησι Καλλίμαχος,

   ἀμφίδυμος Φαίηξ[1]

[1] Φαίηξ Schneider ad fr. 336: Φαίαξ codd.

b Apollodorus in Strabo, *Geography*

And he rebukes those who say that the wandering of
Odysseus in Homer was around Sicily . . . and that there
should be forgiveness for some, but for Callimachus not
at all because he pretends to be a grammarian, but says
that Gaudus is the island of Calypso[1] and the Corcyra is
Scheria.

[1] Calypso, a nymph, daughter of Atlas (Hom. *Od.* 1.51–54)
who rescued Odysseus when he was shipwrecked and kept him
on her island for seven years, until ordered by Zeus to set him
free.

14 Pliny the Elder, *Natural History*

Corcyra . . . was called Scheria and Phaeacia by Homer,
but Drepane[1] by Callimachus.

[1] And Apollonius (Ap. Rhod. 4.1223).

15 Scholia to Dionysius Periegetes

There are two Corcyras, one now called Phaeacis . . . and
it has two harbors, one of Alcinous and the other of Hyllus.
Therefore Callimachus says,

Phaeacia . . . with double doors.

16 Schol. s ad Lyc. *Alex.* 1319 Scheer

λάληθρον τὴν Ἀργὼ λέγει· λάληθρον δὲ ἐπειδή, φα-
σιν, ἐκ τῆς φηγοῦ τῆς ἐν Δωδώνῃ ξύλον εἶχε φωνῆεν
καὶ Καλλίμαχος φωνήεσσαν αὐτὴν ἐκάλεσε.

17 (17 Pf. + *SH* 250–51) 1–13 (init.) *P.Oxy.* 2079 fr. 2 col.
II, 1–13; 8–10, *P.Mich.* inv. 3688 recto, 13–16

```
   ε . . [
     τω . . [ . ] . [ . ]δ . [
   τείρεα δεκρ[
   ἀπταίστου [
5  οὐ μέν θην[
   ἀλλ᾽ ἐς ἀδελ[φει-
   φ . [ . . ] . [
     ἔνθ᾽ ὁ μ‚ὲν ἠδμώλει πῆ[ι. . . . . . . .]ῳ‚
   Τῖφυς ἄ‚γοι πομπ[. . . . . . .] λετο Νωνακρίνη‚¹
10 Καλλιστ‚[ὼ λιβά]δων ἄβροχος Ὠκεαν[οῦ‚
   ἔδδεισα[ν
     . . τετιτ[
   ἀλλατι . . [
     χ‚εὶρ Πολ‚υδευκείη²
15 . . . ] . μο . [
   ἀ]μβλυνν[
   εἰρ]εσίην [
```

16 Scholia to Lycophron, *Alexandra*

He says that the Argo[1] was vocal.[2] They say it talked because it had wood that could speak from the oak in Dodona[3] and Callimachus called it "articulate."

[1] Ship of the Argonauts built with the help of Athena.

[2] The Argo shouts in the harbor urging the Argonauts to depart (Ap. Rhod. 1.524–27).   [3] An oracle of Zeus in Epirus that delivered its responses through rustling leaves of the sacred oak or from doves sitting in the tree (Hdt. 2. 55; Hes. frr. 240, 319 M.-W.). Odysseus consulted it (Hom. *Od.* 14.327–30 = 19.299) and also Achilles prays to Dodonaean Zeus (Hom. *Il.* 16.233–35).

17 Oxyrhynchus papyrus; Michigan papyrus

constellations gleaming . . . infallible . . . not . . . but for a sibling[1] . . . then he was uncertain where . . . let Tiphys[2] guide the mission . . . [10] Callisto, the daughter of Nonacris not dampened by the springs of Ocean,[3] they feared . . . the hand of Polydeuces[4] . . . the rowers

[1] Perhaps Idas, brother of Lynceus, both Argonauts.

[2] Steersman of the Argo (Ap. Rhod. 1.105–10).   [3] The Bears, Ursa Major and Minor, never set (Arat. *Phaen.* 48).

[4] One of the Dioscuri who were among the Argonauts rowing.

---

[1] *Suda* ν 551   [2] Schol. ad Dion. Thrax 532 Hilgard μέμφονται τὸν Ζηνόδοτον, ἐπειδὴ τὸ "ἀρνέων ἐκ κεφαλέων" (Hom. *Il.* 3.273) κτητικὸν ἔλεγε, καὶ τὸν Καλλίμαχον· "χεὶρ ἡ Πολυδευκείη" καὶ "σφυρὸν Ἰφίκλειον" (Call. *Aet.* 75.46), ὅτι ἐπὶ ζώντων ἐχρήσατο κτητικοῖς ἐπὶ σωματικοῦ μέρους.

18 1–12, *P.Oxy.* 2167 fr. 3; 9–15 (fin.), *P.Oxy.* 2168 recto

```
              ]τε. τ[  Τυ]νδαρίδαι
           ].μνης[        ]ς Δία πρῶτον ἵκ[ο]ντο
             ] .ἄλλους ητεσαν ἀ[θ]ανάτους
           ἀοσ]σητῆρας εὐστείρ[. . . .]ελέ[.] ο .[.]·
   5    ἀλλ᾽ ὅγ᾽ ἀνι]άζων¹ ὃν κέαρ Αἰσονίδης
        σοὶ χέρας ἠέρ]ταζεν,² Ἰήιε, πολλὰ δ᾽ ἀπείλει
        ἐς Πυθὼ πέ]μψειν, πολλὰ δ᾽ ἐς Ὀρτυγίην,
        εἴ κεν ἀμιχ.θαλόεσσαν ἀπ᾽ ἠέρα νηὸς ἐλάσσῃς·³
              ] .ὅτι σήν, Φοῖβε, κατ᾽ αἰσιμίην
  10    πείσματ᾽]⁴ ἔλυσαν ἐκ[λ]ηρώσαντό τ᾽ ἐρετμά
              ] .πικρὸν ἔκοψαν ὕδωρ·
                 ] .ἐπώνυμον Ἐμβασίοιο
                    ] . . .εν . . Παγα.σ.αῖς
                        ]´.ρηνα
  15                   ]´. του·
```

. . . .

¹ Suppl. Pf.   ² Suppl. Pf.   ³ Schol. T ad Hom. *Il.*
24.753a–b Erbse οἱ δὲ ὀμιχλώδη καὶ ἀπροότατον τοῖς πλέουσι
διὰ τὰ ἐργαστήρια Ἡφαίστου· ʽεἰ—ἐλάσσῃςʼ
⁴ Suppl. Pf.

19 Choerob. in Theod. (*Gramm. Gr.* vol. 4.1, p. 268
Hilgard)

ὅτι γὰρ τοῦ μέλας μέλαντος ἦν ἡ γενική, δηλοῖ τὸ
ʽΜελαντείους-πέτρας,ʼ διὰ τοῦ ντ ἐξενεχθέν.

Μελαντείους δ᾽ ἐπὶ πέτρας

18 Oxyrhynchus papyri

the Sons of Tyndareus[1] . . . first they supplicated Zeus[2] . . . and they [prayed to?] the other immortals . . . helpers . . . with a good keel.[3] [5] And the son of Aeson,[4] grieving in his heart, held up his hands to you,[5] Ieios,[6] and promised to send many [gifts] to Pytho and many to Ortygia[7] if ever you would drive from the ship the deep fog. That in accordance with your oracle, Phoebus, [10] they let loose the ropes and allotted the oars.[8] They cleaved the bitter water . . . [Apollo] named from the embarkation[9] . . . Pagasae[10]

[1] The Dioscuri, Castor and Polydeuces (Ap. Rhod. 4.592–95).
[2] Their divine father, though they were born in the house of Tyndareus (Ap. Rhod. 2.30).   [3] The Argo (Ap. Rhod. 1.388).
[4] Jason (Ap. Rhod. 1.45–47).   [5] Apollo.   [6] The epithet is from *hiē*, a ritual cry associated with Apollo (Pind. *Pae.* 2.35).   [7] Pytho was Apollo's shrine and oracle at Delphi; Ortygia, an old name for Delos, his other major cult site (Call. *Hymn* 2.59; Ap. Rhod. 1.418–19).   [8] Rowing positions in the Argo were assigned by lot (Ap. Rhod. 1.358).   [9] Apollo Embasius, for whom Jason builds an altar (Ap. Rhod. 1.404).
[10] The harbor near Iolcus where the Argo embarked (Ap. Rhod. 1.238; Hyg. *Poet. astr.* 2.37).

19 Choeroboscus

Because *melantos* was the genitive of *melas*, [the meaning of] *"melanteious-petras"* is clear because it was created with *nt*.

At the Melantian Rocks[1]

[1] Near the island of Thera (Schol. ad Ap. Rhod. 4.1707), but there were also others with the same name (E. Delage, *La Géographie dans les Argonaitiques d' Apollonios de Rhodes* [Paris: de Boccard, 1930], 273).

20 Ἐκλογαὶ διαφόρων λέξεων (AO vol. 2, p. 453 Cramer) s.v. κύφελλα

τὰ νέφη οἷον κρύφελλα, ἀποκρύπτοντα τὴν σελήνην. Καλλίμαχος,

    ἐτμήγη δὲ κύφελλα

21 P.Oxy. 2209A, 1–12; 6–14 (fin.), P.Mich. inv. 5475c

```
       .   .   .   .   .   .   .
                    ].λεινιλιο[
                    ]ἐπὶ βλεφ[αρ
        τόφρα δ' ἀνιήσου.σα λόφον βοὸς ἔ.γρετο Τιτώ¹
        Λαομεδοντείῳ]² παιδὶ χροϊσσαμ[ένη
5                   ]μετὰ δμωῇσι[
                    ]ξείνιον Ἀλκινο[ο
    δ   [           ] Φαιηκίδας, αἵ ῥα τ[
        τερπ[..]. υ..ισ..τινος ἡδομέναις
        χλεύ[..]δει....ος ἀπεκρύψαντο λαθεσθ....[
10      νήστ[ι]ες ἐν Δηοῦς ἤμασι Ῥαριάδος
        ].[.]..δ..[....] ἐπεσβολίῃσι μέλι.σσαι[
        ]..τ...ναι πρωτατουαρχ.ν..[
                    ]νασα[
                    ]ναγ[
       .   .   .   .   .   .   .
```

¹ Schol. Tz. ad Lyc. *Alex.* 941 Scheer, Τιτὼ λέγεται ἡ Ἡμέρα
διὰ τὸ ἀρχαιοτάτην εἶναι. καὶ Καλλίμαχος· τόφρα—Τιτώ
² Init. e.g. suppl. Pf.

20 Anonymous, *Collections of Various Words*

Clouds, such as *kruphella* (sic.), hiding the moon. Callimachus,

> The clouds were dispersed

21 Oxyrhynchus papyrus, Michigan papyrus

eyelids . . . meanwhile Tito[1] roused herself to torment the
neck of the oxen after she had lain with the son of Laomedon.[2] . . . [Medea] among her slaves [5] . . . a guest-gift
of Alcinous[3] . . . the Phaeacians who . . . pleasantries . . .
to the women enjoying themselves . . . jokes . . . they concealed . . . [10] fasting . . . on the days of Rarian Demeter[4]
. . . with abuse

---

[1] Eos, the dawn (*Suda* τ 694).   [2] Tithonus, her husband
(Hom. *Il.* 20.237).   [3] King of the Phaeacians who gives refuge to Medea and the Argonauts when they escape from her
father. His wife, Arete, gives Medea twelve female slaves (Ap.
Rhod. 4.1219–222).   [4] The Eleusinian rites of Demeter.
Eleusis was near the Rarian plain in Attica (*Hymn. Hom. Dem.*
2.450–52).

21a (vol. 1, p. 17 Pf.) Schol. Flor. 38–43; *PSI* 1219 fr.
1.38–43

Κῶς ͵δέ, θ͵εαί, ͵[. . .] μὲν ἀν͵ὴρ Ἀνα͵φαῖος ἐπ᾽
͵αἰσ͵χροῖς

ζητεῖ δ(ιὰ) τίνα αἰ[τίαν ἐν Ἀνάφῃ μ(ετὰ) αἰσχρ(ῶν)
εἰς ἀλλήλους λόγων Ἀπόλλω[νι, ἐν δὲ Λίνδῳ Ἡρακλεῖ
μ(ετὰ) κ(ατα)ρῶν θύουσι. [πρῶτον οὖν Καλλιόπη
ἱστορεῖ ὡς ὅ] τε Ἰάσων ἐ[κ Κόλχων ....]ς̣[

21b (vol. 1, p. 19 Pf.) Schol. Berol. in *P.Berol.* 11521, 1–25

7c.5 (?)

.......]ὑπὲρ τῶ[ν......]ν· φοινικ͵[
....].κοθωράκων χ[....] ὑπέροπλοι π[

7c.7

.....]γνηταιγιαλ̣[.....]ο̣ντες· Κυτα[ίου· Κύτα
... πατρὶ]ς τῆς Μηδεί[ας..]....υστ̣ε̣ρ̣[

7c.8 (?)

5   ....] ἡ νῦν Θετταλία τ[ὸ] παλαιὸν Ἑλλὰ[ς
......].νις ἐστιν αὐτῆς, Κόλχοι δὲ καλοῦ[νται οἱ
ἐν] τῇ Αἴᾳ πολῖται, ἡ δὲ ὅλη χώρα Κολχίς [

21a (vol. 1, p. 17 Pf.) Florentine Scholia

How is it, Goddesses,[1] that an Anaphian[2] man [sacri-
fices] with shameful words?

He asks the reason that men sacrifice to Apollo on Anaphe
with insults against one another and to Heracles at Lindos[3]
with curses. First Calliope[4] relates how Jason [fled] from
Colchis.[5]

[1] The Muses.   [2] Anaphe is the island revealed to the
Argonauts by Apollo (*Aet.* 7c, n. 2, above).   [3] Dorian city on
the island of Rhodes.   [4] A Muse.   [5] The home of Me-
dea on the Black Sea, where Jason had gone seeking the golden
fleece.

21b (vol. 1, p. 19 Pf.) Berlin Scholia

7c.5   (?) . . . on account of these . . . Phoenician . . .
bronze armor . . . insolent

7c.7   . . . Cytian: Cyta,[1] the homeland of Medea.

[1] An ancient name of Colchis (*Aet.* 7c, n. 8, above).

7c.8   (?) . . . [Haemonia], which is now Thessaly,
long ago was called Hellas . . . and the Colchians are called
citizens of Aea[1] which is the whole district of Colchis.

[1] Ap. Rhod. 2.417–18.

7c.11–16

```
..] κα [...] ἔθνος Ἰήονες αλλα μενε...[
       ]πάντα δ᾽ ἀνατράπελα σο...[
  ἐ̣ποιήσαντό με φόρτον σου[
     ].ν ὅ σφε φέρει αὔτανδ̣[ρον
       ]Ἥλιος ἴστω καὶ Φᾶσις [ποταμῶν
ἡμε]τέρων βα̣σ̣ιλεύς·] νῦν τοὺς Ἕλληνας Ἰή[ονας
κέ[κλ]ηκεν ἀπὸ τῶν Ἀθηναίων πάντ[ας κοι-
νῶ[ς·] οὗτοι γὰρ πρότερ[ο]ν Ἰάονες ἐκαλοῦν[το· καὶ
Ὅμηρος ἐπὰν λέγῃ· Ἰάο̣νες ἑλκεσίπεπλ[οι
τοὺς Ἀθηναίους λέγει· ποδήρει̣ς γὰ̣ρ χιτῶνας
ἐφόρ[ο]υν κατ᾽ ἀρχάς, ὃν τρόπον καὶ Πέρσα[ι
Σ]ύρ[οι Καρχη[δ]όνιοι. ἱστορεῖ δὲ ταῦτα
Κλείδ[ημος ἐν] Ἀτθίδι. ἀπὸ μέρους οὖν τοὺς
Ἕλ[ληνας Ἀθηναίους εἴρηκεν, ὃν τρόπον καὶ
Πίνδαρος· Ἑ[λλάδος ἔρεισμ᾽ Ἀθῆναι᾽, Ἰάονες δὲ
κέκληντα[ι ἀπὸ Ἴωνος τοῦ Ξούθου τοῦ Αἰόλου τοῦ
Ἑ[λλάδος ἔρεισμ᾽ Ἀθῆναι᾽, Ἰάονες δὲ κέκληντα[ι
ἀπὸ Ἴωνος τοῦ Ξούθου
τοῦ Αἰόλου τοῦ Ἕ[λ]ληνος
..[.].. ἀντὶ τοῦ ἔκτανον [
κ[αθάπε]ρ καὶ Ὅ[μ]ηρος ..[
```

21c (*SH* 251) in fr. 18.8 (?) *P.Mich.* inv. 3688 recto

```
πέμψ]ειν πολλά σοι [
    ἐπ]ηγγέλλετο εἰσ[
ἐάν τὴν] δυσπροσόρμισ[τον
```

7c.11–16 the Ionians with respect to their tribe . . . they sold me out . . . and he with his men carry her off . . . Let the Sun be my witness and Phasis the king of our rivers. . . . Now all the Greeks are commonly called Ionians from the Athenians, for these were called Ionians previously. And Homer when he says, "the Ionians with their trailing robes"[1] means the Athenians, since they wore garments reaching to their feet in the old days, which was the fashion even of the Persians, Syrians and Carthaginians. Clidemus in his *History of Athens* relates these things. He says that the Athenians were a part of the Greeks. As Pindar puts it, "the Athenians are the pillar of Greece."[2] The Ionians are named from Ion the son of Xuthus of Greek Aeolus. . . . they killed . . . in front of him . . . as Homer[3] . . .

---

[1] *Il.* 13.685   [2] Pind. fr. 76.2 Maehler.   [3] Homer was perhaps cited for his use of the verb *ektanon* (vol. 1, p. 19 Pf.).

21c (*SH* 251) Michigan papyrus

he[1] proclaimed that he would send many [gifts to Pytho and Ortygia] if you would drive away the darkness that

---

[1] Jason. The scholiast is quoting fr. 17 above, perhaps in a discussion of "foggy."

σ]κοτίαν ἀπελά[σηις
5]. εἴρημεν.[
κα]ταγωγοῦ καὶ δυσπ[ροσορ-
μίστου]. εὕρηκε γὰρ ἐπιθ[
τ]οῦτο δ᾽ ἐστιν.[
Καλλί]μαχος ἀμιχ[θαλόεσσαν
10 τὴν] μὴ προσβίβα[στον
ἐκ θαλ]άσσης εἰς τὴν [γῆν
  ].ιν καὶ γὰρ ελε[
ἔν]θ᾽ ὁ μὲν ἠδμώλει πη[
  ]ῳ Τῖφυς ἄγοι πομπ[
15]λετο Νωνακρίνη Κα[λλιστώ
  ].ων ἄββροχος Ὠκεαν[οῦ
  ] διὰ τὴν σκοτίαν ε[
  ].ι προσπελάσαι κατ[
  ]ροπον οἱ Ἀργοναῦτ[αι
20]ται διὰ τί οὖν ουκα[
  ]ος αὐτὴ προσαγορεύε[ται
ἀμιχ]θαλόεσσα η ποι.[
  ].ς δυσβάτως [
προσπ]ελάζειν ἢ καὶ δυσπρος[όρμι-
25 στος κ]αὶ δυσμιγὴς επ[
  ].ιμεθα τὴν ἀμι[χθα-
λόεσσα]ν ὁμιχλ[ώδη].
  ].σιν ἦ κατηκολ[ούθηκεν
καὶ ὁ] Καλλίμαχος ὡς δυσ[
30]ποιησομένου[
  ]...ν...επ.[

makes landing difficult . . . [5] having spoken . . . fit for landing and difficult for landing . . . Callimachus says . . . this is . . . [10] lest the approach from the sea into the foggy land . . . then he did not know . . . Let Tiphys guide the mission . . . [15] Callisto the daughter of Nonacris not dampened by the springs of Ocean,[2] through the darkness . . . to approach . . . the Argonauts . . . [20] on account of what therefore . . . she[3] herself addresses . . . foggy . . . impassable . . . to approach or difficult to approach [25] and hard to mix with, . . . smoky, misty . . . where he followed . . . and Callimachus, how difficult [30] to be made . . .

[2] The constellation Ursa Major (fr. 17, n. 3, above).
[3] Perhaps the Argo.

CALLIMACHUS

21d (Schol. interlin. 21.4 et 5 Pf.) *P.Oxy.* 2209A 4 et 5

21.4 χροϊσσαμ[ένη]· παρακοιμηθεῖσα

21.5]μετὰ δμῳῆσι· μετὰ δμωίδων ἢ σὺν δ[

22–23c *Sacrificium Lindium*

22 *Et.Gen.* AB s.v. γειόμορος

γειόμορος· ὁ γεωργός· Καλλίμαχος· "τέμνοντας περι-
μὴν αὔλακα γειόμορον." εἴρηται ἀπὸ τοῦ περὶ τὴν γῆν
μορεῖν, ὅ ἐστι πονεῖν· γειόμορος γοῦν ὁ γεωπόνος.

τέμνοντα σπορίμην αὔλακα γειόμορον

23 *P.Berol.* 1162b recto

ἀστέρα, ναὶ κεραῶν ῥῆξιν ἄριστε βοῶν."
ὣ]ς ὁ μὲν ἔνθ᾽ ἠρᾶτο, σὺ δ᾽ ὡς ἁλὸς ἦχον ἀκούει
Σ]ελλὸς ἐνὶ Τμαρίοις οὔρεσιν Ἰκαρίης,

---

[1] Heracles, or perhaps the ox, as Trypanis (1958, 20 n. *a*) first
suggested, citing Theoc. *Id.* 25.138–44. [2] A priest at the
oracle of Zeus at Dodona (cf. Hom. *Il.* 16.234–35). Commenta-
tors on the *Iliad* disagreed about the spelling of this name. This
is the first of four examples of "not hearing," as Heracles does not

21d Oxyrhynchus papyrus

21.4 *chroissamenē*: after she slept alongside

21.5 *meta dmōēsi*: among the slaves or with . . .

22–23c The Sacrifice at Lindos

The tale of Heracles and the Lindian farmer, which answers the question posed in *Aet.* 7c.1 and relates the origin of the ritual at Lindos.

22 *Etymologicum Genuinum*

geiomoros: a toiler on the land; an agricultural worker; Callimachus, *temnontas—geiomoron*. He inquires from him about toiling, which is to labor. Therefore someone who toils on the land is a farmer.

The farmer cutting a furrow for sowing

23 Berlin papyrus

star,[1] yes, you best at tearing up horned oxen!" In this way he cursed there, but you, as a Sellus[2] in the mountains of Tmarus[3] hears the echo of the Icarian sea,[4] as the wanton

hear the curses of the farmer.   [3] Mountain in Epirus near Dodona (Strabo 7.7.11).   [4] Where Icarus fell as he flew over the Aegean in his flight from Crete, or was careless in the way he disembarked (Diod. Sic. 4.77.6). It is another example of "not listening."

ἠ]θέων ὡς μάχλα φιλήτορος ὦτα πενιχροῦ,

5   ὡς ἄδικοι πατέρων υἱέες, ὡς σὺ λύρης

—ἐσσ]ὶ γὰρ οὐ μάλ᾽ ἐλαφρός, ἃ καὶ λι̣.οσ

    ουσεχελέξ ..—,

λυ]γρῶν ὡς ἐπέων οὐδὲν ὀπι̣ζόμ[εν]ος

...].......[.].......[

  [ἕνεκεν

10 τοιαύτης,.....[   ]....[

         ]....[,μακτήρια,¹

[

    .....].ινιλι ...[

....]απην Λίνδοιο τ̣[

15 θέντες, ἀμίστυλλον τ̣.αῦρον ἐπισχαδ( )²

.......]πάντες[

.....].αυηκειν[

      ].̣.[

      ].̣[

20   ].̣[

· · · · · · ·

,χαῖρε βαρυσκίπων, ἐπίτακτα μὲν ἑξάκι δοιά,

ἐκ δ᾽ αὐταγρεσίης πολλάκι πολλὰ καμών,³

· · · · · · ·

,ἔμμοτον,⁴

· · · · · · ·

---

¹ 9–11 Schol. ad *Aet.* 23c, inseruit Wilamowitz   ² *Et. Gen.*
AB α 653 (vol. 1, p. 408.1 Lasserre-Livadaras) s.v. ἀμίστυλλον·
σημαίνει τὸν μὴ κεκομμένον θέντες—ἐπισχαδ( )

ears of youth listen to an impoverished lover, [5] as recalcitrant sons pay attention to their fathers, as you listened to the lyre[5]—for you are not very easygoing—so you, caring nothing for his ill-omened words, . . . on account [10] of such . . . food . . . of Lindos . . . [15] the bull, not cut up into pieces,[6] with dried figs . . . all [20] . . . Hail, you with a heavy club, who under orders[7] twice [completed] six labors and often toiled over many of your own free choice.

[5] Heracles killed his music instructor, Linus, with his own lyre (Diod. Sic. 3.67.2; Paus. 9.29.9).   [6] The ritual imitates the way Heracles himself ate the bull whole (cf. Hes. fr. 265 M.-W.).

[7] Eurystheus, king of Tiryns, commanded Heracles to complete his canonical twelve labors (Diod. Sic. 4.9.5).

---

[3] Schol. BDP ad Pind. *Nem.* 3.42c (vol. 3, p. 48.18 Drachmann) ἰδίᾳ· οὐκέτι προστάξαντος Εὐρυσθέως, ἀλλ᾽ ἀφ᾽ ἑαυτοῦ καὶ κατὰ τὸ φιλόπονον αὐτοῦ διηρεύνησεν, ὅθεν δυνατὸν ἐπανελθεῖν τινας. Καλλίμαχος χαῖρε—καμών, τουτέστι τὰ πάραθλα.   [4] Wilamowitz e scholiis fr. 23c

23a (vol. 1, p. 31 Pf.) Schol. Flor. 44–54; *PSI* 1219 fr. 2.44–54

```
....]...[.]ειστι[.]ιη[
....] των θύου[σ]ι τω.[
....]σαντο τοῦ ἔθους
ν]ομιζόμ(εν)α τὰ ἱερὰ π[
5  .].πάντ(ων) πέτρων κ(αὶ) [
.]. μετεδιδάχθησαν [
. ]ασθαι Λίνδιοι κ(αὶ) τοῦτο[
α]ὐτοῖς. π(αρα)τίθεται δ(ὲ) κ(αὶ) αλλ[
.. ὅ]μοιον, ἠνίκα απαι[
10 ......] π(ερι)έτυχεν Θειοδά[μαντι
]ν κ(αὶ) τω[
].[
. . . . . . .
```

23b (vol. 2, p. 107 Pf.) *Dieg.* 1.26–31a; *P. Oxy.* 2263 fr. 1 col. I, 14–19

```
. . . . .
].. .
]ερι[.]ω(ν)
].ων
].την
5 ]νδ[.]ας
]
```

23a (vol. 1, p. 31 Pf.) Florentine Scholia

. . . they sacrifice . . . of the custom . . . the traditional rites . . . of all the rocks and [5] . . . they were instructed . . . the Lindians even this . . . [the account] is added . . . similar to the other, when . . . [Heracles] happened to meet Thiodamas[1] . . . and

[1] King of the Dryopes. Heracles killed one of his oxen and made off with his son Hylas (Ap. Rhod. 1.1211–20). Here it is a second story of Heracles killing oxen and eating them.

23b (vol. 2, p. 107 Pf.) Oxyrhynchus papyrus (*Diegeseis*)

. . .

23c (23 Pf.) Schol. in marg. *P.Berol.* 11629b recto

23.3   in marg. dext.

ἀπ(ὸ) Ἰκάρ(ου) τ(οῦ) υἱ(οῦ) τ(οῦ) Δαιδ[ά]λ[ου·
Σελλ(οὶ) τὸ Θρᾳκ(η)ς ἔθν(ος) ηπε…οιοη[

23.5   in marg. sup.

ἄδικοι· νουθετ(ού)μ(ε)νοι ὑπὸ τῶν ἑαυτῶν γονέων καὶ
μη[δενὸς] αὐτὰ] πο̣ι(ού)μ(ε)νοι

23.6   in marg. dext.

Λίνον γ(άρ) ποτε ε̣.̣.[
……[
….[

23.9   in marg. sup.

ἔνεκεν τοιαύτ(ης)· ὅτι ἡδίους· μάλιστ[α γ(ὰρ) ἥδον-
τ(αι) ὅσοι τὰ] ἀλλότρια ἐσθίουσι

23.11   in marg. sup.

μακτήρια· ἀπ(ὸ) τ(οῦ) μάττειν κ(αὶ) φα[γεῖν·
μᾶζα γ(άρ)· (ἐστιν) ἡ τροφή

23c (23 Pf.) Berlin papyrus (marginal scholia)

23.3   (right margin)

From Icarus, the son of Daedalus[1]
Selli, a Thracian tribe

   [1] Daedalus, an engineer who made the wings that he and his
son, Icarus, used in their escape from Crete (Diod. Sic. 4.77.1–9).

23.5   (top margin)

Unjust: doing the same things after being chastised by
their parents

23.6   (right margin)

For Linus[1] once

   [1] The story of Linus and Coroebus is in *Aet.* 25e–31b, below.

23.9   (top margin)

on account of such that it was sweeter: especially they take
pleasure whoever devours the things of another

23.11   (top margin)

maktēria (food): from *mattein* and *phagein* (to devour)
mazda is nourishment.

23.19 in marg. sup.

ἐπίτακτα μὲν ἑξάκι διοά· τουτ(έστι) τὰ ἐπιτα[σσ-
όμ(ε)]να ἆθλα αὐτῷ ὑπὸ τοῦ Εὐρυσθέως·

23.21 in marg. sup.

Μότα δ(ὲ) λέγεται τὰ λ[ε]πτὰ ῥάκη τὰ βαλλόμενα
ἐπὶ τὰ ἕλκη, ὅθεν ἔμμοτον ἐλέγετο

24–25d Thiodamas Dryops

With his wife Deianira and his son Hyllus, Heracles arrived in the
land of the Dryopians. When his son became hungry he ap-
proached the farmer Thiodamas and asked for food. When it was
refused, Heracles took and ate the farmer's plow ox, which led to

24 *P.Berol.* 11629b verso

σκῶλος[1] ἐπεί μιν ἔτυψε ποδὸς θέναρ·[2] αὐτὰρ ὁ πείνῃ[3]
    θυμαίνων λάχνην στήθεος εἷλκε σέθεν
δραξάμενος· τὶν δ᾽ ὦνα γέλως ἀνεμίσγετο λύπῃ,
    εἰσόκε τοι τρίπολον νειὸν ἀνερχομένῳ
5 ὠμογέρων[4] ἔτι πουλὺς ἀνὴρ ἀβόλησε βοωτέων
    Θει]οδάμας· δεκάπ[ο]υν δ᾽ εἶχεν ἄκαιναν ὅγε,
ἀμφότερον κέντρον τε βοῶν, καὶ μέτρον ἀρούρης·[5]

---

[1] Hapax legomenon, *Il.* 13.564
[2] Hapax legomenon, *Il.* 5.339
[3] Hapax legomenon, *Od.* 15.407
[4] Hapax legomenon, *Il.* 23.791

23.19 (top margin)

The orders six time two: these are the labors commanded by Eurystheus.

23.21 (top margin)

Mota are said to be light rags thrown on wounds from which it is said that something is "treated with lint."

24–25d Thiodamas Dryops

a battle with the Dryopians and the death of Thiodamas. The Dryopians were forced to migrate to the Peloponnesian towns of Asine and Hermione (cf. *Aet.* 25b below; Apollod. *Bibl.* 2.7.7; Ap. Rhod. 1.1211–19).

24 Berlin papyrus

Since a thorn pierced the sole of his foot; and [your son], raging with hunger, grabbed the hair from your chest and pulled it; and for you, Lord, laughter was mingled with pain; [5] until the plowman Thiodamas, a vigorous old man, still strong, met you as you were going over newly thrice-plowed land. He held a ten-foot rod, both a goad for the oxen and a measure of the land . . . "Hail! . . . of

---

⁵ Schol. ad Ap. Rhod. 3.1323b Wendel ἀκαίνῃ· ἀντὶ τοῦ κέ-ντρῳ. ἄκαινα δέ ἐστι μέτρον δεκάπουν Θεσσαλῶν εὕρεμα, ἢ ῥάβδος ποιμενικὴ παρὰ Πελασγοῖς ηὑρημένη· περὶ ἧς Καλλίμαχός φησιν 'ἀμφότερον—ἀρούρης.

...]...ου ξείνων χαῖρε [......]μενων
....]η μέγ' ἀρητὲ προσ[......]s, αἶψα δ', ἄνωγα,
10 εἴ τι κα]τωμαδίης οὐλάδ[ος ἐστὶ]ν ἔσω
τόσσο]ν ὅσον τ' ἀπὸ πα[ιδὶ κακὴν β]ούπειναν
     ἐλά[σσαι,
δός μοι].⁶ καὶ φιλίης [μνήσομ' ἀεὶ δό]σιος."
αὐτὰρ ὅ]γ' ἀγρεῖον [καὶ ἀμείλιχον ἐξ]εγέλασσε
          ].ε........[   ]τε
     βοῶν
15   ].ε ταῦροι
                                      ]ος·
οἵ κεν βρωσείοντες ἐμὸν παρίωσι.ν ἄροτρον⁷
          ].ων
     Λ.έπ.αργε

20 .έκλυε <˘>, τῶν μηδὲν ἐμοὺς δι' ὀδόντας ὀλίσθοι,
     Πηλεύς.⁸
          . . . .
          .ἀδάμας.⁹

6 δός μοι suppl. Castiglioni: ἔξελε suppl. Maas   7 Ap.
Soph. *Lexicon Homericum* (vol. 1, p. 125.34 Bekker) s.v. ὀψείον-
τες (*Il.* 14.37)· ὀπτικῶς ἔχοντες. ὁ δὲ τύπος τῆς λέξεως Ἀττι-
κός . . . καὶ Καλλίμαχος οἱ—ἄροτρον ἀντὶ τοῦ βρωτικῶς
ἔχοντες.   8 Schol. ad Pind. *Nem.* 5.25b (3.93.3 Drachmann)
οἶδεν οὖν ὁ Πίνδαρος τὸν Φώκου θάνατον, ἀλλ' ἐκτρέπται
εἰπεῖν. μήποτε δὲ καὶ τὸ παρὰ Καλλιμάχῳ ἔκλυε—Πηλεύς
οὕτως ἀποδοτέον, ὅτι αἱ γυναῖκες ὠνείδιζον αὐτῷ τὸν Φώκου
θάνατον.   9 ex scholiis Pf.: dub. Harder

strangers . . . much prayed for . . . at once I ask you, [10]
if there is anything inside your shoulder bag as much as
will drive away evil hunger from the child? Give it to me
and I will always remember your gracious gift." But he
laughed in a boorish and implacable way . . . of the oxen
. . . [15] the bulls . . . "whoever desiring to eat go past my
plow" . . . white coat[1] . . . Peleus [20] heard [things] of
which may none slip through my teeth[2] . . . adamant.

---

[1] One of the oxen, perhaps its name.   [2] Callimachus says
that he will not repeat words that are offensive. Peleus, father of
Achilles, was told that he either murdered his brother or killed
his wife. It is not clear why this example is relevant here (Harder
vol. 2, 250).

CALLIMACHUS

25 *Et. Gen.* AB a 1272 (vol. 2, p. 243.7 Lasserre-Livadaras)
s.v. Ἀσινεῖς

Ἀσινεῖς· οἱ Δρύοπες οἱ τὴν Ἀσίνην κατοικοῦντες·
Καλλίμαχος,

    δειλαίοις Ἀσινεῦσιν ἔπι τριπτῆρος †ἁπάσας†[1]

[1] ἐπὶ τριπτῆρος ἁπάσας A omit B: ἐπὶ τριπτῆρες ἁρπάσας
EM: ἔπι τριπτῆρα πιάσσας Barber, *CQ* 53 (1955): 241: ἐπὶ
τριπτῆρ ὅσα παίσας Pf.

25a Pf. = *Aet.* 23a.8–12

25b (vol. 1, p. 31 Pf.) Schol. ad Ap. Rhod. 1.1212–19a

Ἡρακλῆς γήμας Δηιάνειραν τὴν Οἰνέως θυγατέρα
καὶ διάγων ἐν Καλυδῶνι, ἐν συμποσίῳ Κύαθον . . .
ἀνεῖλεν . . . φεύγων οὖν τὸν φόνον καὶ σὺν τῇ γαμετῇ
στελλόμενος ἀνεῖλεν ἐν Εὐήνῳ ποταμῷ Νέσσον Κέν-
ταυρον . . . ἔπειτα προϊὼν ἔφερεν καὶ Ὕλλον τὸν υἱὸν
καὶ ἐλθὼν εἰς τὴν Δρυοπίαν—ληστρικὸν δὲ τὸ ἔθνος
[5] ὁμοροῦν τοῖς Μηλιεῦσιν, ὡς Φερεκύδης ἐν τῇ γ΄
φησίν—, τοῦ παιδὸς πεινῶντος καὶ τοῦ παιδαγωγοῦ
Λίχα ἀπολιμπανομένου, συντυχὼν τῷ Θειοδάμαντι
ᾔτειτο ὀλίγην τροφήν. ὁ δὲ οὐκ ἐδίδου. ὀργισθεὶς δὲ

---

[1] A cupbearer whom Heracles killed accidently. The name
means "ladle," used for serving wine.   [2] Nessus sexually as-
saulted Deianira while he was carrying her across the river. She
cried out to her husband, who shot him with an arrow. While

25 *Etymologicum Genuinum*

Asines: the Dryopes, the ones settling in Asina. Callima-chus,

> Upon the wretched people of Asine . . . a pestle.[1]

[1] Apparently a metaphor describing their distress.

25a Pf. = *Aetia* 23a.8–12

25b (vol. 1, p. 31 Pf.) Scholia to Apollonius of Rhodes, *Argonautica*

After marrying Deianira, the daughter of Oeneus, Hera-cles crossed over into Calydon and killed Cyathus[1] at a symposium . . . and fleeing from that murder and prepar-ing to depart with his wife, he killed the Centaur Nessus in the river Euenus.[2] . . . then going forward he brought along his son Hyllus and went into the territory of the Dryopians—a tribe of brigands [5] who shared borders with the Melieis, as Pherecydes says in Book 3.[3] And since the child was hungry and his tutor Lichas had been left behind, he happened upon Theiodamas and asked for a little food. He did not give it.

dying, the Centaur taught Deianira how to make a love potion out of his blood and semen (Diod. Sic. 4.36.4–5).   [3] Pherecydes of Athens (6th c. BC), author of mythography and cosmogony (*BNJ* 3 F 19).

ὁ Ἡρακλῆς καὶ ἀποσπάσας αὐτοῦ τὸν ἕνα βοῦν, θύ-
σας εὐωχεῖτο. ὁ δὲ Θειοδάμας ἐλθὼν εἰς τὴν [10] πό-
λιν ἐστράτευσε καθ' Ἡρακλέους, καὶ εἰς τοσαύτην
ἀνάγκην κατέστη ὁ Ἡρακλῆς, ὡς καὶ τὴν γυναῖκα
Δηιάνειραν καθοπλίσαι, καὶ λέγεται καὶ κατὰ τὸν μα-
ζὸν τότε τετρῶσθαι. περιγενόμενος δὲ αὐτῶν καὶ
ἀνελὼν τὸν Θειοδάμαντα ἐδέξατο τὸν τούτου υἱὸν
Ὕλαν, καὶ τὸ πᾶν δὲ ἔθνος διὰ τὴν λῃστείαν μετῴκι-
σεν <εἰς τὴν [15] Πελοπόννησον>, ἵνα τῇ πολλῇ τῶν
ἀνθρώπων ἐπιμιξίᾳ τοῦ λῃστρικοῦ ἤθους ἀπόσχων-
ται. <. . .> περὶ Τραχῖνα τὴν Θεσσαλικὴν πόλιν καὶ
τὴν Οἴτην τὸ ὄρος πρὸς τοῖς ὄροις τῆς Φωκίδος. τού-
των δὲ καὶ ὁ Καλλίμαχος μέμνηται.

25c (vol. 1, p. 31 Pf.) Schol. PB ad Ov. *Ib.* 485

Thiodamas fuit quidam, qui inermis inermes suos duxit ad
proeliam, ut dicit. h.[1]

---

[1] Fortasse κ (Καλλίμαχος)

25d (24 Pf.) Schol. in marg. *P. Berol.* 11629b verso

24.1

] .. [

24.6 in marg. dext.

το[

Then Heracles was furious, and dragged away one of the oxen, which he sacrificed and feasted on. Thiodamas went into the city [10] and organized an attack against Heracles. In the face of this necessity Heracles was in such a state that he armed even his wife Deianira and it is said that she was wounded at that time in her breast. When he prevailed and killed Thiodamas, he received Thiodamas' son Hylas and he forced the whole tribe on account of their lawlessness to migrate to the Peloponnese [15] so that after mixing with a number of people they would turn away from their custom of banditry . . . around Trachis, a Thessalian city and Mt. Oeta near the border of Phocis. Callimachus also recalls these things.

25c (vol. 1, p. 31 Pf.) Scholia to Ovid, *Ibis*

There was a certain Thiodamas who lead his men unarmed into battle, as ?Callimachus[1] said.

[1] The *h* may be an error for *k* (i.e., Callimachus). There is no indication of this style of fighting in the other fragments.

25d (24 Pf.) Berlin papyrus (marginal scholia)

24.1

] . . . [

24.6 (right margin)

. . .

24.12–16 in marg. dext.

ε̣. [
ε[
τ[
ε̣[
·[

24.19 in marg. sup.

Λ[έπ]αργε· ὄν(ομα) τ(οῦ) ταύρ(ου)· ἐὰν δὲ λεπαργέ,
λευκὲ κ(α)τ(ὰ) τ(ὸ) τ(ὸ) λέπο[ς ἀργὸν ἔχειν]

24.20 in marg. sup.

ἤκ(ου)σεν ὁ Πηλεὺς ὡς εἴη φονεύσας τὸν ἑαυτ(οῦ)
ἀ[δ]ελφὸν [Φῶκον] ἢ ὅτι ἐφόνευσεν τ(ὴν) ἑαυτ(οῦ) γυ-
ναῖκα Ἀντιγόνην, ἐξ ἧς ἔ[σχε Πολυδώραν¹

    ¹ Suppl. Pf.

24.22 in marg. sup.

οὐδ(έ)ποτε δὲ ὁ ἀδάμας ῥήσσεται εἰ μὴ ὅτι προ‹σ›-
χέετ(αι) αἷμ[α τράγου

24.12–16 (right margin)

. . .

24.19 (top margin)

Leparge: the name of the bull; if it is [called] *leparge* it is white on account of having a white hide.

24.20 (top margin)

Peleus[1] heard that he was the murderer of his own brother, [Phocus,] or that he had killed his wife Antigone, who had borne Polydorus.

[1] King of the Myrmidons of Thessaly, husband of Thetis, and father of Achilles.

24.22 (top margin)

Never is adamant broken unless the blood of a he-goat is poured on it.

25e–31b Linus et Coroebus

25e (27 Pf.) Stobaeus 4.24 (περὶ νηπίων)

ἄρνες τοι, φίλε κοῦρε, συνήλικες, ἄρνες ἑταῖροι
ἔσκον, ἐνιαυθμοὶ δ᾽ αὐλία καὶ βοτάναι

25f (28 Pf.) Ap. Dysc. *De coni*. 83.4

τόν σε Κροτωπιάδην

26 P.Ryl. 13 col. II

. . . .

Ἀρνεῖος μ[
Ἀρνῆδας[
    καὶ θάνε .[
τοῦ μενα[
5   καὶ τὸν ἐπ.ὶ ῥάβδῳ μῦθον ὑφαινόμενον¹
ἀνέρες ε[
    πλαγκτὺν [
ἠνεκὲς ἀε.ίδω δειδεγμένος²
    ουδεμενα[
10 νύμφης αι[
    παιδοφόνῳ [

¹ Schol. ad Pind. *Nem*. 2.1d (vol. 3, 29.19 Drachmann) τοὺς ῥαψῳδοὺς οἱ μὲν ῥαβδῳδοὺς ἐτυμολογοῦσι διὰ τὸ μετὰ ῥάβδου δηλονότι τὰ Ὁμήρου ἔπη διεξιέναι. Καλλίμαχος· "καὶ—ὑφαινόμενον" "ἠνεκὲς—δειδεγμένος"   ² Schol. ad Pind. *Nem*. 2.1d (vol. 3, pp. 29–30 Drachmann)

25e–31b Linus and Coroebus

25e (27 Pf.) Stobaeus

Lambs were your age-mates, dear boy;[1] lambs, your companions. Sheepfolds and pastures were your abodes.

[1] Linus was a son of Apollo by Psamathe, who gave the infant to a shepherd. He was later killed by the shepherd's dogs (Stat. *Theb.* 1.575–90).

25f (28 Pf.) Apollonius Dyscolus, *On Conjunctions*

You, the grandson of Crotopus[1]

[1] Grandfather of Linus, who had his daughter Psamathe killed when he found out about his grandson (Paus. 1.43.7).

26 Rylands papyrus

The month of Arneus[1] . . . Arnean [days][2] . . . and he[3] perished . . . [5] and the story woven on a staff . . . men . . . wandering . . . I received and sing continually . . . [10] of the bride[4] . . . to the child killer[5] . . . She[6] went to

[1] When the Arnean festival, commemorating Linus' death, was held in Argos.   [2] The festival days when the Argives killed every dog they met because the shepherd's dogs had killed Linus (Conon, *BNJ* 26 F 1.19).   [3] Linus.   [4] Perhaps Psamathe.   [5] If singular, Crotopus, who killed his daughter; if plural, the dogs who killed Linus.   [6] Poena (Punishment). In an alternative version of the story, she was sent by Apollo to avenge Linus' death by killing the Argives' children. Coroebus later kills her.

ἧκεν ἐπ᾽ Ἀρ[γείους
    ἤ σφεων [
μητέρας ‚ἐξεκένωσεν, ἐκούφισθεν δὲ τιθῆναι
15   οὐχ οὕτω[
Ἄργος ἀνα[

27 Pf. = *Aet.* 25e

28 Pf. = *Aet.* 25f

29 *Anth. Pal.* 7.154 adesp., titulus

εἰς Κόροιβον, οὗ μέμνηται Καλλίμαχος ἐν α΄ Αἰτίων.

30 *Et. Gen.* AB s.v. δασπλῆτις

δασπλῆτις· ἡ Ἐρινύς. Καλλίμαχος,

    δασπλῆτα Κόροιβος

the Argives . . . their . . . desolated the mothers, and nurses
were lightened of their burdens . . . [15] not thus . . . Argos.

27 Pf. = *Aetia* 25e

28 Pf. = *Aetia* 25f

29 Title of an anonymous epigram

Regarding Coroebus, whom Callimachus recalls in Book 1
of the *Aetia*

30 *Etymologicum Genuinum*

Frightful: The Erinys. Callimachus,

horrid Coroebus

30a (31a Pf.) *P.Oxy.* 2261 fr. 1 col. I

. . . . .

```
] αι.
]
] όντας
]
]ασι
]ες
] ετε Πυθώ
]ς ἐμέ·
    ]ς ὀλ[ί]σθη
]
] οντο
]
```

. . . . .

31 Steph. Byz. τ 195 Billerbeck s.v. Τριποδίσκος καὶ
Τριποδίσκοι

Τριποδίσκος καὶ Τριποδίσκοι· κώμη τῆς Μεγαρίδος.
λέγεται καὶ Τριποδίσκη. Ἡρωδιανὸς δωδεκάτῃ. ὁ κω-
μήτης Τριποδίσκιος. Καλλίμαχος δ᾿ ἐν Αἰτίων <. . .>
πόλιν αὐτὴν εἶναί φησι.

31a Pf. = *Aet.* 30a

31a (vol. 2, pp. 107–8 Pf.), 7–25, *Dieg.* 1.26–31a; 1–11,
P.Oxy. 2263 fr. 1 col. I, 20–30; 12–19, fr. 1 col. II, 1–8

112

30a (31a Pf.) Oxyrhynchus papyrus

. . . Pytho[1] [7] . . . me . . . it should slip

---

[1] The oracle at Delphi, which ordered Coroebus to found the city of Tripodiscus wherever the tripod, which he was given, should fall (Paus. 1.43.7–8).

31 Stephanus of Byzantium

Tripodiscus and Tripodisci: a village of Megara. It is also called Tripodisce. Herodian in Book 12, "The Tripodiscian village." Callimachus in the *Aetia* says it is a city.

31a Pf. = *Aetia* 30a

31a (vol. 2, pp. 107–8 Pf.) Oxyrhynchus papyrus (*Diegeseis*)

. . .

```
                    ].
              ]ερι[ ]ω(ν)
                 ]ων
                ]την
  5             ]νδ[ ]ας
                ]
              ] ικεν
          ζη]τεῖ δι-
        ὰ τίνα αἰτίαν ......]ατην
 10                    ]ρτο(ν)
                    ].ν
                    ]ολ
                    ].ρα
                    ]υσε
 15                    ]
                    ]
                        ]
```

. . .

```
       κ]ατῴκησαν πόλιν ὀνο-
       μαζομένην] Τριποδίσκον. ὅθε[ν
 20    Ἀργεῖοι κ]ατὰ [τ]ὸν καλούμε-
       νον Ἀρν]εῖον [μ]ῆνα τοὺς πα-
       ρα]τ[υχόν]τας κ[ύ]νας ἀναιροῦ-
       σιν. ἔ]λαβ[ε] δὲ τὴ[ν] ἱστορίαν ὁ Κα[λ-
       λί]μαχ[ο]ς παρὰ Ἀγία καὶ Δερ-
 25    κ]ύλ[ο]υ
```

114

He seeks an explanation . . . they colonized the city named Tripodiscus. Hence [20] the Argives in the month called Arneius kill the dogs they happen on. Callimachus took this tale from Agias and [25] Dercylus.[1]

[1] Attic historians, see note on 7a, above.

31b Schol. marg. in fr. 31a.5

30a.5 τρίποδες

31c–g Diana Leucadia

31c (31b Pf.) P.Oxy. 2263 fr. 1 col. II, 9–10

Τὼ]ς[1] μὲν ἔφη· τὰς δ' εἶθαρ ἐμὸς πάλιν εἴρετο θυμός

[1] Τὼ]ς Lobel: ὣ]ς fort. Pf.

31d (31c Pf.) P. Oxy. 2261 fr. 1 col. II

        .   .   .
           ].. [
        ἠοῖος πρὸ ποδῶν[
        ἤματ᾽ ἐπεὶ τρία τοῦτο[
        ἤλυθον· ὠπόλλω[ν
5   εὔαδε τῇ κούρῃ [
          ερ.[
        .   .   .   .

31b Oxyrhynchus papyrus (marginal scholia)

30a.5 tripods

31c–g Diana Leucadia

31c (31b Pf.) Oxyrhynchus papyrus

Thus she[1] spoke, and at once my heart asked them again

[1] A Muse who was narrating the previous *aetion*.

31d (31c Pf.) Oxyrhynchus papyrus

[the golden crown] placed in the morning [now] at her feet
. . . when this [happened] on the third day . . . they went
. . . Apollo [said] it pleased the goddess[1]

[1] Artemis.

31e (31d Pf.) *P. Oxy.* 2261 fr. 2

<blockquote>

· · ·

]..[

].ηδέ[

]νεχο[

]θόναχ[

]..ύβ.[

</blockquote>

31f (31e Pf.) *P.Oxy.* 2261 fr. 3

<blockquote>

· · ·

].....[

]τε καὶ τεσσε[ρ

</blockquote>

31g (vol. 2, pp. 110–11 Pf.) *Dieg.* 1.31b–e; *P.Oxy.* 2263 fr. 1 col. II, 9–30

Τὼ]ς μὲν ἔφη· τὰς δ᾽ εἶθαρ ἐμὸς πάλιν εἴρετο θυμός.

τῆς ἐν Λευκαδίᾳ Ἀρτέμιδος τὸ ξόανον ἐ]πὶ τῆς κεφαλῆς θυείαν [5] ἔχει δι᾽ αἰτίαν ταύτην· Ἠπειρῶται τ[.]ν.[.].η.[.]..η[.]...κατατρέχοντες τὴν Λευκάδα ἐσύλων. ἐλθόντες δὲ καὶ εἰς τὸ τῆς Ἀρτέμιδος ἱερὸν [10] εὗρον τὴν θεὸν ἐστεμμένην χρυσῷ στεφάνῳ· τοῦτον ἐπιχλευάσαντες ἀφεῖλον καὶ τὴν θυείαν, ἐν ᾗ σκόρδα τρίψαντες ἔφαγον, τῇ θεῷ [15] ἐπέθηκαν. ἐπι.ν.[.]... δ᾽ οἱ Λευκάδι[οι]..

31e (31d Pf.) Oxyrhynchus papyrus

. . .

31f (31e Pf.) Oxyrhynchus papyrus

. . .

31g (vol. 2, pp. 110–11 Pf.) Oxyrhynchus papyrus (*Diegeseis*)

Thus she[1] spoke, and at once my heart asked them again. The statue of Artemis at Leucadia[2] has a mortar on its head for this reason. The Epirotes[3] . . . ravaged Leucadia and pillaged it. When they came into the shrine of Artemis they found the goddess wearing a golden crown. This they took away and as an insult they replaced it with the mortar in which they had mashed the garlic for their meal. . . . On the next day the Leucadians constructed another crown

[1] The Muse.
[2] Island off the west coast of Greece.
[3] Residents of Epirus in northwestern Greece.

θ' ἡμ[έ]ρα[ν ἕ]τερον κατεσκεύασαν στέφανον καὶ
ἀντὶ τῆς θυεία[ς] ἔθηκαν, ἀποπεσόντα δ' αὐτὸν
προσήλωσαν [20] τῷ ξοάνῳ. πάλιν δὲ μεθ'
ἡμέ[ρας] τρεῖς ἐπιτιθεμένου κα[ὶ] ..
    με[ί]να[ν]το[ς̣].̣ης

.   .   .   .   .

Diegesis fabulae incertae

31h (vol. 2, pp. 111–12 Pf.) *Dieg.* 1.31f; *P.Oxy.* 2263 fr. 1
col. III, 1–31

ρησαια[
λως ηε.[
γν[.]υς̣.[θυ-
γατρος̣ [
5 .]ον κα.[
..]εμων[
.[.]ο̣[.]δαν[
χα[.]πυ.[
δι.νου.[
10 τοστομι.[
εφη μη.[
πεισασπ[
νησενε.[
θυσια.[
15 γε[
ουλ.[

120

and placed it on the statue instead of the mortar, and when this fell off they nailed it to the statue. Then again after three days of being put back and not remaining . . .

Summary of an Unknown Tale

31h (vol. 2, pp. 111–12 Pf.) Oxyrhynchus papyrus (*Diegeseis*)

. . . of the daughter [5] . . . [10] he (or she) said . . . I persuaded . . . sacrifice [15]. . .

θ.[.]κα[
θω.υτ[
ρουσιφ.[
20 ας περι.[
τυρανν[
επεμψ[
αναδ.α[
.]η ...[
25 παντο.[
παραν[
νιδαε[
ειν τοισ.[
30 οι θεοι.[
των θα.[
..].. [

.   .

31i (vol. 2, p. 112 Pf.) *Dieg.* 1.31g [?]; *P.Oxy.* 2263 fr. 2

.   .   .
       ]...[
].ε ἐπιφω.[
]ο παρη..[
  ]ερι τ(ὴν) τα.[

.   .   .

[20] king . . . sent . . . [25] all . . . [30] the gods

31i (vol. 2, p. 112 Pf.) Oxyrhynchus papyrus (*Diegeseis*)

. . .

CALLIMACHUS

Cetera fragmenta libri primi

32 *Et. Gud.* s.v. Πηληϊάδεω

Πηληϊάδεω· Ὅμηρος . . . ἐν ἡρωϊκῷ δὲ μέτρῳ τὰς ἀπὸ
τῶν εἰς ης εὐθειῶν γενικας, οἱ ποιηταὶ οὐ προφέρον-
ται εἰς ου, ἀλλὰ ἢ διὰ τοῦ εω Ἰωνικῶς, ὡς Πηλεΐδεω,
ἢ διὰ τοῦ αο Δωρικῶς, ὡς Ὀρέσταο. Καλλίμαχος δὲ
ἐν πρώτῳ Αἰτίων ἐχρήσατο τῇ εἰς ου,

    ταῦρον †ἐρυκιμὴν εἰς ἑνὸς ἀντερέτου†

33 Lydus *Mens.* 4.1 (p. 64 Wünsch)

Λογγῖνος δὲ Αἰωνάριον αὐτὸν ἑρμηνεῦσαι βιάζεται
ὡσεὶ τοῦ αἰῶνος πατέρα, ἢ ὅτι ἕνον τὸν ἐνιαυτὸν Ἕλ-
ληνες εἶπον, ὡς Καλλίμαχος ἐν πρώτῳ Αἰτίων,

    τετράενον Δαμάσου παῖδα Τελεστορίδην

34 Schol. AD ad Hom. *Il.* 8.48

Γάργαρον· Τὸ ἀκρωτήριον τῆς Ἴδης . . . Τρία δέ εἰ-
σιν ἀκρωτήρια τῆς Ἴδης· Λεκτόν, Γάργαρον, Φαλά-
κρη· τούτου μνημονεύει Καλλίμαχος ἐν Α τῶν Αἰτίων.

AETIA BOOK I

Other Fragments of Book 1

32 *Etymologicum Gudianum*

Peleïadeō (son of Peleus): Homer in the heroic meter makes genitives [in the form of *eō*] from nominatives in *ēs*. The poets do not render it by *ou*, but either in the Ionic manner, *eō*, like *Peleïdeō*, or in the Doric manner, *āo*, like *Orestāo*.[1] Callimachus, in the first book of the *Aetia*, uses *ou*,

> The widely-lowing bull . . .[2]

[1] *Od.* 1.40.   [2] The text is corrupt and translation uncertain.

33 John the Lydian, *On the Months*

Longinus argues that January can be explained as the "father of the epoch" or what the Greeks call the "year," as Callimachus in Book 1 of the *Aetia*,

> The four-year-old child of Damasus and descendant of Telestor[1]

[1] For suggestions of where this fragment may belong, see Harder vol. 2, 285–86.

34 Scholia to Homer, *Iliad*

Gargaron: the peak of Mt. Ida. There are three peaks of Ida: Lecton, Gargaron, and Phalacre. Callimachus recalls this in Book 1 of the *Aetia*.

35

a Schol. AD ad Hom. *Il.* 13.66 (3.411.30 Erbse)

Αἴας Λοκρὸς μὲν ἦν τὸ γένος, ἀπὸ πόλεως Νά[ρυ]κος, πατρὸς δὲ Ὀϊλέως. οὗτος μετὰ τὴν Ἰλίου πόρθησιν αἴτιος τοῖς Ἕλλησιν ἀπωλείας ἐγένετο· Κασσάνδραν γὰρ τὴν Πριάμου ἱκέτιν οὖσαν Ἀθηνᾶς ἐν τῷ τῆς θεοῦ σηκῷ κατῄσχυνεν, ὥστε τὴν θεὸν τοὺς ὀφθαλμοὺς τοῦ ξοάνου εἰς τὴν ὀροφὴν τρέψαι. τοῖς δὲ Ἕλλησιν [5] ὑποστρέφουσι καὶ κατὰ τὴν Εὔβοιαν γενομένοις χειμῶνας διήγειρε μεγάλους, ὥστε πολλοὺς αὐτῶν διαφθαρῆναι. διανηξάμενος δὲ Αἴας εἰς τὰς Γυράδας καλουμένας πέτρας ἔλεγεν χωρὶς θεῶν γνώμης διασεσῶσθαι. Ποσειδῶν δὲ ἀγανακτήσας διέσχισεν τὴν πέτραν καὶ τὸν Αἴαντα τῷ κλύδωνι παρέδωκεν. ἐκριφέντα δὲ [10] αὐτὸν κατὰ Δῆλον νεκρὸν Θέτις ἐλεήσασα θάπτει. Ἀθηνᾶ δὲ οὐδ᾽ οὕτως τῆς ὀργῆς ἐπαύσατο, ἀλλὰ καὶ τοὺς Λοκροὺς ἠνάγκασεν ἐπὶ χίλια ἔτη εἰς Ἴλιον ἐκ κλήρου παρθένους πέμπειν. Ἡ ἱστορία παρὰ Καλλιμάχῳ ἐν Α Αἰτίων καὶ παρὰ τῷ ποιητῇ ἐν τῇ Δ τῶν Ὀδυσσείων παχυμερῶς.

b Schol. ss[3] ad Lyc. *Alex.* 1141 (p. 335.12 Scheer)

λοιμοῦ κατασχόντος τὴν Λοκρίδα διὰ τὴν εἰς Κασάνδραν ἀθεμιτομιξίαν Αἴαντος ἔχρησεν ὁ θεὸς ⟨β΄⟩ παρθένους ἐνιαυσιαίας εἰς Τροίαν τῇ Ἀθηνᾷ ἀποστέλλειν εἰς χίλια ἔτη. πεμπόμεναι δὲ αὗται ἐφονεύ-

35

a Scholia to Homer, *Iliad*

By birth, Ajax was Locrian,[1] from the city of Naryx, and Oileus was his father. This man was the cause of the destruction of the Greeks after the fall of Troy. He raped Cassandra, the daughter of Priam, who was a suppliant of Athena in the goddess' precinct, so that the goddess turned the eyes of her statue toward the roof. And for the returning Greeks [5] she roused up great storms when they were opposite Euboea, so that many of them were destroyed.[2] But Ajax swam toward the rocks called Gyrades and said that he was saved despite the wish of the gods. Poseidon was displeased and split the rock giving Ajax over to the waves. [10] Thetis[3] took pity on him and buried his castaway body in Delos. But Athena did not cease from her anger, but compelled the Locrians for a thousand years to send girls by lot into Ilium. The story is told by Callimachus in Book 1 of the *Aetia* and summarily by the poet in Book 4 of the *Odyssey*.[4]

[1] A Greek settlement in southern Italy.   [2] Lyc. *Alex.* 361–64.   [3] A sea nymph who was the mother of Achilles.   [4] *Od.* 4.499–511.

b Scholia to Lycophron, *Alexandra*

When a plague took hold of Locris on account of the rape of Cassandra by Ajax, the goddess ordered that two girls be sent each year to Athena at Troy for a thousand years. And the girls who were sent were killed by the Trojans who

οντο ὑπὸ τῶν Τρώων· προυπαντῶντες γὰρ οἱ Τρῶες
ἐλιθοβόλουν αὐτὰς· [5] εἰ δέ τινες ἐκφύγοιεν ἀνελθοῦ-
σαι λάθρᾳ εἰς τὸ τῆς Ἀθηνᾶς ἱερόν, τὸ λοιπὸν αὗται
ἱέρειαι ἐγίνοντο. τὰς δὲ ἀναιρεθείσας ἔκαιον ἀκάρποις
καὶ ἀγρίοις ξύλοις, τὰ δὲ ὀστᾶ αὐτῶν ἀπὸ Τράρωνος
ὄρους τῆς Τροίας εἰς θάλασσαν ἔρριπτον· [10] καὶ πά-
λιν οἱ Λοκροὶ ἀπέστελλον ἑτέρας. ταύτης δὲ τῆς ἱστο-
ρίας καὶ Καλλίμαχος μέμνηται.

36 Steph. Byz. a 236 Billerbeck s.v. Ἀραχναῖον

Ἀραχναῖον· ὄρος Ἄργους. Καλλίμαχος Αἰτίων α΄.

37 1 Steph. Byz. a 270 Billerbeck s.v. Ἄσβυστα; 2–3
comm. anon. in *P.Oxy.* 2260 col. II, 14–18

⸤οἵη τε Τρίτωνος ἐφ᾽ ὕδασιν Ἀσβύσταο⸥
    Ἡφαίστου λόχιον θηξ[α]μένου[1] πέλεκυν
βρέγμ[α]το[ς] ἐκ δίοιο σὺν ἔντ[ε]σιν ἧλαο πατρός

  [1] θηξ[α]μένου Pf.: θεξ[Pap.: δεξ[α]μένου Lobel

38 Steph. Byz. μ 40 Billerbeck s.v. Μαλλός

Μαλλός· πόλις Κιλικίας. Καλλίμαχος Αἰτίων πρώτῳ.
ἀπὸ Μάλλου κτίσαντος αὐτήν. ὁ πολίτης Μαλλώτης
καὶ θηλυκὸν Μαλλῶτις.

threw stones at them as they approached. [5] If any of them escaped and went up in secret to the shrine of Athena, they became priestesses for the rest of their lives. The ones who were killed they burned with wood that grew in the wild and had no fruit, and threw their bones into the sea from Mt. Traron in the Troad. [10] And again the Locrians sent other girls.[1] The story is told by Callimachus.

[1] Lyc. *Alex.* 1141–73.

36 Stephanus of Byzantium

Arachnaeum: a mountain of Argos. Callimachus, *Aetia* Book 1.

37 Stephanus of Byzantium; Oxyrhynchus papyrus

just as, by the waters of the river Triton[1] at Asbysta, after Hephaestus sharpened the birth ax, you leaped in your armor from the head of your divine father

[1] On Athena's birth by the river Triton in Libya, see Hes. fr. 343.11–12 M.-W.; Aesch. *Eum.* 292–93; Ap. Rhod. 4.1310–11.

38 Stephanus of Byzantium

Mallus: A city of Cilicia. Callimachus in Book 1 of the *Aetia*. Founded by Mallus. A citizen of Mallus [is called] *Mallōtēs* and the feminine, *Mallōtis*.

39 Steph Byz. μ 157 Billerbeck s.v. Μεσοπόντιος

Μεσοπόντιος· ὁ Ἐρέσιος Ποσειδῶν· οὕτω γὰρ ἐν
Ἐρέσῳ τιμᾶται, πόλει τῆς Λέσβου. Καλλίμαχος Αἰ-
τίων α΄.

40 Steph. Byz. τ 190 Billerbeck s.v. Τρινακρία

Τρινακρία· ἡ Σικελία, παρὰ τὸ τρεῖς ἔχειν ἄκρας. τὸ
ἐθνικὸν Τρινακριεύς. Καλλίμαχος δ᾽ Αἰτίων α΄ "Τρι-
νάκριον πόντον" φησίν. ἐκλήθη δ᾽ οὕτως ἢ ὅτι τρεῖς
ἄκρας ἔχει ἢ ὅτι θρίνακί ἐστιν ὁμοία.

41 Stobaeus 4.50.11

γηράσκει δ᾽ ὁ γέρων κεῖνος ἐλαφρότερον,
κοῦροι τὸν φιλέουσιν, ἑὸν δέ μιν οἷα γονῆα[1]
χειρὸς ἐπ᾽ οἰκείην ἄχρις ἄγουσι θύρην.

[1] γονῆα Apol. Dysc. *Pron.* 112: τοκῆα Stob.

42 *Et. Gen.* AB β 207 (vol. 2, p. 477.4 Lasserre-Livadaras)
s.v. Βουκεραΐς

Βουκεραΐς· κρήνη ἐν Πλαταιαῖς, ἥτις ὠνομάσθη, ὅτι
Πόλυβος ἐξ Ἄργους ἐπέκτισεν Πλαταιὰς μετὰ τὸν ἐπὶ
Δευκαλίωνος κατακλυσμόν, βοὸς αὐτοῦ ἡγουμένης
κατὰ χρησμόν, ὥς ποτε Κάδμου· ἦν ἐκεῖσε κατακλι-
θεῖσαν τῷ κέρατι πατάξαι τὴν γῆν καὶ κρήνην ἀνα-
φανῆναι, ἣν ἀπὸ τοῦ κέρατος τοῦ βοὸς Βουκεραΐδα

39 Stephanus of Byzantium

Mesopontios: The Eresian Poseidon. He is honored in this way in Eresus, a city of Lesbos. Callimachus in Book 1 of the *Aetia*.

40 Stephanus of Byzantium

Trinacria: Sicily, because it has three capes. A native is called *Trinacrieus*. Callimachus in Book 1 of the *Aetia* mentions the Trinacrian Sea. It has this name either because of the three capes of Sicily or because it resembles a trident.

41 Stobaeus

That elderly man grows old more lightly whom the boys love, and whom like their father they lead by the hand up to the doorway of his house.

42 *Etymologicum Genuinum*

Bouceraïs: a spring in Plataea which was called by this name from the time when Polybus from Argos founded Plataea after the Deucalion flood,[1] when an ox led him according to an oracle, as once was the case for Cadmus.[2] When the cow lay down it struck the earth with its horn and the spring appeared which was called Bouceraïs from

[1] A mythical deluge sent by Zeus that was survived by Deucalion, a son of Prometheus, and his wife, Pyrrha (Ov. *Met.* 1.283–347). [2] Mythical founder of Thebes who was told by the oracle of Delphi to follow a certain cow until she collapsed in exhaustion and found a city on that spot (Apollod. *Bibl.* 3.4.1).

καλεῖσθαι. οὕτως Θέων ἐν τῷ Ὑπομνήματι τοῦ αʹ
Αἰτίων Καλλιμάχου, οὕτω καὶ Σερῆνος ἐν τῇ Ἐπι-
τομῇ τῶν Φίλωνος Περὶ πόλεων, Πολύϊδον λέγων τὸν
λαβόντα τὸν χρησμόν.

ΑΙΤΙΩΝ Βʹ

43–43a De Siciliae urbibus

43 1–45 (fin.), *P.Oxy.* 2080 col. I, 1–47; 8–19 (init.),
P.Oxy. 2210 fr. 16.1–12; 12–17, Stob. 2.4.9 Περὶ λόγου
καὶ γραμμάτων, 2.28.14 Wachsmuth; 46–83, *P.Oxy.* 2080
col. II, 48–85

$$\begin{array}{ll}
&].αλ.[.].ο[\\
&].κουρειαννπ.[\\
&]νο.[..]υδε.[\\
&]..δες ἠρίον η[\\
5 &].ει σκοπελο[\\
&]ειθετις ἐν π[\\
&]ερος ηθελε[\\
ω[&].ωδ' ἀπο[.]αι.[\\
οικ[& πε]ρισσοτερο.[\\
10 κα.[&].ρεκες οὔατα [\\
α.[.]θ.[&]ι φυλακη.[\\
\end{array}$$

καὶ γὰρ ἐγὼ τὰ μὲν ὅσσα καρή.ατι τῆμος ἔδωκα

the horn (*ceras*) of the ox (*bous*). Theon[3] tells the story in this way in his commentary on the first book of the *Aetia* of Callimachus and Serenus in his epitome of Philon's *On Cities*,[4] who says that Polyidus received the oracle.

[3] Augustan scholar who also wrote commentaries on Callimachus and his contemporaries Apollonius of Rhodes, Theocritus, Nicander, and Lycophron (Dickey 2007, 60–68).   [4] Philon of Byblos (2nd c. AD; *BNJ* 790 F 18).

AETIA II

43–43a On Sicilian Cities

43 Oxyrhynchus papyri; Stobaeus

cuttings . . . tomb . . . [5] rock . . . Thetis . . . she wished . . . abundant . . . [10] ears . . . guard

And I, whatever I put on my head at that time, the

ξα‚νθὰ σὺν εὐόδμοις ἁβρὰ λίπ‚η στεφάνο‚ις,
ἄπνοα ‚πάντ' ἐγένοντο παρὰ χ‚ρέος, ὅσσα τ'
   ‚ὀδόντων

15 ἔνδοθ‚ι νείαιράν τ' εἰς ἀχάριστον ἔ‚δυ,
καὶ τῶν οὐ‚δὲν ἔμεινεν ἐς αὔρι‚ον· ὅσσα δ' ἀ‚κουαῖς
εἰσεθέ‚μην, ἔτι μοι μοῦνα πάρεσ‚τι τάδ‚ε.

‚]ννε‚[   ]‚αλλ[‚]με[
  ]‚[   ]‚ε‚ην[
20   ]‚...‚[

duo versus desunt

       ]‚[‚]‚α‚ς
      ]‚‚σαντο θαλ‚[
25   ἑ]σπερίους‚[
      ]‚τε τέθμιον [....]‚[
      ]‚...‚μεναις
      ]‚πόλιν ἄλλα τε[....]
      ]‚ρου Κατάνην
30   ]‚‚νεστε προέδ[ρ]ας
     ]‚‚ εην
    ] ἄλλον ἀΰτει
    ]‚ς παρ' ὕδωρ
   .]‚... ἔπλετο πασέ[ω]ν
35   ]‚τι καλεῖν
  Θεοκλ]έες, ἔρχεο Νάξ[ον
     ]‚‚ δημοσίην
     ]ως Ἱέρωνα
     ]ε, Θάψε, βοή

delicate golden oils with sweet-smelling wreaths, all became lifeless at once, and whatever sank through my teeth [15] into my ungrateful belly, none of these remained until morning. But whatever I put into my ears, those alone are still present.

. . .

. . . the sea . . . [25] western . . . the custom . . . but the city[1] . . . Catana[2] . . . [30] seats in the first row[3] . . . he invokes[4] another . . . beside the water . . . it was of all [35] . . . to call . . . Theocles, you came to Naxus[5] . . . public . . . Hieron[6] . . . O Thapsus!,[7] a cry . . . [40] the autumnal seasons

---

[1] Probably Syracuse (*Aet.* 43a.28–30), founded by Archias (Thuc. 6.3.2). [2] Founded by Euarchus (Thuc. 6.3.3). It is located on the east coast of Sicily. [3] Of the theater, designated for dignitaries and other honorees. [4] Or "invoked," perhaps as founder. [5] Thucydides calls him Thucles (Thuc. 6.3.3). He brought his colonists from Chalcis on Euboea. Naxus was the first Greek colony in Sicily. [6] Hieron, tyrant of Syracuse, deported the Naxians later and resettled them in Leontini (Diod. Sic. 11.49.2). [7] Founded on the east coast of Sicily by Lamis of Megara (Thuc. 6.4.1).

40   φθιν]οπωρίδες Ὧραι
μείλια πεμφίγων ⟨αἰ⟩ὲν ἄγουσι νέα.
φήσω καὶ Καμάριναν ἵν' Ἵππαρι<ς> ἀγκύλος ἕρ<π>ει[1]
            ]λειν
          ]γύλοσῃ[
45   ]ν
"οἶδα Γέλ<α> ποταμο<ῦ> κεφαλ<ῇ> ἔπι κεί<μεν>ον ἄστυ[2]
Λίνδοθεν ἀρχαίη [σ]κιμπτ[όμενο]ν γενε[ῇ,
Μινῴη[ν] καὶ Κρῆσ[σ]αν, ἵ[να ζείον]τα λοετ[ρά
χεῦαν ἐπ' Εὐρώπης υἱέι Κ[ωκαλί]δες·
50 οἶδα Λεοντίνους [ ]δεδρα[........] .....[
καὶ Μεγαρεῖς ἕτερ[οι] τοὺς ἀ[πέ]νασσαν ἐκεῖ
Νισαῖοι Μεγαρῆες, ἔχω δ' Εὔβοιαν ἐνισπε[ῖν
φίλατο κα[ὶ] κεστ[ο]ῦ [δ]εσπότις ἦν Ἔρυκα·
τάων οὐδεμιῇ γὰ[ρ ὅτ]ις πο[τὲ] τεῖχος ἔδειμε
55 νωνυμνὶ νομίμην ἔρχετ' ἐπ' εἰλαπίνην."
ὣς ἐφάμην· Κλειὼ δὲ τὸ [δ]εύτερον ἦρχ[ετο μ]ύθ[ου
χεῖρ' ἐπ' ἀδελφειῆς ὦμον ἐρεισαμένη·
"λαὸς ὁ μὲν Κύμης ὁ δὲ Χαλκίδος, ὃν Περιήρης
ἤγαγε καὶ μεγάλου λῆμα Κραταιμένεος,
60 Τρινακρίης ἐπέβησα[ν], ἐτείχισσαν δὲ πόληα
ἅρπασον οἰωνῶν οὐχὶ φυλα[σσόμενοι]
ἔχθιστον κτίστῃσιν, ἐρῳδιὸ[ς εἰ μὴ ἐφέ]ρπει·

---

[1] Schol. A ad Pind. *Ol.* 5.27a (vol. 1, p. 146.19 Drachmann)
φήσω—ἕρπει   [2] Schol. A ad Pind. *Ol.* 2.7g (vol. 1, p. 78.25
Drachmann) οἱ δὲ Γέλα—ἄστυ

always bring new appeasements for the ghosts.[8] I will also [45] speak of Camarina where the sinuous Hipparis[9] creeps . . .

"I know of a city lying at the mouth[10] of the river Gela, secure in its ancient ancestry from Lindos, and Cretan Minoa, where the daughters of Cocalus poured boiling water on the son of Europa.[11] [50] I know Leontini[12] . . . and the other Megarians whom the Megarians from Nisa[13] sent there; and I can speak of Euboea[14] and Eryx, which the Mistress of the Belt loved.[15] In not one of these cities did the founder who built its walls [55] come to the customary feast anonymously."

So I spoke; and Clio began her second story, resting her hand on her sister's shoulder. "The people, some from Cuma, some from Chalcis, whom Perieres lead and the mighty and arrogant Crataemenes,[16] [60] disembarked on Trinacia,[17] and were walling a city[18] without guarding against the *harpasos*,[19] the most hateful of birds to builders, if a heron does not follow it.[20] For it casts a spell on a

---

[8] D'Alessio 2006; 2007, vol. 2, 424n14. [9] A river near Camarina in Sicily (Pind. *Ol.* 5.12). [10] Literally, the "head." The city was also called Gela. [11] City near Acragas named for Minos, the son of Europa. He came to Sicily pursuing Daedalus, who was in flight from Crete (Diod. Sic. 4.79.1). [12] In eastern Sicily, founded by Thucles of Naxus (Thuc. 6.3.3). [13] The harbor of Megara. [14] On Euboea in Sicily (Hdt. 7.156; Strabo 10.1.15). [15] Aphrodite; for her association with Eryx, a mountain and city in northwest Sicily, see Theoc. *Id.* 15.100–101; Ap. Rhod. 4.917–19. [16] On the founders of Zancle (Thuc. 6.4.5). [17] Sicily. [18] Zancle, in northeastern Sicily, which later became Messina. [19] An otherwise unknown bird of prey. [20] Perhaps drawing on Callimachus' prose work *On Birds* (*Fr. Doct.* 414–28).

137

καὶ γὰρ ὁ βασκαίνει πύργον ἐ[γειρόμεν]ον,
γεωδαῖται κα‚ὶ‚ σπάρτα³ διην‚εκὲς εὖτε‚ βάλωνται,⁴
65 στείνεα καὶ λευρὰς ὄφρα τάμ[ωσιν ὁ]δούς.
μέρμν[ο]ν μοι πτερύγεσσι ....[......]ου τε νέοιο,
εἴ κοτ᾽ ἔτιξ[.]‚ην λαὸν ἔποικον ἄ[γοις.
ἀλλ᾽ ὅτε δὴ μόσσυνας ἐπάλξεσι [καρτυνθέ]ντας
οἱ κτίσται δρέπανον θέντο πε[ρὶ Κρόνιο]ν,
70 —κεῖθι γὰρ ᾧ τὰ γονῆος ἀπέθρισε ‚μήδε᾽ ἐκ‚ε‚ῖν‚ος⁵
κέκρυπται γύπῃ ζάγκλον ὑπὸ ‚χθονίῃ,—
.[ ].ισαν ἀμφὶ πόληος· ὁ μὲν θε[........]εσθαι
....ν, ὁ δ᾽ ἀ‚ντίξουν εἶχε διχο[φροσύνην,
ἀλλήλοις δ᾽ ἐλύησαν ἐς Ἀπόλ[λωνα δὲ βάν]τ‚ες⁶
75 εἴρονθ᾽ ὁπποτέρου κτίσμα λέγοιτ[ο νέον.
αὐτὰρ ὁ φῆ, μήτ᾽ οὖν Περιήρεος ἄ[στυ]ρ[ον εἶ]ναι
κεῖνο πολισσούχου μήτε Κραταιμέ[νεος."
φῆ θεός· οἱ δ᾽ ἀΐοντες ἀπέδραμον, ἐ[κ δ᾽ ἔτι κεί]νου
γαῖα τὸν οἰκιστὴν οὐκ ὀνομαστὶ κ[αλε]ῖ,
80 ὧδε δέ μιν καλέουσιν ἐπ᾽ ἔντομα δημ[ι]οεργοί·
"ἵ]λα‚ος ἡμετέρην ὅστις ἔδειμε [πόλ]ιν
ἐ]ρχέσθω μετὰ δαῖτα, πάρεστι δὲ καὶ δύ᾽ ἄγεσθαι
κ]αὶ πλέας· οὐκ ὀλ[ί]γως α[ἷ]μα βοὸς κέχυ[τ]αι."

³ Hapax legomenon, *Il.* 2.135   ⁴ *Et. Gen.* AB s.v. γαιο-
δόται . . . Καλλίμαχος, γαιοδόται—βάλωνται   ⁵ *Et. Gen.*
AB s.v. ἔθρισεν. Καλλίμαχος, κεῖθι—ἐκεῖνος   ⁶ Suppl. Pf.

138

tower being built and on the surveying cords, when the surveyors lay them out [65] to delimit the narrow streets and the level roads. May you go on the wings of a hawk, as far as I am concerned, if you ever lead a people as colonists . . .

"But when the builders had reinforced the wooden towers with battlements for defense around the sickle of Cronus, [70] for the sickle with which he cut off the genitals of his father[21] is hidden there in a cavern under the earth . . . around the city. And he . . . but the other had an opposite view. They quarreled with one another. And they went to Apollo and asked [75] which of the two should be called possessor of the new colony. But he replied that the city was neither Perieres' nor would it have Crataemenes as patron." The god spoke, and after they heard him they went back, and from this time ever since the land does not invoke its founder by name, [80] but the leaders call him to the sacrifices in this way: "Whoever built our city, be propitious and come to the feast. He may bring two or more [guests]. The oxblood has not been shed in small quantities."

[21] The details of the story are in Hes. *Theog.* 174–82.

CALLIMACHUS

43a Schol. marg. *P.Oxy.* 2080 ad 43 Pf.

43.15   νείαιρ(αν) [
           τῷ ἐ(πι)θ[
           ἐχ.[

43.23   ].ͺ.[

43.25   ]τα ἑσπερι
5   ].

43.28–30   Συρα]κὼ ἀ(πὸ) Συρα[κο(ῦς)
            λίμν(ης) ἤτοι Σ[υ]ράκος-
            [σαι ἀ(πὸ) Ἀρ]χίου γυν[αικ(ὸς)] ἢ ἀ(πὸ)
10   Σύρα(ς) καὶ Κόσσης θυγατέρ(ων)

43.31–32   Εὔαρχος [ἐρ]χόμ(εν) ος ε[ἰ]ς Σικελ(ίαν)
            εἶχε[ναῦς] πλετηλ() ἀγούσας, κ(αὶ) μία
            κ(ατ)αχ[θ(εῖσα)] ε̣ἰ̣[ς]
            πέτραν ἀπώλ( ) κατάνην
15   ου τ(ὴν) πόλιν ( )

43.33   Σελινοῦσσα[1] πόλ(ις) ἀ(πὸ)
            Σε̣[λι]ν(οῦντος) ποταμ(οῦ)

[1] Σελινοῦσσα Hunt: λελινουσσα P

43.37   .[
           ε[

140

43a Oxyrhynchus papyrus (marginal scholia)

43.15   lower
     on which

43.23   . . .

43.25   in the evening

43.28–30 Syraco from the wetland of Syracuse or Syracu-
sae from the wife of Archius or from his daughters Syra
and Cosse.

43.31–32 Euarchus coming into Sicily had boats and one
of them was destroyed against the rock shaped like a
cheese grater (Catane), or the city

43.33   the city Selinussa from the river Selinontes

43.37   . . .

20 43.38–39 ηϲ[
               ἐκε[
               Λ̣εο[ντ
               α̣ρχε[

    43.41   ἐκβλη[θ
25   Αἴτνην.[

    43.51   .[

    43.53–55 Ἔρυξ [υἱὸ(ϲ) Βού̣τ(ου) ,]¹
               ἀφ' οὗ [ἡ πόλιϲ]
               κ(αὶ) Ἀφρο̣[δ(ίτη) Ἐρυκ(ίνη)]
30   ου̣[

    ¹ Βού̣τ(ου) Pf.: Ποϲειδ(ῶνος) Hunt

    43.61   ἅρπαϲοϲ· εἰ[δ(οϲ)] ὀρνέου βάϲκαν(ον)

    43.66–67 α̣ι̣[
               ογ[..]..[ ]
               ]. τονὲ` κτιϲ( )κ´ πολ[.].[ ]

35 43.68   μόϲϲυναϲ [προ-
               μα̣χεῶνα̣[ϲ

    142

43.38–39 Leontini

43.41   they were cast out.[1]
           Etna[2]

[1] Perhaps the Naxians.   [2] Mountain above Catania.

43.53–55 Eryx, son of Butes, from whom the city . . . and
Aphrodite Eryc(ine)

43.61   *harpasus*: a malevolent kind of bird.[1]

[1] The common root *harp-* ("seize" or "snatch") perhaps connects this bird with Harpies.

43.66–67 he founded . . .

43.68   wooden walls: a battlement

43.71 ζάγ]κλον· δρέπαν[ο]ν
κ(ατὰ) Σι]κελ[ο]ύς

43b–c Haliartus

43b (43.84–133 Pf.) *P.Oxy.* 2080 col. II, 86–94

Ὣ]ς ἡ μὲν λίπε μῦθον, ἐγὼ δ᾽ ἐπὶ καὶ [τὸ πυ]θέσθαι
ἤ]θελον—ἦ γάρ μοι θάμβος ὑπετρέφ[ε]τọ—,
Κ]ισσούσης παρ᾽ ὕδωρ Θεοδαίσια Κρῆ[σσαν
  ἑ]ορτὴν
ἡ πόλις ἡ Κάδμου κῶς Ἀλίαρτος ἄγ[ει
5 κ]αὶ στυρὸν ἐν μούνοισι πολίσμασι [. . . . .]. ι.τω.
κ]αὶ Μίνω μεγάλοις ἄστεσι[1] γαῖα φ[έρει,
..]ωθεδετι κρήνη Ῥαδαμάνθο[ς . . . .].[. . .]ν
ἴ]χνια τῆς κείνου λοιπὰ νομογραφ[ίης
..].[.]αμọν· ἐν δέ νυ τοῖσι σοφὸν τόδε τηι[

(9 versus desunt)

20 τη[
  ην[
  κα.[
  τοσ[
  Κνῳ[σ
  αγ.[
25 πεμ[
  ὁππ[ο

(3 versus desunt)

30 [..]ν[

[1] ἄστεσι Massimilla 1990a, 20: ἄγγεσι Hunt

43.71   a sickle (*zanklon*): sickle (*drepanon*)
             according to the Sicilians

43b–c Haliartus

43b Oxyrhynchus papyrus

So she[1] left off the story, but I wanted to learn this in addition—for indeed my amazement kept growing—why Haliartus,[2] the city of Cadmus, holds a Cretan festival, the Theodaesia, by the water of the Cissusa, and the earth bears *styron*[3] only [here] in towns and in the big cities of Minos . . . the spring of Rhadamanthys[4] . . . and the traces left of that lawgiver . . . among which this wise

[1] The Muse.

[2] A city near Lake Copais in Boeotia (Hom. *Il.* 2.503).

[3] Sometimes called *styrax*, a tree that also grew in Asia and Syria, that produced a gum from which incense was made. For its connection with Dionysus and its alternate name, *storax*, see Ath. 14.626f.; Plut. *Vit. Lys.* 28.4.

[4] Son of Zeus and Europa, brother of Minos, and lawgiver. On Radamanthys' flight to Boeotia, see Apollod. *Bibl.* 2.4.11, 3.1.2. There he married Alcmene and was exiled in Ocalea. In this version he becomes a judge in Hades after his death, but cf. Diod. Sic. 5.84.2.

νασσ[
  κοπρ[
ἐνθ[
  υἷα Διώνυσον Ζαγρέα γειναμένη (?)
35 τὸν μ[
  μι..[
ο[.]..[
  ἀμφω[
ἀλλ᾽ ὁμ[
40 ἔθρω[σκ
κε[
  μη[
....[
  σωζε[

(4 versus desunt)

.[
  μ[
. . . . .

43c Schol. marg. *P.Oxy.* 2080 ad 43 Pf.

43b.3–4 θεοξέν(ια)
  ].τειν ὁ Διόνυ(σος) τοῖς
  ].ἐ(πι)γ......[

43b.5 ισ[
5]εφ( ) ....[...

[saying] . . . Cnossus . . . she brought forth [34] a son Dionysus Zagreus[5] . . . both . . . [40] he jumped

[5] A Cretan deity in the Orphic tradition; son of Zeus and Persephone (Diod. Sic. 5.75.4).

43c Oxyrhynchus papyrus (marginal scholia)

43b.3–4 theoxenia[1]
         of Dionysus

[1] The entertaining of gods by humans.

43b.5   . . .

43b.6   .] .[.....].…[…

43b.8   .....] ..[
         Ῥα]δαμαν[θ…

44–47 *Busiris et Phalaris*

44 *Et.Gen.* AB s.v. ποῖα

ποῖα· ὁ ἐνιαυτός. Καλλίμαχος,

　Αἴγυπτος προπάροιθεν ἐπ᾽ ἐννέα κάρφετο ποίας

45 Schol. ss³s⁴ Tzetz. ad Lyc. *Alex.* 717

ὁ Φάληρος τύραννος ἦν ἐν Σικελίαι τοὺς ἐπίξενουμέ-
νους πρὸς αὐτὸν δεινῶς κολάζων καὶ ἀναιρῶν. μέμνη-
ται δὲ αὐτοῦ καὶ Καλλίμαχος ἐν β′ Αἰτίων λέγων,

　τὴν κείνου Φάλαρις πρῆξιν ἀπεπλάσατο

46 (46 Pf. + *SH* 252.1–2) Schol. DEFQG ad Pind. *Pyth.*
1.185; 2–11, *P.Sorb.* inv. 2248 fr. 1

τὸν δὲ τοῦ Φαλάριδος ταῦρον οἱ Ἀκραγαντῖνοι κατε-
πόντωσαν, ὥς φησι Τίμαιος· τὸν γὰρ ἐν τῇ πόλει δει-
κνύμενον μὴ εἶναι τοῦ Φαλάριδος, καθάπερ ἡ πολλὴ

---

[1] Timaeus of Tauromenium (4th–3rd c. BC), historian (*BNJ*
566 F 28c).

43b.6   . . .

43b.8   Radamanthys

44–47 Busiris and Phalaris

44 *Etymologicum Genuinum*

poia: the year. Callimachus,

> Long ago Egypt dried up for nine summers.[1]

[1] To end this drought, the Egyptian king Busiris sacrificed strangers who sought his hospitality. He was later killed by Heracles (Apollod. *Bibl.* 2.5.11).

45 Tzetzes on Lycophron, *Alexandra*

Phalaris was a tyrant in Sicily who dreadfully injured and killed those seeking his hospitality. Callimachus mentions him in the second book of the *Aetia* saying,

> Phalaris modeled his actions on that one.[1]

[1] "That one" is Busiris. Both killed their guests, though only Phalaris roasted them in a bronze bull (Pind. *Pyth.* 1.95–96; Diod. Sic. 9 fr. 19).

46 Scholia to Pindar, *Pythian Odes*; Sorbonne papyrus

The people of Acragas threw the bull of Phalaris into the sea, as Timaeus says.[1] And he says that the bull displayed in the city is not that of Phalaris, although it gives that

κατέχει δόξα, ἀλλ' εἰκόνα Γέλα τοῦ ποταμοῦ. κατα-
σκευάσαι δὲ αὐτόν φασι Περίλαον καὶ πρῶτον ἐν
αὐτῷ κατακαῆναι. Καλλίμαχος, . . .

πρῶτος ἐπεὶ τὸν ταῦρον ἐκαίνισεν, ὃς τὸν ὄλεθρον
   εὗρε τὸν ἐν χαλκῷ καὶ πυρὶ γιγνόμενον
     ]θμον· οτεφ[
     ]ων ἦλθεν α.[
5   ]ῶσινἐπαν[
     ]αντακύην[
     ]λατίθ[.]..[
     ].ς βάλλ' ε.[
     ]ί. ον· οσ[
10   ] εἰν ἁλὶ .[
     ]..[..].ο.[

47 [Plut.] *Par. min.* 39a, 315c

Φάλαρις Ἀκραγαντίνων τύραννος ἀποτόμως τοὺς
παριόντας ξένους ἐστέβλου καὶ ἐκόλαζε. Πέριλλος δὲ
τῇ τέχνῃ χαλκουργὸς δάμαλιν κατασκευάσας χαλκῆν
ἔδωκε τῷ βασιλεῖ, ὡς ἂν τοὺς ξένους κατακαίῃ ζῶν-
τας ἐν αὐτῇ· ὁ δὲ τότε μόνον γενόμενος δίκαιος αὐτὸν
ἐνέβαλεν, ἐδόκει δὲ μυκηθμὸν ἀναδιδόναι ἡ δάμαλις·
ὡς ⟨Καλλίμαχος⟩ ἐν δευτέρῳ Αἰτίων.

impression, but a statue of the river god Gela. They say that Perilaus built it and that he was the first killed in it. Callimachus, . . .

> Since he invented the bull, he was the first who found his death in bronze and fire . . . they went . . . he cast it . . . [10] into the sea

47 Pseudo-Plutarch, *Parallel Stories*

Phalaris, tyrant of Acragas, severely tortured and injured passing strangers. Perillus, a worker in bronze made a bronze heifer and gave it to the king so that he could burn strangers alive in it. And Phalaris then, acting justly for once, threw him into it and the heifer seemed to bellow. So Callimachus [wrote] in the second book of the *Aetia*.

CALLIMACHUS

Certa fragmenta libri secundi

48 Schol. AD ad Hom. *Il.* 1.609

Κρόνου καὶ Ῥέας ἐγένοντο υἱοὶ ἄρρενες Ζεὺς καὶ Πο-
σειδῶν καὶ Ἅιδης, θυγατέρες δὲ Ἑστία, Δημήτηρ,
Ἥρα. τούτων, φασὶν ἐπὶ τῆς Κρόνου δυναστείας ἠρά-
σθησαν < . . . > τὸν δὲ Δία καὶ τὴν Ἥραν ἐπ' ἐνιαυ-
τοὺς τριακοσίους, ὥς φησιν Καλλίμαχος ἐν β′ Αἰτίων,

ὥς τε Ζεὺς ἐράτιζε τριηκοσίους ἐνιαυτούς

49 Schol. A ad Hom. *Il.* 9.193

ταφών· Ἰωνικῶς λέγεται κατὰ τροπὴν τοῦ θ εἰς τὸ τ·
. . . οἱ αὐτοὶ δὲ καὶ τὸ Ἀθάμας κατ' ἀφαίρεσιν τοῦ α
καὶ τροπῇ τοῦ θ εἰς τὸ τ, Τάμμας λέγουσι· Καλλίμα-
χος ἐν δευτέρῳ Αἰτίων,

Τάμμεω θυγατέρος

50 Steph. Byz. κ 263 Billerbeck s.v. Κυνέτεια

Κυνέτεια· πόλις Ἄργους. Καλλίμαχος δευτέρῳ (sc.
Αἰτίων).

Established Fragments of Book 2

48 Scholia to Homer, *Iliad*

The sons of Cronus and Rhea were Zeus and Poseidon and Hades, the daughters were Hestia, Demeter and Hera. And in the dominion of Cronus they say that these made love . . . Zeus and Hera for three hundred years, as Callimachus says in Book 2 of the *Aetia*,

how Zeus loved [Hera] for three hundred years

49 Scholia to Homer, *Iliad*

taphōn is written by the Ionians following the change from theta to tau. Some even call "Athamas" "Tammas" following the removal of the initial alpha and the change from theta to tau, as Callimachus in the second book of the *Aetia*,

of the daughter of Athamas[1]

[1] The son of Aeolus, king of Orchomenus, or a descendant of the same name who founded Teus in Asia Minor.

50 Stephanus of Byzantium

Cynetia: a city of Argos. Callimachus in the second book [of the *Aetia*].

50a Schol. ad Pind. *Isthm.* fr. 6a Maehler in *P.Oxy.* 2451B
fr. 14 col. I, 2–7

$$νο̣μεν[ ]κ̣ι̣.[(ca. 20 litt.)$$
]ιαι· ὅλον τὸ διήγημα τοῦ[το] τ̣ης...[(ca. 16
litt.)
]ν π(αρα)φέρει. ὅτι δ' οἱ Π[έ]λοπος φ[.]̣.τ̣.[ ].
[..]οι κ(αὶ) τ̣.[(ca. 12 litt.)
]ἐκτίσθη τοῦ Πέλοπος ἐ̣[π]εργήσαντος ευ..ισ[
(ca. 9 litt.)
5 Καλλί]μαχος ἐν τῷ Β′ τῶν Αἰτίω[ν· ο]ὗτος γ(ὰρ) τον[
(ca. 16 litt.)
].. ὡμοιωμ(έν)ος

51 Schol. LRM ad Soph. *OC* 258

τί δῆτα δόξης: ὡς μάτην τῆς περὶ τῶν Ἀθηνῶν κατ-
εχούσης δόξης, ὅτι ἄρα φιλοικτίρμων τις εἴη καὶ ἱκε-
ταδόκος. καὶ ὁ Κυρηναῖος, ἐν τῷ τέλει τοῦ β τῶν
Αἰτίων,

οὕνεκεν οἰκτείρειν οἶδε μόνη πολίων

Epaphroditi et Theonis
commentaria in librum secundum

Marcus Mettius Epaphroditus of Chaeroneia (1st c. AD), gram-
marian, author of commentaries on Homer, Hesiod, and Callima-
chus' *Aetia*; and Theon of Alexandria (1st c. BC), grammarian and

50a Scholia to Pindar, *Isthmian Odes*

This whole tale of . . . he presents. That the . . . [people]
of Pelops[1] . . . it was founded by Pelops' work, Callimachus
in the second book of the *Aetia*.[2] For this man . . . being
likened to . . .

[1] The son of Tantalus, who cut him into pieces and offered
them to the gods. Only Demeter ate his shoulder, which was re-
placed by an ivory prosthesis when his body was reassembled. His
cult was at Olympia (Pind. *Ol.* 1.23–98).   [2] This may relate
to a story told in Paus. 5.13.4–6 about the shoulder of Pelops
preserved at Elis (Harder vol. 2, 380).

51 Scholia to Sophocles, *Oedipus at Colonus*

How in vain does this notion persist among the Athenians
that someone should give due honors at burial and be a
receiver of suppliants? And the man from Cyrene (Calli-
machus) at the end of Book 2 of the *Aetia*,

> therefore alone among cities she [Athens] knows how
>   to take pity

The Commentaries of Epaphdroditus
and Theon on Book 2

critic, author of scholarly notes on Aristophanes, the *Odyssey*,
and Apollonius of Rhodes, as well as the *Aetia*.

52 Schol. M ad Aesch. *Eum.* 16

Ἐπαφρόδιτος ἐν ὑπομνήματι Καλλιμάχου Αἰτίων β′
φησί· Μελανθοῦς τῆς Δευκαλίωνος καὶ Κηφισοῦ τοῦ
ποταμοῦ γίνεται Μέλαινα τοὔνομα, Μελαίνης δὲ καὶ
Ποσειδῶνος Δελφός, ἀφ᾽ οὗ Δελφοί.

53 Steph. Byz. δ 146 Billerbeck s.v. Δωδώνη

Δωδώνη· ὠνόμασται δὲ (sc. Δωδώνη) κατὰ Θρασύβου-
λον, ὡς Ἐπαφρόδιτος ὑπομνηματίζων τὸ β′ Αἰτίων
ἀπὸ Δωδώνης μιᾶς τῶν Ὠκεανίδων νυμφῶν.

53a Tzetz. Schol. ad Thuc. 6.4.3 Hude

οὕτως Ἐπαφρόδιτος ὡς λέγεις γράφε· Γέλας δ᾽
ἐκλήθη τῷ πάχνην πολλὴν φέρειν, κλῆσιν ἐκεῖ γὰρ ἡ
πάχνη ταύτην φέρει. ὁ Πρόξενος δὲ σύν τισι ἄλλοις
λέγει Γέλωνος ἀνδρὸς ἔκ τινος Γέλαν πόλιν. ἐξ Ἀντι-
φήμου δ᾽ αὖ γελωτός τις λέγει· χρησμῷ μαθὼν γὰρ
ὡς πόλιν μέλλει κτίσαι γελᾷ δοκήσας τῶν ἀνελ-
πίστων τόδε· κλῆσιν ὅθεν τέθεικε τῇ πόλει Γέλαν.

52 Scholia to Aeschylus, *Eumenides*

Epaphroditus[1] in his commentary on Book 2 of Callimachus' *Aetia* says: Melantho, the daughter of Deucalion and the river Cephisus[2] gave birth to Melaena,[3] by name. Then Melaena and Poseidon produced Delphus from whom the Delphians descended.[4]

[1] Fr. 56 Braswell-Billerbeck.   [2] A river flowing through Phocus and Boeotia.   [3] It is not clear whether Melaena was mentioned in Callimachus' text. Paus. 10.8.10 relates Cephisus to the fountain Castalia.   [4] See *Fr. Inc. Sed.* 517 for alternate explanations.

53 Stephanus of Byzantium

According to Thrasybulus,[1] as Epaphroditus[2] says in his commentary on Book 2 of the *Aetia*, it is named after Dodona, one of the nymphs who were daughters of Ocean.

[1] *FHG* vol. 2, p. 464, fr. 4.   [2] Fr. 57 Braswell-Billerbeck.

53a Tzetzes on Thucydides, *History of the Peloponnesian War*

Epaphroditus[1] writes as you (sc. Thucydides) say: Gelas gets its name because it carries much ice, for ice there has the same name. Proxenus[2] with some others says that the city was named Gela from some man called Gelon. Some say it was named for the laughter of Antiphemus. For when he learned from an oracle that he was about to found a city he laughed, since he believed that this was unhoped for. From this he gave the name Gela to the city.

[1] Fr. 63a Braswell-Billerbeck.
[2] Proxenus of Epirus (3rd c. BC), historian (*BNJ* 703 F 4).

53b *Et. Gen*. AB α 1316 (vol. 2, p. 268 Lasserre-Livadaras)
s.v. ἄστυρον

ἄστυρον· τὸ ἄστυ. Καλλίμαχος· εἴρηται παρὰ τὸ
ἄστυ ὑποκοριστικῶς ἄστυρον. οὕτως θέων ἐν Ὑπο-
μνήματι τοῦ β′ Αἰτίων.

ΑΙΤΙΩΝ Γ′

54–60j Victoria Berenices

54 Pf. = *Aet*. 60c

54 (*SH* 254 + 383 Pf.) 1–19 (init.), *P.Oxy*. 2173; 2–9 (fin.),
P.Lille 82

Ζηνί τε κα‸ὶ Νεμέῃ τι χαρίσιον ἔδνον ὀφείλω‸,
  νύμφα κα[σιγνή]των ἱερὸν αἷμα θεῶν,
ἡμ[ε]τερο.[......] .ων ἐπινίκιον ἵππω[ν.
  ἁρμοῖ γὰρ ‸Δαναοῦ γ‸ῆς ἀπὸ βουγενέος[1]
5 εἰς Ἑλένη[ς νησῖδ]α καὶ εἰς Παλληνέα μά[ντιν,

---

[1] Hesch. β 882 Latte s.v. βουγενέων

---

[1] A nymph, daughter of Aesopus, the eponym of Nemea in
Argolis in the northern Peloponnese (Paus. 2.15.2), where there
was a shrine of Zeus. Every two years it was the site of Panhel-
lenic games featuring a variety of contests, including horse races.

[2] The bride, who is the addressee, is Berenice II, wife of
Ptolemy III Euergetes. The sibling gods are Ptolemy II Philadel-
phus and his sister/wife, Arsinoe II. In contemporary inscriptions

53b *Etymologicum Genuinum*

Astyron; the city. Callimachus. He says that *astu* is a diminutive of *astyron*.[1] Thus Theon in his commentary on *Aetia* Book 2.

[1] *Hec.* 71.1–2.

AETIA III

54–60j The Victory of Berenice

54 Pf. = *Aetia* 60c

54 (*SH* 254 + 383 Pf.) Oxyrhynchus papyrus, Lille papyrus

To Zeus and Nemea[1] I owe a lovely gift, dear bride, sacred offspring of the sibling gods,[2] a victory song for your horses. For just now from the land of Danaus,[3] descendant of Io,[4] [5] to the island of Helen[5] and the Pallenean Seer,[6]

they are the notional parents of both Berenice and her husband, though her actual parents were Magas of Cyrene, Philadelphus' stepbrother, and his wife, Apame (Clayman 2014, 128 and n. 33).   [3] Argos in Greece, where Danaus became king after fleeing Egypt with his fifty daughters.   [4] The mother of Danaus, who fled from Greece to Egypt after she was impregnated by Zeus and turned into a cow by his furious wife, Hera (Paus. 1.25.1).   [5] Pharos, off the coast of Alexandria, where in one tradition Helen of Sparta virtuously sat out the Trojan War (Eur. *Hel.* 1–67).   [6] Pharos was also associated with Proteus (Posid. 115.1 AB = 11 G.-P.), the seer from Pallene (Hom. *Od.* 4.383–424).

ποιμένα [φωκάων], χρύσεον ἦλθεν ἔπος,
Εὐφητηϊάδ[αο παρ'] ἠρίον οὔ[νεκ'] Ὀφέλτου
   ἔθρεξαν προ[τέρω]ν² οὔτινες ἡνιόχων
ἄσθματι χλι[. . . .] . . πιμιδας, ἀλλὰ θε‚ό‚ν‚ι‚ων‚
10   ὡς ἀνέμων ‚οὐδεὶς εἶδεν ἁματροχιάς³
ἠμὲν δή πο[
   καὶ πάρος Ἀργει[
καιρωτους τε[
   Κολχίδες ἢ Νείλῳ [
15 λεπταλέους ἔξυσαν‚[
   εἰδ‚υῖ‚αι φαλιὸν τ‚α‚ῦ‚ρον ἰηλεμίσαι‚
. . . .]υκων ὅτε[
   . . . .]‚ν κομα[
. . . . . .]. . .[.]. .[

. . . .

² προ[τέρω]ν Barigazzi *PP* 6 (1951): 419
³ 9–10 Porphyr. 1.15.9 Sodano ἀλλὰ—ἁματροχιάς

54a 1–23a *PSI* 1500

. . . .

   ]‚[
   Ἰναχ[ίδα]ι‚σ κει[
δωδ[ε]κάκις π‚ερὶ δίφρον ἐπήγαγεν ὄθματα † δίφρου
   καὶ τ[.]. . Ἀμυμών[η
5 κρή[ν]η καλὰ νάουσα κ[
   δρωμ[ῶ]σιν· Δαναοῦ δε[
ἵππα[στ]ῆρ' ἅτ‚ε τοῦτο φε‚

shepherd of seals, the golden news came that your horses ran beside the mound of Opheltes,[7] the son of Euphetes, none warming with their breath the shoulders of the charioteers in front, but they ran [10] like the wind, and no one saw tracks of wheels . . . and formerly, Argive (women) . . . well-woven . . . Colchian women or those by the Nile . . . [15] they wove the finest [garments].[8] . . . [the women] knowing how to mourn for the bull with a white spot on its forehead.[9]

[7] A landmark at Nemea honoring Opheltes, in whose memory the contest was founded by the Seven Against Thebes (Paus. 2.15.2–3). There is also a parallel tradition that the founder was Heracles, slayer of the Nemean lion.   [8] The relevance of the skillful weavers is not clear from the fragments. Thomas (1983, 96–112) argues with parallels from Latin poetry that the weaving may depict the story of Heracles and Molorcus that follows.   [9] The Apis bull, a key feature of the Pharaonic cult. Its mourners are Egyptians (Plin. *HN* 8.184–86).

54a Papyrus fragment

to the descendants of Inachus[1] . . . twelve times around [the turning posts] the chariot led the eyes of . . . and Amymone[2] . . . [5] a lovely spring flowing . . . they ran. Of Danaus . . . the gadfly just as this . . . the blood of the race

[1] The Argives, whose first king was the river-god Inachus (Dion. Hal. *Ant. Rom.* 1.25.4).   [2] A daughter of Danaus and name of a spring in Argos (Apollod. *Bibl.* 2.1.4).

Αἴγυπτος γενεῆς αἷμ᾽ α̣[
δ̣ηθάκ[ι] μου τὸν Νε̣ῖλο[ν
10 κεῖνος ος ἐν Προίτου ξ[
ὡς ἔνεπεν· τοὶ δ᾽ ἦχο̣υ[
ἐκ λαγόνων [. .] θερ[
ἔσταθεν· ἤκου[
αυτα̣ δ[
15 οὐκ ἐρέω [
αὔριον [
σ]υρίζει [
ἀ]λλαποδ[
ὅ]θμα̣ χρ̣.[
20]ισομεν· ε̣[
.....]ο̣σο[
....]ν· α[
.....]ν ιθ[
] νκ[23a (m²)

54b (SH 257.21–34; 176 Pf.) 1–23, P.Lille 76d col. II;
21–34, P.Oxy. 2170 fr. 3; 23, P.Lille 76 col. II m² in marg.
inf.; 24–43, P.Lille 79

εἰς ἔριν ηνικ̣[
δῶκε Ταναγ[ραι-
παιδὶ κασιγν[ητ-
ὼς ἀέκων ε̣[
5 λῃτιαὶ Ταφιο̣[
λήνεα γουνα̣[

162

of Aegyptus[3] . . . often the Nile . . . me . . . [10] that man who in the . . . of Proetus[4] . . . So he spoke and the sound . . . from the flanks . . . the heat . . . they stood . . . They heard . . . [15] I will not speak . . . tomorrow . . . it hisses . . . eye

[3] The brother of Danaus whose fifty sons forcibly married Danaus' fifty daughters (Apollod. *Bibl.* 2.1.5).   [4] King of Argos and Tiryns and brother of Acrisius (Apollod. *Bibl.* 2.4.1). Artemis cured his daughters from madness (Call. *Hymn* 3.233–36).

54b (*SH* 257.21–34; 176 Pf.) Oxyrhynchus papyrus, Lille papyrus

into the battle when . . . (at) Tanagra[1] he gave . . . to the child of his brother . . . how unwilling [5] . . . Taphian[2]

[1] City in Boeotia.
[2] Amphitryon had defeated the Taphians, famous brigands (Hom. *Od.* 15.427).

πωτηθεὶς αν[
   κυπωθεὶς τα[
ὄφρα δεταισ[
10   τόφρα δετω[
τόξα διαπλη[
   καὶ μὲν οτοι.[
σκῶλός μοι β.[
   [
15 αὐλείην παρ' ἄχ[ερδον
   ἐξέρυσ' ἑρμαίο[υ
λέξας κεν ταδ.[
   ὣς φάτο, τῷ δ' ο.[
τὴν προτέρην [
20   δοῖεν, ὁ δ' ἁρπακ[τ-
αἰνολέων ἀπόλ.οιτο .ε[
   καὶ θεὸς η καινε[ ].......[.] ..μ.[
ὄφρα κεπιω.[ ]ω σε πάλιν πυρὶ δ[ε]ῖπνον
   ...]μενον δυερῇ μηδὲ σὺν ἀξ.υλίῃ
25 ...]α νυν, δρεπάνου γὰρ ἀπε.υ.θέ.α τέρχνα[ε]ᾳ [
   ...]α πολύσκαρθμος τοῦτον ἔχειν[...].[
...].ε καὶ λίπτουσα δακεῖν κυτί.σοιο [χίμαιρα
   βληχ]άζει πυλέων ἐντὸς ἐερ[γομένη
...] δυσηβολίοιο τράγου [...]...[
30   ....].ιος ἀλγῆσαι πᾶς κεν ἰδὼ[ν
....] νομοῦ ποίμνησιν ἐελδ[
   ....]θασσόντων ὡς περι.[
   ....]οὐχ ὡς ὑδ‹έ›ουσιν ἵνα.[

booty . . . wool . . . knees . . . flew . . . overthrown . . . as long as . . . so [10] . . . the bow.[3] . . . and . . . a palisade for me . . . [15] beside the prickly pear at the outer door . . . I drew out from the stone wall . . . after saying these things[4] . . . so he spoke[5] . . . the former (prayer) . . . [20] may they grant that the predator, the terrible lion perish and may the god(dess) who . . . new [circumstances] . . . in order that I may feed you when I have [given] food to the fire again and not with a wretched lack of wood as now, [25] for the young shoots are ignorant of the sickle and the leaping [kid longs] to have . . . and the she-goat enclosed within the gates eager to graze on the moon-trefoil bleats . . . of the he-goat, hard to meet, . . . [30] everyone would grieve seeing . . . and for the herds a desire for the meadow . . . besieging thus around . . . not as they sing[6] . . .

---

[3] Presumably Heracles' bow, which proved to be ineffectual against the lion (Apollod. *Bibl.* 2.5.1). [4] This appears to be the end of Heracles' speech to Molorcus on his initial visit to the hut. For speculation about the topics covered, see Parsons and Kassel 1977, 15. [5] The beginning of Molorcus' speech describing his inability to offer Heracles a proper meal on account of the ravages of the lion. [6] Molorcus is about to tell an alternative version of a story.

35 ....εο.[...]. σκληρὸν ἔτικ[τ-
....].............[
  .....].αρ Ἀργείων οὐκέτι β..[
  ....σθαι πατερε..αμεμ..[
  ].........ε..[
40].ν.ι..ισ.οσανα..ν.[
 ].........ισ Ἄργος εκ...[
 ].........τε..[
 ].........κτη...[

54c (*SH* 259; 177.1–37 Pf.) *PSI* 1218 fr. a.

 . . . .

       ]υια[
  δίκρον, φιτρὸ,ν ἀειρ,αμέν,η
   ] λελα[....]..ι στέγος οὐδ' ὅσον ε..[
   ]παιδὶ νέμουσα μέρος.
5 ἀστὴρ δ' εὖτ'] ἄρ' ἔμελλε βοῶν ἄπο μέσσαβα
   [λύσειν
  αὔλιος], ,ὃς δυθμὴ,ν εἶσιν ὕπ' ἠελίου
   ] ὡς κεῖνος Ὀφιονίδῃσι φαείν[ει
   ] θεῶν τοῖσι παλαιοτέροις,
   ]τηρι θύρην· ὁ δ' ὅτ' ἔκλυεν ἠχ[ήν,
10 ὡς ὁπότ' ὀκν]ηρῆς ἴαχ' ἐπ' οὖς ἐλάφου
 σκ]ύμνος [μέ]λλ[ε] μὲν ὅσσον ἀκουέμεν, ἦκα δ'
  ἔλ[εξεν·
  "ὀχληροί, τί τό[δ'] αὖ γείτονες ἡμέ[τ]ερον

166

[35] she[7] gave birth to something hard . . . . . . no longer
of the Argives . . . father . . . [40] Argos

[7] Rhea, who in one tradition gave birth to a stone, which be-
came the Nemean lion (Parsons and Kassel 1977, 25).

54c (*SH* 259; 177.1–37 Pf.) Papyrus fragment

After raising up a wooden fork, she . . . (toward) the roof
. . . dealing out a share not even as much as for a child.[1]
[5] When the evening star was about to loosen the leather
straps from the oxen, which comes at the setting of the
sun, when that one shines on the sons of Ophion,[2] the
older of the gods . . . And when he[3] heard a sound at the
door, [10] as when a lion cub roars in the distance and the
faint sound reaches the ears of a timid fawn, he said softly,
"Annoying neighbors, why have you come to scrape away

[1] A small portion for Heracles' large appetite (Harder vol. 2,
440–41).   [2] The generation of gods before Cronus and the
Titans, who were said to dwell in the underworld (Ap. Rhod.
1.503–6).   [3] Molorcus.

ἤκατ᾽ ἀποκνα[ί]σοντες, ἐπεὶ μάλα [γ'] οὔτι φέρο[ισθε;
ξ]είνοις κωκυμ|οὺς ἔπλασεν ὔμμε θεός."
15 ὢ]ς ἐνέπων τὸ μὲν ἔργον, ὅ οἱ μετὰ [. . .] ινε[
ρῖ]ψεν, [ἐ]πεὶ σμίνθοις κ[ρ]υπτὸν ἔτευχε δόλον·
ἐν͵ δ᾽ ἐτ͵ίθ͵ε͵ι π͵αγίδεσσιν ὀλέθρια δείλατα δο͵ιαῖς
αἴ]ρινο[ν ἐ]λλεβ[όρῳ μί͵γδα μ͵άλευρον ἑλὼν
. .]ντ[.]͵ωιτα͵α[. . . . .].͵. θάνατον δὲ κάλ[υψε
20 . .]͵κ͵[.]͵[. . .]γειη͵[. . . .]͵αγωσιν ἔπι
. .]ημ͵ν͵[. ὢ]ς κίρκο[ι͵. . .]͵. ἄρτι πεσόν[τες
πο͵λλάκις ͵ἐ͵κ λύχνου πῖον ἔλειξαν ἔαρ
ἀλ]καίαις ἀφύσαντες, ὅτ᾽ οὐκ ἐπὶ πῶμα[τ᾽ ἔκειτο
ἄλ]μαις καὶ φιάλης, ἢ ὁπότ᾽ ἐξ ἑτέρης
25 εἴ]λησαν χηλοῖο, τά τ᾽ ἀνέρος ἔργα πενιχροῦ
. . .]ο͵οκ . . .σκληροῦ σκί<μ>π[τετο λ]ᾶο͵ς ὕπο
κλι]σμὸν α . . .τεπ[. . . . . . ὠ]ρχήσα[ντο
βρέγματι, καὶ κανθ͵ῶν ἤλασ͵αν ὦρον ἄπο.
ἀλλὰ τόδ᾽ οἱ σίνται βρα[χέ]ῃ ἐνὶ νυκτὶ τέλεσσαν
30 κύντατον, ᾧ πλεῖστ[ον] μήνατο κεῖνος ἔπι·
ἄμφ[ιά] οἱ σισύρην [τ]ε κακοὶ κίβισίν τε διέβρον.
τοῖσ]ι [δὲ] διχθαδίους εὐτύκασεν φονέας,
ἱπό͵ν͵͵τ᾽ ἀνδίκτην τε μάλ᾽ εἰδότα μ͵α͵κρὸν ἅλε͵σθαι.
. . . . .]͵[.]͵. ἀνέλυσε θύρην
35 . . . .]ἐπεὶ θαμὰ μίσγετο κεί[ν
. . . .]ιν ἐννάετης
. . . .]͵.ο[. . .]ν οὔτε Κλεων[άς
. . . .].[

at this household, since you will leave with nothing at all?
A god made you a bane for guests." [15] Speaking in this
way, he went to work, since he was preparing a secret trap
for the mice. In two traps he put death-dealing bait, wheat
meal mixed with hellebore . . . concealed death . . . [20]
like hawks who have just now fallen on . . . often they had
licked up the rich oil from the lamp, scooping it up with
their tails, when the lid did not lie on the pickling brine
and bowls, or when they pilfered [25] from the other
chest, the labors of a poor man, or skittered under his bed
of hard stone, . . . they danced on his brow and drove sleep
from his eyes, but this, the most shameless thing the rav-
ening mice did in one short night, [30] at which that man
was most angry, the pests ate up his clothes, his goatskin
cloak and his bag. But for them he made ready double
deaths: a spring and weight poised to crush at a long dis-
tance. . . . he loosened the door . . . [35] often it was mixed
for those . . . an inhabitant . . . nor Cleonae[4]

4 A village east of Nemea where there was a temple of Hera-
cles (Diod. Sic. 4.33.3).

54d (*SH* 260) *P. Lille* 78b

```
          ] ονεστιφ  [
          ]πιχορη  [
          ]διον καὶ απλης [
          ]ε χρήσομαι τη
5         ]ζευσσηνδιψαρ[
          ]πενίαν [
          ] εισιναθωιος  [
   –∪∪–∪∪–ο]ὔτισι δῶκαλυρ [
          ] ιν  μοιγερον [
10         ] κμα[ ] [
            ] [
```

   .   .   .   .   .

54e (*SH* 260A et fr. 333 [?] et 557 Pf.) *P.Lille* 78a

```
       ] δε κανὼν τέρα[ς
   εἴτε μιν Ἀργεί ων χρή με καλεῖν ἀ άτην
       ] ωναιτεπαρηχειε [
       ] Δαναοῦ φρείατι πὰρ μεγα[λ
5      Ἰ]φίκλειος ἀδελφε<ι>οῖο νεμ [
       ]σμήξας ἀντι γετης γε[
       ] πελάσαιμι μόνον περιβα[
       ] ἔσεα<ι> καὶ τάχα βουκτέανο[ς
       ] ς ἔτι μᾶλλον ἐπικλ{ε}ινες [
10     ] πε[ί]σω Ζεὺς ὅτι παιδογό[νος
       ] πέσω δ᾽ ὑπ᾽ ὀδόντ[ι
   ] ρμαλλονυπο[
```

54d (*SH* 260) Lille papyrus

insatiable . . . I will consult . . . [5] a leather garment . . .
poverty . . . he goes unharmed . . . I have given to no one
songs without a lyre[1] . . . to me, old man[2]

[1] Songs of lament.   [2] An address to Molorcus.

54e (*SH* 260A + fr. 333 [?] + 557 Pf.) Lille papyrus

after I kill the monster,[1] whether I should call it the ruin
of the Argives or . . . the echoing . . . beside the great
cistern of Danaus[2] . . . [5] the Iphicleian[3] pasture of his
brother . . . after wiping out . . . let me only approach [the
lion] . . . soon you will be a possessor of cattle[4] . . . if the
scales incline even more against me . . . [10] I will per-
suade [them] that Zeus is my father . . . but should I fall
beneath its teeth . . . [sacrificial] beast . . . hospitality

[1] Heracles speaks. The monster is the lion.   [2] An un-
known location in Argos.   [3] Iphicles is the son of Phylacus,
whom Melampus cured of sterility. Phylacus rewarded him with
cattle that he gave to his brother Bias, who needed them as a bride
price (Hom. *Od*. 15.225–38; Apollod. *Bibl*. 1.9.12). The events
took place in Argos, but the relevance of the story to the poem is
unclear.   [4] Addressed to Molorcus, who gets only a mule
(*Aet.* 54i.19 below).

```
        ]...[ ] ...ινησα[
15      ]                    [
        ] .αιτεγεος[
        ]ομοι βοτὸν εν . [
        ξ]εινοσύνησα .[
        ] . εοσδο . . σω[
        ] . . νο . [ ]ιοσδ .[
20      ]...[ ] . η [ ] . ναι
        ]... νειν[
```

54f (*SH* 262) *P.Lille* 78c

```
    .   .   .   .   .
        ]νκ[
        ] ομ[
        ] . .[
        ] .[
    .   .   .   .   .
```

54g (*SH* 263) *P. Lille* 84

```
    .   .   .   .   .
    ] . μ[
    ].....[
    ] . .....[
    π]ενιχρὸν δ[
    ]λλ . . ω . και [
    ]οχ . [...] . ν [
```

54f (*SH* 262) Lille papyrus

. . .

54g (*SH* 263) Lille papyrus

Poor . . . and

54h (57 Pf.; *SH* 264) *P.Berol*. 11629a recto

αὐτὸς ἐπιφράσσαιτο, τάμοι δ' ἄπο μῆκος ἀοιδῇ·
   ὅσσα δ' ἀνειρομένῳ φῆ[σ]ε, τάδ' ἐξερέω·
'ἄττα γέρον, τὰ μὲν ἄλλα πα[ρὼν ἐν δ]αιτὶ μαθήσει,
   νῦν δὲ τά μοι πεύσῃ Παλλὰ[ς .....]..[
5 .]ạ[   ].α
  .   .   .   .

54i (59 Pf.; *SH* 265.1–11) *P.Oxy*. 2212 fr. 18.1–11; 5–9,
Plut. *Quaest. conv.* 5.3.3 (676f–77b)

  .   .   .   .
            ].ν.[
            ]. στέφοṣ[
            ]λλ' ὅτεμ[
            ]χρυσοιο.[
5   καί μιν Ἀλη.τεῖδαι π.ουλὺ γεγειότερον
   τοῦδε παρ' Αἰ.γαίωνι .θεῷ τελέοντες ἀγῶνα
   θήσουσιν ν.ίκης σύ.μβολον Ἰσθμιάδος
   ζήλῳ τῶν Ν.εμέηθε· πίτυν δ' ἀ.ποτιμήσουσιν,
   ἢ πρὶν ἀγων.ιστὰς ἔστεφε το.ὺς Ἐφύρῃ.
10   ].νῳητετεοί, γέρ[ον
            ]. οὐδ' ἱερὴ π.[
            ]σεμοὶ προμ[
               ]ον Παλλὰς ἔ[
               ]αρενῳ τοδ[
15   σ]ὴν κατ' ἐπω[νυμίην.

54h (57 Pf.; *SH* 264) Berlin papyrus

One should learn for oneself and cut short my song's length. But whatever he said to the one inquiring, this I will tell. Dear old man,[1] you will learn the rest when you are present at dinner, but now you will learn what Pallas told me.

[1] Molorcus.

54i (59 Pf.; *SH* 265.1–11) Oxyrhynchus papyrus; Plutarch, *Table-Talk*

a crown . . . than gold . . . [5] and the Aletidae,[1] performing games much older than this[2] at the shrine of the Aegean god,[3] will present it as a token of an Isthmian victory in rivalry with those from Nemea;[4] they will no longer honor the pine which before crowned the contestant in Ephyra[5]. . . . [10] old man[6] . . . not sacred . . . Pallas . . .

[1] The Corinthians were called the Aletidae, from Aletes, a descendant of Heracles and king of Corinth (Pind. *Ol.* 13.14, with scholia).   [2] The Nemean games.

[3] Poseidon, who presided at the Isthmian games in Corinth. He is called Aegean after his cult center at Aegae (Hom. *Il.* 8.203; *Od.* 5.381).   [4] This passage is from a prophecy Athena made to Heracles, who is here relating it to Molorcus.

[5] Corinth (Hom. *Il.* 6.152; Ap. Rhod. 4.1212).

[6] Heracles addresses Molorcus. Pallas' prophecy has apparently ended.

]υς τε Μολόρ[κ
  ]. θυμὸν ἀρε[σσάμενος,
ν]ύκτα μὲν αὐτόθι μίμνεν, ἀπέστιχε δ᾽ Ἄργος ἑῷος·
  οὐδὲ ξεινοδόκῳ λήσαθ᾽ ὑποσχεσίης,
20 πέμψε δέ οἱ τὸ[ν] ὀρῆα, τίεν δέ ἑ ὡς ἕνα πηῶν.
  νῦ]ν δ᾽ ἔθ᾽ [ἁ]γιϲ[τείη]ν οὐδαμὰ παυσομένην
..]...[ ]. Πελοπη.[ ]....ς
  ].. ἔσχον ἀνα[
  ]έστησαν ὅσ[
25]παισὶν ἀνασ[

55 (*SH* 267) Schol. BD ad Pind. *Nem.* 10.1c (vol. 3, p. 165.4 Drachmann)

τὸ Ἄργος, ἥτις πόλις Ἀργείων οἰκητήριον θειωδέστα-
τόν ἐστι τῆς Ἥρας . . . ἔστι δὲ παρὰ τὸ Ὁμηρικόν
. . . καὶ Καλλίμαχος,

  τὸν μὲν ἀρισκυδὴς εὖνις ἀνῆκε Διός
Ἄργος ἔθειν, ἴδιόν περ ἐὸν λάχος, ἀλλὰ γενέθλη
  Ζηνὸς ὅπως σκοτίῃ τρηχὺς ἄεθλος ἔοι

56 (*SH* 267A) Steph. Byz. a 356 Billerbeck s.v. Ἀπέσας

Ἀπέσας· ὄρος τῆς Νεμέας, ὡς Πίνδαρος καὶ Καλλί-
μαχος ἐν γ΄, ἀπὸ Ἀφέσαντος ἥρωος βασιλεύσαντος
τῆς χώρας, ἢ διὰ τὴν ἄφεσιν τῶν ἁρμάτων ἢ τοῦ
λέοντος· ἐκεῖ γὰρ ἐκ τῆς σελήνης ἀφείθη.

57 Pf. = *Aet.* 54h

[15] named after you . . . Molorcian . . . satisfying his heart [with food and drink],[7] he remained there for the night and went to Argos in the morning. Nor did he forget his promise to his host, [20] but sent the mule to him and honored him as one of his kinsmen. And even now a ritual that will never cease . . . the Peloponnesians . . . brought . . . to the children

[7] Heracles is the subject.

55 (*SH* 267) Scholia to Pindar, *Nemean Odes*

Argos, a city which is the habitation of the Argives most sacred to Hera . . . it is in Homer[1] and Callimachus,

> The very angry wife of Zeus sent him to destroy Argos, although it was her own allotment, so that it would be a difficult ordeal for the secret offspring of Zeus.[2]

[1] Hom. *Il.* 4.52. [2] Heracles, whose mother was Alcmene.

56 (*SH* 267A) Stephanus of Byzantium

Apesas: a mountain of Nemea as in Pindar[1] and Callimachus in Book 3, from the hero Aphesas who was king of the place, or on account of the starting point of the chariots or of the lion, for it was sent there from the moon.

[1] Pind. fr. 295 Maehler.

57 Pf. = *Aetia* 54h

CALLIMACHUS

58 (*SH* 268) *Et. Gen.* AB s.v. ἐχῖνος

ἐχῖνος· χερσαῖον ζῷον . . . καὶ ὁ λέβης ὁμοίως ἐχῖνος·
Καλλίμαχος,

> ἄξονται δ᾽ οὐχ ἵππον ἀέθλιον, οὐ μὲν ἐχῖνον
> βουδόκον

59 Pf. = *Aet.* 54i

60 Pf. = *Aet.* 62a

60a (677 Pf.; *SH* 268B) *Suda* κ 1052

κατηναρισμένας· τὸ γὰρ σκυλεύειν ἐναρίζειν: ὅτι τὰ
ἔναρα σκῦλα, . . . Καλλίμαχος ἐπὶ τῆς λεοντείου
δορᾶς,

> τὸ δὲ σκύλος ἀνδρὶ καλύπτρη
> γιγνόμενον, νιφετοῦ καὶ βελέων ἔρυμα

60b (597 Pf.; *SH* 268C) Schol. ad Ap. Rhod. 1.1243–48a
(p. 112.23 Wendel)

ἠύτε τις θήρ· κυρίως οἱ ποιηταὶ τὸν λέοντά φασι
θῆρα, ὡς καὶ Καλλίμαχος,

> θηρὸς ἀερτάζων δέρμα κατωμάδιον[1]

---

[1] Hapax legomenon, *Il.* 23.431

58 (*SH* 268) *Etymologicum Genuinum*

echinos: a land animal . . . and a basin such as a large jar. Callimachus,

> They will not carry off a horse as a prize, nor a jar big
> enough for an ox.

59 Pf. = *Aetia* 54i

60 Pf. = *Aetia* 62a

60a (677 Pf.; *SH* 268B) *Suda*

katēnarismenas: the verb means to strip the enemy: *skūla* is booty . . . Callimachus uses it of a lion skin,

> The hide[1] became a covering for the hero, a defense
> against snow and arrows

[1] Probably Heracles' lion skin.

60b (597 Pf.; *SH* 268) Scholia to Apollonius of Rhodes, *Argonautica*

"like some beast": the poets correctly call the lion a beast, as even Callimachus,

> Raising up the skin of the beast to hang from his
> shoulder.[1]

[1] Heracles takes up the skin of the Nemean lion to carry it to Cleonae. See G. Massimilla, "Il leone nemeo nella *Victoria Berenices* di Callimaco," in *La cultura ellenistica*, ed. R. Pretagostini and E. Dettori, 29 (Rome: Bompiani, 2003).

60c (54 Pf.; *SH* 266) [Prob.] ad Verg. *G.* 3.19

"Lucos Molorchi" Nemeam dicit. Molorchus fuit Herculis hospes, apud quem is diversatus est, cum proficisceretur ad leonem Nemeum necandum. Qui cum immolaturus esset unicum arietem, quem habebat, ut Herculem liberalius acciperet, impetravit ab eo Hercules, ut eum servaret, immolaturus vel victori tamquam Deo vel victo et † interfecto leone cum solutus esset † vel odio Iunonis, ne ei caelestes honores contingerent, vel fatigatus, experrectus mira damnum celeritate correxit, sumptaque apiacea corona, qua ornantur, qui Nemea vincunt. <. . .> supervenit itaque et Molorcho paranti sacrificium Manibus, ubi et aries immolatus erat. Inde Nemea instituta sunt: postea Archemori Manibus sunt renovata a septem viris, qui Thebas petebant. Sed Molorchi mentio est apud Callimachum in Αἰτίων libris.

60d (*SH* 255) Scholia interlinea in *P. Lille* 82 ad fr. 54

54.2 θυγάτηρ τῶ]ν θεῶν ἀδελφῶν, οἵ ἐ[ισιν Πτολεμαῖος καὶ Ἀρ]σινόη ὧν ἀνηγόρευ[ον τὴν Βερενίκην. ἦν δὲ ἐπ'] ἀληθείας θυγάτηρ Μ[άγα τοῦ θείου τοῦ Ε]ὐεργέτου.

60c (54 Pf.; *SH* 266) [Probus] on Virgil, *Georgics*

By the "woods of Molorcus" he means Nemea. Molorcus
was the host of Hercules in whose house he was enter-
tained when he set out to kill the Nemean Lion. When he
was about to immolate the only ram that he had so he
could welcome Hercules more graciously, he was asked by
Hercules to preserve him so that he could be sacrificed
either to the victor as to a god. Or if after killing the lion,
he was undone either by the hatred of Juno that he might
not partake of heavenly honors, or exhausted. He roused
himself, repaired the injury with admirable speed, and the
crown of celery was taken up which adorned those who
are victorious at Nemea. And so he interrupted Molor-
cus as he was preparing a sacrifice for the shades of the
departed, where the ram was sacrificed. From this the
Nemean games were founded. Afterward they were re-
newed for the shades of Archemorus by the Seven Against
Thebes. But there is a mention of Molorcus in Callima-
chus in the books of the *Aetia*.

60d (*SH* 255) Lille papyrus (interlinear scholia)

54.2   The daughter of the sibling gods, who were Ptol-
emy and Arsinoe,[1] whose daughter they proclaimed Bere-
nice.[2] She was in truth the daughter of Magas,[3] the uncle
of Euergetes.[4]

    [1] Ptolemy II Philadelphus and his sister/wife, Arsinoe II.
    [2] Berenice II, who married Ptolemy III Euergetes.
    [3] Philadelphus' half brother. His parents were Berenice I and
the otherwise unknown Philip.   [4] Ptolemy III, the husband
of Berenice II.

54.4 ....]

54.5 ....]λαντος υἱός

54.7 ....] Ἀρχέμορος ἐκαλεῖτο [
10   ....]

54.8 ....]ειν

54.9 ....]ερον ἠγωνισμ.....[
    ....].[ ].ν ην τῶν προτ...[
    ....]ην οὕτινες ἔδραμον ω...[
    ....]ντων ἄ‹ς›θματι χλιᾶναι ἵππῳ.[
15   ....] βασιλίσσης ἄρμα ἡνιοχ[
       .   .   .   .

60e (*SH* 256) Scholia interlinea in *P.Lille* 76 col. I

]
].νεννε
].τιτουμεγα
]
5]
   ]
   ]
   ]

182

54.4   . . .

54.5   son

54.7   he was called Archemorus[1]

    [1] His original name was Opheltes, and he was the son of Lycurgus, king of Nemea. He was killed by a snake when the Seven Against Thebes came to Nemea, and his cult was celebrated with the Nemean games (Paus. 2.15.2–3; Apollod. *Bibl.* 3.6.4).

54.8   . . .

54.9   the contest . . . of those in front . . . no one ran . . . with the warm breath of the horse . . . the chariot of the queen

60e (*SH* 256) Lille papyrus (interlinear scholia)

. . .

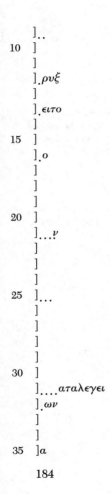

AETIA BOOK III

```
]
]
]
]ται
```

60f *P.Oxy.* 2258B fr. 2 verso

```
        .   .   .   .
          ].‧.[
        ]λωσατ̣ρ̣[
     ]‧ρ̣οιγαροιθε̣‧[
     ]‧αυτα̣‧‧ ϊπ[
5   ]εντωτρε̣‧[
   ]‧ν‧‧τονμε̣λ̣‧[
        ]‧ξενοσ‧λα‧[
        ]‧ινευμεγεθη‧[
        ]‧‧σεω[‧]‧νεπ‧λ‧[
10       ]‧[‧]ν‧[‧]χαλκε̣‧[
       ]‧[‧‧]δρ[‧]αντα[‧]‧[
          ]‧‧‧[‧]‧[‧]τα̣δ[
```

60g (*SH* 258) 1–15, Schol. interlin. *P.Lille* 76; 16–34,
Schol. interlin. *P.Lille* 79

54b.6   ἔρια ἐπι[

60f Oxyrhynchus papyrus
[7] visitor . . . [8] very large [10] . . . bronze

60g (*SH* 258) Lille papyrus (interlinear scholia)

54b.6   wool

54b.13   αναπω.[
        κλινεν [
        Ταναγρα.[
5   γὰρ τὸ τοξ[

54b.14   τόξον επ[
        βατιή οιον[

54b.15   ἄχερδος [

54b.17   δῶρον επα[

10 54b.19   ἐπεὶ προτε[
        βούλεται ε[
        δη τὸ σῳζ[
        εὐχήν [

54b.21   δεινολέω[ν

15 54b.23   οὐκ ἠδυνα[
        λέοντα. ἐὰν οὖν α .[....].. [
        ὁ Μό[λ]ορκος λέγει.[.]ευξο .[
        ὑποδέξασθαι τ..[.].....[
        λίζεσθαι. ἐὰν δὲ απο.....[

20 54b.26   σκαρθμὸς κίνησις μηνα.[
        θμον διὰ τὸν ἀγῶνα εὐκαρ[θμ-
        ΐ]ππων εὐκείνητα τέρχνε[α
        δένδρον τι

54b.13   . . . Tanagra . . . for the bow

54b.14   the bow . . . bush

54b.15   wild pear

54b.17   gift

54b.19   when earlier . . . he wishes . . . prayer

54b. 21   dreadful lion

54b.23   not sweet . . . the lion. If therefore . . . Molorcus
says . . . to have welcomed . . . if

54b.26   a leap . . . movement . . . the moon . . . because
of the contest . . . the bounding of horses . . . pliable shoots
. . . a tree

25   54b.27   ἐ]πιθυμοῦσα τῆς κυτίσ[ου
            .].....η αἲξ οὐ δύναται[ι
            .].....

       54b.29   .]....εντος δυσόσμου [

       54b.30   .].ι. ον τὸν ἀετὸν διασκε.[
             .].....

30   54b.32   π]ερικαθημένων

       54b.34   οὐ]χ οἷον [ἵ]να τὸν Κρόνον ε.[
             ].ειν ἀλλὰ τῳ ὄντι λίθο[ν
             ]ννηκέναι

       54b.36   ]....τι Ἥρας ἐστιν τ..[

60h (vol. 1, p. 503 Pf.) Schol. marg. infer. fr. 177.2–4
P.Oxy. 2258B fr. 2 recto

54b (?)   ἀνα]κτορίῃσι· βασι[λικαῖς

54c.4 (?)   ]σ..μήτ[η]ρ.[
           ] ....β.α.[
           ] ..νρ.[.].οδιᵃ..[¹

¹ Vestigia 2 linearum infra.

54b.27   eager for the chest . . . the goat is not able

54b.29   ill-smelling

54b.30   the eagle

54b.32   of those blockaded

54b.34   not even so that . . . Cronus . . . but indeed a stone
. . .

54b.36   Hera's is . . .

60h (vol. 1, p. 503 Pf.) Oxyrhynchus papyrus (marginal scholia)

54b (?)   by royal sovereignties

54c.4 (?) mother

60i (*SH* 261) Schol. interlin. in *P.Lille* 78a

54e.2 ....] .τα καλεῖν δεῖ αὐτο̣.[
........]

54e.8 ......]οκτέανος, τοῦτο δὲ πο.[

54e.10 ....]........σ... εὐπειθη.[

60j Schol. in marg. dext. *P.Berol.* 11629a verso

54i.20 τὸν ὄνον

54i.21 τ(ου) τ(έστιν) αιω .. [

Fragmenta incertae sedis libri tertii

61 Prisc. *Inst.* 2.12 (*Gramm. Lat*. vol. 2, p. 52.9 Hertz)

τὼς μὲν ὁ Μνησάρχειος ἔφη ξένος, ὧδε συναινῶ

62 Steph. Byz. λ 109 Billerbeck s.v. λυκώρεια

λυκώρεια· κώμη ἐν Δελφοῖς. Καλλίμαχος τρίτῳ.

60i (*SH* 261) Lille papyrus (interlinear scholia)

54e.2   it is necessary to call

54e.8   . . . this

54e.10   . . . he obeyed

60j Berlin papyrus (marginal scholia)

54i.20   the ass

54i.21   this is

Fragments of Uncertain Location in Book 3

61 Priscian, *Institutes of Grammar*

So the stranger, son of Mnesarchus,[1] said, and so I
    agree.

[1] The father of Pythagoras (Heraclitus, fr. 129 DK), who has
just been quoted.

62 Stephanus of Byzantium

Lycoreia: a village in Delphi. Callimachus in the third
book.

62a–c Phalaecus Ambraciotes

62a (60 Pf.; *SH* 268A) *Et. Mag.* 212.36 Gaisford s.v. βρέ-
φος

βρέφος· τὸ νεογνὸν παιδίον. κυρίως ἐπὶ ἀνθρώπου·
Καλλίμαχος ἐν τρίτῳ τῶν Αἰτίων καὶ ἐπὶ σκύμνου
τίθησι.

62b *P.Mil.Vogl.* inv. 1006.1–7

```
      ]στ.[.]ν...[
        ]..λεσενε[
      τ]ῶν οἰκείων [
      ] τὰς χεῖρας, ἀπες[φάγη
5   ὑπὸ τῆς ἀπο]τεκούσης λεαίν[ης
      παρέ]σχοντο τῇ Ἀρτέμ[ιδι
```

. . . .

62c (665 Pf.) Schol. B (a* b*) ad Ov. *Ib.* 501

Pegasus Epirotes, cum circumsideret Ambraciam, exiuit
venatum et leanae catulum nactus sustulit; quem conse-
cuta leaena laniavit, auctore Callimacho.

62d Fabula incerta

62d *P.Mil.Vogl.* inv. 1006.8–9

```
]. [.]ν[..].[......] ε[
   ]. [......]. στ[
```

. . . . .

62a–c Phalaecus of Ambracia

62a (60 Pf.; *SH* 268A) *Etymologicum Magnum*

brephos: a newborn child. Properly of a human. Callimachus in the third book of the *Aetia* applies it to a lion cub.

62b Milan papyrus

. . . of kinsmen . . . hands . . . he was killed [5] by the lioness who had given birth . . . they granted to Artemis

62c (665 Pf.) Scholia to Ovid, *Ibis*

Pegasus of Epirus, when he was besieging Ambracia, went out to the hunt and when he found the cub of a lioness he lifted it up; The lioness pursued him and tore him to pieces, as Callimachus wrote.

62d Unknown Story

62d Milan papyrus

. . .

63 Thesmophoria Attica

63 1–3, *P.Oxy.* 2211 fr. 1 verso, a–c; 4–12, *P.Oxy.* 2211
fr. 1 verso, 1–9

]δοι σὺν παιδί· θ.[..]....άει..[......]..[
  π]ολλὸν κῆρι βαρυ[νομέ]νη
]καλέουσα γυνὴ τ.[....]..[.]ν.άν· .[....].[
  ].ηι γρηῢς γείτο[ν.].[.]ρχομένη
5].' ἰδεῖν οὐ γάρ μιν [...] κλήϊσσεν[.]οντα
    ].ς· ἄφαρ δ' ἀνὰ μὲν θυμὸς [ἔ]γεντο θε[ῆ]ς
].τος· πολλὸν δὲ περὶ φρεσὶν ἀχθήνασα
  ]θη κούρη π[ό]τνα χαλεψαμένη.
τοὔν]εκεν οὔ πως ἐστὶν ἐπ' ὄθμασιν ο[ἷ]σιν ἰδέ[σθ]αι
10 παρθενι]καῖς Δηοῦς ὄργια Θεσμοφόρου
  ]πόσιν ἐλθέμεναι πρὶν νύμφια λέκτρα τελέσσαι
  ]ες ἐκ κείνου χρήματος Ἀκτιάσιν.

64 Sepulcrum Simonidis

64 1–19, *P.Oxy.* 2211 fr. 1 verso; 7–9 et 11–14, *Suda* σ 441

Οὐδ' ἄ]ν τοι Καμάρινα τόσον κακὸν ὀκκόσον
ἀ[ν]δρός
  κινη]θεὶς ὁσίου τύμβος ἐπικρεμάσαι·
καὶ γ]ὰρ ἐμόν κοτε σῆμα, τό μοι πρὸ πόληος
ἔχ[ευ]αν
  Ζῆν'] Ἀκραγαντῖνοι Ξείνι[ο]ν ἁζόμενοι,

63 *The Attic Thesmophoria*

63 Oxyrhynchus papyrus

with a child . . . [a woman] much distressed at heart . . , a
woman calling . . . an old woman going to a neighbor . . .
[5] calling out to her not to look at it. And at once the
anger of the goddess[1] rose up. She grieved much in her
heart and the deity was enraged at the girl. Therefore
there is no way for young girls to see with their own eyes
[10] the rites of Demeter Thesmophorus until a bride-
groom comes to celebrate a marriage . . . and from that
affair comes [the prohibition] for Attic girls

[1] Demeter, whose principal festival at Athens was the Thes-
mophoria, a fertility festival that took place in the fall when seeds
were sown. On the details of the ritual, see Schol. ad Lucian, *Dial.
meret.* 2.1.

64 *The Tomb of Simonides*

64 Oxyrhynchus papyrus; *Suda*

Not even does Camarina[1] threaten so great an evil as
moving the tomb of a pious man. For once an evil
man tore down my tomb, which the people of Acragas
raised for me before the city, honoring Zeus Xenios,[2]

[1] A lake near a Sicilian town of the same name. When the
people wanted to drain it, they were forbidden by an oracle that
said, "Do not move Camarina." They ignored the warning, and
the town was destroyed when their enemies attacked them over-
land (*Anth Pal.* 9.685; Steph. Byz. κ 45 Billerbeck s.v. Kama-
rina).   [2] The god who protects strangers (Hom. *Il.* 13.623–
25; Ap. Rhod. 2.1131–32).

5 ... κ]ατ᾽ οὖν ἤρειψεν ἀνὴρ κακός, εἴ τιν᾽ ἀκούει[ς
  Φοίνικ]α πτόλιος σχέτλιον ἡγεμόνα·
 πύργῳ] δ᾽ ἐγκατέλεξεν ἐμὴν λίθον οὐδὲ τὸ γράμμα
  ᾐδέσθη τὸ λέγον τόν ̣μ̣ε Λεωπρέπεος
 κεῖσθα̣ί Κήϊον ἄνδρα τὸν ἱερόν, ὃς τὰ περισσά
10   .....] μνήμην πρῶτος ὃς ἐφρασάμην,
 οὐδ᾽ ὑμ̣έας, Πολύδευκες, ὑπέτρεσεν, οἵ με
  μελά̣θ̣ρου
  μέλλο̣ντος πίπτειν ἐκτὸς ἔθεσθέ κοτε
 δαιτυμ̣όνων ἄπο μοῦνον, ὅτε Κραννώνιος ̣αἰ̣αῖ
  ὤ̣, λισ̣θ̣ε̣ν μεγάλο̣υς̣ οἶκος ἐπὶ
 ̣Σ̣κ̣ο̣πάδ̣α̣ς.
15 ὦνακες, ἀλ̣ ̣ ̣ἱ[̣ ̣] γὰρ ἔτ᾽ ἦν [
 ]...ωοῦμεδ[......] βοσιν[
....λμοὺς[.......] ϊουνδο̣[
 .....ηστ̣.[.......]εν ἀνῆγεν [
....[   ].[.] ̣ ετ᾽ ̣κ̣.[
. . . .

198

[5] Phoenix,[3] if you have heard of him, the wicked commander of the city. He built my headstone into the wall, nor did he honor the inscription stating that I, the son of Leoprepes,[4] lay there, the holy man from Ceos, who first made known the extra letters[5] [10] and the art of memory.[6] Nor did he fear you [two], Polydeuces, who once got me outside, alone among the diners, when the palace was about to collapse, when alas! the palace of Crannon fell on the powerful sons of Scopas[7] . . . [15] princes.[8]

[3] Otherwise unknown.   [4] Father of the poet Simonides of Ceos (*Suda* σ 439).   [5] The letters zeta, xi, and psi, which combine two consonants (*P.Oxy.* 1800 fr. 1.45; *Suda* σ 439).   [6] Mnemotechnics (*P.Oxy.* 1800 fr. 1.42; Cic. *De orat.* 2.86.351–54; Quint. *Inst.* 11.2.11–16).   [7] Powerful family in Crannon, Thessaly, in the sixth century BC, and patrons of Simonides.   [8] The story is told by Cicero and Quintilian (n. 6 above). Simonides was commissioned to write a poem for Scopas, who later withheld half of the poet's fee, complaining that he used half the poem to praise the Dioscuri and should ask them for the rest. At this, two young men appeared at the door and insisted that Simonides come outside. Just then the house collapsed, killing everyone inside, including Scopas. Simonides was later able to identify all the corpses by remembering the seating arrangement at dinner. There is no evidence that the story originated with Simonides.

65–66 Fontes Argivi

65 Comm. in Antim. *PRIMI* 1.17 col. II 13

οὐκ ἀ[πὸ] τῆς Φυ[σαδ]είας φησὶν ὁ Καλλ[ίμα]χος τὰς
λεχοῦς λ[ούεσθ]αι, ἀλλ᾽ [ἀπ]ὸ τῆς Αὐτομάτης,

Αὐτομά[της] εὐναὲς ἐπών[υμον, ἀλ]λ᾽ ἀπὸ σ[εῖ]ο
λούονται λοχίην οἰκέτιν[.......]ης

66 1–9, *P.Oxy.* 2211 fr. 1 recto; 2–3, Melet. *De nat. hom.*
(*AO* vol. 3, p. 93.1836 Cramer)

ἡρῶσσαι[. .] ιᾶς[1] Ἰασίδος νέπ[ο]δες·
νύμφα Π[οσ]ειδάωνος ἐφυδριάς, οὐδὲ μὲν Ἥρης
ἁγνὸν ὑ φ αινέμεναι[2] τῇσι μέμηλε, πάτος
στῆναι [πὰ]ρ κανόνεσσι πάρος θέμις ἢ τεὸν ὕδωρ
5   κὰκ κεφ[α]λῆς ἱρὸν πέτρον ἐφεζομένας
χεύασθαι, τὸν μὲν σὺ μέσον περιδέδρομας ἀμφίς·
πότνι᾽ Ἀμυμώνη καὶ Φυσάδεια φίλη
Ἵππη τ᾽ Αὐτομάτη τε, παλαίτατα χαίρετε νυμφέων
οἰκία καὶ λιπαραὶ ῥεῖτε Πελασγιάδες.

[1] [βαλ]ι ᾶς (βαλιῆς) Barber apud Trypanis: [φα]λιᾶς
Lehnus, *ZPE* 142 (2003): 31   [2] ὑφηνέμεναι Melet. A: ὑφη-
γέμεναι Melet. M

65–66 Argive Fountains

65 Commentary on Antimachus

Callimachus says the childbed was not washed in Physa-
deia, but in Automate.

> Fair-flowing river named for Automate,[1] with your
> water they bathe a household slave who has given
> birth.

[1] One of the daughters of Danaus, who created or discovered
springs to water Argos. Others mentioned in the fragments are
Amymone, Physadeia, and Hippe. For the story of their making
Argos "well-watered," see Strabo 8.6.8.

66 Oxyrhynchus papyrus; Meletius, *On the Nature of
Man*

Heroines, descendants of the daughter of Iasus.[1] Water
nymph of Poseidon,[2] nor is it right for those who must
weave the holy cloak of Hera to stand by the weavers' rods
before sitting upon the holy rock around which you flow,
and pouring your water over their heads. Queen Amy-
mone and dear Physadea, Hippe and Automate, hail most
ancient dwelling places of the nymphs, and may you flow
on, shining Pelasgian[3] girls.

[1] Io, ancestor of Danaus (Apollod. *Bibl*. 2.1.3).
[2] Amymone, whom Poseidon saved from a satyr, then became
her lover himself and gave her a spring at Lerna (Apollod. *Bibl*.
2.1.4).
[3] In this context, Argive (Call. *Hymn* 5.4).

CALLIMACHUS

67–75e *Acontius et Cydippa*

67 1–22, *P.Oxy.* 2211 fr. 1 recto, 10–31

Αὐτὸς Ἔρως ἐδίδαξεν Ἀκόντιον, ὁππότε καλῇ¹
    ᾔθετο Κυδίππῃ παῖς ἐπὶ παρθενικῇ,
τέχνην—οὐ γὰρ ὅγ᾿ ἔσκε πολύκροτος—ὄφρα λέγο
    ..[²
    τοῦτο διὰ ζωῆς οὔνομα κουρίδιον.
5 ἦ γάρ, ἄναξ, ὁ μὲν ἦλθεν Ἰουλίδος, ἡ δ᾿ ἀπὸ
        Νάξου,
    Κύνθιε, τὴν Δήλῳ σὴν ἐπὶ βουφονίην,
αἷμα τὸ μὲν γενεῆς Εὐξαντίδος, ἡ δὲ Προμήθ[ου,³
    καλοὶ νησάων ἀστέρες ἀμφότεροι.
πολλαὶ Κυδίππην ὀλ[ί]γην ἔτι μητέρες υἱοῖς
10   ἑδνῆστιν κεράων ᾔτεον ἀντὶ βοῶν·
κείνης ο[ὐ]χ ἑτέρη γὰρ ἐπὶ λασίοιο γέροντος
    Σιληνοῦ νοτίην ἵκετο πιδυλίδα⁴
ἠοῖ εἰδομένη μάλιον ῥέθος οὐδ᾿ Ἀριήδης
    ἐς χ]ορὸν εὐδούσης ἁβρὸν ἔθηκε πόδα·
15   ]ήκησ[.].δ᾿ ἔκστασις, οὔτινος αὐτῆς

---

¹ Paragraphus et coronis in marg. sin.
² λέγοι̯τ̯[ο Lobel: λέγοι τ̯[ις M. Gigante, *SIFC* 84 (1998): 208:
λέγοι̯ε[ν A. Barigazzi, *Prometheus* 1 (1975): 201
³ Προμήθ[ου Harder: Προμήθ[ίς Lobel
⁴ πιδυλίδα Pf.: πηγυλίδα pap.

67–75e Acontius and Cydippe

67 Oxyrhynchus papyrus

Eros himself taught Acontius his arts when the boy burned for the maiden Cydippe—for he was not very cunning—in order that throughout his life he would be called her lawful husband. [5] In truth, Cynthian Lord,[1] he came from Iulis[2] and she from Naxos to your ox sacrifice[3] at Delos; he, a descendant of the family of Euxantius[4] and she, of Prometheus,[5] both lovely stars of the islands. While she was still small, many mothers asked for Cydippe as a bride for their sons [10] in exchange for horned oxen. For no other girl went to the damp spring of the shaggy old man Silenus[6] with a face looking more like dawn, nor did any other put down a more graceful foot in the chorus of sleeping Ariadne.[7] . . . [15] and entrancement than no other girl

---

[1] Apollo, who was born on Delos, where Mt. Cynthus is located (Call. *Hymn* 4.9–10). [2] City on the island of Ceos, which was home to the Ptolemaic fleet. [3] It does not appear that Callimachus refers here to a specific, historical festival. [4] Son of Minos and Dexithea, who survived when the gods destroyed the other Telchines at Ceos (Bacchyl. 1.112–40; Apollod. *Bibl.* 3.1.2). [5] Son of Codrus, king of Athens, which he fled after killing his brother Damasichthon and went to Naxos (Paus. 7.3.3). [6] The father of the Satyrs, who follow Dionysus (Eur. *Cyc.*). A specific cult of Silenus at Naxos is not attested, but see Catull. 64.252–54. [7] On a historical cult of Ariadne on Naxos (Plut. *Thes.* 20.3–4). Callimachus refers here to a well-known version of Ariadne's story in which Theseus leaves her sleeping on Naxos, where he abandoned her after she helped him escape from Crete, and she is rescued by Dionysus (Ap. Rhod. 3.997–1007).

].ν κε.[   ]ς ἔχειν ἵ[.].ον·
]ασιν ᾠκίσ[σα .].
ἀ]πειπάμεν[
].[.]ν ἐπιτιμ[   ]α
μ]οῦνον ἔμεν .α[
].[.]ν ὄθμασιν [
].[

20

68 *Et. Gen.* AB s.v. εἰσπνήλης

εἰσπνήλης· ὁ ἐρώμενος· Καλλίμαχος,

    μέμβλετο δ᾽ εἰσπνήλαις ὁππότε κοῦρος ἴοι
φωλεὸν ἠὲ λοετρόν

69 Ath. 15.668b

τοῦτο δὲ λέγοντες παρ᾽ ὅσον τῶν ἐρωμένων ἐμέ-
μνηντο, ἀφιέντες ἐπ᾽ αὐτοῖς τοὺς λεγομένους κοσσά-
βους. διὸ καὶ Σοφοκλῆς . . . καὶ Εὐριπίδης (Fr. 631
K) . . . καὶ Καλλίμαχος δέ φησι,

    πολλοὶ καὶ[1] φιλέοντες Ἀκόντιον[2] ἧκαν[3] ἔραζε[4]
οἰνοπόται Σικελὰς ἐκ κυλίκων λάταγας

[1] καί Ath.: δέ Schol. ad Ar.   [2] Ἀκόντιον Bentley: ἀκόν-
τιον codd.: Ἀκοντίῳ Maas   [3] ἧκαν Ath.: ἧκον Schol. ad Ar.
[4] ἔραζε Schol. ad Ar.: ἔργαζε Ath.

204

. . . to have . . . she colonized . . . denying . . . honored . . .
[20] to be alone . . . with the eyes

68 *Etymologicum Genuinum*

eispnēlēs: the beloved. Callimachus,

> And lovers took an interest in him whenever the boy
> went to the school or to the baths.

69 Athenaeus, *The Learned Banqueters*

The expression "speaking" is used because the players
mention their lovers as they toss the *kossaboi* for them.
Therefore Sophocles in the *Inachus*[1] . . . and Euripides[2]
. . . and Callimachus says,

> And many of the wine drinkers who loved Acontius
> let Sicilian drops fall from their cups to the ground.[3]

[1] Soph. fr. 277 Lloyd-Jones.   [2] Eur. fr. 631 Collard and
Cropp, from *Pleisthenes*.   [3] The game of cottabus was Sicil-
ian in origin and was played in different ways. Generally, drops
of wine were shot at various kinds of targets, and there were
prizes for accuracy (Ath. 15.666c–668f). Here the lovers are dis-
tracted by Acontius and do not shoot at all.

70 *Et. Gen.* AB a 1137 (vol. 2, p. 180.8 Lasserre-Livadaras) s.v. ἄρδις

ἄρδις· ἡ ἀκὶς τοῦ βέλους· Καλλίμαχος,

ἀλλ᾽ ἀπὸ τόξου
αὐτὸς ὁ τοξευτὴς[1] ἄρδιν ἔχων ἑτέρου

[1] Hapax legomenon, *Il.* 23.850

71 Steph. Byz. δ 61 Billerbeck s.v. Δῆλος

Δῆλος· ἐξ αὐτοῦ Δήλιος καὶ Δηλία καὶ Δηλιάς. καὶ Δηλίτης ὁ εἰς Δῆλον ἐρχόμενος χορός, Καλλίμαχος τρίτῳ.

72 Schol. L R (ed. Rom.) ad Soph. *Ant.* 80 (V. De Marco, *MAL* VI.6 [1937]: 192)

ἄγραδε τῷ πάσῃσιν ἐπὶ προχάνῃσιν ἐφοίτα

73 Schol. E Γ ad Ar. *Ach.* 144

ἴδιον ἐραστῶν ἦν τὸ τὰ τῶν ἐρωμένων ὀνόματα γράφειν ἐν τοῖς τοίχοις [ἢ δένδροις], ἢ φλοιοῖς δένδρων οὕτως· "ὁ δεῖνα καλός'" καὶ παρὰ Καλλιμάχῳ,

ἀλλ᾽ ἐνὶ δὴ φλοιοῖσι[1] κεκομμένα τόσσα φέροιτε
γράμματα, Κυδίππην ὅσσ᾽[2] ἐρέουσι καλήν.

[1] φλοιοῖσι Bentley: φύλλοις codd.   [2] ὅσσ᾽ Bentley: ὡς codd.

70 *Etymologicum Genuinum*

ardis: the tip of the arrow; Callimachus,

> from the bow of another, the bowman[1] himself feeling the arrow's point

[1] Acontius, who has fallen in love with Cydippe.

71 Stephanus of Byzantium

Delos: From the Delian one himself (*Dēlios*) come both *Dēlia* (the Delian woman) and *Dēlias* (the mission to Delos). And *Dēlitēs*, the chorus coming into Delos, Callimachus in the third book.

72 Scholia to Sophocles, *Antigone*

> He used to visit the country on every pretext

73 Scholia to Aristophanes, *Acharnians*

It was typical of lovers to write the names of their beloveds on walls [or on trees] or on the bark of trees in this way: "He is very beautiful!" And in Callimachus,

> On your bark may you bear as many engraved
> letters as will say "Cydippe is beautiful."

CALLIMACHUS

74 (74 Pf. + vol. 1, p. 501 Pf.) *P.Oxy.* 2258B recto; Hsch.
λ 547 Latte s.v. λειριόεντα

λειριόεντα] . . . τὸ δὲ λιρός, ὃ δηλοῖ τὸν ἀναιδῆ, διὰ
τοῦ ι (γραπτέον). Καλλίμαχος,

. . . .

```
      ] . . [
      ] . απ[
λιρὸς, ἐγώ, τ.ί δέ σοι τόνδ᾽¹ ἐπέθηκα² φόβον;
      ] . ελα . [
```

. . . .

¹ τί δέ σοι τόνδ Bentley: τίδες, ὅταν δε codd.
² ἐπέσεισα Meineke: ἐνέθηκα Schneider

75 (75.1–41 Pf.) *P.Oxy.* 1011 fol. 1 verso; 3–6 (fin.),
P.Oxy. 2258 B fr. 1 verso; 11–15 (init.), *P.Oxy.* 4427; 42–
77, *P.Oxy.* 1011 fol. 1 recto; 50–58 partes, *P.Oxy.* 2213 fr.
11 a–c

ἤδη καὶ κούρῳ παρθένος εὐνάσατο,
τέθμιον ὡς ἐκέλευε προνύμφιον ὕπνον ἰαῦσαι
ἄρσενι¹ τὴν τάλιν παιδὶ σὺν ἀμφιθαλεῖ.
Ἥρην γάρ κοτέ φασι—κύον, κύον, ἴσχεο, λαιδρὲ
5   θυμέ, σύ γ᾽ ἀείσῃ καὶ τά περ οὐχ ὁσίη·
ὤναο κάρτ᾽ ἕνεκ᾽ οὔ τι θεῆς ἴδες ἱερὰ φρικτῆς,
ἐξ ἂν ἐπεὶ² καὶ τῶν ἤρυγες ἱστορίην.

¹ ἄρσενι P: αὐτίκα Schol. ad Soph. *Ant.* 629
² ἐξ ἂν ἐπεὶ Hunt 1910: εξανεπει P

208

74 (74 Pf. + vol. 1, p. 501 Pf.) Oxyrhynchus papyrus; Hesychius

leirioenta and *liros*, which means "shameless" [should be written] with an iota. Callimachus,

> Why did I in my shamelessness put this cause for fear on you ?

75 (75.1–41 Pf.) Oxyrhynchus papyri

Already the bride was in bed with the boy, as custom demanded that the bride sleep on the night before the wedding with a boy whose two parents were both alive.[1] For they say that once upon a time Hera—dog, dog, hold back, impertinent [5] soul! You will sing even what is not lawful to tell![2] It is to your advantage that you did not see the holy rites of the awful goddess,[3] since you would have spit up

---

[1] This was apparently a fertility rite. On the relevance of this passage to Callimachus' patron, Berenice II, see Clayman 2014, 92–93.   [2] An allusion to the *hieros gamos*, the sacred union of Zeus and Hera, which they kept secret from their parents (*Il.* 14.292–96), a passage also used to justify the brother/sister marriage of Ptolemy II and Arsinoe II (Theoc. *Id.* 17.131–34).

[3] The secrets of the Eleusinian Mysteries of Demeter.

ἢ πολυιδρείη χαλεπὸν κακόν, ὅστις ἀκαρτεῖ
    γλώσσης· ὡς ἐτεὸν παῖς ὅδε μαῦλιν ἔχει.
10 ἠῷοι μὲν ἔμελλον ἐν ὕδατι θυμὸν ἀμύξειν
    οἱ βόες ὀξεῖαν δερκόμενοι δορίδα·
δειελινὴν τὴν δ' εἷλε κακὸς χλόος, ἦλθε δὲ νοῦσος,
    αἶγας ἐς ἀγριάδας τὴν ἀποπεμπόμεθα,
ψευδόμενοι δ' ἱερὴν φημίζομεν· ἦ τότ' ἀνιγρὴ
15   τὴν κούρην Ἀίδεω μέχρις ἔτηξε δόμων.
δεύτερον ἐστόρνυντο τὰ κλισμία, δεύτερον ἡ πα[ῖ]ς
    ἑπτὰ τεταρταίῳ μῆνας ἔκαμνε πυρί.
τὸ τρίτον ἐμνήσαντο γάμου κάτα,[3] τὸ τρίτον αὖτ[ις
    Κυδίππην ὀλοὸς κρυμὸς ἐσῳκίσατο.
20 τέτρατον [ο]ὐκέτ' ἔμεινε πατὴρ ἐ....]φ..ο..[
    Φοῖβον· ὁ δ' ἐννύχιον τοῦτ' ἔπος ηὐδάσατο·
"Ἀρτέμιδος τῇ παιδὶ γάμον βαρὺς ὅρκος ἐνικλᾷ·
    Λύγδαμιν οὐ γὰρ ἐμὴ τῆμος ἔκηδε κάσις
οὐδ' ἐν Ἀμυκλαίῳ θρύον[4] ἔπλεκεν οὐδ' ἀπὸ θήρης
25   ἔκλυζεν ποταμῷ λύματα Παρθενίῳ,
Δήλῳ δ' ἦν ἐπίδημος, Ἀκόντιον ὁππότε σὴ παῖς
    ὤμοσεν, οὐκ ἄλλον, νυμφίον ἐξέμεναι.
ὦ Κήϋξ, ἀλλ' ἤν με θέλῃς συμφράδμονα[5] θέσθαι,

---

[3] κάτα Pf.: κοτέ Hunt   [4] θρύον corr. Hunt: θριον Pap.
[5] Hapax legomenon, Il. 2.371

---

[4] The sacrifices were to be conducted on the morning of the
wedding when the animals will see their own reflection in the
lustral water. This does not occur, because the bride becomes ill
in the afternoon of the previous day.

even the contents of these. Much learning is a terrible thing, and whoever does not control his tongue, how truly is he like a child with a knife.—[10] In the morning the oxen were about to lacerate their hearts, looking at the sharp, sacrificial knife in the water;[4] but in the afternoon an evil pallor seized her,[5] a disease came that we banish into the wild goats.[6] Falsely we call it "sacred."[7] Then that painful, wasting malady [15] brought the girl almost to the house of Hades. Then a second marriage bed was made and a second time the girl was sick with a quartan fever for seven months. Then a third time they thought of marriage and again for a third time a deadly chill settled on Cydippe.

[20] The fourth time, the father no longer stayed at home, but [went to inquire of] Phoebus.[8] And he pronounced this word at night, "A solemn oath of Artemis frustrates the marriage for your child. For my sister was not then vexing Lygdamis,[9] nor in Amyclae[10] was she plaiting rushes, nor was she washing off [25] the filth from the hunt in the river Parthenius,[11] but she was at home in Delos when your child swore that she would have Acontius, no other, as her bridegroom. O Ceyx,[12] if you want to appoint me as counselor, you will fulfill the oath of your

---

[5] Cydippe, the bride.   [6] That is, a disease that could be cured only by magic.   [7] Epilepsy (e.g., Hdt. 3.33).

[8] At Apollo's oracle at Delphi.   [9] King of the Cimmerians, who threatened the temple of Artemis in Ephesus (Strabo 1.3.21).   [10] On the banks of the river Eurotas near Sparta, where there was a temple of Apollo.   [11] The "Virgin" river in Paphlagonia, appropriate for a virgin goddess.

[12] The father of Cydippe.

211

..]ν .. τελευτήσεις ὅρκια θυγατέρος·
30 ἀργύρῳ οὐ μόλιβον⁶ γὰρ Ἀκόντιον, ἀλλὰ φαεινῷ
    ἤλεκτρον χρυσῷ φημί σε μειξέμεναι.
Κοδρείδης σύ γ' ἄ̣ν̣ωθεν ὁ πενθερός, αὐτὰρ ὁ Κεῖος
    γαμβρὸς Ἀρισταίου [Ζη]ν̣ὸς ἀφ' ἱερέων
Ἰκμίου οἷς̣ι μέμ[η]λεν ἐπ' οὔρεος ἀμβώνεσσιν⁷
35 πρηΰνειν χαλ[ε]πὴν Μαῖραν ἀνερχομένην,
αἰτεῖσθαι τὸ δ' ἄημα παραὶ Διὸς ᾧ τε̣ θαμεινοί
    πλήσσονται λινέαις ὄρτυγες ἐν νεφέλαις."
ἡ θεός· αὐτὰρ ὁ Νάξον ἔβη πάλιν, εἴρετο δ' αὐτήν
    κούρην, ἡ δ' ἀπ' ἑτῶς πᾶν ἐκάλυψεν ἔπος
40 κῆν αὖ σῶς· ... λοιπόν, Ἀκόντιε, σεῖο μετελθεῖν
    ⁸......ηνιδιην ἐς Διονυσιάδα.
χἠ θεὸς εὐορκεῖτο καὶ ἥλικες αὐτίχ' ἑταίρης
    ἦιδον⁹ ὑμηναίους οὐκ ἀναβαλλομένους.
οὔ σε δοκέω τημοῦτος, Ἀκόντιε, νυκτὸς ἐκείνης
45 ἀντί κε, τῇ μίτρης ἥψαο παρθενίης,
οὐ σφυρὸν Ἰφίκλειον¹⁰ ἐπιτρέχον ἀσταχύεσσιν
    οὐδ' ἃ Κελαινίτης ἐκτεάτιστο Μίδης
δέξασθαι, ψήφου δ' ἂν ἐμῆς ἐπιμάρτυρες εἶεν
    οἵτινες οὐ χαλεποῦ νήιδές εἰσι θεοῦ.

---

⁶ Hapax legomenon, *Il.* 11.236   ⁷ *Et. Gen.* AB α 613 s.v.
ἄμβων (vol. 1, p. 389.13 Lasserre-Livadaras)   ⁸ Lacuna, P.
Graindor, *Musée Belge* 15 (1911): 58   ⁹ ἦιδον Wilamowitz
ap. Hunt: ειδον Pap.: εἶπον Pf.   ¹⁰ Schol. Lond. ad Dion.
Thrax 532.2 Hilgard

daughter. [30] But [in a marriage with] Acontius I say that you will not be mingling lead with silver, but electrum with shiny gold. You, the father-in-law, are a descendant of Codrus[13] and the Cean son-in-law, from the priests of Zeus Aristaeus the Icmian.[14] To these it is a care [35] to calm terrible Maera[15] when she is rising, and to ask from Zeus the wind by which many quails will be swept into linen nets."

So the god spoke; and her father returned to Naxos and questioned his daughter herself, and she revealed the whole story truthfully, [40] and was well again. . . . for the rest, Acontius, it will be yours to go to the Island of Dionysus[16] . . . And the oath to the goddess was fulfilled, and at once girls of the same age sang the marriage hymns for their companion, deferred no longer.

Then, Acontius, I do not think that you would exchange that night [45] on which you touched the belt of the maiden for the ankle of Iphicles[17] running on the corn, nor for the possessions of Midas of Celaenae.[18] And may the witnesses of my verdict be those who are not ignorant of

---

[13] For Codrus, see *Aet.* 67 n. 5 above.   [14] For the origins of this cult, see Ap. Rhod. 2.516–27. Aristaeus was the son of Apollo and Cyrene, who built an altar to Icmian Zeus on a mountain top in Ceos to ameliorate the heat of Sirius. In response, the Etesian Winds began to blow.   [15] A name for Sirius, the dog star.   [16] Naxos, where Dionysus married Ariadne (Diod. Sic. 5.52.1).   [17] Son of Phylacus and proverbially swift runner who could run on the corn growing in the fields without doing any damage (Hes. fr. 62 M.-W.; Paus. 5.17.10). He was sterile until cured by Melampus (*Aet.* 54e.5 above).   [18] Proverbially rich man, king of Celaenae in Phrygia. For the story that everything he touched turned to gold, see Ov. *Met.* 11.100–145.

50 ἐκ δὲ γάμου κείνοιο μέγ' οὔνομα μέλλε νέεσθαι·[11]
    δὴ γὰρ ἔθ' ὑμέτερον φῦλον Ἀκοντιάδαι
    πουλύ τι καὶ περίτιμον Ἰουλίδι ναιετάουσιν,
    Κεῖε, τεὸν δ' ἡμεῖς ἵμερον ἐκλύομεν
    τόνδε παρ' ἀρχαίου Ξενομήδεος, ὅς ποτε πᾶσαν
55 νῆσον ἐνὶ μνήμῃ κάτθετο μυθολόγῳ,
    ἄρχμενος ὡς νύμφῃσι[ν ἐ]ναίετο Κωρυκίῃσιν,
    τὰς ἀπὸ Παρνησσοῦ λῖς ἐδίωξε μέγας,
    (Ὑδροῦσσαν τῷ καί μιν ἐφήμισαν), ὥς τε
        Κυρή[νης[12]
    .... θυσ[.]το.. ᾤκεεν ἐν Καρύαις·
60 ὥς τέ μιν ἐννάσσαντο τέων Ἀλαλάξιος αἰεί
    Ζεὺς ἐπὶ σαλπίγγων ἱρὰ βοῇ δέχεται
    Κᾶρες ὁμοῦ Λελέγεσσι, μετ' οὔνομα δ' ἄλλο
        βαλέσθ[αι[13]
    Φοίβου καὶ Μελίης ἶνις ἔθηκε Κέως·
    ἐν δ' ὕβριν θάνατόν τε κεραύνιον, ἐν δὲ γόητας
65 Τελχῖνας μακάρων τ' οὐκ ἀλέγοντα θεῶν
    ἠλεὰ Δημώνακτα γέρων ἐνεθήκατο δέλτ[οις
    καὶ γρηῦν Μακελώ, μητέρα Δεξιθέης,

11 μέλλε νέεσθαι Hunt: μέλλεν ἔ<σ>εσθαι A. Brinkmann, *RhM* 72 (1917–18): 478: μέλλεν ἔ<π>εσθαι A. Platt, *CQ* 4 (1910): 112   12 Κυρή[νης Storck 1912, etc.: Κιρώ[δης Murray ap. Hunt   13 βαλέσθ[αι Lobel ap. Pf.: βαλεισθ[pap.: καλεῖσθ[αι

19 Eros.   20 Acontius.
21 Xenomedes of Chios (5th c. AD), historian (*BNJ* 442 F 1).

the stern god.[19] [50] And from the marriage a great name
was destined to arise; for still your tribe, the Acontiadae,
dwell numerous and much honored in Iulis; and Cean,[20]
we heard the story of your passion from ancient Xeno-
medes,[21] who once recorded [55] the whole island in a
mythological memoir, beginning with how it was settled
by the nymphs of Corycia,[22] whom a great lion drove from
Mt. Parnassus. And for that reason they call it Hydrusa.[23]
And how the son of Cyrene [Aristaeus] lived in Caryae.[24]
[60] And how they settled in the country whose sacrifices
Zeus Alalaxius[25] always receives to the sound of trumpets.
Carians and the Leleges together,[26] and how Ceos,[27] son
of Phoebus and Melia, caused it [the island] to take an-
other name.

And in his tablets the old man put *hubris* and deadly
lightning, and in them he put those sorcerers [65] the
Telchines, and crazed Demonax, who did not care for the
blessed gods, and the old woman Macelo,[28] the mother of

[22] For the nymphs who dwelled in the Cory-
cian Cave, see Strabo 9.3.1; Paus. 10.32.2.   [23] The "well-hydrated," per-
haps because the nymphs were hydriades, water nymphs.

[24] One of two possible places of that name in Arcadia, very
likely related to the story of Aristaeus (Harder vol. 2, 641–42).

[25] Zeus of the war cry ("alala," Xen. *An.* 6.5.27).

[26] Tribes originally from Asia Minor who migrated to the
Greek islands (Hdt. 1.171).

[27] Perhaps one of the Carians or Leleges or someone who
brought new settlers and became the eponymous founder. Cal-
limachus wrote a prose work on the foundation of islands and
cities and their name changes (*Fr. Doct.* 412).

[28] Demonax, here, is king of the Telchines, and Macelo is his
wife.

ἃς μούνας, ὅτε νῆσον ἀνέτρεπον εἵνεκ' ἀλ[ι]τρῆς
ὕβριος, ἀσκηθεὶς ἔλλιπον ἀθάνατοι·
70 τέσσαρας ὥς τε πόληας ὁ μὲν τείχισσε Μεγακλῆς
Κάρθαιαν, Χρυσοῦς[14] δ' Εὔπ[υ]λος[15] ἡμιθέης
εὔκρηνον πτολίεθρον Ἰουλίδος, αὐτὰρ Ἀκαῖος
Ποιῆσσαν Χαρίτων ἵδρυμ' ἐυπλοκάμων,
ἄστυρον Ἄφραστος δὲ Κορή[σ]ιον, εἶπε δέ, Κεῖε,
75 ξυγκραθέντ' αὐταῖς ὀξὺν ἔρωτα σέθεν
πρέσβυς ἐτητυμίη μεμελημένος, ἔνθεν ὁ παιδὸς
μῦθος ἐς ἡμετέρην ἔδραμε Καλλιόπην.

[14] Χρυσοῦς Wilamowitz ap. Hunt: χρεισους vel χροισους
sscr. δ' pap.: Βρισοῦς vel Βριζοῦς G. Huxley, GRBS 6 (1965):
243   [15] Εὔπ[υ]λος Hunt, sed Εὔπ[α]λος vel Εὔπ[ο]λος Pf.

75a (vol. 1, p. 71 Pf.) Dieg. 6.1–7; P.Mil.Vogl. 1.18 col. VI,
1–7

```
              ]ς παρθένου ἐκ
           Κυδί]ππης μήλῳ καλ-
λίστῳ ........"μὰ τὴ]ν Ἄρτεμιν, Ἀκον-
τίῳ γαμοῦμαι" ........].σενηδεηδε
5          ]νετο· ὡς δε.ε
           ]ηθει[...]ιν..ρω
           ].γαμ[
```

. . . .

Dexithea, the two of whom alone the gods left unharmed when they overturned the island on account of wicked arrogance.[29]

[70] And in regard to the four cities,[30] [he told] how Megacles built Carthaea, and Eupylus, son of the demigoddess Chryso, the city of Iulis with its many fountains, and how Acaeus built Poeessa, the shrine of the Graces with lovely hair, and Aphrastus, the city of Coresus; and he told, Cean, [75] of your urgent love blended in among these [foundation stories], the old man who cared for the truth, from whom the account of this boy ran to our Calliope.[31]

[29] Cf. Schol. B ad Ov. *Ib.* 475.   [30] Cf. Strabo 10.5.6; Plin. *HN* 4.62.   [31] One of the principal Muses who provided information for the poet in Books 1 and 2. Here the name seems to stand for this poem, or perhaps Callimachus' art.

75a (vol. 1, p. 71 Pf.) Milan papyrus (*Diegeseis*)

. . . of the maiden from . . . with the loveliest apple of Cydippe . . . "By Artemis, I will marry Acontius" . . . how . . . marriage

75b Aristaenet. 1.10 (1–99, 106–10 Mazal)

Ἀκόντιος τὴν Κυδίππην καλὸς νεανίας καλὴν ἔγημε
κόρην. ὁ γὰρ παλαιὸς λόγος εὖ ἔχει, ὡς ὅμοιον ὁμοίῳ
κατὰ θεῖον ἀεὶ προσπελάζει. τὴν μὲν ἅπασι τοῖς ἑαυ-
τῆς φιλοτίμοις κεκόσμηκεν Ἀφροδίτη, μόνου τοῦ κε-
στοῦ φεισαμένη· καὶ τοῦτον πρὸς τὴν παρθένον εἶχεν
ἐξαίρετον ἡ θεός. καὶ [5] τοῖς ὄμμασι Χάριτες οὐ τρεῖς
καθ᾽ Ἡσίοδον, ἀλλὰ δεκάδων περιχορεύει δεκάς. τὸν
δὲ νέον ἐκόσμουν ὀφθαλμοὶ φαιδροὶ μὲν ὡς καλοῦ,
φοβεροὶ δὲ ὡς σώφρονος, καὶ φύσεως ἔρευθος εὐαν-
θὲς ἐπιτρέχον ταῖς παρειαῖς. οἱ δὲ φιλοθεάμονες τοῦ
κάλλους εἰς διδασκάλου προϊόντα περιεσκόπουν συν-
ωθοῦντες [10] ἀλλήλους, καὶ ἦν ὁρᾶν τούτων πλη-
θούσας μὲν ἀγορὰς στενοχωρουμένας δὲ λαύρας. καὶ
πολλοί γε διὰ τοῦτο τὸ λίαν ἐρωτικὸν τοῖς ἴχνεσι τοῦ
μειρακίου τοὺς ἑαυτῶν ἐφήρμοζον πόδας.

οὗτος ἠράσθη Κυδίππης. ἔδει γὰρ [15] τὸν καλὸν
τοσούτους τετοξευκότα τῷ κάλλει μιᾶς ἀκίδος ἐρω-
τικῆς πειραθῆναί ποτε καὶ γνῶναι σαφῶς, οἷα πε-
πόνθασιν οἱ δι᾽ αὐτὸν τραυματίαι. ὅθεν ὁ Ἔρως οὐ
μετρίως ἐνέτεινε τὴν νευράν (ὅτε καὶ τερπνὴ πέφυκεν
ἡ τοξεία), ἀλλ᾽ ὅσον εἶχεν ἰσχύος προσελκύσας τὰ
τόξα σφοδρότατα διαφῆκε τὸ [20] βέλος. τοιγαροῦν
εὐθέως, ὦ κάλλιστον παιδίον Ἀκόντιε, δυοῖν θάτερον,
ἢ γάμον ἢ θάνατον διελογίζου βληθείς.

πλὴν αὐτὸς ὁ τρώσας ἀεί τινας παραδόξους μη-
χανὰς διαπλέκων ὑπέθετό σοι καινοτάτην βουλήν,

75b Aristaenetus

Acontius, a beautiful youth, married Cydippe, a beautiful girl, for the old saying holds true, how according to divine law, like inclines to like. Aphrodite adorned her with all of her own endowments, holding back only the *cestos*.[1] This the god retained to distinguish herself from the maiden. And [5] in her eyes not three Graces dance around, as in Hesiod,[2] but ten times ten. And bright eyes adorned the youth as befits the good-looking, but awe-inspiring like a wise man's; and a rose color blossoming naturally spread over his cheeks. And those who loved to contemplate beauty would watch as he went to school, jostling [10] one another, and you could see them filling the marketplaces and the narrow alleys. And many, on account of this excessive love, fit their own feet into the boy's footsteps.

This boy was in love with Cydippe. For it was inevitable [15] that this beautiful boy, who had wounded so many with his beauty, would someday experience a single arrow-point of Eros and know clearly the sufferings of those who were wounded by him. Hence Eros stretched his bow not moderately (when archery is actually pleasant), but drawing back the bow with all his strength, he loosed the most forceful [20] shot. Therefore, at once after you were struck, o most beautiful child Acontius, you decided it was one of two things: marriage or death.

Except the one who deals the wound always weaves some surprising complications, but in your case he offered

---

[1] The embroidered belt of Aphrodite, which contains various charms (love, desire, dalliance, and persuasion), that steals the wits even of the wise (*Il*. 14.214–17).   [2] Hes. *Theog.* 907.

τάχα που τὸ σὸν αἰδούμενος κάλλος. αὐτίκα γοῦν
κατὰ τὸ Ἀρτεμίσιον ὡς ἐθεάσω [25] προκαθημένην
τὴν κόρην, τοῦ κήπου τῆς Ἀφροδίτης Κυδώνιον ἐκλε-
ξάμενος μῆλον ἀπάτης αὐτῷ περιγεγράφηκας λόγον
καὶ λάθρᾳ διεκύλισας πρὸ τῶν τῆς θεραπαίνης πο-
δῶν. ἡ δὲ τὸ μέγεθος καὶ τὴν χροιὰν καταπλαγεῖσα
ἀνήρπασεν, ἅμα διαποροῦσα τίς ἄρα τοῦτο τῶν παρ-
θένων μετέωρος [30] ἀπέβαλε τοῦ προκολπίου· "ἆρα,"
φησίν, "ἱερὸν πέφυκας, ὦ μῆλον; τίνα δέ σοι πέριξ
ἐγκεχάρακται γράμματα; καὶ τί σημαίνειν ἐθέλεις;
δέχου μῆλον, ὦ κεκτημένη, οἷον οὐ τεθέαμαι πρότε-
ρον. ὡς ὑπερμέγεθες, ὡς πυρρωπόν, ὡς ἐρύθημα φέ-
ρον τῶν ῥόδων. εὖγε τῆς εὐωδίας· ὅσον καὶ [35] πόρ-
ρωθεν εὐφραίνει τὴν αἴσθησιν. λέγε μοι, φιλτάτη, τί
τὸ περίγραμμα τοῦτο;" ἡ δὲ κόρη κομισαμένη καὶ
τοῖς ὄμμασι περιθέουσα τὴν γραφὴν ἀνεγίνωσκεν
ἔχουσαν ὧδε· "μὰ τὴν Ἄρτεμιν Ἀκοντίῳ γαμοῦμαι."
ἔτι διερχομένη τὸν ὅρκον εἰ καὶ ἀκούσιόν τε καὶ νόθον
τὸν ἐρωτικὸν λόγον ἀπέρριψεν [40] αἰδουμένη, καὶ
ἡμίφωνον καταλέλοιπε λέξιν τὴν ἐπ' ἐσχάτῳ κειμένην
ἅτε διαμνημονεύουσαν γάμον, ὃν σεμνὴ παρθένος
κἂν ἑτέρου λέγοντος ἠρυθρίασε. καὶ τοσοῦτον ἐξεφοι-
νίχθη τὸ πρόσωπον, ὡς δοκεῖν ὅτι τῶν παρειῶν ἔνδον
εἶχέ τινα ῥόδων λειμῶνα, καὶ τὸ ἐρύθημα τοῦτο μηδὲν
τῶν χειλῶν [45] αὐτῆς διαφέρειν. εἶπεν ἡ παῖς, ἀκή-
κοεν Ἄρτεμις· καὶ παρθένος οὖσα θεός, Ἀκόντιε, συν-
ελάβετό σοι τοῦ γάμου.

a most novel plan, perhaps somehow deferring to your beauty. As soon as you saw the girl sitting by the temple of Artemis, [25] you selected from the garden of Aphrodite a Cydonian apple, and you wrote on it a legend of deceit and secretly rolled it under the feet of her attendant. Then she, struck by its size and color, snatched it up, and wondering which of the servants had distractedly [30] dropped it from her lap, said "Are you sacred, o apple? What are the letters carved around you? And what do you wish to signify? Take the apple, mistress, such as I have never before beheld. How very big it is, how red, having the redness of roses. And an excellent fragrance! How [35] from a distance it gladdens the senses. Tell me, dearest, what is this inscription?" The maiden took it, and with her eyes examining the writing recognized its meaning: "By Artemis, it is Acontius I will marry." While still completing the oath, however involuntary and spurious, she threw away the declaration of love, embarrassed, [40] and left half-spoken the reading at the end, which mentioned marriage, at which a decent girl blushes even when someone else speaks of it. And her face turned so red that on her cheeks a meadow of roses seemed to have blossomed. And this redness differed not at all from that [45] of her lips. The girl spoke and Artemis listened. Although a virgin goddess, she joined in with you, Acontius, in your marriage plot.

τέως οὖν τὸν δείλαιον—ἀλλ᾽ οὔτε θαλάττης τρικυ-
μίας οὔτε πόθου κορυφούμενον σάλον εὐμαρὲς ἀφη-
γεῖσθαι· δάκρυα μόνον, οὐχ ὕπνον αἱ νύκτες ἐπῆγον
τῷ μειρακίῳ· κλαίειν [50] γὰρ αἰδούμενος τὴν ἡμέραν
τὸ δάκρυον ἐταμιεύετο ταῖς νυξίν. ἐκτακεὶς δὲ τὰ μέλη
καὶ δυσθυμίαις μαραινόμενος τὴν χροιὰν καὶ τὸ
βλέμμα δεινῶς ὡρακιῶν ἐδεδίει τῷ τεκόντι φανῆναι
καὶ εἰς ἀγρὸν ἐπὶ πάσῃ προφάσει τὸν πατέρα φεύγων
ἐφοίτα. διόπερ οἱ κομψότεροι τῶν ἡλικιωτῶν [55] Λα-
έρτην αὐτὸν ἐπωνόμαζον, γηπόνον τὸν νεανίσκον οἰό-
μενοι γεγονέναι. ἀλλ᾽ Ἀκοντίῳ οὐκ ἀμπελῶνος ἔμελεν,
οὐ σκαπάνης, μόνον δὲ φηγοῖς ὑποκαθήμενος ἢ πτε-
λέαις ὡμίλει τοιάδε· "εἴθε, ὦ δένδρα, καὶ νοῦς ὑμῖν
γένοιτο καὶ φωνή, ὅπως ἂν εἴπητε μόνον· Κυδίππη
καλή.᾽ ἢ γοῦν [60] τοσαῦτα κατὰ τῶν φλοιῶν ἐγκεκο-
λαμμένα φέροιτε γράμματα, ὅσα τὴν Κυδίππην ἐπ-
ονομάζει καλήν. Κυδίππη, καλήν σε καὶ εὔορκον
ὁμοίως προσείπω ταχύ, μηδὲ Ἄρτεμις ἐπί σοι ποι-
ναῖον βέλος ἀφῇ καὶ ἀνέλῃ· μένῃ δὲ τὸ πῶμα προσ-
κείμενον τῇ φαρέτρᾳ. ὦ δυστυχὴς ἐγώ. τί δέ σοι
τοῦτον ἐπῆγον [65] τὸν φόβον; ὁπότε καί φασι τὴν
θεὸν ἐπὶ πάσαις μὲν ἁμαρτάσι κινεῖσθαι δεινῶς, μά-
λιστα δὲ τοὺς ἀμελοῦντας τῶν ὅρκων πικρότερον τι-
μωρεῖσθαι. εἴθε μὲν οὖν ὡς ἀρτίως ηὐχόμην εὔορκος
εἴης, εἴθε γάρ· εἰ δὲ ἀποβαίη, ὅπερ μηδὲ λέγειν κα-
λόν, ἢ Ἄρτεμις ἔσται σοι, παρθένε, πραεῖα· οὐ σὲ
γάρ, [70] ἀλλὰ τὸν δόντα τῆς ἐπιορκίας τὴν πρόφασιν
κολαστέον. μαθήσομαι μόνον ὡς μεμέληκας τῶν

Meanwhile, the wretched one—but neither the triple waves of the sea nor the crest of roiling desire are easy to describe; to the young man the nights brought only tears, not sleep. Being ashamed [50] to cry during the day, he stored up his tears for the nights. His limbs melting, his flesh wasting away from despair, and his appearance looking terribly weak, he feared to encounter his father and went to the country on every pretext to avoid him. On that account the more clever of his agemates began to call him [55] Laertes, thinking that the youth had become a farmer. But the vineyard was not of interest to Acontius, nor the mattock, but sitting alone under the oaks or elms he kept company with them with words such as these: "I wish, O trees, that you had a mind and a voice so that you could only say, 'Cydippe is beautiful.' [60] Or you could at least bear as many letters engraved on your bark as pronounce Cydippe beautiful. And may I soon call you both beautiful, Cydippe, and faithful to your oath; and may Artemis not send to you a punishing arrow and carry you off, but may the cover lie on her quiver. Oh I am unlucky! Why did I bring to you [65] this peril? When they say that the goddess is terribly agitated by all sins, punishing with special severity those who do not take their oaths seriously. I wish that you would be a respecter of oaths as I prayed just now, how I wish! But if the result is what is not good even to say, Artemis will be kind to you, maiden. For you should not [70] be punished, rather the one who furnished the pretext for your perjury. I will only confirm that you took

γραμμάτων, καὶ τοῦ σοῦ πρηστῆρος τὴν ἐμὴν ψυχὴν
ἀπαλλάττων οὐχ ἧττον αἵματος ἀφειδήσω τοῦ ἡμετέ-
ρου ἤπερ ὕδατος εἰκῆ χεομένου. ἀλλ' ὦ φίλτατα δέν-
δρα, τῶν ἡδυφώνων ὀρνίθων οἱ θῶκοι, [75] ἆρα κἂν ἐν
ὑμῖν ἐστιν οὗτος ὁ ἔρως, καὶ πίτυος τυχὸν ἠράσθη
κυπάριττος ἢ ἄλλο φυτὸν ἑτέρου φυτοῦ; μὰ Δία, οὐκ
οἶμαι· οὐ γὰρ ἐφυλλορροεῖτε καὶ τοὺς κλάδους ἁπλῶς
ὁ πόθος κόμης ὑμᾶς καὶ ἀγλαΐας ἐψίλου, ἀλλὰ καὶ
μέχρι στελέχους τε καὶ ῥιζῶν ὑπονοστήσας τῷ πυρσῷ
διικνεῖτο." [80] τοιαῦτα μὲν τὸ παιδίον Ἀκόντιος διελέ-
γετο πρὸς τῷ σώματι μαραινόμενος καὶ τὸν νοῦν.

τῇ δὲ Κυδίππῃ πρὸς ἕτερον ηὐτρεπίζετο γάμος. καὶ
πρὸ τῆς παστάδος τὸν ὑμέναιον ᾖδον αἱ μουσικώ-
τεραι τῶν παρθένων καὶ μελλιχόφωνοι (τοῦτο δὴ
Σαπφοῦς τὸ ἥδιστον φθέγμα). ἀλλ' ἄφνω νενόσηκεν
[85] ἡ παῖς, καὶ πρὸς ἐκφορὰν ἀντὶ νυμφαγωγίας οἱ
τεκόντες ἑώρων. εἶτα παραδόξως ἀνέσφηλε, καὶ δεύ-
τερον ὁ θάλαμος ἐκοσμεῖτο· καὶ ὥσπερ ἀπὸ συνθήμα-
τος τῆς Τύχης αὖθις ἐνόσει. τρίτον ὁμοίως ταῦτα
συμβέβηκε τῇ παιδί, ὁ δὲ πατὴρ τετάρτην οὐκ ἀνέ-
μεινε νόσον, ἀλλ' ἐπύθετο τοῦ [90] Πυθίου, τίς ἄρα
θεῶν τὸν γάμον ἐμποδίζει τῇ κόρῃ. ὁ δὲ Ἀπόλλων
πάντα σαφῶς τὸν πατέρα διδάσκει, τὸν νέον, τὸ μῆ-
λον, τὸν ὅρκον, καὶ τῆς Ἀρτέμιδος τὸν θυμόν· καὶ
παραινεῖ θᾶττον εὔορκον ἀποφῆναι τὴν κόρην. "ἄλ-
λως τε," φησί, "Κυδίππην Ἀκοντίῳ συνάπτων οὐ μό-
λιβδον ἂν συνεπιμίξαις [95] ἀργύρῳ, ἀλλ' ἑκατέρωθεν
ὁ γάμος ἔσται χρυσοῦς."

in my writing, and freeing my soul from your whirlwind, I will be no less sparing of my own blood than if it were water carelessly spilled. But, o dearest trees, perches of sweetly-singing birds, [75] do you ever feel this kind of love, and does it happen that the pine is loved by the cypress, or any plant by another? By Zeus, I think not. For you would not merely drop your leaves, and desire would not simply strip the branches of your foliage, their adornment, but it would penetrate by its fire even down to your trunks and roots." [80] Such things did the child Acontius say, wasting away in his body and mind.

And for Cydippe a marriage was prepared with someone else. And the most musical of the maidens sang the wedding hymn with smiling voices (to use the loveliest term of Sappho)[3] in front of the marriage chamber, but the girl suddenly became ill [85] and her parents were looking at a funeral rather than a wedding, when unexpectedly she recovered, and a second bridal chamber was prepared. And as if there were an arrangement with Fortune, she fell sick again. And when a third time the same thing happened to the girl, her father did not wait for the illness a fourth time but inquired of [90] Pytho whch of the gods was blocking the marriage of his child. And Apollo explained everything to the father clearly: the youth, the apple, the oath, and the anger of Artemis. And he advised that the maiden fulfill her oath forthwith. "Besides" he said, "connecting Cydippe to Acontius will not be mixing [95] lead with silver, but the marriage will be golden on each side."

[3] Fr. 71.6 Voigt.

ταῦτα μὲν ἔχρησεν ὁ μαντῷος θεός, ὁ δὲ ὅρκος ἅμα
τῷ χρησμῷ συνεπληροῦτο τοῖς γάμοις. αἱ δὲ τῆς παι-
δὸς ἡλικιώτιδες ἐνεργὸν ὑμέναιον ᾖδον οὐκ ἀναβαλ-
λόμενον ἔτι οὐδὲ διακοπτόμενον νόσῳ . . . [106] . . .
Τῆς νυκτὸς ἐκείνης Ἀκόντιος οὐκ ἂν ἠλλάξατο τὸν
Μίδου χρυσόν, οὐδὲ τὸν Ταντάλου πλοῦτον ἰσοστά-
σιον ἡγεῖτο τῇ κόρῃ. καὶ σύμψηφοι πάντες ἐμοί, ὅσοι
μὴ καθάπαξ τῶν ἐρωτικῶν [110] ἀμαθεῖς· τὸν γὰρ ἀνέ-
ραστον οὐκ ἀπεικὸς ἀντίδοξον εἶναι.

75c (T 65) Ov. *Rem. am.* 381–82

Callimachi numeris non est dicendus Achilles,
    Cydippe non est oris, Homere, tui.

75d (vol. 1, p. 501 Pf.) Schol. in marg. dext. *P.Oxy* 2258B

75, 4–5   φαν[
          νυμ[

75e Schol. in marg. sup. *P.Oxy.* 4427

. . . .

          ]..[ ].[

75.23   ]θη ὑπὸ τη..[
          ]. περὶ τὸν Λύγδ[αμιν
          ]σων [

The prophetic god uttered all this, and the oath and the oracle were together fulfilled by the marriage. And the girl's age-mates sang a marriage hymn that did the job, no longer delayed or cut short by illness . . . [106] . . . For that night Acontius would not have exchanged the gold of Midas, nor did he think the wealth of Tantalus equal in value to his bride. All my fellow jurymen are those who are not entirely without knowledge of love [110], for it may seem otherwise to someone without experience.

75c (T 65) Ovid, *The Remedies for Love*

> Not in the meters of Callimachus should Achilles be spoken,
> > nor is Cydippe suited to your mouth, Homer.

75d (vol. 1, p. 501 Pf.) Oxyrhynchus papyrus (marginal scholia)

75.4–5   appear . . . bride

75e Oxyrhynchus papyrus (marginal scholia)

75.23   by . . . around Lygdamis . . .

75.25   Παρθένιο]ς· ποταμὸς τῆς Παφλα[γονίας
ποτ]αμῷ Παρθενίος ποτα[μός (?)

76 Fabula ignota

76 *P.Oxy.* 1011 fol. 1 recto, 78–80

..αρτηπολλ.κοιμίσσασασομ.....
εστισε Πισαίου Ζηνός οπισπ...ιθην
ἀλλ' ι..νησ.κρουτοναικ.υ......ος

76a Fabulae ignotae

76a *P.Mil.Vogl.* 1.18 inv. 28b col. VI, 26–44

     . . . .
      ]..[
      ].τ[
      ]υυ[
      ]
5   ]ωοσ
      ]
      ]
      ]τ[
     ].ωσε.[
10   ]νομενων
     ].λουμε-
     ]τίμημα

75.25   Parthenius: a river of Paphlagonia; to the river,
         the river Parthenius (?)

76 *Unknown Tale*

76 Oxyrhynchus papyrus

. . . of Pisaean[1] Zeus . . .

[1] Pisa was a village at Olympia where there was a sanctuary
for Zeus (Pind. *Ol.* 10.43–45). Olympia is called Pisa in *Aet.* 84,
Aet. 98, and *Ia.* 196.12.

76a *Unknown Tales*

76a Milan papyrus

Fragments of *Diegeseis* of three *aitia* between *Acontius and
Cydippe* and the *Nuptial Rite at Elis*.

. . .

```
              ]
              ]νδε γενέσθαι
15      ]ρου καὶ τ[
        ]μιοσα.[
        ] .ν καί
        ] .εχει
        ] .ιαν
20  ....] κ.[...]μ.χ[ .......... ].[π]ροχείρως πα-
    ....]
```

76b–77d Eleorum ritus nuptialis

76b *P.Mil.Vogl.* 1.18 col. I, 3

Εἴπ' ἄγε μοι.. [ ].. α[......].]...... αιηνισ

77 Schol. BCDEQ ad Pind. *Ol.* 10.55c

καὶ Καλλίμαχος δὲ τὴν ῏Ηλιν Διὸς οἰκίον εἶπεν ἀντὶ τοῦ Πίσαν,

῏Ηλιν ἀνάσσεσθαι, Διὸς οἰκίον, ἔλλιπε Φυλεῖ

77a *P.Oxy.* 2213 fr. 2.1–4

```
.    .    .
η[.]...[
  φρασσ[
μυθο[
  ἦν μ[
```

AETIA BOOK III

76b–77d Marriage Rites of the Eleans

76b Milan papyrus

come tell me . . .

77 Scholia to Pindar, *Olympian Odes*

And Callimachus said that Elis was the home of Zeus be-
fore Pisa,

He[1] left to Phyleus to rule Elis, the home of Zeus.

[1] Heracles. Phyleus was the son of Augeas, king of Elis, who
refused to pay Heracles after the latter had cleaned his stables.
Heracles then destroyed the city and left Phyleus to rule over
what was left while he founded the Olympic games (Pind. *Ol.*
10.23–30; Apollod. *Bibl.* 2.5.5, 2.7.2).

77a Oxyrhynchus papyrus

. . . he (or she) told a story . . . there was

77b (vol. 1, p. 85 Pf.) *Dieg.* 1.3–8; *P.Mil.Vogl.* 1.18 col. I, 3–9

Εἴπ' ἄγε μοι.. [ ]..α[.......].[.]......αιήνις

φ]ησὶν ἐν Ἤλιδι ε.[.......]...ντ[.], [γ]αμου-
μένας παρθ[ένους   ]..ο[.].ου π[έ-
πλους ἐχούσας σ[   ].[.....]ου[

5   ..] δόρυ δὲ ἐν[
.δε φησιν α.[
ἄνδρα καθωπ[λισμένον

.   .   .   .

77c Schol. D ad Hom. *Il.* 11.698 Thiel

Ἡρακλῆς προστάξαντος Εὐρυσθέως, ἀνεκάθηρε τὴν
Αὐγέου κόπρον, ἀπαιτοῦντι δὲ αὐτῷ τὸν μισθὸν, οὐκ
ἀπεδίδου λέγων, ἐξ ἐπιταγῆς αὐτὸν πεποιηκέναι. Φυ-
λεὺς δὲ ὁ τούτου παῖς, κριτὴς γενόμενος, κατέκρινε
τὸν πατέρα, ὁ δὲ ἀγανακτήσας, ἐξέβαλεν αὐτὸν
τῆς χώρας. Ἡρακλῆς δὲ ἐπιστρατευσάμενος Ἦλιν
[5] ἐπόρθησεν, καὶ, μεταπεμψάμενος τὸν Φυλέα ἐκ
Δουλιχίου παραδίδωσιν αὐτῷ τὴν βασιλείαν. Ὀλι-
γανδρίας δὲ οὔσης διὰ τὸ πολλοὺς ἐν τῷ πολέμῳ συν-
εφθάρθαι, Ἡρακλῆς συγκατέκλινε τὰς τῶν τετελευ-
τηκότων γυναῖκας τῷ στρατῷ· οὕτως τε πολλῶν
γεννηθέντων, ἔθηκε Διὶ τὸν Ὀλυμπιακὸν ἀγῶνα καὶ
αὐτὸς [10] πρῶτος τῶν ἀγωνισμάτων ἤψατο. ἱστορία
παρὰ Καλλιμάχῳ.

77b (vol. 1, p. 85 Pf.) Milan papyrus (*Diegeseis*)

come tell me . . . cow

They say in Elis . . . maidens being married . . . having dresses . . . [5] with a spear in . . . they say . . . an armed man[1]

---

[1] An explanation of this unusual marriage ritual is in *Aet.* 77c below.

77c Scholia to Homer, *Iliad*

At the command of Eurystheus Heracles cleaned the manure of Augeas, but he did not pay his wages when he asked, but said that he had done it on orders. Phyleus, the son of this man, was made judge and ruled against his father, who became furious and cast him from the country. Heracles took up arms against [5] Elis and destroyed it, then recalled Phyleus from Dulichium and gave him the kingdom. It was short on men because many had been killed in the war, so Heracles made the wives of the fallen lie with his army. And when many were born in this way, he dedicated the Olympic contest to Zeus and he himself [10] engaged in the games first. The story is in Callimachus.

CALLIMACHUS

77d Schol. D ad Hom. *Il.* 2.629 Thiel

(Φυλεύς) ὃς εἰς τὸ Δουλίχιον ποτὲ ἀπῳκίσθη διὰ τὸ
καταμαρτυρῆσαι τοῦ πατρὸς Αὐγείου πρὸς Ἡρακλέα
περὶ τοῦ μισθοῦ ὃν ὑπέσχετο παρέξειν τῷ Ἡρακλεῖ ὁ
Αὐγείας, εἰ καθάρειεν αὐτοῦ τὰς ἐπαύλεις μεστὰς οὔ-
σας τῆς κόπρου τῶν βοῶν. Ἡ ἱστορία καὶ παρὰ Καλ-
λιμάχῳ.

78–78c Hospes Isindius

78 *P.Oxy.* 2213 fr. 2.5–6; 1, *P.Mil.Vogl.* 1.18 col. I, 10

Ὤφε‚λες οὐλοὸν ἔγ[χος,
 μηδ[

78a Steph. Byz. ι 101 Billerbeck s.v. Ἴσινδος

Ἴσινδος· πόλις Ἰωνίας. ὁ πολίτης Ἰσίνδιος

78b (vol. 1, p. 86 Pf.) *Dieg.* 1.10–26; *P.Mil.Vogl.* 1.18 col.
I, 10–26

Ὤφελες οὐλοὸν ἐγ[
  ]εις Ἰσίνδιον δ[
  ]῀υπα[
  ]σισ[

          11 lineae desunt

..].[..].[
οισφ[.]‚ια[

234

77d Scholia to Homer, *Iliad*

(Phyleus) who once was deported into Dulichium on account of bearing witness against his father Augeas in favor of Heracles on the matter of a wage that Augeas had promised to give him, if he would clean his stables which were full of cattle dung. The story is in Callimachus.

78–78c The Host of Isindus

78 Oxyrhynchus papyrus; Milan papyrus

if only the deadly sword

78a Stephanus of Byzantium

Isindos: the Ionian city; Isindius, a citizen of Isindus.

78b (vol. 1, p. 86 Pf.) Milan papyrus (*Diegeseis*)

I wish the deadly sword . . . of Isindus . . .

78c Schol. G ad Ov. *Ib.* 621

Isi‹n›dius, a loco sic dictus, ‹Ae›t‹h›alon, hospitem suum, occidit ; quare Io‹n› omnes homines illius regionis a sacrificio suo repellit.

79–79a Diana Lucina

79 *P.Mil.Vogl.* 1.18 col. I, 27

Τεῦ δὲ χάριν .ọ. [κικλήσ]κουσιν

79a (vol. 1, p. 87 Pf.) *Dieg.* 1.27–36; *P.Mil.Vogl.* 1.18 col. I, 27–36

Τεῦ δὲ χάριν .ο. [κικλής-] Κουσιν

ἐξῆ[ς] φ[ησι γυναῖκας δ]υστοκούσας τὴν Ἄρτε[μιν
5 καίπερ ο]ὖσαν παρθένον ἐπ[ικαλεῖν, ὅτι .ọ]... τη ἀπεκυ-
ήθη, ἢ ὅτι δ[ιὰ ἐφημος]ύνην τοῦ Διὸς ἡ Εἰλείθυια
[αὐτὴν] τοῦτ' ἔχειν ἔδωκεν ἐξ[α]ίρετον, ἢ διότι τὴν
ἑαυτῆς μητ[έρα ἐ]λύσατο τῶν ὠδίνων ὅτε ἀπέτικτεν
10 τὸν Ἀπόλλωνα.

78c Scholia to Ovid, *Ibis*

An Isindian, so called from the place, murdered his guest
Aethalus;[1] therefore Ionia rejects all men of that region
from the sacrifice.

1 Otherwise unknown.

79–79a Diana Lucina

79 Milan papyrus

for the sake of what . . . they call

79a Milan papyrus (*Diegeseis*)

for the sake of what . . . they call

Next he says that women who are having difficult births
call on Artemis, although she is a virgin, because she was
conceived . . . because Eileithyia[1] gave her this special
honor by an order of Zeus, or because she freed her own
mother from birth pains when she gave birth to Apollo.

1 Goddess of childbirth (Hom. *Il.* 16.187–88).

80–83b Phrygius et Pieria

80 (80 et 82. Pf. 1–12 [init.] et 7–8 [med.]) *P.Oxy.* 1221
fr. 4a.1–12 et 4b.1–2; 3–22 (fin.); *P.Oxy.* 2213 fr. 1 (a + b),
1–20

ἂν νέφος αν[
εἴτε γὰρ οὐκατ[
   τοῦτ᾽ εἰπεῖν [   ] [
ἐ]ξ ἐμέθεν τε[   ]ντα."

5   ἦ] ῥα· σὲ δ᾽ οὐ πυλ.εών   οὐ κά]λυκες,
   Λ]ύδιον οὐ κα[ίρωμα   ]ι Κάειρ[α]ι
   λάτριες, οὐκαγ[..].ικο[   ]s,   K
   τ]οῖς ἔπι θηλύτ[ερ]αι.[   ] ἰαίνεσθε
   ἔξαιτον, πυκιι[νοῦ γ]νώματος ἐξ[έ]βαλ[ο]ν·
10   αἰδοῖ δ᾽ ὡς φοί[νικι] τεὰς ἐρύθουσα παρειὰς
   ἔνν]επες ὀφ[θαλμο]ῖς ἔμπαλι.[...]ομεν[.].[
   ]..[   ]ε χρήζοιμι [νέ]εσθαι
          ]..[. μετὰ πλ]εόνων."
         ].ε, νόον δ᾽ ἐφ[ρ]άσσατο σεῖο
15   ] πατρίδι μαιομένης
       ]Μυ[όε]ντα καὶ οἳ Μίλητον ἔναι[ον
      ]η· μούν[ης νηὸν ἐς] Ἀρτέμιδος
   π]ωλε[ῖσθαι Νη]ληΐδος· ἀλλὰ σὺ τῆμος
   βουκτ]ας[ι]ῶν ἀρ[τὺν πιστο]τέρην ἔταμες,
20   ἔνδει]ξας καὶ Κύπ[ρι]ν ὅτι ῥητῆρας ἐκείνου
   Τ]εύχει τοῦ Πυλί[ου κρ]έσσονας οὐκ ὀλίγον·
   ἐ]ξεσίαι πολέε[ς γὰρ ἀπ᾽ ἀμφοτέροιο μο]λοῦσαι
   ἄστ]εος ἀπρήκτ[ους οἴκαδ᾽ ἀνῆλθον ὁδούς
   ].σθ[.]θε[

80–83b Phrygius and Pieria

80 (80, 82 Pf.) Oxyrhynchus papyri

cloud . . . whether . . . to say this . . . from me."[1] He said;
[5] but you,[2] not a tiara nor earrings . . . nor a Lydian
textile . . . nor Carian slaves . . . [nor other things] in which
you women especially take delight did drive you from your
shrewd judgment. [10] And in shame turning red in your
cheeks as if with scarlet dye, you spoke with eyes looking
away . . . "I would wish to come . . . with more people."[3]
He perceived your thoughts . . . [15] you sought for the
fatherland . . . that those who live in Myus and Miletus go
only to the temple of Neleid[4] Artemis, but you then made
an agreement more trustworthy than [those ratified by]
the sacrifice of oxen, [20] and you showed that Cyprus[5]
creates speakers far more powerful than that man from
Pylos.[6] For many embassies coming from both cities re-
turned to their homes unsuccessful

[1] Apparently the end of a speech of Phygius offering Pieria
whatever she wants.

[2] Pieria, here addressed by the narrator.

[3] Pieria speaks to King Phrygius asking to come to Miletus
with more of her people. Now they are limited to visiting only
during the festival of Artemis. See *Aet.* 83b below.

[4] Neleus founded Miletus from Athens and was its first king
(Hdt. 9.97; Strabo 14.1.3). Artemis was his patron (Call. *Hymn*
3.225–27).

[5] Aphrodite, after Cyprus, the place of her birth (Hes. *Theog.*
199).

[6] Nestor (Hom. *Il.* 1.247–49), whose words were sweeter than
honey.

81 *P.Oxy.* 2213 fr. 17.1–5

. . . .

]κτεαν[ον
]δ᾽ ακου[σ
Φρύ]γιος·
κατ]ένευσεν[
5   ἀ]προστρέ[φεται

. . . .

82 Pf. = *Aet.* 80.19–24

83 *P.Oxy.* 2212 fr. 1b.1–3

. . . .

].[.].[
]..[....]σιων.[
Φρύ]γιοσ[..].μ[.].Πιε[ρί-

83a v. *Aet.* 78b.5–6

83b Aristaenet. 1.15.16–68 Mazal

[16] Μίλητος τοίννν καὶ Μυοῦς αἱ πόλεις ἐπὶ μήκιστον χρόνον πρὸς ἀλλήλας ἀνεπίμικτοι διετέλουν, πλὴν ὅσον ἐς Μίλητον οἱ τῆς ἑτέρας ὑπόσπονδοι βραχὺ προσεφοίτων, καιρὸν ἔχοντες καὶ μέτρον τῆς αὐτόθι τιμωμένης Ἀρτέμιδος [20] τὴν πανήγυριν καὶ σμικρὰν ἀνακωχὴν ἑκάτεροι τὴν ἑορτὴν ἐποιοῦντο.

81 Oxyrhynchus papyrus

. . . property . . . unwilling . . . the Phrygian; . . . he nodded in assent[1] . . . (s)he turns away

[1] Typically the gesture of a god, but here perhaps Phrygius.

82 Pf. = *Aetia* 80.19–24

83 Oxyrhynchus papyrus

. . . the Phrygian . . . Pieria

83a See *Aetia* 78b.5–6 (where perhaps the story of Phrygius and Pieria ends)

83b Aristaenetus

[16] Even so the cities Miletus and Myus continually avoided contact with each other for the longest time, except to the extent that those from the other city visited Miletus briefly under a treaty when they celebrated the all-night festival of Artemis, [20] who was honored there on that occasion and for that extent of time, and each of

τούτους Ἀφροδίτη κατελεοῦσα διήλλαξεν, ἀφορμὴν
εἰς σύμβασιν μηχανησαμένη τοιάνδε.

κόρη γάρ τις τοὔνομα Πιερία, φύσει τε καλὴ κὰκ
τῆς Ἀφροδίτης ἐπισημότερον κοσμηθεῖσα, ἐκ τοῦ
Μυοῦντος ἐγκαίρως ἐπεδήμησε [25] τῇ Μιλήτῳ. καὶ
τῆς θεοῦ τὸ πᾶν διεπούσης μετὰ τοῦ πλήθους εἰς Ἀρ-
τέμιδος ἐχώρουν, ἡ μὲν παρθένος ταῖς Χάρισιν ἀγλα-
ϊζομένη, Φρύγιος δὲ ὁ τοῦ ἄστεος βασιλεὺς πρὸς τῶν
Ἐρώτων κατατοξευόμενος τὴν ψυχὴν ἐπὶ τῇ κόρῃ τὴν
πρώτην αὐτίκα φανείσῃ. καὶ θᾶττον ἄμφω συνῆλθον
[30] εἰς εὐνή, ἵνα καὶ πρὸς εἰρήνην ὅτι τάχιστα συν-
αφθῶσιν αἱ πόλεις.

ἔφη δ᾽ οὖν ὁ νυμφίος ἐρασμίως ἐναφροδισιάσας τῇ
κόρῃ καὶ σπεύδων αὐτῇ πρέπουσαν ἀμοιβὴν ἀποδοῦ-
ναι· "εἴθε γὰρ θαρροῦσα λέξειας, ὦ καλή, τί ἄν σοι
χαριέστατα γένοιτο παρ᾽ ἐμοῦ. καὶ διπλασίαν ἡδέως
[35] τὴν αἴτησιν ἀποπληρώσω." τοιαῦτα μὲν ὁ δίκαιος
ἐραστής· σὲ δέ, ὦ πασῶν ὑπερφέρουσα γυναικῶν καὶ
κάλλει καὶ γνώμῃ, τῆς ἔμφρονος οὐ παρήγαγεν εὐ-
βουλίας οὐχ ὅρμος, οὐχ ἑλικτῆρες, οὐ πυλεῶν ὁ πο-
λύτιμος, οὐ περιδέραιον, οὐ Λύδιός τε καὶ ποδήρης
χιτών, οὐ πορφυρίδες, [40] οὐ θεράπαιναι τῆς Καρίας
οὐδὲ Λυδῶν ὑπερφυῶς ἱστουργοῦσαι γυναῖκες, οἷς
ἅπασιν ἀτεχνῶς ἀγάλλεσθαι τὸ θῆλυ πέφυκε γένος,
ἀλλ᾽ εἰς γῆν ἑώρας τὸ πρόσωπον, ὥσπερ τι συννοου-
μένη. εἶτα ἔφης ἐπιχαρίτως πεφοινιγμένη τὰς παρειὰς
καὶ τὸ πρόσωπον ἐξ αἰδοῦς ἀποκλίνασα [45] καὶ πῇ
μὲν τῆς ἀμπεχόνης ἄκροις δακτύλοις ἐφαπτομένη τῶν

them considered the festival a short pause [in their usual hostility]. Aphrodite, who had compassion for them, devised a starting point for their reconciliation by the following means.

A young woman from Myus, Pieria by name, beautiful by nature and adorned even more remarkably by Aphrodite, visited [25] Miletus at the opportune time. Under the management of the goddess, they went with the crowd to the temple of Artemis—both the maiden, gleamingly ornamented by the Graces, and Phrygius, king of the city, who was shot in the heart by the Erotes at the first appearance of the girl. And before long they went [30] to bed together, so that the cities could be joined in peace as soon as possible.

After the bridegroom made love to the girl passionately and was eager to give her something suitable in return he said, "I hope you will tell me straight out, my beauty, what gift from me would please you the most, and I will be delighted [35] to fulfill your request twice over." So spoke the righteous lover. But you, most eminent of all women in both beauty and wisdom, neither a necklace led astray from your wise, good counsel, nor earrings, nor an expensive tiara, nor a collar, nor a floor-length gown from Lydia, nor clothes dyed [40] purple, nor enslaved women from Caria, nor Lydian women extraordinary at weaving, all those things that utterly enthrall the female race; no, you turned your face to the ground [45] as if thinking something through. Then you spoke, your cheeks blushing in a

κροσσῶν, πῇ δὲ περιστρέφουσα τοῦ ζωνίου τὸ ἄκρον,
ἔστε δὲ ὅτε καὶ τοὖδαφος περιχαράττουσα τῷ ποδί
(ταῦτα δὴ τὰ τῶν αἰδουμένων ἐν διαπορήσει κινή-
ματα), ἔφης οὖν μόλις ἠρεμαίᾳ φωνῇ· "ἐπίνευσον, ὦ
βασιλεῦ, [50] ἐμέ τε καὶ τοὺς ἐμοὺς συγγενεῖς εἰς
τήνδε τὴν εὐδαίμονα πόλιν ὅταν ἐθέλοιμεν ἐπ' ἀδείας
ἰέναι."

ὁ δὲ Φρύγιος τῆς φιλοπάτριδος γυναικὸς ὅλον
κατενόησε τὸν σκοπόν, ὡς διὰ τούτων ἐκείνη σπονδὰς
πρὸς Μιλησίους πραγματεύεται τῇ πατρίδι, κατέ-
νευσέ τε βασιλικῶς, καὶ τὸ σπουδασθὲν [55] ἐκύρωσε
τῇ φιλτάτῃ, πιστότερον ἢ κατὰ θυσίαν ἐμπεδώσας ἐξ
ἔρωτος τοῖς ἀστυγείτοσι τὴν εἰρήνην· φύσει γὰρ εὐ-
διάλλακτον ἄνθρωπος, ὅταν εὐτυχῇ· αἱ γὰρ εὐπραξίαι
δειναὶ τὰς ὀργὰς ὑφαρπάζειν καὶ τοῖς εὐτυχήμασι τὰ
ἐγκλήματα διαλύειν.

οὕτως οὖν ἐκφανῶς δεδήλωκας, [60] ὦ Πιερία, τὴν
Ἀφροδίτην ἱκανὴν εἶναι παιδεύειν ῥήτορας οὐκ ὀλί-
γον ἀμείνους καὶ τοῦ Νέστορος τοῦ Πυλίου· πολλοὶ
γὰρ πολλάκις ἑκατέρωθεν τῶν πόλεων σοφώτατοι
πρέσβεις ἐξ ἑτέρας εἰς ἑτέραν ὑπὲρ εἰρήνης εἰσιόντες
διὰ κενῆς ὅμως κατηφεῖς τε καὶ ἀσχάλλοντες ἄπρα-
κτον [65] ἀνέλυον τὴν πορείαν· ἐντεῦθεν τοιοῦτος εἰκό-
τως παρὰ ταῖς Ἴωσι πάτριος ἐπεκράτησε λόγος· "εἴθε
με παραπλησίως ὁ σύνοικος τιμήσειε τὴν ὁμόζυγα,
ὥσπερ ὁ Φρύγιος τὴν καλὴν τετίμηκε Πιερίαν."

244

graceful way, your face bowing modestly, on one side touching the fringe of your shawl with the tips of your fingers and on the other twisting the top of your belt, sometimes making figures on the ground with your foot (for these are the gestures of the modest when perplexed), you said with a soft and gentle voice, "Grant, o king, [50] that I and my household may come without fear into this blessed city whenever we wish."

Phrygius understood completely the goal of that patriotic woman—how in this way she was bringing about treaties with the Milesians on behalf of her fatherland— and assented in a kingly way, granting his beloved's wish [55], and through love he brought about a peace for his citizens more trustworthy than one [ratified] with sacrifices. For people naturally can be reconciled when they are fortunate. For skillful good dealings take away anger and good fortune puts an end to accusation.

In this way you showed clearly, [60] Pieria, that Aphrodite is quite capable of educating orators better by no small degree than even Nestor of Pylus. For many a very wise ambassador had come from either city to the other on a mission of peace but [65] concluded his failed mission dejected and aggrieved. This is probably the origin of the traditional saying among Ionian women: "I wish my husband would honor me, his wife, just as Phrygius honored the beautiful Pieria."

84–85a Euthycles Locrus

84 *P.Oxy.* 2212 fr. 1b.4

ᵓΗλθες ὅτ᾽ ἐκ Πίσ˙ης, Εὐθˌύκˌλεες, ἄνδρας ἐˌλέγξας
                                   ] [

. . . .

85 *P.Oxy.* 2213 fr. 8

. . . .

].[.].[
δ]ήμιον ε[κατὰ] χρέος .[
  ἴκ]εο Μυσ[   ].[   ]οικ.[
ἔν]θεν ἀνερχόμε[νος] πάλιν [
5   δῶ]ρον ἀπηναίους ἦλθες ὀρῇ[ας ἄγων·
  ὡς] δέ σ᾽ ἐπὶ ῥήτρῃσι λαβεῖν καˌ[τὰ πατρίδος εἶπε
  δῆ]μος [ἐπ᾽] ἀφνειοῖς αἰὲν ἀπαγχόμενος,
πά]ντες ὑπὸ ψηφῖδα κακὴν βάλον· ἦν δ᾽ ἀπὸˌ[
  εἰκόν]α¹ σὴν αὐτὴ Λοκρὶς ἔθηκε [πόλ]ις,
10   ....]άσται Τεμεσαῖον ἐπειπ[   ]ν
  ]ˌαμελισσάων ἀμφὶσολοιτυπ[
π]ολλά τε καὶ μακάρεσσιν ἀπεχ[θέα]χρˌιˌ
  τ]ῷ σφισιν ἐν χαλεπὴν θῆκ[ε τελεσφο]ρίην,²
ὅν]τινα κικλήσκουσιν Ἐπόψ[ιον,]ˌὅστις ἀˌλιτρούς
15   αὐˌγάζειν ἰθˌαραῖς οὐ δύναται λογάσιν
                                ]νˌειστη
                                   ] [

. . . .

84–85a Locrian Euthycles

84 Oxyrhynchus papyrus

when you came from Pisa,[1] Euthycles, after you put the men to shame

1 Olympia (cf. *Aet.* 76.2).

85 Oxyrhynchus papyrus

public . . . in due fashion. . . . you went . . . coming back again from there . . . [5] you came bringing driving mules as a gift. And when the people, always choking with indignation against the rich, said that you had gotten them for covenants against the fatherland, they all secretly cast a hostile vote. And your statue which the city of Locri itself had put up . . . [10] Temesaean[1] bronze . . . many things hateful to the blessed ones . . . for that reason he put on them a dreadful [curse] . . . , the one whom they call Epopsius,[2] [15] who is not able to look upon sinners with kindly eyes

1 From Temesa (Hom. *Od.* 1.184), either the city of that name in southern Italy or the one in Cyprus.   2 "The watcher from above," Zeus (Call. *Hymn* 1.81; Ap. Rhod. 2.1123).

---

1 εἰκόν]α suppl. E. Barber et P. Maas, *CQ* 44 (1950): 168

2 τελεσφο]ρίην suppl. Lobel ap. Pf.: ἀλαστο]ρίην D'Alessio 2007, vol. 2, 499n103

85a (vol. 1, p. 91 Pf.) *Dieg.* 1.37–2.8; *P.Mil.Vogl.* 1.18 col. I, 37–44; col. II, 1–8

Ἦλθες ὅτ᾽ ἐκ Πίσης, Εὐθύκλεες, ἄνδρας ἐλέγξας

φη[σ]ὶν Εὐθυκλῆν τὸν Ὀλυμπιονίκην, πεμφθέν-
τα [5] πρεσβευτὴν καὶ ἀνακάμψαντα οἴκαδε σὺν
ἡμιόνοις ἃ εἰλήφει δῶρα παρά τινος ξένου,
συκοφαντηθῆναι ὡς κατὰ τῆς πόλε[ως εἰλ]ηφότα·
ἐφ᾽ ᾧ κατεψήφ[ισα]ν[1] αἰκίσασθαι [10] [τ]ούτου τὸν
ἀνδριάντα. ἐπεὶ δὲ λοιμ[ὸ]ς ἐπικατ[έ]π[εσ]εν,
ἔγνωσαν οἱ πολῖται αὐ[το]ῦ παρὰ τοῦ [Ἀ]πόλλωνος
ὡς διὰ τὴν ἀτιμίαν αὐτο[ῦ π]ροσβέβλητ[αι α]ὐτοῖς.
τὸ μὲν ἄγαλμα τ[οῦ Εὐ]θυκλ[έο]υς [15] κατ᾽ ἴσον τῷ
τοῦ Διὸς ἐτ[ίμη]σαν, ἔτι δὲ καὶ βωμὸν
ποιήσαντε[ς . .].τ[.].. [. .]υ.[.ἱ]σταμένου μηνός.

[1] κατεψήφ[ισα]ν Pf.: κατεψηφ[ίσθη Vogliano 1937

ΑΙΤΙΩΝ Δ´

86–89a Daphnephoria Delphica

86 *P.Mil.Vogl.* 1.18 col. II, 10

Μοῦ]σαί μοι βασιλη[　　　　ἀεί]δειν[1]

[1] Fin. suppl. Maas 1937, 161

85a (vol. 1, p. 91 Pf.) Milan papyrus (*Diegeseis*)

> When you came from Pisa, Euthycles, after you put
> the men to shame

They say that Euthycles, the Olympic victor, when he was
sent [5] as an ambassador and returned home with mules
that he had as gifts from some host, was falsely accused of
taking them against the interests of the city. And they
voted against him to deface [10] his statue. When a plague
fell upon them his citizens learned from Apollo that it
struck them on account of dishonoring him. They honored
the statue of Euthycles [15] equally to that of Zeus and in
addition, after they made an altar . . . at the beginning of
the month.[1]

---

[1] Presumably the time when sacrifices were made.

AETIA IV

86–89a Daphnephoria at Delphi

86 Milan papyrus

Muses for me to sing of kings . . .

87 Steph. Byz. δ 40 Billerbeck s.v. Δειπνιάς

Δειπνιάς· κώμη Θεσσαλίας περὶ Λάρισσαν, ὅπου φασὶ τὸν Ἀπόλλωνα δειπνῆσαι πρῶτον, ὅτε ἐκ τῶν Τέμπεων καθαρθεὶς ὑπέστρεψεν· . . . Καλλίμαχος δ',

   Δειπνιὰς ἔνθεν μιν δειδέχαται

88 Schol. ad Ap. Rhod. 2.705–11b

Δελφύνην· ὅτι Δελφύνης ἐκαλεῖτο ὁ φυλάσσων τὸ ἐν Δελφοῖς χρηστήριον, Λεάνδριος καὶ Καλλίμαχος εἶπον· δράκαιναν δὲ αὐτήν φησιν εἶναι, θηλυκῶς καλουμένην Δέλφυναν, αὐτὸς ὁ Καλλίμαχος.

89 Tert. *De cor.* 7.5 Fontaine

Habes Pindarum atque Callimachum, qui et Apollinem memorat interfecto Delphico dracone lauream induisse, qua supplicem.

89a (vol. 1, p. 95 Pf.) *Dieg.* 2.10–28; *P.Mil.Vogl.* 1.18 col II, 10–28

   Μοῦ]σαί μοι βασιλη[ἀεί]δειν

87 Stephanus of Byzantium

Deipnias: village in Thessaly near Larissa, where Apollo dined after returning purified from Tempe . . . Callimachus, Book 4,

> From there Deipnias received him

88 Scholia to Apollonius of Rhodes, *Argonautica*

Delphyne: Leandrius[1] and Callimachus have said that the one guarding the oracle in Delphi was called Delphyne. Callimachus himself says she is a snake, calling her by the feminine form Delphyna.

[1] Maeandrius (*FHG* vol. 2, p. 337, fr. 10).

89 Tertullian, *De Corona*

You have Pindar and Callimachus, who recalls that even Apollo, after he had killed the Delphic snake, put on a laurel branch as a suppliant.

89a (vol. 1, p. 95 Pf.) Milan papyrus (*Diegeseis*)

> Muses to sing to me of kings . . .

Α]ὔτη πρώτη ἐλ[ε]γ[εία   ]τρου[
    ]ν ἱστορία[   ]απερ[
[   ]σαι.[   ].ει[

ll. 5–11 desunt

    ]ε
    ]οπε[
[..]ι..[   ]ω[[15] Ἀπ]όλλων γὰρ
παῖς ὢν κ[ρατήσας τὸν] Πυθοῖ δράκοντα
ἀ[πενύψα]το [τὰς] χεῖρας ἐν τῷ Πη[ν]ει[ῷ..]νδ[.]
πα[ρα]κειμένην δάφνην ειδ[..].ει[..].
ἐκτεμὼν περιβάλλει τῷ [....]ειω.ι.

90–90b Abdera

90 *P.Mil.Vogl.* 1.18 col. II, 29

    Ἔνθ', Ἄβδηρ', οὗ νῦν . [...]λεω φαρμακὸν ἀγινεῖ

90a (vol. 1, p. 97 Pf.) *Dieg.* 2.29–40; *P.Mil.Vogl.* 1.18 col.
II, 29–40

    Ἔνθ', Ἄβδηρ', οὗ νῦν.[...]λεω φαρμακὸν ἀγινεῖ

Ἀβδήροις ὠνητὸς ἄνθρωπος καθάρσιον τῆς
ὄλεως, ἐπὶ πλίνθου ἑστὼς φαιᾶς, θοίνης ἀπολαύων
[5] δαψιλοῦς, ἐπειδὰν διάπλεως γένηται, προάγεται
ἐπὶ τὰς Προυρίδας καλουμένας πύλας· εἶτ' ἔξω τοῦ
τείχους περίεισι κύκλῳ περικαθαίρων αὐτῷ τὴν
πόλιν, καὶ τότε ὑπὸ τοῦ βασιλέως καὶ τῶν ἄλλων
λιθοβολεῖται, ἕως ἐξελασθῇ τῶν [10] ὁρίων.

This first elegy . . . the story . . . [15] Apollo, being a boy, when he overpowered the snake at Pytho, washed his hands in the Peneius[1] . . . and cutting the laurel which was lying beside him he put it round [his head]

[1] River in the valley of Tempe (Hom. *Il.* 2.751–54).

90–90b Abdera

90 Milan papyrus

There, Abdera,[1] where now he drives out the
scapegoat

[1] Town on the coast of Thrace founded by Heracles in honor of Abderus, a son of Hermes (Apollod. *Bibl.* 2.5.8) or of Poseidon (Pind. *Pae.* 2.1–2), who was killed by the horses of Diomedes.

90a (vol. 1, p. 97 Pf.) Milan papyrus (*Diegeseis*)

There, Abdera, where now he drives out the
scapegoat

In Abdera, a man purchased as an offering for the purification of the city, stands on a gray brick enjoying an abundant [5] feast, and when he is totally full, he is brought to the gates called "Prurian";[1] then outside the walls he goes around in a circuit purifying the city, and then he is stoned by the king and others until he is driven from the [10] boundaries.

[1] Perhaps equivalent to Attic *phrouros*, i.e., gates with guards. See L. Deubner, "Der Pharmakos von Abdera," *Studi Italiani di Filologia Classica* (1934): 189.

90b

(a) Schol. C (F* D*) ad Ov. *Ib.* 467

Callimachus dicit quod Abdera est civitas in qua talis est mos, quod quoque anno cives totam civitatem publice lustrabant; et aliquem civium quem in illa die habebant devotum pro capitibus omnium lapidibus occidebant.

(b) Schol. B (a*) ad Ov. *Ib.* 467

Abdera terra est, in qua pro more antecessorum in capite anni in festis Iani unus exponitur morti pro populo, ut ait H.

91–92a Melicertes

91 *P.Mil.Vogl.* 1.18 col. II, 41

α . . . . Μελικέρτα, μιῆς ἐπὶ πότνια Βύνη

92 1–3 (init.), *P.Oxy.* 2170 fr. 1.1–3; 1–3 (fin.), *PSI* 1218C fr. 1–3

    ] . [   ] . . . [   ] . ε . . [
 ση . . [.] τ̣ [. . .] φ [Λε]α̣νδρίδες εἴ τι παλαιαὶ
 φθ̣[έγγ]ο̣νται[   ]υφαν ἱστορίαι.

---

¹ Leandrius of Miletus, author of a history of Miletus and often identified with the historian Maeandrius of Miletus (*BNJ*

90b

(a) Scholia to Ovid, *Ibis*

Callimachus says that Abdera is a city in which this is the custom, that in each year the citizens publicly purified the city. And on that day they killed with stones one of the citizens whom they believed was sacrificed for the lives of all.

(b) Scholia to Ovid, *Ibis*

Abdera is a land in which, by the custom of their ancestors, at the start of the year in the festival of Janus, one [person] is put to death for the public, as H.[1] says.

    [1] H is K(allimachos): Pf. vol. 1, 499.

91–92a Melicertes

91 Milan papyrus

Melicertes, on one . . . queen Byne[1]

    [1] Ino (*Fr. Inc. Loc.* 745). Princess of Thebes (daughter of Cadmus and Harmonia) who escaped her mad husband, Athamas, by jumping into the sea with her son Melecertes (Eur. *Med.* 1284–89). They were saved by a dolphin and became marine divinities Leucothea and Palaemon (Paus. 1.44.8).

92 Oxyrhynchus papyrus; papyrus fragment

if the ancient tales of Leandrius[1] say anything [true],

    491–92). On Leandrius as a source for Callimachus, see *Aet.* 88 (with Pf. vol. 1, 91); Diog. Laert. 1.28.

92a (vol. 1, p. 98 Pf.) *Dieg.* 2.41–3.11; *P.Mil.Vogl.* 1.18
col. II, 41–col. III, 11

A .... Μελικέρτα, μιῆς ἐπὶ πότνια Βύνη

Ἑξῆς· ἐπεὶ ⟨σὺν⟩ Μελικέρτῃ τῷ παιδὶ ἑαυ-
τὴν κατεπόντισεν Ἰνώ, ἐξέπε-
σεν εἰς αἰγιαλὸν τῆς Τενέδου τὸ σῶ-
5 μ[α] τοῦ Μελικέρτου· τοὺς δὲ ἐκεῖ πο-
τε κατοικοῦντας Λέλεγας ποιῆσαι
αὐτῷ βωμόν, ἐφ' οὗ ἡ πόλις ποιεῖ
θυσίαν, ὅταν περὶ μεγάλων φο-
βῆται, τοι[ά]νδ[ε]· γυνὴ τὸ ἑαυτῆς βρέ-
10 φος κα[ταθύσα]σα παραχρῆμα τυφλοῦ-
ται. τοῦ[το δ' ὕσ]τερον κατελύθη, ὅτε
οἱ ἀπὸ Ὀ[ρέστου] Λέ[σβ]ον ᾤκησαν.

93–93b *Theudotus Liparensis*

93 1–18 (init.), *P.Oxy.* 2170 fr. 1.4–21; 1–7 (fin.), *PSI*
1218c fr. 4–10; 1 *P.Mil.Vogl.* 1.18 col. III, 12

Νέκταρος α[......], ν, γλύκιον γένος ηραπ, εδο[
   κ[.]. δονηδυ[........]ς ἀμβροσίης
ὑμέας γαῖ ἀνέδ[ωκε, τ]ὰ καὶ τερπνίστατα πά[ντων
   νεῖσθε διὰ γλῶσ[σαν γλεύ]κεος ὅσσα πέρα.
5 δείλαιοι, τυ[τθόν] μιν ἐπὶ πλ⟨έ⟩ον ἢ ὅσον ἄκ[ρον
   χείλος ἀναγλ[......]π[.]ρ ἀναινομένου
ἀνδρὸς ανουν[.........]ς ἐπέτασσεν [.] .[
   ω.[.] μίαν νησ.[

92a (vol. 1, p. 98 Pf.) Milan papyrus (*Diegeseis*)

A . . . Melicertes, on one queen Byne

Next, when Ino threw herself into the sea with her child Melicertes, the body of Melicertes washed up on the beach of Tenedos.[1] And he says that the Leleges[2] who were living there then made an altar to him, on which the city makes a sacrifice in this way whenever it is terrified by great things: a woman sacrifices her own baby and at once is blinded. Later this rite was eliminated when the descendants of Orestes[3] colonized Lesbos.[4]

[1] An island in the Aegean located near the Hellespont.

[2] A pre-Hellenic people in Asia Minor and on various Greek islands (Hdt. 1.171).   [3] Orestes' son Penthilus was the founder of Tenedos (Paus. 3.2.1).   [4] The largest Greek island, off the coast of Asia Minor.

93–93b *Theudotus of Lipara*

93 Oxyrhynchus papyrus; papyrus fragment; Milan papyrus

a race sweeter than nectar . . . [sweeter] than ambrosia the earth has sent you up and the most pleasurable of all things, even more than must,[1] you who pass over the tongue. [5] Wretches, a little bit further than the tip of the lip . . . a man refusing . . . he commanded . . . one island

[1] Intensely sweet crushed grapes with their juice.

οἰκήσας Λιπά[ρ
10   της ω. Τυ[ρσην
ἤλυθ᾽ ἄγων π[
    πολλά, τὸ δ᾽ ἐκ.[
φη[.]αρ ἀποτρ[
    ἱερὸς εἰ Φοίβου [
15 δημόθεν ωσ.[
    τουτο ενει[
  ]στ᾽ ἐπὶ τὴν ν[
    ]ηξαιον προτ[

93a (vol. 1, p. 99 Pf.) *Dieg.* 3.12–24; *P.Mil.Vogl.* 1.18 col. III, 12–24

Νέκταρος.[......]ν. νθιον γένος η-
    ραπεδο[   ]Λιπαραιο[.......]ο
    Τυρσην[   ]ιας[
5 ...]ετης[   ]δο[
      ]..[

ll. 6–12 desunt

    ].τε[

93b Schol. C (F* D*) ad Ov. *Ib*. 465

Thyrreni, obsidentes Liparium castrum, promiserunt Apollini quod, si faceret eos victores, fortissimum Liparensium ei sacrificarent. habita autem victoria promissum reddiderunt, immolantes ei quendam nomine Theodotum. Unde Gallus: "Theodotus captus Phoebo datus hostia, quamvis nequaquam sit homo victima grata deo."

... after colonizing Lipara[2] ... [10] Etruscan ... he came leading ... many things, the one from ... sacred if Phoebus ... [15] from among the people ... this ... at the

[2] An island off the north coast of Sicily colonized by Pentathlus of Cnidus (Paus. 10.11.3).

93a (vol. 1, p. 99 Pf.) Milan papyrus (*Diegeseis*)

a sort [sweeter] than nectar ... Liparaean ... Etruscan

93b Scholia to Ovid, *Ibis*

The Etruscans, when they were besieging the camp of Lipara, promised Apollo that if he made them victors they would sacrifice to him the bravest Liparian. When they were victorious they made good on their promise, immolating for him a man by the name of Theodotus. From this Gallus[1] says, "The captive Theodotus was given to Phoebus as a sacrificial offering although a human victim is by no means pleasing to a god."

[1] Pf. (vol. 1, 99) believes that Callimachus is meant.

94–95c Leimonis

94 *P.Mil.Vogl.* 1.18 col. III, 25

Τὸν νεκρ[ὸ]ν .[......].τ[....]υβατονιστιναευω

95 *P.Oxy.* 2170 fr. 2

. . . .
  .. [
πατρο ..[
  δακρυσασ .[
αἰαῖ καὶ μαλ[‘ Ἵππου]
  καὶ Κούρης· ạ[

95a (vol. 1, p. 101 Pf.) *Dieg.* 3.25–33; *P.Mil.Vogl.* 1.18 col.
III, 25–33

Τὸν νεκρ[ὸ]ν .[......].τ[....]υβατονις τιναευω

      [......]μ̣[.]νη ενουσπως αὐτοῦ
πα[ῖ]δ[α Λειμ]ώνην φθαρεῖσαν λάθρα εἰς τὸν
θ[άλα]μọν [σ]υγκατακλείσας ἵππῳ διὰ το[ύτ]ọ[υ]
διέφθειρεν· ὅθεν Ἀθήνησιν [5] τόπο[ς] Ἵππου καὶ
Κόρης· τὸν δὲ συγγενόμενον αὐτῇ δόρατι παίσας
νεκρὸν ἐξέδησεν ἵππου, ὥστε κατὰ τοῦ ἄστεος
σύρεσθαι.

94–95c Of Leimone

94 Milan papyrus

the corpse[1]

[1] Probably the body of the man who had raped Leimone. He was killed by her father, Hippomenes, and his corpse was dragged by a horse through the town (Aeschin. *In Tim.* 182). She was killed by being shut up with a horse in a room, which was later called the Place of the Horse and the Maiden.

95 Oxyrhynchus papyrus

. . . of the father . . . you wept . . . "aiai" and . . . of the Horse and the Maiden

95a (vol. 1, p. 101 Pf.) Milan papyrus (*Diegeseis*)

The corpse

After he secretly confined his daughter Leimone, who had been seduced, in a room with a horse and through this [method] killed her. Therefore at Athens [5] is the place "Of the Horse and Maiden." And after he struck the one who had assaulted her with his spear, he tied the corpse to a horse so that it was dragged through the city.

95b Schol. a m g V x L S ad Aeschin. *In Tim.* 182 (p. 365.53 Dilts)

Ἱππομένης ἀπὸ Κόδρου καταγόμενος, ἡ δὲ θυγάτηρ Λειμωνίς. οὕτω Καλλίμαχος.

95c Schol. B (a* G* C* F* D* Conr.*) ad Ov. *Ib.* 335 (p. 67 La Penna)

Limone, Hippomenis filia, cum quodam adultero deprehensa est, qui cum curru Hippomenis tractus dilaceratus est. illa vero cum quodam equo ferocissimo inclusa ab eo dilacerata est. unde Clarius: "Limone moritur, sed causa est mortis adulter: altera causa fuit moechus et altera equus."

96–96a Venator Gloriosus

96 *P.Oxy.* 2170 fr. 2.6–7; 1 *P.Mil.Vogl.* 1.18 col. III, 34

Θ‚εοὶ πάντε‚ς κομποῖς νεμεσήμονες, ἐκ δέ τε πάντων
  Ἄρτεμις α[

96a (vol. 1, p. 102 Pf.) *Dieg.* 3.34–41; *P.Mil.Vogl.* 1.18 col. III, 34–41

  Θεοὶ πάντες κομποῖς νεμεσήμονες, ἐκ δέ τε
    πάντων

κυνηγὸς †αλωιος† ἑλὼν κάπρον ἐπεῖπεν οὐ δέον

95b Scholia to Aeschines, *Against Timarchus*

Hippomenes, a descendant of Codrus,[1] his daughter was Limone, as Callimachus says.

[1] The last king of Athens (Lycurg. *Leoc.* 84–87).

95c Scholia to Ovid, *Ibis*

Limone, the daughter of Hippomenes, was caught with some adulterer, who was torn apart, dragged by the chariot of Hippomenes. She was dismembered after she was shut up with a very ferocious horse, and from this Clarius[1] says: "Limone is dead, but the cause of her death is the adulterer; another cause was the seducer and another, the horse."

[1] Clarius (or Darius) is Callimachus (Massimilla 1996, vol. 2, 188 on fr. 283); cf. *Fr. Inc. Sed.* 795–96.

96–96a The Braggart Hunter

96 Oxyrhynchus papyrus; Milan papyrus

All the gods are angry at boasts, and out of all of these, Artemis

96a (vol. 1, p. 102 Pf.) Milan papyrus (*Diegeseis*)

> All the gods are angry at boasts, and out of all of these

A hunter who had taken a boar said that it was not neces-

Ἀρτέμιδι ἀνατιθέναι τοὺς ἡγουμένους ἐκείνης [5]
καὶ ἑαυτῷ ἀνήρτησε τὴν κεφαλὴν τοῦ ὑὸς ἐξ
αἰγείρου, ὑφ᾿ ᾗ καθυπνώσας ἐπιπεσούσης αὐτῷ τῆς
κεφαλῆς ἀπέθανεν.

97–97a Moenia Pelasgica

97 P.Mil.Vogl. 1.18 col. III, 34

Τυρσηνῶν τείχισμα Πελασγικὸν εἶχέ με γαῖα

97a (vol. 1, p. 102 Pf.) Dieg. 3.34–41; P.Mil.Vogl. 1.18 col.
III, 34–41

Τυρσηνῶν τείχισμα Πελασγικὸν εἶχέ με γαῖα·

Ἱστορεῖ περὶ τῶν Ἀθήνησιν Πελασγικῶν ὅρων (?)
καὶ τοῦ ποιηθέντος ὑπ᾿ αὐτῶν τείχους.

98–99b Euthymus

98 P.Mil.Vogl. 1.18 col. IV, 5

Εὐθύμου τὰ μὲν ὅσσα παραὶ Διὶ Πῖσαν ἔχοντι

---

[1] Euthymus was an Olympic victor in boxing who defeated
the "hero of Temesa" and freed the people of Locri from an
odious ritual (Paus. 6.6.4–11; Str. 6.1.5).

sary to dedicate it to Artemis for those who thought themselves better than her. He hung the head of the swine from a poplar in honor of himself, then fell asleep under the tree and perished when the head fell on him.

97–97a *Pelasgian Walls*

97 Milan papyrus

the earth holds me, the Pelasgian Wall[1] of the Tyrrhenians

[1] The Cyclopian wall around the Acropolis at Athens dating from the thirteenth century BC (Paus. 1.28.3). It was associated with the Pelasgians, a pre-Hellenic people who migrated to various places, including Italy, where they were identified with the Tyrrhenians (i.e., the Etruscans; Thuc. 4.109.4).

97a (vol. 1, p. 102 Pf.) Milan papyrus (*Diegeseis*)

The earth holds me, the Pelasgian Wall of the Tyrrhenians

He tells about the Pelasgian landmarks at Athens and the wall that was made by them.

98–99b *Euthymus*

98 Milan papyrus

whatever feats of Euthymus[1] beside the [sanctuary of] Zeus who holds Pisa[2]

[2] That is, at the Olympic games.

CALLIMACHUS

99 Plin. *HN* 7.152

Consecratus est vivus sentiensque eiusdem oraculi iussu
et Iovis deorum summi adstipulatu Euthymus pycta, sem-
per Olympiae victor et semel victus, patria ei Locri in
Italia; ibi imaginem eius et Olympiae alteram eodem die
tactam fulmine Callimachum ut nihil aliud miratum video
deumque iussisse sacrificare, quod et vivo factitatum et
mortuo, nihilque de eo mirum aliud quam hoc placuisse
dis.

99a (vol. 1, p. 103 Pf.) *Dieg.* 4.5–17; *P.Mil.Vogl.* 1.18 col.
IV, 5–17

Εὐθύμου τὰ μὲν ὅσσα παραὶ Διὶ Πῖσαν ἔχοντι

Ὅ[τ]ι ἐν Τεμέσῃ ἥρως περίλοιπος τῆς Ὀδυσσέως
νεὼς ἐδασμοφόρει ἐπιχωρ[ίου]ς τε καὶ ὁμόρους, οὓς
10 κομίζοντας αὐτῷ κλίνην καὶ κόρην ἐπίγαμον
ἐάσαντας ἀπέρχεσθαι ἀμεταστρεπτεί, ἔωθε[ν] δὲ
τοὺς γονεῖς ἀντὶ παρθέ[ν]ου γυ[ναῖ]κα κομίζεσθαι.
τὸν δὲ δ[ασ]μὸν [τοῦ]τον ἀπέλυσεν Εὔθυμος
15 πύκτης [.] λέξας τὰς [τῷ ἥρ]ωϊ
κυν . . ζ[. . . . . .]φηαφησ[. . . . . .] . . . πρ . [   ]το . [
       συ[   ] . . [

lineae 14–17 desunt

266

99 Pliny the Elder, *Natural History*

While alive and aware, Euthymus the boxer was conse-
crated at the order of the oracle and the agreement of
Zeus, the highest of the gods, because he was always a
victor at Olympia and was defeated only once. His father-
land was Locri[1] in Italy. I see that Callimachus was more
amazed than he had been at anything else that his statue
there and at Olympia were touched by lightning on the
same day, and by order of the gods there was a sacrifice
and that was frequently done for him while still living and
after death, and that there is nothing amazing about this
other than that it pleased the gods.

[1] A Greek colony on the east coast of southern Italy. It was
known for its law code, recorded in the 7th century BC and as-
sociated with the Pythagorean Zaleucus (Diod. Sic. 12.21).

99a (vol. 1, p. 103 Pf.) Milan papyrus (*Diegeseis*)

Whatever feats Euthydemus accomplished beside
the [sanctuary of] Zeus who holds Pisa . . .

[He says] that the hero[1] in Temesa,[2] left by the ship of
Odysseus, exacted tribute from the locals and their neigh-
bors, who [10] had to provide to him a bed and a marriage-
able maiden, and to go away, leaving her behind, without
turning around. In the morning her parents took home a
woman instead of a maiden. Euthymus [15] the boxer
freed them from this tribute to the hero . . .

[1] In Callimachus' account, the hero is not given a name, but
Pausanias calls him Lycas (Paus. 6.6.11) and Strabo, Polites
(Strabo 6.1.5).   [2] A Greek city in Italy whose precise loca-
tion is not known.

99b Schol. ad Paus. 6.6.4

τὰ κατὰ Εὔθυμον τὸν πύκτην, οὗ καὶ Καλλίμαχος μέ-
μνηται

*100–100a Iunonis Samiae simulacrum
antiquissimum*

100 Euseb. *Praep. evang.* 3.7.5–3.8.1

οὔπω Σκέλμιον ἔργον ἔξοον, ἀλλ’ ἐπὶ τεθμὸν
  δηναιὸν γλυφάνων ἄξοος ἦσθα σανίς·
ὧδε γὰρ ἱδρύοντο θεοὺς τότε· καὶ γὰρ Ἀθήνης
  ἐν Λίνδῳ Δαναὸς λιτὸν ἔθηκεν ἕδος.

100a (vol. 1, p. 105 Pf.) *Dieg.* 4.22–29; *P.Mil.Vogl.* 1.18
col. IV, 22–29

                ]γι.αφ[
...... τὸ ξόα]νον τῆς Ἥρας [ἀνδρι-
αντοειδὲ]ς ἐ[γέ]νετο ἐπὶ βασιλέως
Προκ[λέους· τὸ] δὲ ξύ[λο]ν, ἐξ οὗ εἰργάσθη
5 ε..η[....].αμ[.]ς..ν, ἐξ Ἄργους δέ Φα-
σι[.......]οτας ἔτι πάλαι σανιδῶ-
δες [κομι]σθῆναι κάταργον ἄτε μηδέ-
πω π[ροκ]εκοφυίας τῆς ἀγαλματομικῆς.

AETIA BOOK IV

99b Scholia to Pausanias, *Description of Greece*

Concerning Euthymus the boxer, whom Callimachus mentions.

100–100a The Most Ancient Image of Juno at Samos

100 Eusebius, *Preparation for the Gospel*

Not yet were you the well-cut work of Scelmis, but following ancient custom, a plank uncarved by chisels.[1] For then they set up the gods in this way. And Danaus dedicated a simple statue of Athena in Lindos.[2]

[1] The addressee is the statue of Hera at Samos, originally aniconic and later a work of art by Smilis of Aegina (Paus. 5.17.1). For an explanation of Callimachus' spelling, see Harder vol. 2, 762–63.　[2] A city on the island of Rhodes where Danaus and his daughters were said to stop on their way from Egypt to Argos (Hdt. 2.182.2).

100a (vol. 1, p. 105 Pf.) Milan papyrus (*Diegeseis*)

The wooden statue of Hera took the form of a statue when Procles[1] was king. The wood from which it was made . . . they say was brought from Argos long ago, still a plank, unwrought since the art of sculpture had not yet advanced.

[1] Presumably an early king of Samos. Otherwise unknown.

101–101b Iunonis Samiae simulacrum alterum

101 *P.Mil.Vogl.* 1.18 col. IV, 30

Ἥρῃ τῇ Σαμίῃ περὶ μὲν τρίχας ἄμπελος ἕρπει

101a (vol. 1, p. 106 Pf.) *Dieg.* 4.30–35; *P.Mil.Vogl.* 1.18 col. IV, 30–35

Ἥρῃ τῇ Σαμίῃ περὶ μὲν τρίχας ἄμπελος ἕρπει

λέγεται ὡς τῇ Σαμίᾳ Ἥρᾳ περιέρπει τὰς τρίχας
ἄμπελος, πρὸς δ᾽ ἐδάφει λεοντῇ βέβληται, ὡς
λάφυρα τῶν Διὸς νόθων παίδων, Ἡρακλέους
[5] καὶ Διονύσου.

101b (vol. 1, p. 106 Pf.) Tert. *De cor.* 7.4

Iunoni vitem Callimachus induxit. ita et Argi signum eius
palmite redimitum subiecto pedibus corio leonino, insul-
tantem ostentat novercam de exuviis utriusque privigni.

102–102a Pasicles Ephesius

102 *P.Mil.Vogl.* 1.18 col. IV, 36

Ἠισύμνας Ἐφέσου, Πασίκλεες, ἀλλ᾽ ἀπὸ δαίτης

101–101b Another Statue of Juno at Samos

101 Milan papyrus

On the Hera at Samos a vine creeps around her hair

101a (vol. 1, p. 106 Pf.) Milan papyrus (*Diegeseis*)

On the Hera at Samos a vine creeps around her hair

It is said that vine entwines the hair of Hera at Samos and at the base a lionskin[1] is tossed as spoils of the bastard[2] children of Zeus, Heracles, [5] and Dionysus.

[1] On Heracles and the lion skin, cf. *Aet*. 60a and 60b above.
[2] On Zeus' mistresses, cf. Hom. *Il*. 14.315–28.

101b (vol. 1, p. 106 Pf.) Tertullian, *De Corona*

Callimachus draped a vine on Juno. And so at Argos a statue of her is bound with vine shoots and at her feet a lion's skin is placed. It shows the stepmother scoffing at the spoils of each stepson.

102–102a Pasicles of Ephesus

102 Milan papyrus

you ruled Ephesus, Pasicles, but from a feast

102a (vol. 1, p. 106 Pf.) *Dieg.* 4.36–5.2; *P.Mil.Vogl.* 1.18 col. IV, 36–col. V, 2

Ἠισύμνας Ἐφέσου, Πασίκλεες, ἀλλ᾽ ἀπὸ δαίτης

Φησὶν ὅτ[ι] Πασικλῆς Ἐφεσίων ἄρχων ἐξ εὐωχίας
ἀνέλυεν· ἐπιτιθέμενοι δέ τινες αὐτῷ ὑπὸ τοῦ
σκότους [5] ἐδυσθέτουν, ὅτε δὲ προῆλθον ⟨πρὸς⟩
τὸ Ἥραιον, ἡ μήτηρ τοῦ Πασικλέους ἱέρεια οὖσα
διὰ τὸν ψόφον τοῦ διωγμοῦ λύχνον ἐκέλευσεν
προενεγκεῖν ⟨οἱ⟩· οἱ δὲ τυχόντες φωτὸς ἀνεῖλον
[10] αὐτῆς τὸν παῖδα.

103–103a Androgeos

103 *P.Mil.Vogl.* 1.18 col. V, 3

Ἥρως ὦ κατὰ πρύμναν, ἐπεὶ τόδε κύρβις ἀείδει

103a (vol. 1, p. 107 Pf.) *Dieg.* 5.3–8; *P.Mil.Vogl.* 1.18 col. V, 3–8

Ἥρως ὦ κατὰ πρύμναν, ἐπεὶ τόδε κύρβις ἀείδει

φησὶν ὅτι ὁ καλούμενος "κατὰ πρύμναν ἥρως"
Ἀνδρόγεώς ἐστιν· ⟨. . .⟩ πάλαι γὰρ ἐνταῦθα τὸν
Φαληρικὸν [5] ὅρμον εἶναι, οὗ τὰς ναῦς ὁρμίζεσθαι
πρὶν γενέσθαι τὸν Πειραιᾶ.

102a (vol. 1, p. 106 Pf.) Milan papyrus

You ruled Ephesus, Pasicles, but from a feast

He says that Pasicles, the ruler of Ephesus, departed from a banquet. Some people attacking him were doing badly on account of the darkness, [5] but when they came to the temple of Hera Pasicles' mother, who was a priestess, ordered a lamp to be brought on account of the noise of the chase. And when they obtained the light, they killed [10] her son.

103–103a Androgeos

103 Milan papyrus

O hero at the [ship's] stern, since the tablet[1] sings of this

[1] A *kyrbis* is a wooden or stone tablet on which were inscribed laws or religious regulations. At Athens there were *kyrbeis* containing the laws of Draco and Solon.

103a (vol. 1, p. 107 Pf.) Milan papyrus (*Diegeseis*)

O hero at the [ship's] stern, since the tablet sings of this

They say that the one called "hero of the stern" is Androgeos.[1] Long ago Phalerum [5] was the harbor there where ships anchored before Piraeus[2] existed.

[1] The son of Minos (*Aet.* 7a.5 above). He had a cult at Phalerum (Paus. 1.1.4).   [2] The harbor at Athens which preceded the Piraeus built by Themistocles in 493/2 BC (Hdt. 6.116; Paus. 1.1.2).

104–104a Oesydres Thrax

104 *P.Mil.Vogl.* 1.18 col. V, 9

Οἰσύδρεω Θρήϊκος ἐφ᾽ αἵματι πολλὰ Θάσοιο

104a (vol. 1, p. 108 Pf.) *Dieg.* 5.9–17; *P.Mil.Vogl.* 1.18 col. V, 9–17

   Οἰσύδρεω Θρήϊκος ἐφ᾽ αἵματι πολλὰ Θάσοιο

Φησὶν Παρίους Οἰσύδρην τὸν Θρᾶκα
φονε[ύ]σαντας διαπολιορκηθῆναι Θασι[. . .]ως τὸ
ἀρέσκον Βισάλταις [5] [ἐ]πιτίμιο[ν τ]ίνειν ἔχρησεν
ὁ θεός· οἱ δετειχο.[. . .]αννοθ..[. . .]Θασίοις
ἐρ[ω]τῶσι[. . .]ειν.η.[. . . . .]πέμπειν πα[
.[. . . . .]. [.].α.[. . . . . .]..πλη.κο.[

   105–105b Syrma Antigones (?)

105 *P.Mil.Vogl.* 1.18 col. V, 18

.]δε[. . . . . .]ν[. . . . . .]ιδετονδ..[

104–104a Thracian Oesydres

104 Milan papyrus

at the killing of Oesydres[1] of Thrace many things at
Thasus[2]

[1] A Thracian name otherwise unknown.   [2] An island op-
posite the coast of Thrace colonized by settlers from Paros around
680 BC, led by Telesicles (the father of Archilochus) and the poet
himself (Strabo 10.5.7). A war between the Thracians and the
Thasians ensued.

104a (vol. 1, p. 108 Pf.) Milan papyrus (*Diegeseis*)

> At the killing of Oesydres of Thrace many things at
> Thasus

He says that after the Parians killed the Thracian Oesydres
they were besieged. . . . the god commanded them to
pay a penalty [5] pleasing to the Bisalti[1] . . . they ask the
Thasians . . . to send

[1] A Thracian tribe (Hdt. 7.115).

105–105b The Dragging of Antigone (?)[1]

[1] A place-name so-called because it was there that Antigone
dragged the body of her brother Polynices to the pyre of their
brother Eteocles after the two had killed one another. The flame
on the pyre divided itself in two to mark their mutual hostility
(Paus. 9.25.2).

105 Milan papyrus

. . .

105a (vol. 1, p. 109 Pf.) *Dieg.* 5.18–24; *P.Mil.Vogl.* 1.18 col. V, 18–24

```
.]δε[.......].ν[..........]ιδετονδ..[
φ[.......]πισο[..........]νο.[......]ταιομ[........
...]καγ[......]σχι[..].[..........]εναγι[
.....].φοραν α.[......]σημαιν.[.....]σδεου.ε
φι[..] .[..]. ον ἀπολελ[... τ]ὴν Ἀν[τ]ιγόνην ὡς
οὐδὲ ἐκειν[
```

105b Ov. *Tr.* 5.5.33–39

Consilio, commune sacrum cum fiat in ara
    fratribus, alterna qui periere manu,
35   ipsa sibi discors, tamquam mandetur ab illis,
    scinditur in partes atra fauilla duas.
Hoc, memini, quondam fieri non posse loquebar,
    et me Battiades iudice falsus erat:
omnia nunc credo.

106–7a Gaius Romanus

106 *P.Mil.Vogl.* 1.18 col. V, 25

Ὧδε[....]γείνεσθε, Πανελλάδος ὧδε τελέ[σ]σαι

107 Plin. *HN* 3.139

Arsiae gens Liburnorum iungitur usque ad flumen Titium.
pars eius fuere Mentores, Himani, Encheleae, Bulini et

105a (vol. 1, p. 109 Pf.) Milan papyrus (*Diegeseis*)

. . . the sacrifice was split . . . gave a sign of the division . . . that Antigone in order not [to deprive] that one

105b Ovid, *Tristia*

By design, when a joint sacrifice is made on the altar to the brothers who each perished by the other's hand, [35] the very conflict between them, as though at their command, splits the black cinders into two parts. Once, I recall, I used to say that this could not happen, and that the son of Battus was wrong in my judgment. Now I believe it all.

106–7a Roman Gaius

106 Milan papyrus

Thus be . . . of the whole of Greece and thus . . . to accomplish

107 Pliny the Elder, *Natural History*

The tribe of the Liburnians extends to Arsia and even to the river Titus. Parts of it were the Mentores, the Himani, the Encheleae, the Bulini, and those whom Callimachus

quos Callimachus Peucetios appellat, nunc totum uno
nomine Illyricum vocatur generatim.

107a (vol. 1, p. 110 Pf.) *Dieg.* 5.25–32; *P.Mil.Vogl.* 1.18
col. V, 25–32

Ὧδε [. . . .] γείνεσθε Πανελλάδος, ὧδε τελέ[σ]σαι

Φ[η]σὶ Πευκετίων προσκαθημένων [τ]οῖς τείχεσι
τῆς Ῥώμης τῶν Ῥωμαίων Γάϊον ἐναλλόμενον
καταβαλεῖν τὸν [5] ἐ]κείνων ἡγούμενον, τρωθῆναι
δὲ εἰς τὸν μηρόν· μετὰ δὲ ταῦτα ἐπὶ τῷ σκάζειν
δυσφορήσαντα παύσασθαι τῆς ἀθυμίας ὑπὸ τῆς
μητρὸς ἐπιπληχθέντα.

108–9a Ancora Argus navis
Cyzici relicta

108 *P.Mil.Vogl.* 1.18 col. V, 33

Ἀργὼ καὶ σέ, Πάνορμε, κατέδραμε καὶ τεὸν ὕδωρ

calls the Peucetii.[1] Now they are all generally called by one name, Illyrians.

[1] The identity of the Peucetians is not certain. Possibilities are Illyrians (as here) or one of several Italic peoples.

107a (vol. 1, p. 110 Pf.) Milan papyrus (*Diegeseis*)

Thus be . . . of the whole of Greece and thus . . . to accomplish

He says that when the Peucetians were besieging the walls of Rome, one of the Romans, Gaius,[1] leaped down and struck [5] their leader, but was wounded in his thigh. After this he was depressed by his limp, but put off his distress when he was rebuked by his mother.[2]

[1] Apparently a generic Roman name. He has been identified with Horatius Cocles if the Peucetians are the Etruscans, and Spurius Carvilius Maximus, if they are another of the Italic tribes.   [2] Based on parallel stories, she probably reminded him that his limp was a badge of courage.

108–9a The Anchor of the Ship Argo
Left at Cyzicus

108 Milan papyrus

On you too, Panormus,[1] the Argo landed and your water

[1] The harbor at Cyzicus (Schol. ad Ap. Rhod. 1.954).

109 Schol. ad Ap. Rhod. 1.957 (83, 26 Wendel)

κρήνη ὑπ᾽ Ἀρτακ⟨ίῃ⟩· Ἀρτακία κρήνη περὶ Κύζικον,
ἧς καὶ Ἀλκαῖος μέμνηται καὶ Καλλίμαχος, ὅτι τῆς
Δολιονίας ἐστίν.

109a (vol. 1, p. 111 Pf.) *Dieg.* 5.33–39; *P.Mil.Vogl.* 1.18
col. V, 33–39

   Ἀργὼ καὶ σέ, Πάνορμε, κατέδραμε, καὶ τεὸν
      ὕδωρ

Φησὶ τοὺς Ἀργοναύτας ὑδρεύσασθαι ἀποβάντας
εἰς Κύζικον ἀπολιπεῖν τὸν λίθον ἐνθάδε ᾧ ἐχρῶντο
ἀγκύρᾳ, ἅ⟨τε⟩ ἐλαφρότερον ὄντα—τοῦτον δ᾽
ὕστερον [5] καθιερωθῆναι Ἀθηνᾷ—, ἕτερόν γε μὴν
βαρύτερον ἀναλαβε[ῖ]ν.

110–110f Coma Berenices

110 1, *P.Mil.Vogl.* 1.18 col. V, 40; 7–8 Schol. ad Arat.
Phaen. 146 (p. 147 Martin)

1   Πάντα τὸν ἐν γραμμαῖσιν ἰδὼν ὅρον ᾗ τε φέρονται

7   †ἢ† με Κόνων ἔβλεψεν ἐν ἠέρι τὸν Βερενίκης
         βόστρυχον ὃν κείνη πᾶσιν ἔθηκε θεοῖς

13/14 [σύμβολον ἐννυχίης . . . ἀεθλοσύνης?]

109 Scholia to Apollonius of Rhodes, *Argonautica*

behind the spring Artacia: The spring Artacia near Cyzicus[1] from which Alcaeus[2] and Callimachus recall that it was of Dolionia.[3]

[1] Greek city in Anatolia visited by the Argonauts (Ap. Rhod. 1.936–84).   [2] Fr. 440 Voigt.   [3] The Doliones lived around Cyzicus (Ap. Rhod. 1.947–48 with Schol. ad Ap. Rhod. 1.936–49a).

109a (vol. 1, p. 111 Pf.) Milan papyrus (*Diegeseis*)

> On you too, Panormus, the Argo landed and your
>   water

He says that the Argonauts, after disembarking at Cyzicus to fetch water, left the stone there that they used as an anchor because [5] it was too light—this was later dedicated to Athena—and took up another, heavier one.[1]

[1] Apollonius' version of the story (Ap. Rhod. 1.953–60) is similar.

110–110f The Lock of Berenice

110 Milan papyrus; Scholia to Aratus, *Phaenomena*

[1] Looking at the whole [heavenly] region within the lines[1] and where [the stars] are borne . . . [7] Conon[2] saw me in the sky, the lock of Berenice[3] that she dedicated to all the gods [13/14] . . . warrant of the nocturnal tussle . . .

[1] Conon is apparently reading a star chart with sections of the heavens marked off by lines.   [2] Conon of Samos, an astronomer and mathematician in the Ptolemaic court (Verg. *Ecl.* 3.40–42).   [3] Berenice II, wife of Ptolemy III Euergetes (Clayman 2014).

26 [μεγάθυμον?]

.   .   .   .

40 σήν τε κάρην ὤμοσα σόν τε βίον

.   .   .   .

                              ].[
    ἀμνά]μω[ν Θείας ἀργὸς ὑ]περφέ[ρ]ετ[αι,
45 βουπόρος Ἀρσινόη̣ς μ̣η̣τρὸς σέο, καὶ διὰ μέσ[σου
    Μηδείων ὀλοαὶ νῆες ἔβησαν Ἄθω.
    τί πλόκαμοι ῥέξωμεν, ὅτ᾽ οὔρεα τοῖα σιδή[ρῳ
    εἴκουσιν; Χαλύβων ὡς ἀπόλοιτο γένος,
    γειόθεν ἀντέλλοντα, κακὸν φυτόν, οἵ μιν ἔφ̣ηναν
50   πρῶτοι καὶ τυπίδων ἔφρασαν ἐργασίην.
    ἄρτι [ν]εότμητόν με κόμαι ποθέεσκον ἀδε[λφεαί,
       καὶ πρόκατε γνωτὸς Μέμνονος Αἰθίοπος
    ἵετο κυκλώσας βαλιὰ πτερὰ θῆλυς ἀήτης,
       ἵππο[ς] ἰοζώνου Λοκρίκος Ἀρσινόης,
55 .[.]ασε δὲ πνοιῇ με, δι᾽ ἠέρα δ᾽ ὑγρὸν ἐνείκας
       Κύπρ]ιδος εἰς κόλ[πους   ἔθηκε
    αὐτή̣, μιν Ζεφυρῖτις ἐπιπροέ[ηκε(ν)
    ....Κ]ανωπίτου ναιέτις α[ἰγιαλοῦ.
    ὄφρα δὲ] μὴ νύμφης Μινωίδος ο[
60   .....]ος ἀνθρώποις μοῦνον ἐπι .[

---

4 Either the sun, the son of Theia and Hyperion (Hes. *Theog.*
371–74; Pind. *Isth.* 5.1), or the grandson of Theia, viz., Boreas,
the North Wind (Hes. *Theog.* 378–80; see D'Alessio 2007, vol. 2,
524n39).   5 Most likely the obelisk erected in front of the
mortuary temple of Arsinoe II. The first of two examples of iron
cutting through rock. She was only Berenice's honorary mother;
her real mother was Apame, the wife of Magas of Cyrene.

[26] great hearted . . . [40] I swore by your head and your life . . . the bright descendant of Theia[4] is carried above, [45] the ox-piercer of your mother Arsinoe[5] and the deadly Median ships sailed through the middle of Athos.[6] What can we locks do when such mountains yield to iron? May the race of the Chalybes[7] perish, who revealed it rising up from the earth, an evil growth, [50] and first contrived the work of hammers.

My sister locks were mourning for me when I was just newly cut, and at once the brother of Aethiopian Memnon[8] dashed in, moving his dappled wings in circles, a gentle wind, the Locrian[9] horse of purple-belted Arsinoe,[10] [55] and with his breath he took me through the damp air and placed me on the lap of Cypris.[11] Zephyritis herself, an inhabitant of the Canopian coast,[12] had dispatched him, so that not . . . of the bride, daughter of Minos[13] [60] . . . only for men . . . but that I too, the beau-

---

[6] The mountain in northern Greece said to be bisected by Xerxes so that the Persian army could invade Greece in 480 BC (Hdt. 7.22–24, 37; Thuc. 4.109.2–3). In fact, he cut a canal through the isthmus connecting Mt. Athos with Calcidice.

[7] A non-Greek people who lived in the area of the Black Sea, known for their iron work (Ap. Rhod. 2.374–76).

[8] Zephyrus (Hes. *Theog.* 378–80), the West Wind. Like Memnon, a son of Eos.   [9] Perhaps because a west wind would seem to Alexandrians to be coming from Epizephyrian Locri in Sicily.   [10] Arsinoe, deified with Aphrodite's attribute.

[11] Aphrodite.   [12] The temple of Arsinoe-Aphrodite was on Cape Zephyrium on the coast between Alexandria and Canopus.

[13] Ariadne, whose wreath became a constellation, is invoked here as a parallel for Berenice, whose lock will have the same future.

φάεσ]ιν ἐν πολέεσσιν ἀρίθμιος ἀλλ[ὰ φαείνω
καὶ Βερ]ενίκειος καλὸς ἐγὼ πλόκαμ[ος,
ὕδασι] λουόμενόν με παρ' ἀθα[νάτους ἀνάγουσα
Κύπρι]ς ἐν ἀρχαίοις ἄστρον [ἔθηκε νέον.

65   ]
                                                        ]
‚πρόσθε μὲν ἐρχομεν ‚μετοπωρινὸν‚ Ὠκ]εανόνδε
            ].ο[
                  ἀ]λλ' εἰ κα[ι   ]....ν
70   ]..[.]‚τη[
μὴ   ] κοτέσηι[ς   οὔτ]ις ἐρύξει
βοῦς ἔπος‚]η...[ ].[ ].βη
            ].[.]ελε.[   ].θράσος ἀ[στ]έρες ἄλλοι
            ]νδινειε.[   ]ρσοσο[.]τεκ.[.]ω·
75 οὐ‚ τάδ‚ε‚ μοι τοσσήνδε φ‚ε‚ρει χάριν‚ ὅσ[σο]ν
            ἐκείνης
ἀ]σχάλλω κορυφῆς οὐκέτι θιξόμενος
ἧς ἄπο, παρ[θ]ενίη μὲν ὅτ' ἦν ἔτι, πολλ‚ὰ πέ‚πωκα
λι‚τ‚ά, γυναικείων δ' οὐκ ἀπέλαυσα μύρων.

            . . . .

            ο.[
90   με[
νυ[   ].[
    το.[   ]νθι[
γείτ[ονες   ]ως[
        α.[   ].. Ὑδροχ[όος] καὶ [Ὠαρίων.
94a χ[αῖρε], φίλη τεκέεσσι.[
94b   .[   ].....[.]ν.[

tiful lock of Berenice, counted among the many stars
might shine. Cypris placed me, bathed in the waters,[14] up
by the immortals, a new star among the ancient ones. [65]
. . . [67] going in front . . . to Ocean in autumn . . . but if
even . . . that you not be angry . . . no ox will prevent my
speech[15] . . . [my] insolence . . . the other stars . . . [75]
these things do not bring as much gratification to me as
grief that I will no longer touch that head from which I
drank so many simple oils, while she was still a maiden,
but did not enjoy womanly perfumes. . . . neighbors . . .
Aquarius and Orion . . . [94a] farewell, [may you be] dear
to children[16]

[14] A star that rises and sets in the Ocean (Hom. *Il.* 5.5–6,
18.489).

[15] See *Aet.* 110e below.

[16] A wish for Berenice's fertility, which was amply rewarded.
She had six children in seven years (Clayman 2014, 171–78).

110a (vol. 1, p. 123 Pf.) *Dieg.* 5.40–44; *P.Mil.Vogl.* 1.18 col. V, 40–44

Πάντα τὸν ἐν γραμμαῖσιν ἰδὼν ὅρον ᾗ τε
    φέρονται ·

φησὶν ὅτι Κόνων κατηστέρισε τὸν Βερενί-
κης βόστρυχον, ὃν θεο[ῖς] ἀναθήσειν ὑπέσχε-
το κείνη, ἐπειδὰν ἐπανήκῃ ἀπὸ τῆς κατὰ Συ-
5 ρίαν μάχης.

110b Hyg. *Poet. astr.* 2.24

1. Cuius supra simulacrum proxime Virginem sunt aliae septem stellae ad caudam Leonis in triangulo collocatae, quas Crinem Berenices esse Conon Samius mathematicus et Callimachus dicit; cum Ptolemaeus Berenicen Ptolemaei et Arsinoes filiam, sororem suam, duxisset uxorem et paucis post diebus Asiam oppugnatum profectus [5] esset, vovisse Berenicen, si victor Ptolemaeus redisset, se crinem detonsuram; quo voto damnatam crinem in Veneris Arsinoes Zephyritidis posuisse templo, eumque postero die non comparuisse. quod factum cum rex aegre ferret, ut ante diximus, Conon mathematicus cupiens inire gratiam regis dixit crinem inter sidera videri collocatum et quasdam [10] vacuas a figura septem stellas ostendit quas esse fingeret crinem.

110a (vol. 1, p. 123 Pf.) Milan papyrus (*Diegeseis*)

Looking at the whole [heavenly] region within the
lines and where [the stars] are carried

He says that Conon catasterized the lock of Berenice
which she had promised to dedicate to the gods when he[1]
returned from the battle against Syria.

[1] Ptolemy III was absent during the first year of his marriage
with Berenice (246 BC), pursuing the Third Syrian War. He had
instigated it in support of his sister (also named Berenice and now
known as Berenice Syra), who tried to assert the claims of her
infant son to the Seleucid throne following the death of her hus-
band, Antiochus II.

110b Hyginus, *Astronomy*

1. Above the constellation of Leo nearest to Virgo are
seven other stars in a triangle located near Leo's tail, which
the mathematician Conon of Samos and Callimachus say
are the lock of Berenice. When Ptolemy married Bere-
nice, the daughter of Ptolemy and his sister Arsinoe, and
set out a few days later to make war against Asia, [5] Ber-
enice vowed that if Ptolemy returned as victor she would
cut her hair; and that she placed this lock of hair which
was dedicated by the vow in the temple of Venus-Arsinoe-
Zephyritis, but on the next day it was not found. When
the king was angry at what happened, as we said earlier,
Conon the mathematician, who wanted to be in the good
graces of the king, said that the lock was seen located
among the stars and he showed seven stars lacking a shape
[10] which he pretended to be the lock.

2. hanc Berenicen nonnulli cum Callimacho dixerunt
equos alere et ad Olympia mittere consuetam fuisse. alii
dicunt hoc amplius Ptolemaeum Berenices patrem, mul-
titudine hostium perterritum, fuga salutem petisse, filiam
autem saepe consuetam insiluisse in equum et reliquam
copiam [15] exercitus constituisse et complures hostium
interfecisse, reliquos in fugam coniecisse. pro quo etiam
Callimachus eam magnanimam dixit.

110c Catull. 65.15–16

Sed tamen in tantis maeroribus, Hortale, mitto
    haec expressa tibi carmina Battiadae

110d Catull. 66

Omnia qui magni dispexit lumina mundi,
    qui stellarum ortus comperit atque obitus,
flammeus ut rapidi solis nitor obscuretur,
    ut cedant certis sidera temporibus,
5   ut Triviam furtim sub Latmia saxa relegans
    dulcis amor gyro devocet aerio:
idem me ille Conon caelesti <in> lumine vidit
    e Bereniceo vertice caesariem
fulgentem clare, quam multis illa dearum
10   levia protendens bracchia pollicita est,

---

[1] The moon is invisible when she visits Endymion on Mt.
Latmus in Caria (Ov. *Ars. am.* 3.83, *Tr.* 2.299).

2. This Berenice some say with Callimachus raised horses and was accustomed to send them to Olympia.[1] Moreover, others say that Ptolemy, the father of Berenice, when frightened by a multitude of enemies sought safety in flight, but that his daughter jumped on a horse, as she was often accustomed, reorganized the remaining troops, [15] killed several enemy and drove the rest into retreat. For which even Callimachus said she was brave.[2]

[1] Berenice's equestrian victories are celebrated in the "Victoria Berenices" (*Aet.* 54–60j) above, and in Posidippus' *Hippika* (Clayman 2014, 147–58).　[2] There is no corroborating evidence for this incident.

110c Catullus

But nevertheless in such great sadness, Hortalus,[1] I send these songs of the Battiad[2] to you, translated.

[1] Q. Hortensius Hortalus, a distinguished Roman orator, historian, and politician, rival of Cicero (Cic. *Brut.* 1.1–6).
[2] That is, Callimachus. "Son of Battus" refers to his origins in Cyrene, which was founded by Battus (Hdt. 4.150–58).

110d Catullus

He, who observed the lights of the great heavens, who discovered the rising and the setting of the stars, how the fiery glow of the fierce sun is hidden, how the constellations withdraw at certain seasons, [5] how sweet Love, hiding the moon secretly under Latmus' rock,[1] calls her from her aerie orbit, that same Conon saw me in the heavenly light, shining brightly, a lock from Berenice's head, which, [10] stretching out her smooth arms, she promised

qua rex tempestate novo auctus hymenaeo
    vastatum finis iuerat Assyrios,
dulcia nocturnae portans vestigia rixae
    quam de virgineis gesserat exuviis.
15 estne novis nuptis odio Venus? anne parentum
    frustrantur falsis gaudia lacrimulis
ubertim thalami quas intra limina fundunt?
    non, ita me diui, vera gemunt, iuerint.
id mea me multis docuit regina querellis
20   invisente novo proelia torva viro.
et tu non orbum luxti deserta cubile,
    sed fratris cari flebile discidium?
cum penitus maestas exedit cura medullas.
    ut tibi tunc toto pectore sollicitae
25 sensibus ereptis mens excidit! at ⟨te⟩ ego certe
    cognoram a parva virgine magnanimam.
anne bonum oblita es facinus, quo regium adepta es
    coniugium, quod non fortior ausit alis?
sed tum maesta virum mittens quae verba locuta es!
30   Iuppiter, ut tristi lumina saepe manu!
quis te mutavit tantus deus? an quod amantes
    non longe a caro corpore abesse volunt?
atque ibi me cunctis pro dulci coniuge divis
    non sine taurino sanguine pollicita es,
35 si reditum tetulisset. is haud in tempore longo
    captam Asiam Aegypti finibus addiderat.
quis ego pro factis caelesti reddita coetu
    pristina vota novo munere dissolvo.
invita, o regina, tuo de vertice cessi,
40   invita: adiuro teque tuumque caput,
digna ferat quod si quis inaniter adiurarit:
    sed qui se ferro postulet esse parem?

to many goddesses, at the time her husband, enriched with a new marriage, set out to devastate the territory of the Assyrians, carrying the sweet traces of a nocturnal battle which he waged for virgin spoils. [15] Is Venus hated by newlyweds? Or are the joys of their parents deceived by false tears, which they shed abundantly within the bridal chambers? No, may the gods help me, their groans are not true. [20] This my queen taught me with her many complaints, when her new husband went off to savage war. When he deserted you, did you not grieve for your abandoned bed? Or was the departure of a dear brother worthy of tears? How care ate out your sad marrow deep within, so that deeply distressed, with [25] senses totally ripped from your breast, consciousness left you. But certainly I knew you to be bold from the time you were a small girl. Or have you forgotten the noble act, which no stronger person dared, by which you acquired a royal marriage? But then, what unhappy words you spoke as you sent away your husband!

[30] Jupiter, how often did you sadly daub your eyes with your hand? What great god changed you! Is it because lovers do not wish to be separated far from their dear one? And there you promised me to all the gods, not without the blood of bulls, [35] that your sweet husband might return. And he in no long time added captured Asia to the territories of Egypt. And for these accomplishments, I, translated to the celestial assembly, discharge your old vow with a new gift. Unwilling, O Queen, did I leave your tresses, [40] Unwilling: I swear by you and your head. If anyone should swear vainly by these, may he suffer what is fitting. But who claims that he is equal to iron?

ille quoque eversus mons est, quem maximum in oris
    progenies Thiae clara supervehitur,
45 cum Medi peperere novum mare, cumque iuventus
    per medium classi barbara navit Athon.
quid facient crines, cum ferro talia cedant?
    Iuppiter, ut Chalybon omne genus pereat,
et qui principio sub terra quaerere venas
50   institit ac ferri fingere duritiem!
abiunctae paulo ante comae mea fata sorores
    lugebant, cum se Memnonis Aethiopis
unigena impellens nutantibus aera pennis
    obtulit Arsinoes Locridos ales equos,
55 isque per aetherias me tollens avolat umbras
    et Veneris casto conllocat in gremio.
ipsa suum Zephyritis eo famulum legarat,
    Graia Canopeis incola litoribus,
hic, liquidi vario ne solum in lumine caeli
60   ex Ariadneis aurea temporibus
fixa corona foret, sed nos quoque fulgeremus
    devotae flavi verticis exuviae,
uvidulam a flutu cedentem ad templa deum me
    sidus in antiquis diva novum posuit.
65 Virginis et saevi contingens namque Leonis
    lumina, Callisto iuncta Lycaoniae,
vertor in occasum, tardum dux ante Booten,
    qui vix sero alto mergitur Oceano;
sed quamquam me nocte premunt vestigia divum,
70   lux autem canae Tethyi restituit.
pace tua fari hic liceat, Rhamnusia virgo,
    namque ego non ullo vera timore tegam,

For even that mountain was overturned, the greatest on
the shores, which the bright descendant of Theia sails
past, [45] when the Medes created a new sea, and when
young men sailed in a barbarian fleet through the middle
of Athos. What can hair do when such things yield to iron?
Jupiter, may the whole race of Chalybes perish, and who-
ever first resolved to search for veins of iron [50] under
the earth, and to refine its hardness. Just after I was cut
off my sister locks were mourning my fate, when the sib-
ling of Ethiopian Memnon appeared, pulsing the air with
quivering wings, the flying horses of Locrian Arsinoe, [55]
and he, carrying me, flew through the shadowy upper air,
and placed me in the chaste lap of Venus. For this Zephy-
ritis herself, the Greek Goddess who dwells on the shores
of Canopus, selected her own servant. Then Venus depos-
ited me, as I was departing for the regions of the gods,
damp with tears, a new constellation among the old, [60]
that the golden crown from Ariadne's brows not alone be
fixed in the varied lights of heaven, but that we also would
gleam, the promised spoils from Berenice's blond head.
[65] Touching the lights of Virgo and of savage Leo, joined
with Callisto,[2] the daughter of Lycaon, I am turned toward
my setting, leading slow Bootes, who with difficulty sub-
merges late in the deep ocean. Though at night the tracks
of the gods press me, [70] the light of gray Tethys[3] restores
me. With your permission may I be allowed to speak,
Rhamnusian Virgin,[4] for I will not hide the truth on ac-

---

[2] The constellation Ursa Major, the Bear.   [3] Titan daugh-
ter and wife of Oceanus (Call. *Hymn* 3.44–45; Hes. *Theog.* 131–
36); also mother of the Nile (Hes. *Theog.* 337).   [4] Nemesis,
who had a shrine at Rhamnus in Attica (Paus. 1.33.1–3).

nec si me infestis discerpent sidera dictis,
    condita quin nostri pectoris evoluam.
75 non his tam laetor rebus, quam me afore semper,
    afore me a dominae vertice discrucior.
quicum ego, dum virgo quondam fuit, omnibus expers
    unguentis, una vilia multa bibi.
nunc vos optato quas iunxit lumine taeda,
80 non prius unanimis corpora coniugibus
tradite nudantes reiecta veste papillas,
    quam iucunda mihi munera libet onyx,
vester onyx, casto colitis quae iura cubili.
    sed quae se impuro dedit adulterio,
85 illius a mala dona levis bibat irrita pulvis:
    namque ego ab indignis praemia nulla peto.
sed magis, o nuptae, semper concordia vestras,
    semper amor sedes incolat adsiduus.
tu vero, regina, tuens cum sidera divam
90 placabis festis luminibus Venerem,
unguinis expertem non siris esse tuam me,
    sed potius largis effice muneribus.
sidera cur iterent 'utinam coma regia fiam,'
    proximus Hydrochoi fulgeret Oarion!

110e (vol. 1, pp. 114–22 Pf.; vol. 2, pp. 115–16 Pf.) Schol. in *P.Oxy.* 2258

110.45   marg. infer.

        βουπόρ[ος] Ἀρσιν(όης)·
        βουπόρος ὁ ὀβελίσκο[σ].[..].οπορον .. [
        ] .....Ἀ]θων

count of any fear, not even if the constellations rend me for these dangerous words, will I disclose the secrets of a true heart. [75] I am not so delighted with these things, as I am distressed that I will be, always will be, apart from the head of my mistress, with whom I, while she was still a virgin testing all the unguents, I drank many thousands. When the marriage torch has joined you in its hoped-for light, Brides, [80] do not surrender your bodies to your like-minded husbands, baring your breasts with clothing cast aside, before the onyx jar offers charming gifts to me, your jar, you who cherish your vows with a chaste bed. But whoever has given herself to impure adultery, [85] let the light dust drink up her unfavorable and useless gifts, for I seek no gifts from the unworthy. But more, O brides, may concord always dwell in your house, and constant love. And you, Queen, whenever watching the stars, [90] you propitiate Venus with festive lights, let me, your lock, not be without unguents, but rather offer me large gifts. Why do the stars hold me fast? May I become a royal lock again, and let Orion glow next to Aquarius!

110e (vol. 1, pp. 114–22 Pf.; vol. 2, pp. 115–16 Pf.) Oxyrhynchus papyrus (marginal scholia)

110.45   (lower margin)

The Ox-piercer of Arsinoe : the ox-piercer is the obelisk . . . Athos

marg. sinistr.

Ἀρσινόης μητρ(ός)· κατὰ τιμὴν εἶπεν,
ἐπεὶ θυγάτηρ Ἀπάμας καὶ Μάγα

110.48   marg. infer.

[Χ]αλύβων ὡς ἀ[πό]λοιτ(ο) γέν(ος)·
Χάλυβ(ες) Σκυθί(ας) ἔθνος, παρ᾽ οἷς πρώτοις εὑρέθη
ἡ ἐργασία τοῦ σ[ιδ]ήρου κ(αὶ) ἴσως ἐντεῦθεν [λέ]γε-
τ(αι) τὸ περιτεμεῖν τὸ περισκυ[θί]σαι δ̣. [.] τῷ Σκύθῃ
σι]δήρῳ

110.49   marg. infer.

γειό[θ(εν)· εὕρ]ητ(αι) ἐκ τῆς γ[ῆ]ς

marg. sinistr.

τὴν τοῦ σιδήρου γένεσ[ι]ν 'κακὸν φυτὸν' εἶπεν

110.52   marg. sinistr.

π]ρόκ(ατε)· εὐθέως

marg. infer.

καὶ πρόκατε γνωτ(ὸς) Μέμν(ονος)] 'γνωτὸς
Μέμνονος' ὁ Ζέφυρος, Μέμνων γὰρ υἱό[ς
...........].. Ἡσίοδ(ος)· "Ἀστραίῳ δ᾽ Ἠὼς
ἀνέμους, τ.έ.κε." περι μὲν τοῦ Μέμνονος Ὅμ(ηρος)·
"τὸν ῥ᾽ Ἠοῦς ἔκτεινε φαεινῆς ἀγλαὸς υἱό]ς·"

(left margin)

Of her mother Arsinoe: he speaks of her honorific title, since she was the daughter of Apama and Magas.

110.48   (lower margin)

May the tribe of the Chalybes perish: the Chalybes are a Scythian people. Among whom the working of iron was first discovered and perhaps from this *periskythizō* means to cut around with a sword of Scythian iron.

110.49   (lower margin)

geiothen means from the earth.

(left margin)

He said that the genesis of iron is an evil growth.

110.52   (left margin)

prokate: immediately.

(lower margin)

And immediately the brother of Memnon : the brother of Memnon is Zephyrus, for Memnon is the son of . . . Hesiod says, "To Astraeus Eos gave birth to the winds."[1] And Homer says about Memnon, "whom the glorious son of bright

---

[1] Hes. *Theog.* 378.

Ἡσίοδ(ος) δέ· "Τιθωνῷ δ᾽ ⌊Ἠ⌋ὼς τέκε Μέμνονα
χαλκοκορυστή[ν"

110.53   marg. sinistr.

βαλιά· ποικίλα

marg. dext.

θῆλυς ἀήτ[ης]].ρα. [ ].εσ.τιν[.] καὶ ạ[
].......ινπα [

marg. sin.

θῆλυς ἀήτ(ης)· δ]ιὰ τὸ γόνιμον πνοῦς ἁπαλός

110.54–57   marg. inf.

ἁ]ρπασθῆνα[ι] ὑπ[ὸ] τọῦ Ζ[ε]φύρου καὶ εἰς
τοὺς κόλπους τεθῆναι τῆς [ ]ν πεμφθέντος,
ὤ[ς] φησιν· "αὐτή μιν Ζεφυρῖτις" ἐπιπρο.[ ]
Ἀρσινό[η] ἔχει ἐν Ἀλε[ξ]ανδρείᾳ χωρίον τε
....μενον τετρα[μμένον] Λοκροὶ Ἐπιζεφύρι[ο]ί
εἰσι· διὰ τọῦτο ἐκαλεῖτο Λọ[κ]ρίς. λέγεται. [
]δ. Ζέφυρος

110.55   marg. dext.

[.]ạστ..[.] ὑγρόν· ἁπαλόν

298

dawn killed. "[2] And Hesiod says "to Tithonus Eos bore Memnon with the bronze helmet."[3]

[2] Hom. *Od.* 4.188.   [3] Hes. *Theog.* 984.

110.53   (left margin)

balia: dappled.

(right margin)

thēlus aētēs . . .

(left margin)

thēlus aētēs means a gentle breeze on account of its fruitfulness.

110.54–57 (lower margin)

to be snatched by the Zephyr sent by her and placed into her lap, as he says, "Zephyritis herself " . . . onward . . . Arsinoe has a district in Alexandria . . . turned . . . The Locrians are Epizephyrians. On account of this she is called Locrian. Zephyrus is called

110.55   (right margin)

hygros: tender.

110.65–66 marg. dext.

```
                    ]
    ]ν̣[ . . . ]λο̣μ̣ . . α̣ι̣ . . [
       ]νε[ . ] . . ν̣ . [ . ] . . ] . . . [
              . . . . . [
                . . . [
             . ν̣ . ε̣ [
```

110.65–68 marg. infer.

π̣ . . . μ̣ε̣ . [.] . [ ] . . . τ(ως) ἀκουστέον, ἐπεὶ ὁ Λέων
κατηστ[έ]ρ̣ι̣στ̣αι ὑπὸ τῇ Ἄρκτῳ· Ἄρατ̣[ος]·
"ποσσὶ δ' ὑπ' ἀμφοτ̣(έροισι) Λέων ὑπ[ὸ] καλὰ
φα[είν]ει"[1] τῆς Ἄρκτου λέγει· ταῖς δὲ Πλειά[σ]ι
φ(ασὶν) ἐοικένα τὸν Πλόκαμ(ον) κα̣τ̣[ὰ τ]ὸ
σχῆμα διὰ τ[ὸ μικροὺς] κ[α]ὶ πυκνοὺς ἐν [. .] .
ἀ̣στέρας κεῖσθαι, καθὰ καὶ Διόφιλ[ος ἐ̣]ν τῷ
ἐπιγραφομένῳ Προκ[. .]ῳ οὗτ(ως)·

ʼπολλά̣[κι δὴ] ἴδε κεῖνο δι' ἠέ[ρος] ἐμφανὲς
ἄστρον ὄμματ' ἐπιστ[ή]σασα κατ' ἀστ[ερ]
όεσσαν Ἄμαξαν· τὴν ἄρ' ἅπαν ἄ̣[στρον μὲν]
ἀεὶ κ(ατα)κείμενον [. .]η . . ταδιη κέχυται,
πολλοὶ δ‹έ οἱ› ἀστέρες ἀμφί[ς] καὶ θαμέες
τυπόωσιν, ἀτὰρ [κατὰ] | εἴδεται ὤμω[ν

[1] Arat. Ph. 148

110.65–66 (right margin)

. . .

110.65–68 (lower margin)

. . . From this it should be understood, since Leo is placed under the Bear. Aratus says of the Bear, "Under both feet Leo shines brightly."[1] And he says that the Lock is like the Pleiades in shape on account of the small stars lying close together, accordingly even Diophilus in his composition the "*Proc* . . ."[2] says this:

Often he saw that star manifest through the air standing before his eyes set opposite the starry wagon . . . and the whole star always lying opposite . . . it scatters, and many stars on both sides and close together strike [him] but he appears over the

[1] Arat. *Phaen.* 148.
[2] On Diophilus or Diophile and the title of the composition, see *SH* 179–81.

Παρθένο‹υ› οὐ‹δ›ὲ Λέοντος ἀπόπροθεν αἰω-
ρεῖται, οὐρανίοιο Λέοντος ἐπιψαύε[ι [ἰ]ξύος
ἀκροτά[τ(ης), ἕ]πε̣τ(αι) δέ οἱ ἄγχι Βοώτης·
Ἄρκτον ἀποσκοπέων η̣ο̣ι̣α̣μ̣ε̣τ̣α̣σ̣κ̣οοπα [

ου [.] . [. .] . [. Βο]ώτ(ην) τὸν [Π]λ̣[ό]κ̣α̣μ̣(ον) εἶπ̣(ε)
διὰ τὸ τὸν Βοώ[την] μετ᾽ αὐτὸν ἀνατέλλειν τ̣[ε καὶ
δύνειν. ἶνις Ἄκμονος· ὁ Οὐρα]νός· οὗτο̣ς γὰρ
Ἄκμονος υἱ[ό]ς̣. ἶνις δὲ κυρ̣ί̣ω̣[ς] ὁ ὑποτίτθ[ι]ος
ἀπὸ τ(οῦ) [ἰνοῦν τοῦ σημαίνοντος τὸ θηλάζειν] . ν̣ι
κανόνιον. πρόσθε μὲν ἐρχομε̣ν̣ . μ̣ε̣τ̣ο̣π̣ω̣ . . ·
κοινη . [ ]τ̣ε τῆς ἀ̣ν̣[α]τ̣ο̣λῆς κ(αὶ) τῆς δύσεως.
ἀνατέλλ[ει] μὲν γάρ, φ(ησιν), ὁ Πλόκαμος πρ[ὸ
τῆς μετοπωρινῆς ἰσημερίας, δύνε]ι δὲ μετὰ [τὴ]ν̣
ἐαρινὴν ἰ̣σ̣ημερίαν.

110.67–70 marg. dext.

πρόσ]θε μὲν ἔρχ(ομεν)· . . . [ν . ε . [τῇ μὲν]
μετοπωρινῇ ἰσημερίᾳ ἔωθεν ἀνατελλοντ . .
[τροπῇ δὲ] θερινῇ ἔωθεν δυνον̣τ̣[ ] Ἡσίοδος
ἀν(α)τ(ελλοντ), κατ᾽ εὐθεῖα[ν] δὲ δυνοντ . [

110.72   marg. dext.

βοῦς ἔπος· νόμισμ(α)· ὃ ἐδίδοσαν οἱ
φλυ[α]ρο̣ῦντες·[

shoulders of Virgo and rises far from the heavenly
Lion, he touches . . . the highest point of her waist,
and Bootes follows near to him. Looking at the Bear
. . .

He says that Bootes attends the Lock because Bootes rises
and sets with it. "The son of Acmon." Uranus. This is the
son of Acmon. The legitimate son, the one suckled under
the breast from the word *ineo* meaning "to suckle" . . . the
chart. "Coming before . . ." in common . . . of the rising
and the setting. The Lock rises, he says, before the autum-
nal equinox and sets after the spring equinox.

110.67–70 (right margin)

Coming before: at the autumnal equinox rising at dawn
. . . setting at dawn at the summer solstice . . . as Hesiod[1]
says, rising and setting in a straight line.

[1] Fr. 292 M.-W.

110.72   (right margin)

[60] The ox story: A coin which the blabbers paid as a fine.

110.73   marg. dext.

διχ()αμει[.]

110.75–76 marg. dext.

οὐ τ[ά]δε μο[ι] | τοσσ(ήνδε) φέρει·] ο]ὐ τοσοῦτον,
φ(ησίν), ὁ Πλόκα[μ(ος) χ]άριν ἔχει ὅτι ἐν οὐ-
ρα[νῷ] ἐστιν ὅσ[ον] ἄχθεται ἐπὶ τῇ κε[φα]λῇι
μὴ συνπεφυ.[

110.77   marg. inf.

πολλὰ πέπωκα λιτά·

       marg. sin.

     vestigia litt.

110.92   marg. sin.

]ἀστέρι

110.93–94 marg. sin.

γείτονες ἔ]στωσαν ['Υδρο]χ[ό]ος καὶ Ὠρί(ων)

110.73   (right margin)

. . .

110.75–76 (right margin)

Neither did these things distress me as much as he says
the Lock has not as much pleasure from being in heaven
as it is distressed that it is not growing on her head.

110.77   (lower margin)

[65] I drank many light oils

            (left margin)

. . .

110.92   (left margin)

. . . star . . .

110.93–94 (left margin)

They are neighbors, Aquarius and Orion.

110f (vol. 2, pp. 114–15 Pf.) *P.Oxy.* 2258 fr. 12

recto

```
        .   .   .
        ] .ο...[
].......αιη [
 ]. Βερενικ.[
]ανειλεν.....[
 ] Πτολεμαῖος.[
          ]χνι[
          ].[
```

verso

```
        .   .   .
 ].[ ].[
]..[.]..τι[
 ]. πα[ρ]θένου
] ὀλίγος οικα[
 ]...τουτ...τ[
 ]ποιητ( )τονωκο[
]..επε...[.].[
 ].ιχ.[
  ]..[
```

111 Steph. Byz. μ 262 Billerbeck s.v. Μυτιλήνη

Μυτιλήνη· πόλις ἐν Λέσβῳ μεγίστη. Ἑκαταῖος Εὐ-

110f (vol. 2, pp. 114–15 Pf.) Oxyrhynchus papyrus

(recto)

. . . Berenice . . . Ptolemy

(verso)

. . . of the maiden . . . a little house . . . this . . . the poet
. . .

111 Stephanus of Byzantium

Mytilene: the biggest city in Lesbos. Hecataeus' *Europa*,[1]

[1] *BNJ* 1 F 140.

ρώπῃ ἀπὸ Μυτιλήνης τῆς Μάκαρος ἢ Πέλοπος θυγα-
τρός. οἱ δὲ ὅτι Μυτίλης ἦν ὁ οἰκιστής. οἱ δὲ ἀπὸ
Μύτωνος τοῦ Ποσειδῶνος καὶ Μυτιλήνης. ὅθεν Μυτω-
νίδα καλεῖ τὴν Λέσβον Καλλίμαχος ἐν τῷ τετάρτῳ.
Παρθένιος δὲ Μυτωνίδας τὰς Λεσβικάς φησι.

112 (Epilogus) *P.Oxy.* 1011 fol. 2 verso, 1–10

   ...]..ιν ὅτ᾽ ἐμὴ μοῦσα τ[.....]άσεται
  ...]του καὶ Χαρίτων [.....]ρια μοιαδ᾽ ἀνάσσης
   ...]τερης οὔ σε ψευδον[.....]ματι
πάντ᾽ ἀγαθὴν καὶ πάντα τ[ελ]εσφόρον εἶπεν...[..].[
5 κείν.. τῷ Μοῦσαι πολλὰ νέμοντι βοτὰ
  σὺν μύθους ἐβάλοντο παρ᾽ ἴχν[ι]ον ὀξέος ἵππου·
  χαῖρε, σὺν εὐεστοῖ δ᾽ ἔρχεο λωϊτέρῃ.
χαῖρε, Ζεῦ, μέγα καὶ σύ, σάω δ᾽ [ἐμὸ]ν οἶκον
  ἀνάκτων·
αὐτὰρ ἐγὼ Μουσέων πεζὸν [ἔ]πειμι νομόν.

    ΚΑΛΛΙΜΑΧΟΤ [ΑΙΤΙ]ΩΝ Δ´

from Mytilene the daughter of Macar or of Pelops. And they [said] that Mytiles was the founder, those [descending] from Myton the son of Poseidon and Mytilene. From this Callimachus calls Lesbos Mytonis in the fourth book. Parthenius[2] calls the women of Lesbos Mytonides.

[2] Fr. 43 Martini.

112 (Epilogue) Oxyrhynchus papyrus

. . . when my Muse . . . and of the Graces . . . of our queen[1] . . . not falsely you . . . noble in all things and accomplishing everything he said . . . [5] to whom[2] the Muse contributed stories when he was pasturing many cattle beside the footprint of the swift horse.[3] Farewell, and may you return with greater well-being. Farewell greatly you as well, Zeus. And preserve the house of my kings. But I will pass on to the foot pasture of the Muses.[4]

Aetia of Callimachus, Book 4

[1] Probably Berenice II.   [2] Callimachus in imitation of Hesiod (*Theog.* 22–34), echoing *Aet.* 2.1–4, above.   [3] Pegasus, the winged horse of Bellerophon, whose hoof strike made the spring Hippocrene, where the Muses have their home on Mt. Parnassus.   [4] Possibly Callimachus' prose works, but more likely his *Iambi*, which follow directly in *P.Oxy.* 1011 and in the *Diegeseis* (Clayman 1988).

FRAGMENTA INCERTI LIBRI

113 Ciris (?)

Scylla, daughter of Nisus, king of Megara, fell in love with Minos,
who was besieging the city, and cut her father's lock of purple hair
that was magically protecting it. In his wrath Nisus pursued her

113 *P.Oxy.* 2208 fr. 2

. . . . .

```
              ]..[     ]
     ]ρπον δαυ[
     ]οἰωνὸς ἀν' ἐ[
     Κ]εῖριν φῆ πρ[
]ν ῥέξειν α.[
  .].. εμάτη[
  ] .πλεε.[
  ].ττω δ' ἦλθ[
Κ]εῖριν ἰδε.[
  ]...ι.[
```

. . . . .

113a–d Fabulae incertae

113a (*SH* 271) *P.Ant.* 114 fr. 1 recto

. . . .

```
   ].α....εν.[
```

FRAGMENTS WHOSE BOOK
IS UNCERTAIN

113 Ciris (?)

in the form of a sea eagle, and she turned into the bird called Ciris
(Verg. *Ciris* 48–53, 484–541; Verg. *G.* 1.404–9; Ov. *Met.* 8.6–151).
Possibly from Book 1, based on the papyrus, or Book 3, based on
the contents (D'Alessio 2007, vol. 2, 544n1).

113 Oxyrhynchus papyrus

Daulides[1] . . . bird . . . he spoke of Ciris[2] . . . to do . . . she
went . . . he saw Ciris.

[1] Procne and Philomela, girls who were turned into birds at
Daulia in Phocis (Apollod. *Bibl.* 3.14.8).   [2] Scylla's name as
a bird (Ov. *Met.* 8.150–51; [Verg.] *Ciris* 487–89).

113a–d Unknown Tales

113a (*SH* 271) Antinoöpolis papyrus

. . .

```
    ].......[
  ].......ερ.[
  ]ομο........[
].[.].ησεμ...α..[
    ]ετε[
  .    .    .
```

113b (*SH* 272) *P.Ant.* 114 fr. 1b verso

```
  .      .     .
]..α..ωξ.[
]...αμεν.[
]ηδεδιων....[
].ον ἀν' εὐάγκει[αν
]αμενην νυμφ[
 ]θεσθα...ατε..[
        ].[..].[
  .    .    .
```

113c (*SH* 273) *P.Ant.* 114 fr. 2a recto

```
  .      .     .
]ραβαλ.ιτε
].ακες
]..επροσαλλ.[
]
  .    .    .
```

113b (*SH* 272) Antinoöpolis papyrus
. . . with lovely glades . . . the nymph

113c (*SH* 273) Antinoöpolis papyrus
that you might throw

113d (*SH* 274) *P.Ant.* 114 fr. 2b verso

. . . .

η . . [.] . [
ὀξύτατον [
  ὑμέας ω . [
ἐν Δίῃ· τὸ ˌγὰρ ἔσκε παλαίτερον οὔνομα Νάξῳ ˌ
  ενˌθενε[

. . . .

113e–f Onnes

Leodamas, king of the Milesians, was murdered by Amphitres,
and his sons went with his people to Assesus, where Amphitres
besieged them. Two of the Cabiri, Onnes and Tottes, came to

113e (115 Pf.) 1–21 (fin.), *P.Oxy.* 2167 fr. 5.1–21; 11–21
(init.), *P.Oxy.* 2211 fr. 2 recto, 1–11; 11–12, *Et.Mag.* 38,
36 Gaisford (a 543 Lasserre-Livadaras)

. . . .

          ] . . λθαˌ[.]ρειν πόδαˌ[
          ] . . [.] . ιον νο[.] . [.] . [
          ] . [.]τας χορὸς εὐτˌαˌ[
            ] . . . [.]σαγους[
5   ]τˌι παθὼν νο[
      ]αˌρˌκοταναιˌ[
          ]νˌοˌτεπτ[
      ] . [. .] . πατροιˌ[
      ]τˌαιφˌαˌμˌενο[

113d (*SH* 274) Antinoöpolis papyrus

the sharpest . . . you (pl.) . . . on Dia, which was the older
name for Naxos.[1] From there

[1] The island in the Cyclades on which Theseus abandoned
Ariadne after they escaped from Crete, where she had saved him
from the Minotaur. This verse overlaps with Call. *Fr. Inc. Sed.*
601. Naxos also appears in *Aet.* 7a.12 above, where Dionysus and
a nymph from Coronis are parents of the Graces (P. Parsons, *CR*
20 [1970]: 86).

113e–f Onnes

their rescue (Nicolaus of Damascus *BNJ* 90 F 52). Explanations
of how the fragments fit the narrative are in Massimilla 1996,
385–93; and Harder vol. 2, 875–91. Possibly from Book 3.

113e (115 Pf.) Oxyrhynchus papyrus; *Etymologicum
Magnum*

to raise the foot . . . chorus . . . [5] suffering . . . of the

10   . .   ].[.]...ε.[
.[.....]υνη· λάθρη δ ὲ παρ' Ἡφα ί σ τοιο καμίνοις
ἔτραφεν αἰράων ἔργ α διδα σ κόμε νοι.
Ὄννης μὲν νῦν ηχ[....] ...εισιμ[
λαοῖσιν, τότε δ' ην ψ[...].[..]αν.[
15 ἦστο τεὴν κάθ' ὅδον συμεν.[
τω δὲ σιδηρείας ἵμα..σ ἀντυγάδ[ας
ἃς αὐτοὶ χάλκευσαν ἐπ' ἄκμοσιν Ἡφ[αίστοιο
γεντ..κ..τειν νεκ[   ] υσ [
φῶτε δύω κρύπτοντ[   ]....[
20   πατροφόνου λιπάρ[   ].[.]α...[
ἐξ ἕδρης ἐκύλισαν ἐ.[   ]..[

113f (114.1–3 Pf.) *P.Oxy.* 2208 fr. 3.1–3

.   .   .   .

    ]κικλ[.].[.].α[
     ]η πολυγώνιε, χαῖρε [
    πα]ιδὸς ἐπὶ προθύροις.

fathers . . . in secret by the forges of Hephaestus[1] they were brought up learning the art of the hammer. Onnes[2] now . . . with the people, then . . . [15] he sat by your road[3] . . . they beat the iron rims of the shields[4] which they themselves[5] forged on the anvils of Hephaestus. The two spoke, hiding [the sacred objects] . . . of the father slayer[6] . . . they rolled him from his seat

[1] The smithy god who was the father of the Cabiri (Hdt. 3.37). For the Cabiri as smiths, see Nonnus, *Dion.* 14.20–22. They were a group of minor deities with a cult center at Samothrace, similar to the Curetes, Dactyls, and Corybantes. [2] One of the Cabiri. His brother, Tottes, would also have been part of the tale. [3] The subject seems to be Amphitres, who was attacking the town of Assesus and was seated by the battlefield to watch the action. When the people of Assesus, under orders of Onnes and Tottes, left the town in a procession with the sacred objects of the Cabiri at the front, the attackers fled and Amphitres was killed. [4] They were beating the iron rim of their shields, a feature of their ritual, like that of the Curetes and Dactyls (Nonnus, *Dion.* 14.27–32). [5] Onnes and Tottes.
[6] Amphitres, who was killed by the sons of Leodamas in revenge for his slaying their father.

113f (114.1–3 Pf.) Oxyrhynchus papyrus

o featureless one,[1] farewell![2] . . . of the boy at the portico

[1] An aniconic statue with multiple surfaces like a polygon.
[2] Addressed to Milesian Apollo. See D'Alessio, "Apollo Delio, i Cabiri Milesii e le cavalle di Tracia. Osservazioni su Callimaco frr. 114–115 Pf.," *ZPE* 106 (1995): 5–21; Massimilla 1996, 375–83. The *aition* concludes here.

114 Statua Apollinis Delii

114 (114.4–17 Pf.) 1–12, *P.Oxy.* 2208 fr. 3.4–15 ; 11–14,
P.Oxy. 2211 fr. 2 verso 1–4 ; 12–14, *P.Oxy.* 2212 fr. 19.1–3

;] "ναί, Δήλιος." "ἦ σύ γεπη[
  ]ν;" "ναὶ μὰ τὸν αὐτὸν ἐ̣μέ."
;] "ναί, χρύσεος." "ἦ καὶ ἀφα[ρής
  ] ζῶμα μέσον στ[ρέφεται.
5 σκαιῇ μὲν ἔ]χεις χερὶ, Κύνθιε τ[όξον,
τὰς δ' ἐπὶ δεξιτερῇ] σὰς, ἰδανὰς Χάριτας;"
        ]ν ἵν' ἄφρονας ὑβρ[
         ἀ]γαθοῖς ὀρέγω·
        ]ητοῖσι κολασμο[
10   ἀργό]τερος·
          ]ε̣ν φίλα χειρὶ δατ[.]σ̣.α̣ι
        ]ντες ἕτοιμον ἀεί,
        ]ἵν' ἦ μετὰ καί τι νοῆσαι
        ]ἀγαθὸν βασιλεῖ.

114a Fabula Thracia (?) incerta

The fragment perhaps recounts how Diomedes of Thrace was
killed when he took Heracles' man-eating mares for Eurystheus

114 *The Statue of Delian Apollo*

A dialogue with an unknown interlocutor, a form familiar in epigrams, including those of Callimachus. Possibly from Book 3.

114 (114.4–17 Pf.) Oxyrhynchus papyri

"Yes, Delian" . . . "you," . . . "Yes, by myself" . . . "Yes, of gold" "And naked . . .?" "A belt circles my waist"
[5] "You have in your left hand, Cynthian,[1] a bow and in your right, your fair Charites?"[2] ". . . so that [I can hold back] fools from insolence . . . [and] offer to good men . . . [but] punishment to mortals . . . [10] and more clear . . . with my own hand . . . always ready . . . so that it might be possible to repent . . . good for the king."[3]

[1] Apollo was born on Delos, where Mt. Cynthus is located (*Hom. Hym.* 3.25–29).   [2] The Graces, here representing the arts in contrast to the bow.   [3] Usually understood as one of the Ptolemies (D'Alessio 2007, vol. 2, 548n6).

114a *Thracian (?) Tale of Uncertain Location*

in Argolis (Apollod. *Bibl.* 2.5.8). See D'Alessio 2007, vol. 2, 548n7. Possibly in Book 3.

114a (114.18–25 Pf.) *P.Oxy.* 2211 fr. 2 verso 5–12

>   ]ας ἥν κεν ὁδεύσῃ[1]
>   ]νον Ἀργολικήν
>   ]ατος, ἐκ γὰρ ἐκείνων
>   ]. Βιστονίδες
>   ]. ς ὄχον, ὤπασε γάρ τοι
>   ]μηνος ἄναξ
>   ]. τισι χῶς σέ κοτ᾽ ἄνδρες
>   ]τ.[.]ιν Ἰλιακοῦ

[1] Hapax legomenon, *Il.* 11.569

115 Pf. = *Aet.* 113e

116–17 Fabulae incertae

116 *P.Oxy.* 2167 fr. 4

>   .   .   .   .
>   ν . . τ . [
>   μ[.]δε[
>   ]δε[
>   ]δὲ[
>   .[.]ατο[
>   τῆς δέκ[
>   .[.]. πτε.[
>   .[
>   .   .   .   .

114a (114.18–25 Pf.) Oxyrhynchus papyrus

. . . along which [road] you traveled . . . the Argolic . . .
from those . . . Thracians[1] . . . he gave a chariot to you . . .
the king . . . as once the men . . . you . . . of Trojan

[1] Bistonides are Thracians, and Diomedes was their king (Ap.
Rhod. 1.34; Hesychius, B 634 s.v. *Bistonis*).

115 Pf. = *Aetia* 113e

116–17 Tales of Uncertain Location

Possibly from Book 1.

116 Oxyrhynchus papyrus

. . .

117 *P.Oxy.* 2167 fr. 7

```
        .   .   .
        ]. ν.[
       ]ποβ.[
       ]αιλι.[
       ].ρε.ασε[
        ]π.οιο.[
        ]κδρή.[
        ]τρ..δ..[
        ]μητη[
        ].ηεν[
          ].[
        .       .   .
```

118–118a Apollinis templa Delphica

Probably in Book 1. Possibly a chronological list featuring three
temples of Apollo (Harder vol. 2, 906–8; but see Thomas 1983,
97). Similar lists can be found in Pind. *Pae.* 8.58–74; Paus. 10.5.9–

118 *P.Oxy.* 2209B

```
    .   .   .   .
      ].φ.οεις οἵ τε μάλισ[τα
      ]ν.[λ]ειαίνουσι· τὸ δ' ἱερ[ὸν
  ἐξ αὐ]τοσχεδίης κεῖνο τεκ.[
      ].ύ..ι σταφύλῃ.[.]ο.[
5     ].........ν λειαμε.[
      ].......ιησι μελιχροτ[
```

322

117 Oxyrhynchus papyrus

. . .

118–118a The Temples of Apollo at Delphi

13; Strabo 9.3.9. The precise detail is reminiscent of his description of the Statue of Zeus at Elis in *Iamb* 6 (*Ia.* 196).

118 Oxyrhynchus papyrus

. . . who above all polish [the stones]. That temple very simply . . . with a level . . . [5] smooth[1] . . . sweetness . . .

---

[1] Or a tool for smoothing stone.

]ἀ̣κ̣ρ̣ιβὲς καὶ τότε Λητο[ΐδ
]‥ τό δ᾿ ἔμέ̣λ̣λεν ες[
]‥ ἀ̣μφιπερικ[
10   ]ωη‿αν‿‿ε‿[
]‥[

. . . . .

118a (fr. 118 Pf.) Schol. supralin. *P.Oxy.* 2209B

ad 3 ……οἰκοδόμος οἷον εἰκαίω[ς

ad 4 διηκρίβωσαν τὸ ΰ[ψ]ο̣ς

119–37 Fabulae incertae

119 1, Schol. BD ad Pind. *Nem.* 9, 123b; 2–3, Schol. ad Eur. *Hec.* 472; 2–7; *P.Oxy.* 2210 fr. 1

. . . . . .

⌞Μηκώνην μακάρων ἕδρανον αὖτις ἰδεῖν,⌟
ἧχι π‿ά̣λους ἐβά̣λ̣‿οντο, διεκρίναντο δὲ τιμάς
πρῶτ‿α̣ Γιγαντείο‿υ δαίμονες ἐκ πολέμου·
]αρκαταμ[
]θος μεγ‿[
]ις· μουνω[
‿]‥[

. . . .

accurate and once the son of Leto[2] . . . it was about to . . .
those who dwelled around[3]

[2] Apollo.   [3] A reference to the Amphictyons of Delphi,
who built a new temple there circa 325 BC.

118a (118 Pf.) Oxyrhynchus papyrus (supralinear scholia)

(on 3)   a building, as it were, ordinary

(on 4)   they perfected the top

119–37 Unknown Tales

Perhaps from Book 2.

119 Scholia to Pindar, *Nemean Odes*; Scholia to Euripides, *Hecuba*; Oxyrhynchus papyrus

again to see Mecone,[1] the dwelling of the blessed ones
where the gods cast lots and first divided the honors[2] from
the time of their war with the Giants

[1] An old name for Sicyon (Strabo 8.6.25) in the northern Peloponnese, which was particularly dense with temples (Paus. 2.7.5–9, 2.9.6–11.3).   [2] In contradiction to Call. *Hymn* 1.59–64, where the narrator rejects the story of the divine lots.

120 *P.Oxy.* 2210 fr. 2

```
      .        .
  ].os.[
  ].νέω[
  ] κενα[
  ].μεν[
Κύ]πριδο[ς
    ]ων.[
  ] .α.[
.        .        .
```

121 *P.Oxy.* 2210 fr. 3

```
  .        .        .
    ].αμ[
    ]εζε.[
    ]ακ.[
.        .        .
```

122 *P. Oxy.* 2210 fr. 4

```
.        .        .
].α.[
].ει[..]..[..].[
  ]μφομεν[
].ον· εἰσότ.[
].το πίνῳ
].ος· αὐτίκ[
```

120 Oxyrhynchus papyrus

Of Cyrpis[1]

[1] Aphrodite (*Hom. Hymn* 5.1).

121 Oxyrhynchus papyrus

. . .

122 Oxyrhynchus papyrus

. . . until when . . . with dirt . . . at once . . . again . . . as when

]σε πάλιν [
]α̣ δ᾽ ὡς ὅτ[
. . . .

123 *P.Oxy.* 2210 fr. 5

. . . .
].[. . .].[
]ύφεν[
]ενεων[
]ν· ενδε[
].ν ὡσ.[
]μενη[
.[
. . . .

124 *P.Oxy.* 2210 fr. 6

. . .
]..ομ̣[
]σκα̣[
]κπο̣[
]εδρ̣[
. . . .

123 Oxyrhynchus papyrus

. . .

124 Oxyrhynchus papyrus

. . .

125 *P.Oxy.* 2210 fr. 7

```
  .      .      .      .
   ].[..].[
  ]ῳικα .θ .[
 ]κε δυσάγγελ[
  ] .κομεν[
  ] .σινενη[
  ] ..ωσαν[
  ]ωπαρε[
  ]έ .ατογ[
     ] .[
  .      .      .      .
```

126 *P.Oxy.* 2210 fr. 8

```
  .      .      .
    ]επὶν[
   ]λνομ[
  ] .πολυμ[
   ]μον[
    ] ...ρ[
  .      .      .      .
```

127 *P.Oxy.* 2210 fr. 9

```
  .      .      .
   ] .νος[
   ]δογε[
```

125 Oxyrhynchus papyrus

. . . a messenger of evil

126 Oxyrhynchus papyrus

. . .

127 Oxyrhynchus papyrus

. . .

```
      ]....[
     ]λυσε.[
    ]σσιν εφ.[
  .    .    .
```

128 *P.Oxy.* 2210 fr. 10

```
  .    .    .    .
     ]αρ..[
    ].υλη[
   ] δεῆτ..[
    ]ν..λ.[
    ]ευντε.[
    ]ηιπαν.[
   ]ντεδιάκ[
    ].πιδα[
    ].ονιε[
    ].οσσυ.[
 .    .    .
```

129 *P.Oxy.* 2210 fr. 11.a–c

129a

```
  .    .    .    .
    ]νο[
    ]υζ[
  ]σεπατ[
  ]μυκλα.[
```

332

128 Oxyrhynchus papyrus

. . .

129 Oxyrhynchus papyrus

129a

. . .

Amyclae[1]

. . .

[1] Village in Laconia south of Sparta with a sanctuary of Apollo Amyclaeus (Paus. 3.16.2).

].ηνεσ.[
  ]κμ[
. . . . .

129b

. . . . .
  ]νεμε[
  ]ιβιης[
  ]...[
. . . . .

129c

. . . . .
  ]εξ.[
 ].αθενο[
  ]θαρσα[
 ].σσητ.[
  ]αμεν[
  ].ουδ.[
. . . . .

130 *P.Oxy.* 2210 fr. 12.a–b

130a

. . . . .
  ]αν.[

334

129b

. . .

129c

. . .

130 Oxyrhynchus papyrus

130a

. . .

```
      ].ρωι [
      ]πα..[
      ]ν [
      ]..[
```
·   ·   ·   ·

130b

·   ·   ·   ·

```
   ]..[
   ]ωσενε.[
   ]νεσσιν.[
   ]ενη· [
```
·   ·   ·   ·

131 *P.Oxy.* 2210 fr. 13

·   ·   ·   ·

```
    ]σο.[
    ]κρο[
   ]ασσεσ.[
οὐ]χ ὁσίη[
```
·   ·   ·   ·

132 *P.Oxy.* 2210 fr. 14

·   ·   ·   ·

```
    ]δεκ[
    ].
```
·   ·   ·   ·

336

130b

. . .

131 Oxyrhynchus papyrus

. . . Cronus[1] . . .

[1] Titan, father of Zeus and other Olympians (Hes. *Theog.* 137–75).

132 Oxyrhynchus papyrus

. . .

133 *P.Oxy.* 2210 fr. 15

.   .   .   .

   ]ρκ[
   ]νω[

.   .   .   .

134 *P.Oxy.* 2210 fr. 17

.   .   .

    ]..[..].[
  ].[.]ηχει ·[
 ]ατας [
   ] .θει [
 ]εται
 ]νθα[
 ]μεν[
 ]ποτε.[
 ]α.λμ[
  ].[.].[

.   .   .   .

134a *P.Oxy.* 2210 fr. 18

.   .   .   .

  .[
  ζ[
  α.[
  γα[

.   .   .   .

133 Oxyrhynchus papyrus

. . .

134 Oxyrhynchus papyrus

. . . once . . .

134a Oxyrhynchus papyrus

. . .

135 *P.Oxy.* 2210 fr. 19

```
    .  .       .
    ]ῆσα[
]·   [
]οσάνξ[
      ] · [
       ].ν[
   .    .    .
```

136 *P.Oxy.* 2210 fr. 20

```
   .        .
].[ ]..κ.[
]αρζω.[
]νκ...[
  .    .    .
```

137 *P.Oxy.* 2210 fr. 21

```
   .        .
    ]νεπ[
    ]νοσ.[
    ]αρεμ[
    ]....[
  .    .    .
```

135 Oxyrhynchus papyrus

. . .

136 Oxyrhynchus papyrus

. . .

137 Oxyrhynchus papyrus

. . .

137a Epops (?)

137a (*SH* 238) 1–15, *P.Ant.* 113 fr. 1a recto

$$\cdot \quad \cdot \quad \cdot \quad \cdot \quad \cdot \quad \cdot \quad \cdot \quad \cdot$$

```
                ].[        ].[
      ..........].νανερε[..].ρμ.[
      ..........]επεφησα λιθων[.]..[.].στα[
      ..........]ειης χαῖρ' ἀ[.]έπαυσα λυρη[
 5    ..........]ο̣σηρατον[...]ρ̣[.]ω̣ε̣.[.] μουν[
      ..........].ιδων οἱ λιπαροὶ κόρακες
      ..........]πλέουσιν ἐπώπια καλὸν α[
      ..........]῎Ερατὼ δ' ἀνταπάμειπτο τά[δε·
      ......] κο[τ'] ἔκηδον ὁμώλακες..γα.ε.[
10    ....]αιανι.[.]ν ἦν ὑπὸ πάντα δόρε[ι
      ....]ς ῎Εποψ εὖτέ σφιν...δ....[
      .]ανος αἰχμηταῖς ἷκτο μ.[
      .]ναέταις Σικυῶνος επι[
      ......]ἤβα̣ι̣ι̣ὴν οὔ τι κατ.ὰ πρόφασιν
                            ].[
```

137b De paupertate (?)

Perhaps in Book 1 or 2. For the relationship of this fragment with *Iamb* 3 (*Ia*. 193 below), see Clayman 1988, 281–83. Themes in common include contrast of wealth and poverty, the gods' tardi-

AETIA: UNPLACED FRAGMENTS

137a Epops (?)

Perhaps from Book 1 or 2.

137a (*SH* 238) Antinoöpolis papyrus

. . . I agreed . . . of stones . . . farewell . . . I ceased the lyre
. . . [5] alone . . . the glossy ravens . . . watching-posts for
sailors, lovely . . . and Erato[1] answered with these words
. . . Once the neighbors were distressing . . . [10] every-
thing was under the spear . . . when Epops[2] came to them
with his warriors . . . for the inhabitants of Sicyon . . . on
no small pretext

[1] One of the Muses (Hes. *Theog.* 76–79) associated with love
stories (Ap. Rhod. 3.1–3).   [2] Perhaps Epopeus, a king of
Sicyon (Paus. 2.6.1–3), but also the hoopoe.

137b On Poverty (?)

ness or unwillingness to act, and the narrator's claim to rely on
the moral standards he had been taught earlier.

137b (*SH* 239) 1–14, *P.Ant.* 113 fr. 1b verso

. . . . .

$$
\begin{array}{l}
].\omega[.....]\pi[\\
].\omega[....]\mu a\ \dot{\rho}\upsilon\eta\phi\epsilon\nu\dot{\epsilon}s\ o[\\
].\epsilon\pi\lambda[.].\eta\ \phi\hat{\upsilon}\lambda a\ [.]\rho\epsilon\mu o\upsilon\sigma\iota\tau o[\\
]\beta a\lambda o\nu\tau o\mu\epsilon\tau[...]a\iota\phi\eta\mu\iota.[\\
\end{array}
$$

5 –∪∪ο,ὐ δῆκται τὼς κύνες εἰσὶ θ,εοί
–∪μ]ὲν οὖν ἔτι μοί τι δόμοις θο[
–∪∪]μοις αἰδὼς ἷζεν ἐπὶ βλεφ[άροις
]ιν ἐθέλεσκον ἃ μὴ μάθον ευ[..].[
]σεν δ' ἄλλο μέλος σιπύ[η]

10]νη λίπεν ὄθματα σ..τοδε[
] πῦρ ἱέναι
] ..σηχήεσσαν ἐλεγμ[ην
μ]ελαινομένη
].ε..[

. . . . .

137c Fabula Laconica (?)

137c (*SH* 240) *P.Ant.* 113 fr. 2a recto

. . . . .

...........]τ.[
..........κα.[

344

137b (*SH* 239) Antinoöpolis papyrus

the rich . . . the tribes trembled[1] . . . they were cast . . . [5]
the gods are not biters like dogs . . . while still I had some-
thing at home, shame sat upon my eyelids, and I did not
wish [to sing?] what I had not learned well . . . but the
foodbin [urged] another song . . . [10] it left my eyes . . .
this . . . to go [through] fire . . . a resounding reproof . . .
turning black

[1] See *Ia.* 203.59 for trembling Muses, who may be the subject
here.

137c A Laconian Tale (?)

Probably in Books 1 or 2. This seems to be an account of the
Partheniae, disaffected Spartan youth who founded Tarentum
(Harder vol. 2, 941–42).

137c (*SH* 240) Antinoöpolis papyrus

```
        ..........]ηβ.[..].[
   .].ε.[.........].δ.[
5    .]..δ[.........]...[
   ..........]εχα[.].σ..[
      .].[.]νδ' αυ.[..]ζη[
   ..]..τειη δ' ὑπεκυψ[
      .]..ημεν μεγάλω καιπ[
10 Σ]πάρτη δ[ί]ψιον ἄστυ γε.[
      πένθος ἐδάκρυσαν κει.[
   εὖτέ σφεων πόσιες τεκ[
      ......Ἀ]μυκλαίω κα[
15 .......]δ[..].[.]...κεδ[
      .........]μ.ιχο[
   .   .   .   .   .   .
```

137d–m Fabulae incertae

137d (*SH* 241) *P.Ant.* 113 fr. 2b verso

```
   .   .   .   .
   ]..[
   ].τιδ..[
   ]ρεφετο[
   ]νη..[
5  ]....[
   ].οπ...[
   ].ετερον
```

. . . bowed down . . . large and . . . [10] Sparta, a parched city . . . they wept with grief . . . when their husbands . . . to Amyclae[1]

[1] A town in Laconia south of Sparta associated with the rising of the Partheniae (Ant. Syr. *BNJ* 555 F 13).

137d–m Unknown Tales

Probably from Book 1 or 2.

137d (*SH* 241) Antinoöpolis papyrus

```
      ]οιτο ... τα .[
      ]νοι στόματι·
10    ]ιδον ὀπαδούσ
      ]ουσ
      ]θον ἕδρην
      ]ευθα .. ν ..
       ] .ακισεπ[ . ] .[
      .     .     .
```

137e (*SH* 242) *P.Ant.* 113 fr. 3a recto

```
      .     .     .
      ]νκωρυ[
      ] .ελειν .[
      ]εινευ .[
      ]κκειονε .[
5     ]νουτον[
      ]πλησто[
      .     .     .
```

137f (*SH* 243) *P.Ant.* 113 fr. 3b verso

```
      .     .     .
      ] .. ρ .. [
      ]τ .... [
      ] .κιδο .[
      ] .τελ .. [
      ] .ρκετο .[
       ] .[
      .     .     .
```

... the other ... [in] the mouth ... [10] ... the attendants
... seat

137e (*SH* 242) Antinoöpolis papyrus

. . .

137f (*SH* 243) Antinoöpolis papyrus

. . .

137g (*SH* 244) *P.Ant.* 113 fr. 4a recto

.   .   .   .

  ]τω.[
].ινησα[
]εινωτ᾽ εξε[
].τεφοιβε[

.   .   .   .

137h (*SH* 245) *P.Ant.* 113 fr. 4b verso

.   .   .   .

  ]
]αιναισ
].
  ].ει[

.   .   .   .

137i (*SH* 246) *P.Ant.* 113 fr. 5a recto

.   .   .   .

]
]νε
]
  ]νρα[

.   .   .   .

350

137g (*SH* 244) Antinoöpolis papyrus

. . .

137h (*SH* 245) Antinoöpolis papyrus

. . .

137i (*SH* 246) Antinoöpolis papyrus

. . .

137j (*SH* 247) *P.Ant*. 113 fr. 5b verso

```
  .   .   .   .
].[
]π[
]νω[
]οσ[
  .   .   .
```

137k (*SH* 248) *P.Ant*. 113 fr. 6a recto

```
  .   .   .   .
].[
] ακτι[
]
  .   .   .
```

137l (*SH* 249) *P.Ant*. 113 fr. 6b verso

```
  .   .   .
] ͵εδει[
]μουπ[
  .   .   .
```

137m (*SH* 253 1–2) [Plut.] *Cons. ad Apoll.* 26 (*Mor.* 115a); 2–16, *P.Sorb.* inv. 2248 fr. 2

```
  .   .   .   .   .   .
```
⌞† τοιάδε θνητοῖσι κακὰ κακῶν † ἀμφί τε κῆρες⌟
  ⌞εἰλε⌞ῦν⌞τ⌞αι· κ⌞ενε⌟ ἢ δ᾽ εἴσδυσ⌞ις οὐδ᾽ ἀθέρι⌟

137j (*SH* 247) Antinoöpolis papyrus

. . .

137k (*SH* 248) Antinoöpolis papyrus

. . .

137l (*SH* 249) Antinoöpolis papyrus

. . .

137m (*SH* 253 1–2) Pseudo-Plutarch, *Consolation to Apollonius*; Sorbonne papyrus

Such things for mortals are the evils of evils and the demons of death swarm around. Entrance is fruitless, even

```
   ...]υκ[.]ο.[....].ων επιχει[
      ...]ν.[.].ε.[....].αμμινα.[
5  ...]η...........ο...ρυ.[
      ...]νοδ...ο.....υ.[
   ...]υμε..ου........[
      ....]ρουχευ.......υ...η[
   ...]ν.. σεδαησ......[
10    ...]....  ἀνθρωποισε....[
   ...].εταις ἀγαπητὸν ἐνυπν[ι
      αἰεὶ, τοῖς μικκοῖς μικκὰ διδ.οῦσι θεοί
   ...]εω τὸν ὄνειρον.[].ε.[
      ...].μενος Μουσέων ει.[
15 ...]αρ ὁππότ᾽ ἔληξε θεῆς.[
      ...].μ.....μα......[
```

138–74 Fabulae incertae

138 *P.Oxy.* 2212 fr. 3

```
   .   .    .   .
      ]  [
      ]δον [
      ].πετα[
      ]ατον[
        ].[
   .   .    .   .
```

for pollen. . . . you learned [10] . . . for people . . . beloved in sleep . . . Always the gods give small things to the small . . . . the dream[1] . . . of the Muses . . . [15] when [the voice] of the goddess ceased.[2]

[1] Perhaps a reference to Callimachus' programmatic dream of the Muses in *Aet*. 1.2 above.

[2] Apparently a programmatic piece from the end of Book 2 (Harder vol. 2, 945–46; Massimilla 1996, 366–68).

138–74 Unknown Tales

Probably from Book 3.

138 Oxyrhynchus papyrus

. . .

139 *P.Oxy.* 2212 fr. 6

.   .   .   .   .

  ] ωρ[
  ] με[
  ] με[
  ] τοι.[
  ] εν[
  ] λο[

.   .   .   .   .

139a *P.Oxy.* 2212 fr. 7

.   .   .   .   .

  ].ι [
  ] [

.   .   .   .   .

140 *P.Oxy.* 2212 fr. 8

.   .   .   .

        ]ζ[
      ] θ.[
      ] α.[
      ]φ[

.   .   .   .

139 Oxyrhynchus papyrus

. . .

139a Oxyrhynchus papyrus

. . .

140 Oxyrhynchus papyrus

. . .

141 *P.Oxy.* 2212 fr. 9

.　　.　　.　　.

　　]εσ[
　　].α.[

.　　.　　.　　.

142 *P.Oxy.* 2212 fr. 10

.　　.　　.　　.

　　].γρε[
　　].ν

.　　.　　.

143 *P.Oxy.* 2212 fr. 11

.　　.　　.

　　]αρήϊα.[
　　]νοσυ[
　　]μαχ.[
　　]εκρη[
　　].ε[

.　　.　　.

144 *P.Oxy.* 2212 fr. 12

.　　.　　.

　　]ηντελ.[
　　]..τη.[

.　　.　　.

141 Oxyrhynchus papyrus

. . .

142 Oxyrhynchus papyrus

. . .

143 Oxyrhynchus papyrus

. . .

144 Oxyrhynchus papyrus

. . .

145 *P.Oxy.* 2212 fr. 13

.   .   .
   ].ων·[
    ]κοῦσα[
   ]ῳν
   ].̣[
.   .   .   .

146 *P.Oxy.* 2212 fr. 14

.   .   .
   ]άδην[
.   .   .

147 *P.Oxy.* 2212 fr. 15

.   .   .
   ]να.[
.   .   .

148 *P.Oxy.* 2212 fr. 16

.   .   .
   ]λα.[
   ].ττ[
    ]σω[
.   .   .

145 Oxyrhynchus papyrus

. . .

146 Oxyrhynchus papyrus

. . .

147 Oxyrhynchus papyrus

. . .

148 Oxyrhynchus papyrus

. . .

149 *P.Oxy.* 2212 fr. 17

.   .   .   .

    ]. .[
    ]ῢλλο[
     ]υ.[

.   .   .   .

150 *P.Oxy.* 2212 fr. 20

.   .   .   .

    ]νεσθαι.[
    ]πεπλο[
  ]νισονται.[
  ]ἀλλἐπιμε[

.   .   .   .

151 1–3, *P.Oxy.* 2212 fr. 27; 4–6, *P.Oxy.* 2212 fr. 21

.   .   .   .

μ[
οφ[
ν.[
αἶψα δομο[
ὀφθαλμοὺς [
ὡς ἔχ᾽ ἐπωφ.[
]ηπ[

.   .   .   .

149 Oxyrhynchus papyrus

. . .

150 Oxyrhynchus papyrus

. . . robe . . .

151 Oxyrhynchus papyrus

. . . quickly home . . . eyes . . . so it is . . . help . . .

152 *P.Oxy.* 2212 fr. 22

.   .   .   .

  ]χειρα[
  ]τοπον[
  ]ντος [
  ]   [
  ]μησασθαι [
    ].
          ].[

.   .   .   .

153 *P.Oxy.* 2212 fr. 23

.   .   .   .

      ] [
  ]   [
  ]   [
  ]   [
]ρυσσεν[
  ]   [

.   .   .   .

154 *P.Oxy.* 2212 fr. 24

.   .   .

  ] αιν[
  ] αιν[
  ] γαια[

152 Oxyrhynchus papyrus

hand . . . a place . . . to represent

153 Oxyrhynchus papyrus

. . .

154 Oxyrhynchus papyrus

terrible . . . terrible . . . earth

```
]  στε.[
]  ου[
  ].ἀ[
```
.   .   .   .

155 *P.Oxy*. 2212 fr. 25

.   .   .   .

```
]ειτοπ[
  ]νῶ..[
```
.   .   .   .

156 *P.Oxy*. 2212 fr. 26

.   .   .   .

```
]ρὴ[
]υ.[
```
.   .   .   .

157 Pf.   = *Aet*. 151

158 *P.Oxy*. 2213 fr. 3

.   .   .   .

```
].η[
].χο[
]κοδ[
```
.   .   .   .

AETIA: UNPLACED FRAGMENTS

155 Oxyrhynchus papyrus

. . .

156 Oxyrhynchus papyrus

. . .

157 Pf. = *Aetia* 151

158 Oxyrhynchus papyrus

. . .

159 *P.Oxy.* 2213 fr. 4

.   .   .   .
]σειδα.[
]ναυ[
.   .   .   .

160 *P.Oxy.* 2213 fr. 5

.   .   .   .
   ]κο[
  ]μαρ.[
] .ολλ.[
] εγεν.[
] .οιτόν[
]εκυμαλ[
.   .   .   .

161 *P.Oxy.* 2213 fr. 6

.   .   .   .
  ]κο.[
  ]ηρα[
.   .   .   .

159 Oxyrhynchus papyrus

Poseidon . . .

160 Oxyrhynchus papyrus

. . .

161 Oxyrhynchus papyrus

. . .

162 *P.Oxy.* 2213 fr. 10

. . .
ἔ]δεθλον
  ]ε̣.
]ος ἔοις κε̣
πτ]έρυγι·
    ]. αλλων
    ].
        ]ε̣χο[
. . .

163 *P.Oxy.* 2213 fr. 12

. . .
   ].β.[
]Φοίβῳ τ[
  ].ον μ[
. . .

164 *P.Oxy.* 2213 fr. 13

. . .
].ασωσ.[
].ερων[
]αντεχ[
 ]βου[
. . .

162 Oxyrhynchus papyrus

. . . a shrine . . . may you be . . . [on] a wing . . . of others

163 Oxyrhynchus papyrus

. . . To Phoebus

164 Oxyrhynchus papyrus

. . .

165 *P.Oxy.* 2213 fr. 14

.   .   .   .
]κατ[
].ης· [
.   .   .   .

166 *P.Oxy.* 2213 fr. 15

.   .   .   .
            ].[
ἀχρὴς δ' ἀνέ.παλτ.ο
        ]τις ὅτ[
        ] εἴ κοτ' [
.   .   .   .

167 *P.Oxy.* 2213 fr. 16

.   .   .   .
    ].ισα.[
  ].ον μεσσ[
  ] τεθμός οκ[
  ]ραισεν π[

.   .   .   .

165 Oxyrhynchus papyrus

. . .

166 Oxyrhynchus papyrus

. . . he sprang up, pale . . . . . . when . . . if ever

167 Oxyrhynchus papyrus

. . . custom

168 *P.Oxy.* 2213 fr. 18

.   .   .   .

```
        ]...[
      ]πτην[
      ]επαισαρ[
5    ]_πολιη[
      ]_ητελ_[
      ]απηρν[
       ]_σεμ[
         ]εγαλ[
```

.   .   .   .

169 *P.Oxy.* 2213 fr. 19

.   .   .

```
      ]ν_[
      ]ενη[
      ]ηκου[
5    ]_γ᾽ ουθε_[
      ]ιποπτο[
      ]μενω[
       ]η__[
```

.   .   .   .

168 Oxyrhynchus papyrus

. . . gray . . . holy

169 Oxyrhynchus papyrus

. . . not

170 *P.Oxy.* 2213 fr. 20

```
   .      .        .
      ]ετ.[
      ]ηκα[
   .      .        .
```

171 *P.Oxy.* 2213 fr. 21

```
   .      .        .
      ]αν[
      ]ουκ[
   ]οπ.[
   ] δε[
   .      .        .
```

172 *P.Oxy.* 2213 fr. 22

```
   .   .      .        .
].[.].[
  ]κατη.[
    ].ισ
      ]εσθαι[
        ]    [
        ]    [
   .      .        .
```

170 Oxyrhynchus papyrus

. . .

171 Oxyrhynchus papyrus

. . . not

172 Oxyrhynchus papyrus

. . .

173 *P. Oxy.* 2213 fr. 23

```
  .     .   .    .
        ].[
        ].δο[
        ]ο[
       ][ ]στ[
5      ] ..ν[
       ][ ]τ[
  .     .   .    .
```

174 *P.Oxy.* 2213 fr. 24

```
  .     .   .    .
   ]    ανερ[
   ]     ηρ[
   ]     οι[
    ]    ..[
  .     .   .
```

175 Fabula incerta

175 *P.Oxy.* 2170 fr. 4

```
  .     .   .    .
    ].βε[..]ο.[
    ]ο.[..]νος[
    ].ν π[.].εβο.[
    ].α..μ.ον[
```

378

173 Oxyrhynchus papyrus

. . .

174 Oxyrhynchus papyrus

. . . the man . . .

175 Unknown Tale

Perhaps from Book 4.

175 Oxyrhynchus papyrus

]ν[.]ο[.]κεατου[
]πυρκαϊῆς   [
]ναμα κεδνη[
]..νανει [
]αλλ.ναμ[

.   .   .   .   .

176 Pf. = *Aet*. 54b.21–34

177 Pf. = *Aet*. 54c

178–85b Icus

178 1–34, *P.Oxy*. 1362 fr. 1 col. I (1–25) et col. II (26–34);
11–14, Ath. 11.477c; 11–12, Ath. 10.442f; 15–16, Ath.
1.32b–c; 32–34, Stob. 4.17.11; 33–34, Schol. ad Arat.
Phaen. 299

ἠὼς οὐδὲ πιθοιγὶς ἐλάνθανεν οὐδ' ὅτε δούλοις
    ἦμαρ Ὀρέστειοι λευκὸν ἄγουσι χόες·
Ἰκαρίου καὶ παιδὸς ἄγων ἐπέτειον ἀγιστύν,
    Ἀτθίσιν οἰκτίστη, σὸν φάος, Ἠριγόνη,

---

¹ Festival celebrating the opening of jars of new wine (Pha-
nodemus of Athens, *BNJ* 325 F 12).   ² The festival of the
Choes, the wine pitchers, offered special liberties for slaves

. . . he lay where . . . from the pyre . . . with care

176 Pf. = *Aetia* 54b.21–34

177 Pf. = *Aetia* 54c

178–85b Icus

Perhaps the Proem of Book 2 (Harder vol. 2, 956–57).

178 Oxyrhynchus papyrus; Athenaeus, *The Learned Banqueters*; Stobaeus; Scholia to Aratus, *Phaenomena*

The day of the Pithoegia[1] did not escape his notice, nor the time when the pitchers of Orestes[2] bring a bright day[3] for the slaves. And carrying out the annual ceremony of the daughter of Icarius, your day, Erigone,[4] lady pitied by

(Schol. ad Hes. *Op.* 368). For Orestes' role in the founding of the ritual, in which guests drank from their own pitchers in solitude, see Eur. *IT* 949–60.   [3] A holiday, as in *Iamb* 1 (*Ia.* 191.37).

[4] The Aiora, celebrated at Athens honoring Erigone, daughter of Icarius, who was killed by drunken peasants. When his daughter found his body, she hanged herself in grief, along with other Attic women made mad by Dionysus (Apollod. *Bibl.* 3.14.7).

5 ἐς δαίτην ἐκάλεσσεν ὁμηθέας, ἐν δέ νυ τοῖσι
   ξεῖνον ὃς Ἀ[ἰ]γύπτῳ καινὸς ἀνεστρέφετο
   μεμβλωκὼς ἴδιόν τι κατὰ χρέος· ἦν δὲ γενέθλην
   Ἴκιος, ᾧ ξυνὴν εἶχον ἐγὼ κλισίην
   οὐκ ἐπιτάξ, ἀλλ᾿ αἶνος Ὁμηρικός, αἰὲν ὁμοῖον
10 ὡς θεός, οὐ ψευδής, ἐς τὸν ὁμοῖον ἄγει.
   καὶ γὰρ ὁ Θρηϊκίην μὲν ἀπέστυγε χανδὸν ἄμυστιν
   ζωροποτεῖν, ὀλίγῳ δ᾿ ἥδετο κισσυβίῳ.
   τῷ μὲν ἐγὼ τάδ᾿ ἔλεξα περιστείχοντος ἀλείσου
   τὸ τρίτον, εὖτ᾿ ἐδάην οὔνομα καὶ γενεήν·
15 "ἦ μάλ᾿ ἔπος τόδ᾿ ἀληθές, ὅ τ᾿ οὐ μόνον ὕδατος
   αἶσαν,
   ἀλλ᾿ ἔτι καὶ λέσχης[1] οἶνος ἔχειν ἐθέλει.
   τὴν ἡμεῖς—οὐκ ἐν γ[ὰ]ρ ἀρυστήρεσσι φορεῖται
   οὐδέ μιν εἰς ἀτ[ενεῖ]ς ὀφρύας οἰνοχόων
   αἰτήσεις ὁρόω[ν] ὅτ᾿ ἐλεύθερος ἀτμένα σαίνει—
20 βάλλωμεν χαλεπῷ φάρμακον ἐν πόματι,
   Θεύγενες· ὅσσ[α] δ᾿ ἐμεῖο σ[έ]θεν πάρα θυμὸς
   ἀκοῦσαι
   ἰχαίνει, τάδε μοι λ[έ]ξον [ἀνειρομέν]ῳ·
   Μυρμιδόνων ἐσσῆνα τ[ί πάτριον ὕ]μμι σέβεσθαι
   Πηλέα, κῶς Ἴκῳ ξυν[ὰ τὰ Θεσσαλι]κά,
25 τεῦ δ᾿ ἕνεκεν γήτειον ιδ[. .]υτ[. . . .]ρτον ἔχουσα
   ἥρως κα[θ]όδου πα[ῖς
   εἰδότες ὡς ἐνέπου[σιν
   κείνην ἢ περὶ σὴν [

---

[1] Hapax legomenon, *Od.* 18.328

Attic women, [5] he invited some like-minded friends to a feast, and among them was a stranger newly visiting Egypt, having come on some personal business. By birth he was an Ician[5] and I shared a couch with him, not by design, but the saying of Homer[6] is not false, [10] that a god always brings like to like. For he hated chugging neat wine in a long Thracian[7] gulp, but enjoyed a small cup.

And I said this to him, as the bowl went around for the third time and I had learned his name and family: [15] "The saying is true, that wine likes its portion not only of water but of conversation too. Which—for it is not offered in pints, nor by looking at the obstinate expression of the wine pourers would you ask for it, a free man fawning on a slave[8]—[20] let us toss in as a drug against the tiresome drinking, Theogenes.[9] And what my heart longs to hear from you, please tell me as I ask:

Why is it a tradition for your countrymen to worship the king of the Myrmidons, Peleus?[10] What has Thessaly in common with Icus? [25] And why does the girl with an onion . . . at the descent of the hero . . . as those who know

---

[5] Icos, an island opposite the coast of Magnesia.

[6] A restatement of Hom. *Od.* 17.218, where Melanthius, one of the suitors, introduces Odysseus, who is disguised as a beggar, to the swineherd Eumaeus.　　[7] Thracians and other northern peoples were associated with excessive drinking (Pl. *Leg.* 637d–e).　　[8] A reversal of usual roles that is associated with the festival of the Choes (D'Alessio 2007, vol. 2, 558n20).

[9] The stranger's name revealed here for the first time.

[10] Peleus, king of the Myrmidons, was the father of Achilles (Hom. *Il.* 1.1).

οὔθ᾽ ἑτέρην ἔγνωκα· τ[
30   οὔατα μυθεῖσθαι βου‚λομέν[οις ἀνέχων."
τ[αῦτ᾽] ἐμέθεν λέξαντο[ς
    "τ‚ρισ‚μάκαρ, ἦ παύρων ὄ‚λβιός ἐσσι μέτα,
ναυτι‚λίης εἰ νῆιν ἔ‚χεις βίον· ἀλλ᾽ ἐμὸς αἰών
    κύμασιν‚ α‚ἰ‚θυίης μᾶ‚λλον ἐσῳκίσατο."

179 *P.Oxy.* 1362 fr. 2

 .   .   .   .
  ].ευτ[
  ]ην[
  ]ργερ.[
  ]ομη[
  ].νεσσ[
  ].ιπα.[
  ]ρτροι[
  ].[
 .   .   .   .   .

180 *P.Oxy.* 1362 fr. 3

 .   .   .   .
  ]
  ]ακα κεῖθ[εν
  ]ν
 .   .   .   .   .

speak . . . that . . . around your . . . nor do I know another
. . . [30] holding out my ears toward those wishing to tell
a story." And after I said these things, "Thrice blessed, and
lucky as few are, if you lead a life ignorant of seafaring![11]
But my lot is lived more on the waves than the bird called
a shearwater."

[11] This has wrongly been read as proof that Callimachus him-
self never left Africa, but see Introduction.

179 Oxyrhynchus papyrus

. . .

180 Oxyrhynchus papyrus

. . . from there

181 *P.Oxy.* 1362 fr. 4

. . . . . .
..[
καὶ δι[
πληγ[
δείελο[
καί μιν ἀπο[
αὐλίον ὀθν[ει
. . . . . .

182 *P.Oxy.* 1362 fr. 5

. . . . .
ἐ]τείχισαν [
]τέρῳ γο[
]λως κακ[
] ́κε ληθ[
. . . . .

183 (183 Pf. + Add. Pf. vol. 1, p. 504) *P.Oxy.* 1362, ed. Lobel ap. Pf.

. . . .
]αοι βασι[λ
] νε αφν[
]δ᾽ ἡμετε[ρ
]ναος[
] κεν[
] βορε[

181 Oxyrhynchus papyrus

and . . . struck . . . evening . . . and him . . . sheepfold . . . foreign

182 Oxyrhynchus papyrus

they walled up . . . evil

183 (183 Pf. + Add. Pf. vol. 1, p. 504) Oxyrhynchus papyrus

king . . . our . . . the North Wind

]ιοι[

. . . . . .

184 Ammon. *Diff.* 498 (p. 129.1 Nickau)

οὐδ' ἔτι τὴν Φθίων εἶχεν ἀνακτορίην

185 Hsch. ι 469 Latte s.v. Ἰκιάδες

Ἰκιάδες (?)

185a Schol. BDEGQ ad Pind. *Pyth.* 3.166

καὶ τοὺς Κρόνου παῖδας βασιλεῖς ἐθεάσαντο ἐν ταῖς
χρυσαῖς καθέδραις, καὶ δῶρα παρ' αὐτῶν ἐδέξαντο.
ἀλλ' ὅμως, φησί, καὶ οὗτοι ἄπταιστον οὐκ ηὐτύχησαν
βίον. ὁ μὲν γὰρ Κάδμος εἰς ὄφιν μεταβαλὼν ἀπέθα-
νεν, ὁ δὲ [Πηλεὺς] ἐν Ἴκῳ τῇ νήσῳ ἀτυχήσας τὸν
βίον οἰκτρῶς καὶ ἐπωδύνως ἀπέθανεν, ὡς καὶ ὁ Καλ-
λίμαχος μαρτυρεῖ.

184 Ammonius, *On the Differences of Synonymous Expressions*

no longer did he[1] have sovereignty over the Phthians

[1] Peleus, who had been king of Phthia, but after the Trojan War he was exiled by Acastus and shipwrecked at Icus on his way to join his grandson Neoptolemus (Schol. ad Pind. *Pyth.* 3.166).

185 Hesychius

Iciades ("the children of Icus") . . .

185a Scholia to Pindar, *Pythian Odes*

[Cadmus and Peleus] saw the royal children of Cronus[1] on their golden seats, and received gifts from them. But all the same he says that even these men did not enjoy consistent good fortune in their lives. For Cadmus[2] died after being changed into a snake, and the other perished on the island of Icus after suffering pitiful and painful misfortune in his life, as Callimachus attests.

[1] Titan, father of Zeus (Hes. *Theog.* 467–500).   [2] First king of Thebes and culture hero who killed a dragon guarding the Isthmian spring and was himself turned into a snake (Eur. *Bacch.* 1330–39).

185b Ath. 11.477c

Καλλίμαχος . . . λέγων ἐπὶ τοῦ Ἰκίου ξένου τοῦ παρὰ
τῷ Ἀθηναίῳ Πόλλιδι συνεστιασθέντος αὐτῷ

186–186a Hyperborei

The *aition* apparently explains why the sacrifices for Delian
Apollo that were once brought to the island by Hyperborean girls
were later transported by a new system of exchange between

186 1–33, *P.Oxy.* 2214; 9, Schol. ad Ap. Rhod. 4.282–91b

```
].  βρεχμὸν¹ γὰρ ἐπώμοσας ὅττι μεγι[στ
        ]..῾π.νόης νέποδες
     ]σιν ἐτήσια, σὺν δ[ε]κ[α]τ[α]ίῳ
     ]ουσιν δῖα πέτευρα [φόρ]ῳ
5                  ]..[..]ελε..σ[
     ].. δισσ[ά]κι Λητοΐδ.[
         π]αρὲκ θέμιν ἔδρακε.[
     ].ν υἷες Ὑπερβορέων
   Ῥιπαίο.ν πέμπουσιν ἀπ᾽ οὔρεος, ἧχι .μάλιστα
10    τέρπουσιν λιπ.αραὶ Φοῖβον ὀνοσφαγίαι.·
   Ἑλλήν]ων τά γε πρῶτα Πελασγικο.[
     ἐξ Ἀριμα]σπείης δειδέχαται κο[μ]ι[δῆς
        ] ἐπὶ πτόλιάς τε καὶ οὔ[ρεα
     ]υσιν Νάου θῆτες² α̣[
```

¹ Hapax legomenon, *Il.* 5.586   ² Hapax legomenon, *Od.*
4.644

185b Athenaeus, *The Learned Banqueters*

Callimachus . . . speaking of the stranger from Icus who was dining with him at the home of the Athenian Pollis.

186–186a The Hyperboreans

neighboring states after the girls did not return one year (Hdt. 4.33–35; Call. *Hymn* 4.283–99).

186 Oxyrhynchus papyrus; Scholia to Apollonius of Rhodes, *Argonautica*

After swearing by his head, which is the greatest [oath] . . . descendants of . . . yearly, with a tribute of tithes on wooden planks . . . [6] twice to the son of Leto . . . he acted against the law . . . the sons of the Hyperboreans send them[1] from the Rhipaean mountain,[2] where especially [10] rich ass-sacrifices please Apollo. The Pelasgians[3] first of the Greeks . . . receive [the gifts] from the Arimaspean[4] conveyance . . . to cities and mountains . . . servants of Zeus

---

[1] The sacrifices that were sent in a relay from people to people until they reached Delos.   [2] Mountains to the far north of Greece associated with the Hyperboreans (Hellanicus of Lesbos *BNJ* 4 F 187b; Ap. Rhod. 4.286–87). The departure point for the journey.   [3] Who dwell in Dodona (Hdt. 4.33.1), the second stage of the relay.   [4] Another reference to the Hyperboreans, who were confused with the Arimaspi (Call. *Hymn* 4.291; Steph. Byz. α 423 Billerbeck s.v. Arimaspoi).

15   ].τις φηγοῦ[.].μεδ[´
        ]...[
        ].σ δ᾽ ἐξ[
        ]ον ἀκρο..[..].[
        ]σ ἀνάγουσιν, ἀτὰρ.[
20   ]οτ᾽ ὀφρυόειν Ἴλιον[
        ].ου πίνοντες ἀφ᾽ ὕδατ[ος
        ].π..[....]ις Ἀν[τ]ιόπ[η
             ]. ἀμοιβαδὶ[σ..].[
              ] ἔχεν ἐννᾳέτα[ς
25   ]ν χάριν οὐκ ἐδύναν[τ]ο
           ]ατι λιχνο[τά]τῳ·
          ]παραπλω[.]σ.[.] ἀμάλλης
             ].μα πέρι
          ] ἀναιδέος ὄθμ[α]τος ἄλκα[ρ
30   ]ν ἔπαυσε θεή
        ].σα Διὸς κεμαδοσσόε [κο]ύρη
         ].[   ]εμ[.]
             ] γενέθλῃ

186a *P.Oxy.* 2214 (marg. sup et inf.)

        ]...[
        ]..[
    ]..[
    ].[ ]κ[   ]αν.[...].[
5 ...[.]νλεπ[...]π.δεαι...[
      ...[..]π..καιπλει.δ..[
]λιην.[.].κ..ων

Naeus[5] . . . [15] of the oak[6] . . . from . . . the height . . . they bring . . . [20] Ilium on the edge of a steep rock . . . drinking from the water of the . . . Antiope[7] . . . in turn[8] . . . inhabitants . . . [25] a favor . . . they were not able . . . the most lewd . . . sail by . . . a sheaf . . . around . . . defense against the shameless eye . . . [30] the goddess stopped . . . the daughter of Zeus who rouses the deer[9] . . . family

[5] Who presided over the sanctuary at Dodona (Dem. 21.53).
[6] The oracular tree that was consulted at Dodona.
[7] Probably the Amazon Antiope (Ap. Rhod. 2.385–87).
[8] In reference to the handing over of the sacrifices (Massimilla 1996, 427).
[9] Artemis in her capacity as huntress (Call. *Hymn* 3.15–17).

186a Oxyrhynchus papyrus (marginal notes)

. . .

CALLIMACHUS

187–90 Fabulae incertae

187 Clem. Alex. *Protr.* 2.38.2

Ἄρτεμιν δὲ Ἀρκάδες Ἀπαγχομένην καλουμένην προσ-
τρέπονται, ὥς φησι Καλλίμαχος ἐν Αἰτίοις. καὶ Κον-
δυλῖτις ἐν Μηθύμνῃ ἑτέρα τετίμηται Ἄρτεμις

188

a Schol. ss³s⁴ ad Lyc. *Alex.* 570

Σταφύλου τοῦ υἱοῦ Διονύσου θυγάτηρ γίνεται Ῥοιώ·
ταύτῃ ἐμίγη Ἀπόλλων. αἰσθόμενος δὲ ὁ Στάφυλος
ἔβαλεν αὐτὴν εἰς λάρνακα καὶ ἀφῆκε κατὰ τὴν θά-
λασσαν. ἡ δὲ προσεπελάσθη τῇ Εὐβοίᾳ καὶ ἐγέννη-
σεν αὐτόθι περί τι ἄντρον παῖδα, ὃν Ἄνιον ἐκάλεσε
διὰ τὸ ἀνιαθῆναι αὐτὴν δι᾽ αὐτόν. τοῦτον δὲ Ἀπόλλων
ἤνεγκεν εἰς Δῆλον, ὃς γήμας Δωρίππην ἐγέννησε τὰς
Οἰνοτρόπους Οἰνώ, Σπερμώ, Ἐλαΐδα αἷς ὁ Διόνυσος
ἐχαρίσατο, ὁπότε βούλονται, σπέρμα λαμβάνειν. Φε-
ρεκύδης δέ φησιν ὅτι Ἄνιος ἔπεισε τοὺς Ἕλληνας
παραγενομένους πρὸς αὐτὸν αὐτοῦ μένειν τὰ θ᾽ ἔτη·
δεδόσθαι δὲ αὐτοῖς παρὰ τῶν θεῶν τῷ [10] δεκάτῳ ἔτει
πορθῆσαι τὴν Ἴλιον, ὑπέσχετο δὲ αὐτοῖς ὑπὸ τῶν
θυγατέρων αὐτοῦ τραφήσεσθαι· ἔστι δὲ τοῦτο καὶ

187–90 Unknown Tales

187 Clement of Alexandria, *Protrepticus*

The Arcadians supplicate the Artemis who is called "strangled,"[1] as Callimachus says in the *Aetia*. And another Artemis, "Condylitis," is honored in Methymna.[2]

[1] Some children put a rope around the neck of a statue of Artemis Condylitis and said that she was strangled. The people stoned them to death, but then when all their babies were stillborn they asked the oracle at Delphi for a remedy and were told to honor the children as heroes and call the goddess "strangled" (Paus. 8.23.6–7).   [2] A city in northwest Lesbos.

188

a Scholia to Lycophron, *Alexandra*

Rhoeo was the daughter of Staphylus, son of Dionysus. Apollo had sex with her and when her father Staphylus became aware of it, he cast her into a box and threw it into the sea. She was brought to Euboea, and there near a cave gave birth to a child whom she called Anius on account of her suffering through him. And Apollo brought him into Delos, and he married Dorippe and begot Oenotropes Oeno, Spermo, and Elais. And to these Dionysus granted the favor of producing seeds whenever they wished. Pherecydes[1] says that Anius persuaded the Greeks who had come to him to stay there for nine years; that it was given to them by the gods that Ilium would be taken in the tenth year, and he promised that they would be fed by his daugh-

[1] Pherecydes of Athens (5th c. BC), historian and genealogist (*BNJ* 3 F 140).

παρὰ τῷ τὰ Κύπρια πεποιηκότι. μέμνηται δὲ καὶ
Καλλίμαχος τῶν Ἀνίου θυγατέρων ἐν τοῖς Αἰτίοις.

b Schol. ss[3] ad Lyc. *Alex.* 580

αἱ Οἰνότροποι ἐκαλοῦντο Οἰνώ, Σπερμώ, Ἐλαΐς. αὗται
ἔλαβον παρὰ Διονύσου δῶρον, ἵνα, ὅτε θελήσουσι,
καρπὸν τρυγῶσι, καὶ ἡ μὲν Οἰνὼ τὴν οἶνον ἐποίει, ἡ
δὲ Σπερμὼ τὰ σπέρματα, τὸ ἔλαιον δὲ ἡ Ἐλαΐς. αὗται
καὶ τοὺς Ἕλληνας λιμώττοντας ἐλθοῦσαι εἰς Τροίαν
διέσωσαν. μαρτυρεῖ δὲ ταῦτα καὶ Καλλίμαχος.

189 Serv. ad Verg. *Aen.* 1.408

Maiorum enim haec fuerat salutatio, cuius rei *αἴτιον*, id
est causam, Varro, Callimachum secutus, exposuit, adse-
rens omnem eorum honorem dexterarum constitisse vir-
tute.

190

a Serv. ad Verg. *Aen.* 7.778

exponit τὸ *αἴτιον*: nam Callimachus scripsit Αἴτια, in qui-
bus etiam hoc commemorat.

ters. And this is poeticized in the *Cypria*.[2] And Callimachus recalls the daughters of Anius in the *Aetia*.

[2] One of the "cyclic" epics in the Trojan cycle, which told the story from the origin of the Trojan War to the beginning of the *Iliad*. It is dated roughly to the second half of the sixth century BC and attributed to Stasinus or Hegesias of Cyprus. Thirty-one fragments are extant. On this incident, see fr. 26 West.

b Scholia to Lycophron, *Alexandra*

The Oenotropi are called Oeno, Spermo, and Elais. They received a gift from Dionysus so that when they wished they could harvest fruit and Oeno made wine and Spermo, seeds, and Elais, olive oil. And they came to Troy and saved the Greeks who were starving. Callimachus also testifies to these things.

189 Servius on Virgil, *Aeneid*

For this was the salutation of the ancestors whose *aition*, (that is, the cause) this Varro explained following Callimachus, declaring that their every honor was established by virtue of their right hands.

190

a Servius on Virgil, *Aeneid*

He explains the *aetion*:[1] for Callimachus wrote the *Aetia*, in which he does indeed mention this.

[1] When Hippolytus, the son of Theseus, denied the erotic advances of his stepmother, Phaedra, she accused him of sexually assaulting him, and his father put him to death (Eur. *Hipp.*). The story of his resurrection was told by Virgil (*Aen.* 7.761–69).

b Schol. G ad Ov. *Ib.* 279

tangit fabulam de Hippolyto, unde Callimachus: 'noluit
Hippolytus Phaedrae violare pudorem, et quia noluerat,
habuit pro munere mortem. sed qui recta facit quod in
aeternum moriatur, denegat Hippolytus, qui vitae bis re-
paratur.'

190a–c Teuthis

190a (*SH* 276) 1–14 et 17–20 (fin.), *P.Oxy.* 14; 4, *P.Oxy.*
2221 col. II, 17; 5–15 (init.), *P.Mich.* inv. 4761c

. . . .

$$\qquad]ης\ ἀντὶ\ γεωτομίης·$$
$$\Gamma λαύ]κῳ\ Λυκίῳ,\ ὅτε\ σιφλὸς\ ἐπει[$$
$$ἀνθ'\ ἑκατομβοί]ων\ ἐννεάβοια^1\ λαβεῖν$$
$$σ]μινύην\ πέλεκυν\ μετα\ .\ [$$
5 $$..]υροφ....δήκτην\ ἀμφοτέρῳ\ στόμα[τι$$
$$ὡ]ς\ ἀντὶ\ σκαπανῆος\ ὀροιτύπος\ ἐργάζη[$$
$$τ]οῖον\ ἐπεὶ\ κείνης\ ὀκριόειν\ ἔδαφος$$
$$γ]αίης·\ οὔτε\ βάλοις\ κεν\ ἐνὶ\ σπόρον\ οὔτ'\ ἐν[ὶ\ κλῆμα,$$
$$δ]οιὰ\ Μεθυμναίου\ δῶρα\ κυθηγενέος·$$
10 $$ἀγρ[ι]άδας\ δ'\ οὐκ\ ἄλλο\ σαρωνίδας\ οὖδας\ ενε[$$
$$.ω.\ φορον\ Ἀζάνων\ δαῖτα\ παλαιοτάτην·$$

¹ Hapax legomenon, *Il.* 6.236

b Scholia to Ovid, *Ibis*

He touches on the story of Hippolytus. From Callimachus: Hippolytus was unwilling to violate the purity of Phaedra, and because he was unwilling, he had death for a reward. But Hippolytus denies the notion that whoever acts uprightly dies eternally, for he was restored twice to life.

190a–c Teuthis

Probably from Book 1.

190a (*SH* 276) Oxyrhynchus papyrus; Michigan papyrus

. . . instead of tilling the earth. Then Glaucus of Lycia, when soft in the head, accepted [armor worth] nine oxen for armor worth a hundred.[1] . . . a hoe in exchange for an ax . . . [5] a biter with a mouth on both sides . . . work as a cutter instead of a digger . . . so rugged is the soil in that land. Neither could you toss seed on it, nor plant a vine shoot, the two gifts of the Methymnian[2] who was born in secret.[3] . . . [10] no other ground . . . wild oaks. . . . the tribute . . . the most ancient meal[4] of the Azani.[5] From

---

[1] Referring to Hom. *Il.* 6.234–36, where Glaucus was induced to exchange his golden armor for Diomedes' bronze.

[2] Dionysus. Methymna, a city on Lesbos famous for the abundance of its grapevines (Ov. *Ars am.* 1.57).   [3] Zeus concealed Dionysus' birth from his jealous wife, Hera, and carried the baby in his own thigh (*Hymn. Hom. Dion.* 1.7–8; Eur. *Bacch.* 94–98).   [4] Acorns, the proverbial meal of the ancient Arcadians (Hdt. 1.66.2).   [5] Azania is in the northwest of Arcadia (Strabo 8.3.1); Azani can signify Arcadians generally.

τοῦδέ κοτ᾽ Ἀργείοισιν ἐς Αὐλίδα [
  κοίρανος· Ἀτρείδαις δ᾽ εἰς ἔριν ἀντι . [
ἤγειρεν μέγα νεῖκος, ὃ καὶ πα[
15 εἰς ἑόν, ἀλλ᾽ ἔστη‹ς›, παῖ Διὸς ἐμ . [
[   ]
         ]δεν[
         ]νι[
        ]εεις[
       ] . ον[

190b (SSH 276A) *P.Mich*. inv. 6235 fr. 1 et 2

(a) fr. 1

. . . .

                   ]θεν
              ] καὶ ἄλ-
[λ-   ] . . Ἀπολ-
[λων-   ]με[. . .] . ανα
5   ]μένο[υ Ἀ]πόλλω-
[νος (?)   ] . παρει[.]ι δ᾽ ἀσφα-
[λ-   αἴ]τιος ἐγένετο
              ]
           ]ν Ἀθήνης εχον
10   ]λατος ἀπὸ αἰτί . -
[ας τοιαύτης   ]νες ἐπορεύοντο
           ὑπ[ὲρ τῆς Ἑλένης
          ]ν Ἀγαμέμνονα

there once the commander[6] . . . to the Argives at Aulis[7] . . . into strife with the sons of Atreus . . . he stirred up an epic feud, on account of which [he determined to return] [15] to his own country, but you intervened, child of Zeus[8]

[6] Teuthis, king of the Arcadians (Paus. 8.28.4–6).

[7] In Boeotia opposite Euboea, where the Greek forces departed for the Trojan War and Agamemnon sacrificed his daughter Iphigenia (Eur. *IA*).   [8] Athena, who according to Pausanias (Paus. 8.28.5) intervened in the quarrel.

190b (*SH* 276A) Michigan papyrus

(a) fr. 1

. . . Apollo . . . Apollo . . . safe . . . this was the cause . . . of Athena [10] . . . from such a cause they set out . . . for the sake of Helen . . . Agamemnon . . . from Arcadia . . .

```
                    ]ρους τῆς Ἀρκαδί-
15  [ας             ]σης οὐκ ὀλίγης·
                    ]ν στρατεύειν α .
         ἡ Ἀθ]ηνᾶ δ' ἐκήλησε
                    ] .θη φίλῳ αυ[
                    ]ν μὴ ἕως α .[
20                  ]ακτων [ .]πιτ[
                    ]κασεινα[
                    ] . ον μη[
                    ]ν Ἀρκα[δ-
                    ]ωτου ξ[
```

(b) fr. 2

```
         .   .   .   .
                ]ανηα
                ] . ιου -
   . . .
                ]εκει .
                ]...(.)
         .   .   .   .
```

190c (667 Pf.) Schol. ad Paus. 8.28.6

ὅτι φησὶν οὗτος ἑωρακέναι τὸ τῆς Ἀθηνᾶς ἄγαλμα ἐν Τευθίδι τελαμῶνι κατειλημμένον. καὶ ἢ Καλλίμαχος ἢ οὗτος ψεύδεται. ὁ μὲν γὰρ παλαίτερος ὢν φησὶ λῆξαι τοῦ τραύματος τὴν θεραπείαν, ὁ δὲ ἑωρακέναι φησὶν ἔτι ὥσπερ ἐπιδούμενον καὶ θεραπευόμενον.

[15] not small . . . to wage war . . . Athena beguiled . . . to a friend . . . not until . . . Arcadia

(b) fr. 2

. . .

190c (667 Pf.) Scholia to Pausanias, *Description of Greece*

Because this one says that he saw the statue of Athena in Teuthis bound with a bandage. And either Callimachus or this one (Pausanias) is lying. The first, who is older, says that the treatment of the wound had abated, but the other says that he saw it as if it were still dressed and cared for.

CALLIMACHUS

190d–f Fabulae incertae

190d (725a Pf.; vol. 2, p. 123) *P.Oxy.* 2258 fr. 8 recto

]ι Καμαριν()[
    ]θη. [
    ]ης .[

190e (725a Pf.; vol. 2, p. 123) *P.Oxy.* 2258 fr. 8 verso

.   .   .   .
   ]   [
γυ]ναικὶ κατ[
 ]α.[.]ọ..απ[
]ης. [
]ασ[
.   .   .   .

190f (*SH* 277) Phot. *Bibl.* ε 1039; Theodoridis s.v. ἐντὸς ἑβδόμης

ἐντὸς ἑβδόμης· Ἀθήνησιν ἀπείρητο ἐντὸς ἑβδόμης στρατείαν ἐξάγειν. τὴν δὲ αἰτίαν εἴρηκε Καλλίμαχος ἐν Αἰτίοις.

190d–f Unknown Tales

190d (725a Pf.; vol. 2, p. 123) Oxyrhynchus papyrus

. . . Camarina[1]

[1] Lake and town in Sicily, subject of a proverb (*Aet.* 64.1–2 above).

190e (725a Pf.; vol. 2, p. 123) Oxyrhynchus papyrus

to a woman . . .

190f (*SH* 277) Photius; Theodoridis

before the seventh day: it is prohibited in Athens to lead out an army before the seventh day. Callimachus explains the cause in the *Aetia*.

190g (D'Alessio 2007, 794–800) *P. Horak* 4 (*PSI* 3191)[1]

[1] G. Menci, *Gedenkschrift Ulrike Horak*, v. 1 (Florence, 2004), suppl. et comm. D'Alessio, vol. 2, 794–800

col. I fr. A

```
          ‒ ‒ ‒
               ] .[
               ] ενωι
                 ]ταυτου
           ].....[......ν]
               ]
  5          π]ερὶ τήν
             ] δ' αυτόν
             ] ... δε του
           ]ε[......]
           Με]σσηνίασ
           ].. ηπεα διὰ του[
 10        ]
           Πελο]ποννήσωι
           ].. σ Ἡρακλείδαις[
           Πέλο]πο[ν]σ νῆσον [
           ]χρησαμένοις
 15          ]. γωι ἔτυχε
             ]. αιρους ἐπι
           ἵπ]που ὀχούμενος
             ] πεντάθλων
             π]ένταθλοι
```

190g (D'Alessio 2007, vol. 2, 794–800) Papyrus fragment

col. I fr. A

. . . of Messenia . . . [10] on the Peloponnese . . . to the Heraclidae[1] . . . the island of Pelops . . . to those who were proclaimed . . . [15] he happened . . . riding on a horse[2] . . . of pentathons . . . the pentathetes . . . [20] of the contest . . . frightening the horses[3]

---

[1] The descendants of Heracles, who claimed the right to rule the Peloponnese including Argos, Messenia, and Lacedaemonia, (Apollod. *Bibl*. 2.8.4). Their "return" is also called the Dorian invasion.   [2] Oxylus, legendary king of Elis (Paus. 5.4.1–4).

[3] The Taraxippus was a geographic feature in Olympia. Lycophron (42–43) associates it with the Hill of Cronus. See also Paus. 6.20.15–19 on the significance of its name.

20   ] ἀγωνίας
         το]ῦ̣ Ταραξίππο̣[υ

col. I fr. B

       –   –   –
          ] .ον[
          ]
          ] . ιλη
        ].[ ] .ων...σ
5   ]... Πτολεμα[ί]ω παρ[
       ]παλαιέ
      ].. ἥμισυ δ᾽ Ἀσσυρ[ι
      ]ον παρο.....ητρ[
                δεεν[
10   ] .νκι[   ].
         ]α̣στρ[   ].[   ].
         –   –   –

col. II fr. A

[ ]ειτ[ ]σ ἀλ[
[μο]λύβδαι̣να]   [
[τὸ] μέλαν δρυός]   [
[Ἰά]ων] ποταμὸς[
5 [Π]ῖσα] χωριον τη̣[ς Ἤλιδος[   ] ἀπὸ Πί[
    σον βασιλεως...[
[ἀ]μφιμ[άσ]α̣σθε]   περι.[

408

col. I fr. B

[5] Near Ptolemy[1] . . . was wrestling . . . half Assyrian[2]

[1] Either Ptolemy II Philadelphus or Ptolemy III Euergetes.
[2] The second part of *Fr. Inc. Sed.* 506: "half Persians, half Assyrians," perhaps in reference to one of the Syrian Wars.

col. II fr. A

a sinker:
the dark woodland:
Iaon:[1] a river
[5] Pisa:[2] a place in Elis named from King Pisus.
wipe all around:[3]

[1] Call. *Hymn* 1.21.
[2] Olympia, see *Aet.* 84 and 98.
[3] Hom. *Od.* 20.152, of preparations for a feast.

[ὀ]πασσ[ά]μενος   περι. [
[χ]λωρο̣[ν]]   νέον [
10   ἔπισσα]   ἔγγον. [
λαγόνι]   ἐκ μεταφορᾶ[ς
ἄζωστος]   ἀνασεσυρμ[ένος/η
ὀχήνη   ἱερὸν ὀστοῦ[ν
ἀνακλῶν   ποταμὸς [
15   κόσμος   διάκτωρ . [
ἀσύφηλον   ἀπαίδε[υτον
προχάνη   πρόφας[ις
Ἔν̣ν̣α   πολις .. [

— — —

fr. C

]σικελ[
]   [
]σενε. [
] . καλε . [
] . νησ . [
πο]ταμό[ς
]λαισ λ[
] . οσε[

having given:
green: young
[10] the younger daughter: descendant
on the flank: as a metaphor[4]
ungirt: pulled up
ochēnē: the sacred bone
bending back: a river
[15] world order: messenger
headstrong:uneducated
pretext: motive
Enna: name of a city

[4] For "foothills," in *Hec.* 169.

fr. C

　　] a river

frr. D + E + F + G

```
   .. [ ].. [
   ἀρετᾷ[    ] .[
   ἠλεῖον    συ.. [   ]. [
   Πτέριο[ν]    χωρίον τῆς Μ[ηδίας
5     κ[α]ὶ Περσίδος [ .]λεοσ[
   κροτ[ημα  ]το ἔλασμα του. [
        τ[   ]ησ τοιαύτης υλ. [
   κροτειτω   ἐλα[υ]νέτω        [
   [θ]αμβαλέης  πλ[η]κτικῆς [
10 [ ]χιραλεοι   τρα[    ] και απο[
              ]και δι᾽ ἀσφ[α]λείας εχο. [
   [κ]ατακορής  συ[νε]χῶς ὀχλ[ῶν
   κά]ρφο[ς]   χόρ[το]ς αχυρο[ν
```

fr. H

```
    ]οσσ[
```

frr. D + E + F + G

virtue:
of Elis:
Pterios: place of Media
[5] and of Persia
hammerwork: metal plate . . . of such
strike!: Beat!
astonishing: startling
[10] with chapped hands: hard . . . in safety
glutted: continuous troubles
twigs: husks of fodder

fr. H

. . .

IAMBI

INTRODUCTION

THE IAMBIC TRADITION
IN GREEK POETRY

Iambic poetry is characterized by biting invective aimed at named (or more likely, pseudonymous) opponents and composed in a variety of iambic meters. It is frequently written in the first person and purports to be the speech of someone who is angry, self-righteous, and sure of his own moral superiority, who presents himself as abject, belittled by his opponents, and indignant at the injustice of the world he inhabits.[1] Though the iambicist's bitter rants appear to be spontaneous, and his enemies seem like real individuals, his mockery is a literary construct defined by tradition.

Archilochus of Paros (7th c. BC), who was said to be the founder of the genre and inventor of the iambic meter,[2] composed various kinds of verse, including laments, exhortations, monologues, curses, hymns, obscenities, animal fables, and more. His meter, as various as his subject matter, included iambic trimeters, trochaic tetrameters, epodes, and elegies, among others. Though

[1] Rosen 2007, 122, 222–23.
[2] [Plut.] *De mus.* 28.1140f–41b.

extant only in fragments, his poems display the full range of iambic attitudes, and ancient biographers claimed that his attacks on the daughters of Lycambes drove them and their father to suicide.[3]

The other key figure in the history of the iambic genre, Hipponax of Ephesus (6th c. BC), is less well known, perhaps because fewer fragments of his verses have survived. They record a raucous life among denizens of an Ionian underworld, violent and bawdy. His verse features obscene language, graphic sexual acts, and slapstick humor. Like Archilochus, he had a personal *bête noire*, the sculptor Bupalus, whom, it was claimed, he hounded to death along with his brother Athenis.[4] It was Hipponax's signature meter, the choliamb,[5] and his ionic dialect that were adopted by Callimachus for the introduction and conclusion to his own *Iambi*. Callimachus also borrows some specific subject matter from Hipponax, including the Seven Sages (Hipp. 63 and 123 W.; *Ia.* 191.51–77 and *Dieg.* 6.10–21); the story of Branchus (Hipp. 105.6 W.; *Ia.* 194.28–30); the giving of not disinterested advice (Hipp. 118 W.; *Ia.* 195);[6] and the image of the impoverished, starving poet or Muse (Hipp. 32; 39 W.; *Ia.* 203.60–62).

3 Hor. *Epist.* 1.19.25; Dioscor. *Anth. Pal.* 7.351 (17 G.-P.); *P.Dublin* inv. 193a (*SH* 997).

4 *Suda* ι 588.

5 The choliamb, or "limping" iamb, resembles an iambic trimeter, but the last breve is always replaced by a longum, and the third anceps is usually short.

6 For details on how Callimachus borrows Hipponax' rhetorical structure, see Kerkhecker, 143–46.

CALLIMACHUS' *IAMBI*:
CONTENTS, METER, DIALECT,
AND GENERIC FEATURES

Though the Alexandrians gave Archilochus first place in
the iambic canon, Callimachus defined his own contribu-
tion to the genre against the standard of Hipponax. He
literally resurrects him in *Iamb* 1, "Listen to Hipponax!
For I have come from the place where they sell an ox for
a penny,[7] bringing iambic verse that does not sing of the
battle with Bupalus" (*Ia.* 191.1–4). Callimachus is saying
that his own *Iambi* will be Hipponactean, but with a dif-
ference. The precise nature of the difference is unclear at
this point. Hipponax' ghost is addressing an unruly group
of artists and intellectuals[8] in front of a temple of Serapis
in Callimachus' Alexandria. The reanimated Hipponax
uses his own signature choliambs, his Ionic dialect, and his
combative attitude to harangue the crowd and deliver his
ironic message that they should not compete with one
another, though he reserves the right to harass them all.
He also borrows a teaching story from Hipponax to illus-

---

[7] The underworld (cf. *Epig.* 13.6).

[8] The papyrus originally read *philosophoi*, which was cor-
rected to *philologoi*. Though Pfeiffer prints the latter in his own
text, the former was a general word for "intellectual" used in
reference to the members of the Alexandrian Museum as late as
the Roman period. *Philologoi* as a designation for professional
scholars is not used earlier than Erastosthenes, who was Callima-
chus' student. *Philosophoi* in the narrow sense are important in
this scene, which includes references to Euhemerus, a Cynic, the
Pythagoreans, and the Seven Wise Men.

trate his point: how Bathycles' cup was intended as a prize for the best of the Seven Wise Men, but was declined by each of them in turn and finally dedicated to Apollo (*Ia.* 191.32–77). The colorful insults with which he takes leave of the crowd when Charon comes to take him below (*Ia.* 191.78–98) nicely undercut his allegedly good advice.

Iamb 2 is an animal fable also in stichic choliambi, narrated by another Ionian, Aesop of Sardis, "whom the Delphians received ungraciously when he was singing a tale" (*Ia.* 192.15–17). Aesop was publicizing the greed of the Delphian priests, who stole portions of the sacrificial meat, and they responded by throwing him over a cliff or stoning him to death as if he were a scapegoat (*Ia.* 191b). The real Hipponax wrote at length about scapegoats and apparently presented himself in that role (Hipp. 5–10 W.). In *Iamb* 1 his Callimachean ghost reprises that role by likening the raucous crowd to "Delphians" (*Ia.* 191.27). In the second *Iamb*, a Callimachean Aesop tells how certain humans acquired the voices of a dog, an ass, a parrot, and fish, then became verbose and overwordy (*Ia.* 192.10–15). Since his targets include "tragedians [who] have the voice of those living in the sea" (*Ia.* 191.12), this must be a rude variety of literary criticism.

Though composed in Hipponax's meter and dialect, *Iamb* 3 looks to a different model: the moralizing choliambi of Callimachus' Hellenistic contemporaries, such as Phoenix of Colophon.[9] Their targets are the evils of wealth and the degeneracy of the age, which an unidentified narrator is lamenting here (*Ia.* 193.1–20). It soon becomes obvious, however, that his interest is in a youth whose

---

[9] Clayman 1980, 66–70.

mother has prostituted him to a rich man (*Ia.* 193a). Oaths have been broken, and the narrator, who is but a poor poet, ends on an hysterical note, by wishing he were a eunuch devotee of Cybele or Adonis (*Ia.* 193.35–39).

In *Iamb* 4, the poet returns to the fable form and the subject of status seeking with a debate between a laurel and an olive tree about which deserves greater honor. The remains include two passages containing sixty-three lines and fourteen lines linked by a bridge of eight half-lines to create one of the longest stretches of continuous verse in the whole of Callimachus' extant corpus. It offers a rare opportunity to observe the charm of Callimachus' style and also demonstrates his habit of self-reference, which is discussed further below.

Talking trees recall Aesop again, and these two specimens present their cases for priority over the other with the verbal finesse of professional rhetoricians. They also exhibit distinct personalities; the olive is smooth and sophisticated, while the laurel is a feisty iambicist. There has been much scholarly discussion, unresolved and irresolvable, about which of the two truly represents the poet, and it is likely that neither does.[10]

Iamb 5 is the first of the epodes and the last of the diatribes. Its meter combines the choliambic trimeters used in the previous poems with iambic dimeters that appear in several of those that follow. Here a speaker pretends to give advice to a schoolteacher who is abusing his students. The indirection of his speech is characterized as a riddle or an oracle, which are typical of Greek popular literature (*Ia.* 195.31–33). It closely follows a poem of Hipponax in

[10] Rosen 2007, 200–206; Kerkhecker, 113–15.

form and content (118.1–6 W.), offering a unique opportunity to observe how Callimachus adapts his model to his own purposes.[11]

Iamb 6 is the first of the noncholiambic, non-Ionic, non-Hipponactean *Iambi*. Here iambic trimeters are combined with ithyphallics in a *propempticon*, that is, a poem for a friend who is about to depart on a journey. It is written in a Doric dialect inspired by the journey's destination: Olympia, where the main attraction will be Phidias' famous statue of Zeus. The statue is described in minute, technical detail that is amusing in its aggressively unpoetic diction.

Iamb 7 is epodic[12] and Doric like the sixth, though here the dialect is colored with Aeolic forms to suit the location of the tale in Aenus, an Aeolic city in Thrace. It is also about a statue of a god, but this one is a primitive, uncarved wooden log in contrast to Phidias' gold and ivory masterpiece. Some fisherman catch it in their nets but do not recognize its divine nature until they fail in their efforts to destroy it and bring it to the oracle at Delphi, who reveals that it is Hermes. The story is told by the object itself in the manner of an epigram.

For *Iambi* 8 to 11, fragments are few and the *Diegeseis* are the only additional source of information. *Iamb* 8 continues the trend of adapting other genres for the *Iambi*. It is an *epinicion* in iambic trimeters[13] and Ionic dialect honoring Polycles of Aegina for his victory in the hydrophoria. The poem included an account of the contest's ori-

---

[11] Kerkhecker, 143–46.

[12] Also trimeters combined with ithyphallics.

[13] It cannot be determined whether the meter is epodic or stichic.

gins, when the Argonauts landed on Aegina and vied with one another at fetching water (*Ia.* 198a). Like tales of the Argonauts in the *Aetia*, this story was also told by Apollonius (Ap. Rhod. 4.1765–72), and it cannot be determined which version is prior.

Iamb 9 continues the stichic iambic trimeters of *Iamb* 8, but its dialect is Doric, like *Iambi* 6 and 7. Here Callimachus presents another articulate statue of Hermes, this one ithyphallic. A lover of the handsome youth Philetadas asks Hermes whether he is in this condition on account of the same young man, but the statue replies that he is originally Tyrrhenian,[14] that his condition is in accordance with a mystic account, and that the speaker has immoral intentions.

Iamb 10, the fourth and fifth consecutive *aitia*, appear to continue the iambic trimeters of *Iamb* 9 but return to the Ionic dialect for the story of Mopsus of Pamphylia and an explanation of why Aphrodite Castnia accepts the sacrifice of pigs, and Artemis of Eretria welcomes even one-eyed and tailless animals.

Iamb 11, in Doric with a five-footed iamb not attested elsewhere, corrects the popular version of a proverb, "The goods of Connarus are there for the taking." The correct name is Connidas, a wealthy pimp of Selinus, who used to say that he would divide his estate between Aphrodite and his friends, but after his death his will revealed that anyone could take his possessions. Connidas is making this point from his tomb, a familiar convention in epigram.

More fragments are available for *Iamb* 12, written for

[14] On the Athenians adopting images of ithyphallic Hermes from the Pelasgians, see Hdt. 2.51; on the identification of the Pelasgians with the Tyrrhenians (or Tyrsenians), see Hdt. 1.57.

the poet's friend Leon on the occasion of his daughter's seven-day birth party. Here, in Ionic and catalectic trochaic trimeters, Callimachus describes a similar feast that Hera hosted for her daughter Hebe. The celestial party was attended by all the Olympians, who vied with one another in bringing toys cleverly fabricated from precious metals, but who lost the contest to Apollo, who offered a song more valuable than gold. Callimachus is suggesting that his own song is equivalent to Apollo's and therefore the best gift of all.

Iamb 13 is again about rivalries, and here Callimachus, returning to Hipponax's Ionic dialect and choliambic meter, presents himself beleaguered by opponents who question the authenticity of his *Iambi*, "not after associating with the Ionians nor having visited Ephesus . . . where those who are about to give birth to choliambs are learnedly inspired." Callimachus claims a purity of intention, even as he defends the variety in his work. His critics complain, "this is woven in and chattering . . . in Ionic and Doric and mixed [dialects] . . . how far do you dare?" The *Diegeseis* summarize his defense: he models himself on the fifth-century-tragedian Ion of Chios, who composed in various genres. No one blames a craftsman for making objects of various kinds (*Ia.* 203a).

The charge of variety (*polyeideia*) may be aimed at the poets' entire corpus, but it has clear application to the *Iambi* themselves, which rework nine usually distinct genres in six different metrical schemes and three dialects. Yet the alternations are carefully orchestrated to create an aesthetically pleasing whole.[15] The appearance of

---

[15] Clayman 1980, 48–51.

Hipponax himself to introduce the *Iambi* balances Callimachus' energetic defense of his artistic choices at their conclusion, and the frame that they create is a convincing argument that his original book of *Iambi* ended precisely here. Arguments that four additional poems (*Mel.* 226–29) belong to this group are presented below.

RELATIONSHIP TO CALLIMACHUS' OTHER WORKS

In an ancient edition of Callimachus' collected works, the *Iambi* were immediately preceded by the four books of the *Aetia*. This order is reflected in *P. Oxy.* 1011, where the final verses of the *Aetia* (*Aet.* 112.9) are followed in the same column by a *subscriptio* identifying the preceding as *Aetia* Book 4, then a new title, *Iamboi*, and the opening line of *Iamb* 1 (*Ia.* 191.1). The order is confirmed by the *Diegeseis*, where the *Aetia* also concludes with a *subscriptio*.[16] In light of this evidence, it is natural to read the last lines of the *Aetia* as a direct link to the *Iambi*,

> χαῖρε, Ζεῦ, μέγα καὶ σύ, σάω δ᾽ [ἐμὸ]ν οἶκον
>   ἀνάκτων·
> αὐτὰρ ἐγὼ Μουσέων πεζὸν [ἔ]πειμι νομόν.

> Farewell greatly you as well, Zeus. And preserve the
>   house of my kings.
> But I will pass on to the foot pasture of the Muses.

---

[16] In the *Diegeseis* no title is given for the *Iambi*, but it is not consistent in these matters.

The *Aetia* ends with the hymnist's traditional, first-person *envoi* to a patron deity, followed by an announcement of the next song.[17] The identification of the Muses' "foot pasture" with the *Iambi* is made on the authority of Horace, who aligns his *Satires* with a "walking Muse" (*Sat.* 2.6.17) and describes "chats . . . creeping along the ground" (*Epist.* 2.1.250–51).

The formal transition is a cue to look for connections between the two poetic collections, and although they are both fragmentary, some connections emerge. Both the *Aetia* and the *Iambi* encompass a wide variety of subjects, including epinicia (*Aet.* 54–60j; *Ia.* 198), poems on aniconic statues (*Aet.* 100–100a; *Ia.* 197), and more artistic statues of gods (*Aet.* 31g, 35, 46, 101–101b; *Ia.* 196). More specifically, *Iamb* 3 (*Ia.* 193) shares themes with *Aetia* 137b, including the contrast of wealth and poverty, the gods' tardiness or unwillingness to act, and the narrator's claim to rely on the moral standards that he had been taught in his youth.[18] *Iamb* 4 also has links to other poems of Callimachus, for example, the tree where Leto rested when she gave birth to Apollo appears there (*Ia.* 194.84), in *Iamb* 13 (*Ia.* 203.62), and also in his *Hymn to Delos* (*Hymn* 4.209–11). The story of Branchus is found in the fourth *Iamb* (*Ia.* 194.28–31) and the fourth lyric poem (*Mel.* 229), which recounts the tale at length.[19] Particularly noteworthy are the links between the *Iamb* 4 and the *Hecale*, including the narrator's overhearing a long conversation between talking birds (*Ia.* 194.60–82; *Hec.* 73–76),

17 For example, *Hymn. Hom. Ap.* 3.545–46.
18 Clayman 1988, 281–83.
19 Following Hipponax 105.6 W.

the contest for Athens between Athena and Poseidon (*Ia*. 194.66–68; *Hec*. 70–71), and the dinner of various olives enjoyed by Theseus in the hut of Hecale (*Ia*. 194.76–77; *Hec*. 36–37).[20]

DATE

Theseus' dinner of olives is a central scene in the *Hecale*, depicting the legendary hospitality of its impoverished heroine. In contrast, in *Iamb* 4 it is but one item on a list of honors claimed by the olive in her contest with the laurel. It appears then that the poet of the *Iambi* is referring back to a well-known passage in his previous work and that *Iamb* 4 (if not all the *Iambi*) was composed after the *Hecale*. This inference would be more useful if the *Hecale* could be dated, but Callimachus' self-reference suggests at least that his book of *Iambi* was not his earliest work. This is consistent with the only other evidence available for its dating: Hipponax's summoning his babbling contemporaries to "a shrine outside the walls" (*Ia*. 191.9). The *Diegeseis* identify this as the great Serapeum of Parmenion, which stood outside the walls of Rhacotis, built by Ptolemy III after 246 BC (*Dieg*. 6.2–4).[21] Since Callima-

---

[20] On the olives offered to Theseus, see Hollis, 173–74.

[21] Pfeiffer objects to this identification because Euhemerus, who is depicted here scribbling "his blasphemous books" (*Ia*. 191.9–11), was already dead by the second half of the third century BC, but Rees (1961) argues that the poet is not describing the philosopher himself, but a statue that depicts him in the act of writing. Bolstering this argument is a statue group including philosophers and poets outside the Serapeum at Memphis that was likely modeled on the more sumptuous one in the forecourt

chus wrote for and about this Ptolemy and his wife, Berenice, the poem's composition after this date is plausible enough. The *Iambi* belong, then, not to the first part of Callimachus' career, but to the second.

HISTORY AND CONSTITUTION OF THE TEXT

Like the *Aetia*, the text of the *Iambi* is extant only in fragments collected mainly from papyri and quotations from Byzantine scholarship. The first editor to identify and publish a fragment of the *Iambi* (*Ia.* 191.9–11) was Vulcanius in his edition of 1584. Fabri added a second (192.1–3) in her edition of 1675. By 1697 Bentley had identified twenty-five additional fragments, which included about sixty verses in choliambs and iambic trimeters, some not explicitly attributed to Callimachus in their sources. Bentley's attributions, order, and numbering were retained in subsequent editions by Ernesti (1761), Blomfield (1815), and Schneider (1870–1873). These fragments were augmented from papyri, beginning in 1904 with *P.Oxy.* 661, which contains *Ia.* 197.11–25 and 39–51. The following year the publication of *P.Oxy.* 1011 added 334 new lines, including parts of *Iambi* 1–4, 12, and 13. Lobel was able to add a few more from *P.Oxy.* 1363 (published in 1915),

---

of the Serapeum at Rhacotis. See Marianne Bergmann, "The Philosophers and Poets in the Serapieion at Memphis," in *Early Hellenistic Portraiture: Image, Style, Context*, ed. Peter Schultz and Ralf von den Hoff (Cambridge University Press: Cambridge, 2007), 246–63.

which he reexamined in 1934. Several additional fragments of text have been added since, most recently and substantially from *P.Mich.* inv. 4967 (1951), which preserves *Ia.* 12.57–70. A complete list of all papyrus sources of the *Iambi* follow below. In addition to fragments of text, the Scholia Florentina, a scholarly commentary covering the first part of *Iamb* 1, was identified in *PSI* 1094 (1929), and of greatest importance is the *Diegeseis*, published by Vogliano in 1937 and described in the General Introduction, with the first lines and brief prose summaries of all the *Iambi.* Pfeiffer reedited all of the available text for his edition of 1949–1953, and later reviews of the text, notably by Kerkhecker (1999), have yielded only a few minor improvements.

CATALOG OF PAPYRI

The list of relevant papyri below follows the numbering and order of Mertens-Pack[3], the online database of the Centre de documentation de papyrologie littéraire (CEDOPAL) at the Université de Liège, which provides additional information and bibliography.[22] Each entry begins with the inventory number assigned by Mertens-Pack[3], followed by the series name in standard abbreviations, the numbers in the *Supplementum Hellenisticum* and Pfeiffer where applicable, its estimated date, and the verses in the *Iambi* that it supplies.

[22] Additional information about the papyri can also be found in Pfeiffer vol. 2, ix–xxvi; *SH*, pp. 89–122; Kerkhecker, xvii–xx; Lehnus 2011, 23–38; Asper, 537–39.

00211.000: *P.Mil.Vogl.* inv. 1006 (+ *P.Mil.Vogl.* 1.18 + *P.Mil.Vogl.* inv. 28b). Pap. 8 Pf. 1st–2nd c. AD. *Diegeseis* of *Ia*. 191–213.

00211.100: *P.Oxy.* 1011. Pap. 35 Pf. 4th c. AD. *Ia*. 191.1–10, 26–51, 54–73, 78–98; 192.4–17; 193.1–13, 24–39; 194.1–12, 22–106; 212.7–86; 213.2–66.

00218.000: *P.Oxy.* 1363. Pap. 25 Pf. 2nd–3rd c. AD. *Ia*. 191.5–24.

00219.000: *PSI* 1094. Pap. 19 Pf. 2nd c. AD. Schol. Florentina in *Ia*. 191.6 and 191.26–39.

00220.000: *P.Oxy.* 2215. Pap. 27 Pf. 2nd–3rd c. AD. *Ia*. 193.5–24; 194.14–21.

00221.000: *P.Ryl.* 485. Pap. 34 Pf. 4th c. AD. *Ia*. 194.115–17; 195.1–7.

00222.000: *PSI* 1216 (+ *P.Oxy.* 2171 + *P. Oxy.* 2172). Pap. 6 Pf. 1st–2nd c. AD. *Ia*. 194.107–17; 195.1–68; 196.22–62; 197.1–14, 21–25.

00223.000: *P.Oxy.* 661 (+ *P.Oxy.* 20, p. 168). Pap. 21 Pf. 2nd c. AD. *Ia*. 197.11–25, 39–51.

00223.010: *P.Lips.* inv. 290v. *APF* 55.1 (2009): 1–20. Pap. 47 Lehnus; not in Pf. 2nd c. AD. Schol. in *Ia*. 211 and 212.1–3.

00224.000: *P.Oxy.* 2218. Pap. 28 Pf. 2nd–3rd c. AD. *Ia*. 212.1–6.

00225.000: *P.Mich.* inv. 4967. Pap. Lehnus 49; Pf. vol. 2, 118–19. 2nd c. AD. *Ia*. 212.57–70.

AFTERLIFE OF THE *IAMBI*

Like Callimachus and his Greek predecessors, Roman poets understood *iambi* as both a meter and an attitude. In the first century BC, Catullus, Callimachus' great admirer, used the signature choliambs of the *Iambi* for excoriating attacks (Catull. 37,[23] 59), more gentle teasing, and a variety of other subjects.

While Catullus reflects the spirit of the *Iambi*, a generation later Horace's book of seventeen *Epodes* reinterprets Callimachus' iambic project more specifically. Like Callimachus, Horace begins with a string of poems in a signature meter (*Epod.* 1–10, in couplets of iambic trimeters and iambic dimeters), followed by a transition (*Epod.* 11) that looks forward to poems with various metrical combinations, and a concluding *Epode* (*Epod.* 17) that returns to iambic trimeters. This careful architectonic arrangement, which incorporates alternations of subject and theme, is characteristic of both the *Epodes* and the *Iambi*, which also incorporate variations of dialect. It makes perhaps the strongest argument that Horace composed his seventeen *Epodes* with the *Iambi* in mind. This suggests in turn that the Romans read manuscripts with seventeen poems rather than the thirteen in Pfeiffer's edition. More details on this issue are discussed below in the Introduction to Callimachus' lyric poems.

In addition to their formal arrangements, the *Iambi* and *Epodes* both incorporate form and content from a broad range of literary predecessors to explore social, moral, and literary issues. For the last, Horace cites their common Greek predecessors and characterizes himself as a madman and raging bull like Archilochus and Hipponax (*Epod.* 6.11–14), using images for those two forebears found in Callimachus (*Ia.* 191.78–79, 203.52–53); he min-

---

[23] Also on a Callimachean theme, the lover lured away by a richer man (cf. *Iamb* 3).

gles sex and literature, as Callimachus does in *Iambi* 3 and
5;[24] and he includes poems for a friend (*Epod.* 1; *Iambi* 6,
12) and an unusual *propempticon* (*Epod.* 10; *Iamb* 6).

Callimachus is also a model for Horace's first book of
Satires, especially the programmatic *Satires* 1.4 and 1.10.
In *Satires* 1.10, the final poem of Book 1, Horace uses
references to Callimachus' last *Iamb*, the thirteenth, to
argue against the mixing of Latin and Greek.[25] Here Qui-
rinus plays the role of Apollo (*Sat.* 1.10.31–35), who gives
Callimachus advice in *Aetia* 1. There is other content from
the *Iambi* as well, including *Satires* 1.8 on a statue of
Priapus that looks back to the aniconic Hermes of *Iamb* 7
and the ithyphallic Hermes of *Iamb* 9.

The shadow of Callimachus is also visible in Horace's
Roman predecessors in satire. At the beginning of the
second century BC, Ennius begins his *Annales* with a Pro-
logue in which the dreaming poet sees Homer, whose
spirit passes to Ennius through a peacock according to
Pythagoras' theory of metempsychosis (Enn. *Ann.* 1.2–9
FRL). His debt to Callimachus' dream of the Muses in
Aetia 2–2j is clear, but even more to *Iamb* 1, where the
reborn Hipponax appears making fun of Pythagorean veg-
etarianism and Euphorbus, Pythagoras' avatar, is a proto-
geometrician (*Ia.* 191.56–63). The peacock is a humorous
addition to the animals of *Iamb* 2 who once spoke like

---

[24] For example, in *Epodes* 8 and 12, Horace develops an
elaborate metaphor likening bad style to a decaying, overdressed
prostitute (Clayman 1980, 78–80).

[25] K. Freudenburg, *The Walking Muse: Horace on the Theory
of Satire* (Princeton, 1993), 106–7, esp. 104 for other reminis-
cences of the *Iambi* in the *Satires*.

men.[26] Few fragments remain of Ennius' *Satires*, but even so it is clear that they were written in various meters, including iambs. Like Callimachus' *Iambi*, the first-person narrator is at the center participating in dialogues, reciting fables (*Iamb* 2; Enn. *Sat.* 14 *FRL*), and making pronouncements on moral corruption (*Iamb* 3; Enn. *Sat.* 9 *FRL*).

The *Saturae* of Lucilius in the next generation include similar contents and more. Like Callimachus' *Iambi*, they are concerned with literary precedent and production. For example, Lucilius refers jokingly to Archilochus (786 W. = 698 M.), writes in a style that Varro characterizes as *gracilis*,[27] that is, equivalent to Callimachus' *leptos* (in both cases "fine" or "slender"), and includes literary criticism among his various topics.[28] Also like Callimachus, Lucilius ridicules philosophers and philosophy (lib. inc. 1225f. M.; *Iamb* 1) and quotes the charges of his opponents against him when defending himself and his work (1026 M. = 1077 W.; 821–22 M. = 929–30 W.; *Ia.* 203.11–22).

After Horace, Roman poets of the first century AD were still reading and responding to the *Iambi*. Persius presents himself as an anti-Callimachus in the programmatic Prologue to his *Satires*, where he announces that he never wetted his lips in Hippocrene, nor does he remember that he dreamed on Parnassus (Pers. *Prol.* 1–7), like Callimachus who dreams that he met the Muses on Helicon (*Aet.* 2–2j). Persius seems to reject Callimachus here,

[26] Schol. ad Pers. 6.9–11. See O. Skutsch, *The Annals of Quintus Ennius* (Oxford, 1985), 147–67.

[27] Varro ap. Gell. *NA* 6.14.7.

[28] Plin. *HN* Praef. 7.

but in the next lines the Roman poet recalls the talking animals of *Iamb* 2, when he asks who taught the parrot to say "hello" in Greek and tried to instruct the magpie in human speech (Pers. 1.8–14). While insisting that he can write satires without a visit to the Muses' spring where his predecessors have gone before,[29] Persius restates Callimachus' position in *Iamb* 13 that he can write choliambs without visiting Hipponax's home in Ephesus. Both are arguments for authenticity without banal imitation.

Beyond formal satire, Martial evokes Callimachus' *Iambi* in the fourth book of his *Epigrams*, in which a birthday song (Mart. 4.45) recalls *Iamb* 12, a gift in the form of a poem to mark the birth of Leon's daughter, and a portrait of a Cynic in a threadbare cloak (Mart. 4.53) resembles a philosopher in the crowd around Hipponax (*Ia*. 191.29–30). Both are placed shortly after an elegant compliment to Callimachus (Mart. 4.23).

After the first century AD, the *Iambi* seem to disappear from the consciousness of Roman poets along with Callimachus' other works.

---

[29] E.g., Prop. 3.3.1–6.

BIBLIOGRAPHY

Acosta-Hughes, Benjamin. *Polyeideia: The Iambi of Callimachus and the Archaic Iambic Tradition.* Berkeley: University of California Press, 2002.

Clayman, Dee L. *Callimachus' Iambi.* Leiden: Brill, 1980.

———. "Callimachus' *Iambi* and *Aitia.*" ZPE 74 (1988): 277–86.

Dawson, Christopher. "The *Iambi* of Callimachus. A Hellenistic Poet's Experimental Laboratory." *Yale Classical Studies* 11 (1950): 1–168.

Kerkhecker, Arnd. *Callimachus' Book of Iambi.* Oxford: Oxford University Press, 1999.

Rees, B. R. "Callimachus, *Iambus* 1.9–11." *CR* 11 (1961): 1–3.

Rosen, Ralph, M. *Making Mockery: The Poetics of Ancient Satire.* Oxford: Oxford University Press, 2007.

IAM[BOI

IAMBUS I (191–191b)

191 1–5, *P.Oxy.* 1011 fol. 2 verso, 91–96; 6–10 (fin.),
P.Oxy. 1011 fr. 11 verso; 5–34, *P.Oxy.* 1363; 26–47, *P.Oxy.*
1011 fol. 2 recto, 97–118; 47–51, *P.Oxy.* 1011 fr. 2 recto;
54–73, *P.Oxy.* 1011 fol. 3 verso, 119–38; 78–98, *P.Oxy.*
1011 fol. 3 recto, 139–59

Ἀκούσαθ' Ἱππώνακτος· ‸ο‸ὐ γὰρ ἀλλ' ἥκω
ἐκ τῶν ὅκου βοῦν κολλύ‸βου π‸ιπρήσκουσιν,
φέρων ἴαμβον οὐ μάχην ‸ἀείδ‸οντα
τὴν Βο‸υπ‸άλ‸ειον [�]‸νά‸ [...‸ἄ]νθρωπος
5   ]‸‸β̣ [   ]‸ειν
    ὦ]νδρες οἳ νῦν [   ]κέπφ[
    κα]τηύλησθ' οιμε[Διω]νύσου
    ]τε Μουσέων ‸ α[   ]‸. Ἀπόλλωνος
ἐς τὸ πρ‸ὸ τείχευς ἱρὸν ‸ἀλέες‸ δεῦτε,
10 οὗ τὸν‸ πάλαι Πάγχαιο‸ν ὁ πλάσας Ζᾶνα

Poet from Ephesus (6th c. BC), credited with inventing cho-
liambi (Demetr. *De eloc.* 301), the meter Callimachus uses here

IAMBI

IAMB 1 (191–191b)

191 Oxyrhynchus papyri

Listen to Hipponax![1] For I have come from the place
where they sell an ox for a penny,[2] bringing iambic verse
that does not sing of the battle with Bupalus[3] . . . a man
[5] . . . men who are now . . . birdbrain[4] . . . you who were
entranced by the flutes of Dionysus, the Muses and Apollo.
Come here together to the shrine outside the wall,[5]
[10] where the old man who long ago created Panchaean

---

along with Hipponax's Ionic dialect and combative attitudes. He
also treated the story Callimachus tells here of Bathycles' cup (63,
123 W.). Another possible source was the local historian Lean-
drius (or Maeandrius) of Miletus (Diog. Laert. 1.28).

[2] The underworld (cf. Call. *Epig.* 13.6).

[3] Bupalus, the sculptor who was the object of Hipponax's in-
vective (*Suda* ι 588; Plin. *HN* 36.11).

[4] Literally, a sea petrel, which had a reputation for stupidity
(Ar. *Pax* 1067–68).

[5] Identified by the *Diegeseis* (191a below) as the great Sera-
peum of Parmenion, which stood outside the walls of Rhacotis,
built by Ptolemy III after 246 BC. This suggests but does not
prove that *Iamb* 1 was written late in Callimachus' career.

γέρων, λαλάζων[1] ἄδι κα βιβλία ψήχει.

　　　]ι̣ γὰρ ἐντὸς ου[

　　　]άγη τις· η πολ[

　　　]ντα βωμοί τ[

15　　]ν πρὸς Ἅιδην[

　　ἄν]δρες ὁκόσοι βο̣[

　　　]ηδοι Μοῦσα τ̣[

　　　]νον ὅστις ἐμ[

　　　]δ̣ε καὶ τὸν ὃς χ[

20　　]ν ἑταίρην ατ[

　　ἴ]αμβον ὅστι[ς

　　] ὡς τις[2] τοὺς ν[

　　]άμετρα τοις[

　　　]ν ὅστις τηι[

25　　π]ολλούς· ἐν[

ὤπολλον, ὦνδρες, ὡς παρ' αἰπόλῳ μυῖαι

ἢ σφῆκες ἐκ γῆς ἢ ἀπὸ θύματος Δελφ[οί,

εἰ̣λη̣δὸ̣ν [ἐσ]μεύουσιν· ὦ Ἑκάτη πλήθευς.

ὁ ψιλοκόρσης τὴν πνοὴν ἀναλώσει

30　φυσέων ὅκ ως μὴ τὸν τρίβωνα γυμνώσῃ·

σωπῇ γενέσθω καὶ γράφεσθε τὴν ῥῆσιν.

ἀνὴρ Βαθυκλῆς Ἀρκάς—οὐ μακρὴν ἄξω,

ὦ λῷστε μὴ σίμαινε, καὶ γὰρ οὐδ' αὐτός

μέγα σχολάζ[ω·] δ[ε]ῖ με γὰρ μέσον δινεῖν

35　φεῦ φ]εῦ Ἀχέρο[ντ]ος—τῶν πάλαι τις εὐδαίμων

ἐγένετο, πά[ν]τα δ' εἶχεν οἶσιν ἄνθρωποι

θεοί τε λευκ ὰς ἡμέ ρας ἐπίστανται.

Zeus,[6] babbles and scribbles his blasphemous books . . .
inside . . . someone . . . altars . . . [15] to Hades . . . men
as many as . . . Muse . . . whoever . . . and the . . . who . . .
[20] a courtesan . . . an iambus whoever . . . as someone
. . . them . . . unmetrical . . . whoever . . . [25] many.

O Apollo, the men swarm in droves, like flies around a
goatherd, or wasps from the ground,[7] or Delphians[8] re-
turning from a sacrifice. O Hecate[9] the crowd! The baldy
loses his breath [30] puffing in exertion, so that he is not
stripped of his jacket. Be quiet and write down the tale.
Bathycles, an Arcadian man—I will not be long, my good
man, do not make an ape face, for I myself do not have
much leisure. I must whirl back to the middle of—[35]
alas! alas!—Acheron[10]—Bathycles, one of those long ago
who was blessed. He had all the things by which men and

---

[6] Euhemerus (late 4th–early 3rd c. BC), intellectual who
wrote about his trip to the imaginary Panchaea and argued that
Uranus, Cronus, and Zeus were merely human kings long ago
(Diod. Sic. 6.1.1–10).   [7] Similes found at greater length in
Homer (*Il.* 2.469, 16.259).   [8] The greedy priests at Delphi
who cut off portions of the sacrificial meat for themselves (Schol.
Flor. 191b.26–27 below).   [9] A chthonic deity suited to Hip-
ponax, who has just arrived from the underworld (Schol. Flor.
191b.28 below).   [10] River in Hades (Hom. *Od.* 10.513).

---

[1] λαλάζων *P.Oxy* 1011: ἀλαζών D'Alessio 2007, vol. 2,
580n11; Kerkhecker 1999, 24

[2] ὥς τις *P.Oxy* 1011: χὥστις Maas

ἤδη καθίκ[ειν οὗτ]ος ἡνίκ᾽ ἤμελλεν
ἐς μακρὸν [. . . .]—καὶ γὰρ ἐ . . . ος ἔζωσε—,
40 τῶν ᾽ . . . . . [. . . .] τοὺς μὲν ἔνθα, τοὺς δ᾽ ἔνθα
ἔστησε τοῦ κλιντῆρος· εἶχε γὰρ δεσμ[ό]s
μέλλοντας ἤδη παρθένοις ἀλινδεῖσθαι.
μόλις δ᾽ ἐπά[ρας] ὣς πότης ἐπ᾽ ἀγκῶνα
. .] . . . ν ὁ Ἀρκ[ὰς κ]ἀνὰ τὴν στέγην βλέψας
45 .] . . . νοισ. [. . .] . . [
ἔ]πειτ᾽ ἔφ[ησε
"ὦ π . αῖδες ὦ . ἐμαὶ τὠπιόντος ἄγκυραι
. .] . . . λο . . [
β]ούλεσθε ῥέξω[
50 σ]ὺν θεοῖσι καὶ . [.
. . . .] . . [³

. ἔπλευσεν ἐς Μίλητον· ἦν γὰρ ἡ νίκη
Θάλητος, ὅς τ᾽ ἦν ἄλλα⁴ δεξιὸς γνώμην,⁵
καὶ τῆς Ἀμάξης ἐλέγετο σταθμήσασθαι
55 τοὺς ἀστερίσκους, ᾗ πλέουσι Φοίνικες.
εὗρεν δ᾽ ὁ Προυσέληνο[ς] αἰσίῳ σίττῃ
ἐν τοῦ Διδυμέος τὸν γέρ[ο]ντα κωνῴῳ
ξύοντα τὴν γῆν καὶ γράφοντα τὸ σχῆμα,
τοὐξεῦρ᾽ ὁ Φρὺξ Εὔφορβ . ος ., ὅστις ἀνθρώπων
60 τρ . ίγ . ωνα καὶ σκ . αληνά, πρῶτος ἔγρ . α . ψε
καὶ κύκλον ἐπ[. . .] . κ.ἠδίδαξε νηστεύειν

³ Desunt versus fere ca. 15 in pap.   ⁴ ὅς τ᾽ ἦν ἄλλα
Bentley: ὅς τὸν ἄλλα cod. M: ὅς τἄλλα cod. V   ⁵ [Ach. Tat.]
Isagog. in Arat. (vol. 1, 29.20 Maas)

440

gods understand good times.[11] Already when he was about to go down into the great [abyss], for he had lived . . . [40] and [of his sons] he stood some here, some there around his bed. A bond held them, who were already about to roll around with girls. And with difficulty, like a drunkard at a feast, he propped himself on his elbow, . . . the Arcadian looked up at the ceiling [45] . . . then he said, "O sons, my anchors as I depart, . . . [what] you wish . . . I will do . . . [50] with the gods . . .

He sailed to Miletus, for the victory belonged to Thales,[12] who had an ingenious mind and among other accomplishments was said to have measured the [55] little stars of the Wagon,[13] by which the Phoenicians sail. With an auspicious bird omen the Pre-moonman[14] found the old man in the shrine of Didyma,[15] scratching the ground and drawing the shape that Phrygian Euphorbus[16] devised, who was the first person [60] to draw the triangle and unequal triangle and the circle . . . and taught . . . to

[11] Literally, "white days." For the expression, see *Aet.* 178.2 above and discussion in D'Alessio 2007, vol. 2, 582n18.

[12] Presocratic philosopher, mathematician, and astronomer who correctly predicted the eclipse of 585 BC (Diog. Laert. 1.5.24–26). [13] The constellation Ursa Major (Arat. *Phaen.* 93). [14] Pre-moonman, i.e., an Arcadian. They were reputed to be older than the moon (Ap. Rhod. 4.264–65). He is identified as Bathycles' son Amphalces by the *Diegeseis*.

[15] Didyma, sanctuary and oracle of Apollo near Miletus (Hdt. 6.19). [16] Pythagoras (6th c. BC), mystic and mathematician, often the butt of comedy, who espoused vegetarianism and reincarnation. He claimed that one of his own earlier incarnations was the Homeric hero Euphorbus (Diod. Sic. 10.6.1).

τῶν ἐμπνεό̣ντων· ο̣ἱ̣ ᾿Ιταλοὶ[6] δ᾿ ὑπήκουσαν,
οὐ πάντες, ἀλλ᾿ οὓς εἶχεν ̣οὕτερος δαίμων.
πρὸς δή [μ]ιν ὧδ᾿ ἔφησε ̣[

65 ἐκεῖ[νο] τοὐλόχρυσον ἐξ[ελὼν πήρης·[7]
"οὑμὸς πατὴρ ἐφεῖτο τοῦ[το τοὔκπωμα
δοῦ[ναι], τίς ὑμέων τῶν σοφ[ῶν ὀνήιστος
τῶν ἑπτά· κἠγὼ σοὶ δίδωμ[ι πρωτῆον."
ἔτυψε δὲ] σκίπωνι τοὔδα[φος πρέσβυς
70 καὶ τ]ὴν ὑπήνην τήτέρη [καταψήχων
ἐξεῖπ[ε·] "τὴν δόσιν μὲν
σὺ δ᾿ εἰ̣ [το]κ̣εῶνος μὴ λό[γοις ἀπειθήσεις,
Βίης [. . . . . ὐ̣]ε̣ι̣λ̣[[8]
Σόλων· ἐκεῖνος δ᾿ ὡς Χίλων᾿ ἀπέστειλεν[9]

. . . .

75 πάλιν τὸ δῶρον ἐς Θάλητ᾿ ἀνώλισθεν[10]

. . . .

"Θάλης με τῷ μεδεῦντι Νείλεω δήμου
δίδωσι, τοῦτο δὶς λαβὼν ἀριστῆον."[11]

. . . .

ἀλλ᾿ ἢν ὁρῇ τις, "οὗτος ᾿Αλκμέων" φήσει
καὶ "φεῦγε· βάλλει· φεῦγ᾿" ἐρεῖ "τὸν ἄνθρωπον."

---

[6] Lloyd-Jones, *CR* 17 (1967): 125–27; D'Alessio 2007, vol. 2,
586n28   [7] 65–70 suppl. Pf.   [8] Desunt versus ca. 20 in pap.
[9] Choerob. *De orth.* in Hdn. Περὶ ὀρθογραφίας (*Gramm.
Gr.* vol. 3.2, 407–611 Lentz)
[10] *Et.Mag.* sv Θαλῆς   [11] Diog. Laert. 1.29

442

abstain from [eating] living things; the Italians obeyed, not all, but those whom the "other spirit"[17] held back. And to him he said this, [65] after he took the golden cup from his pouch, "My father urged me to give this cup to whomever of you wise men is the best of the Seven.[18] And I am giving it to you first." Then the old man struck the earth with his stick [70] and scratching his beard with the other hand said, "[I will not accept] the gift, but you will not disobey the words of your father if . . . to Bias . . . Solon, and that man sent it to Chilon . . . [75] and again the gift returned to Thales . . . "Thales dedicates me to the Lord of the people of Neleus,[19] after twice receiving this prize of honor."

But if someone sees [me] he will say "This is Alcmeon,"[20] and "Flee! He strikes! and "Flee from the man!"

[17] Misfortune, that is, the poor became vegetarians like Pythagoras. See M. L. West, *CR* 21 (1971): 330.

[18] A canon of Presocratic philosophers and political figures first mentioned by Plato (*Protagoras* 342e–343b). The list changes somewhat in different sources (Diog. Laert. 1.5.27–34). Thales, Bias, Solon, and Chilon appear in the text, and the *Diegeseis* (191b) suggest that Periander, Pittacus, and Cleobulus completed the version that Callimachus was using.

[19] Founder of Miletus (Strabo 14.1.3).

[20] A matricide who was driven mad by the Erinyes (Apollod. *Bibl.* 3.7.5). He was the subject of tragedies by both Euripides and Sophocles.

80 ἕκαστ[ο]ς αὐτὸν .[. .]ᾳ. αρθα κηρύσσει
   ὡς υστ. . .σιν οισ. . .κοτ. . .⌒.
   ὁ δ' ἐξόπισθε Κω[ρ]υκαῖος ἐγχάσκει
   τὴν γλῶσσαν †ελων ὡς κύων ὅταν πίνῃ,
   καί φησι τοὐπι[. . . . .]ς ἐκπλεύς[
85 ε.τᾳ[..]´.[   ].αι.ηξει.[
        τὰ τρά.χηλα γυμνάζει
   ]. . . . .ουσκορ. .μος
   μαν]θάνοντες οὐδ' ἄλφα
   ]. . . κονδύλῳ καπηλεῦσ[αι
90]. . . . . . νι[.]ασυλλο.
   ]ουσερ.ρ. .οσῳ [πέ]πλον
   ]ηρ μοῦνος εἷλε τὰς [Μο]ύσας
   ].οι χλωρὰ σῦκα τρωγούσα[ς
   ]λου καὶ γέλωτος [
95 μὴ] πίθησθε· καὶ γὰρ η.[
   ]. . .ι τοῦ Χάρωνος ιν. . . .ν[
   ]ῴλνε κἀποπλεῖν ὥρη
   ]ήσας ε[   ]τω κυσω¹²

. . . .

¹² Desunt in pap. versus fere 20.

191a *Dieg.* 6.1–21

    Ἀκούσαθ' Ἱππώνακτος· οὐ γὰρ ἀλλ' ἥκω

Ὑποτίθεται φθιτὸν Ἱππώνακτα συγκαλοῦντα τοὺς φι-
λοσόφους¹ εἰς τὸ Παρμενίωνος καλούμενον Σαραπί-
δειον· ἥκουσι [5] δ' αὐτοῖς κατ' εἴλας ἀπαγορεύει φθο-

[80] Each one proclaims that he himself . . . How . . . the Corcyrean[21] gapes behind you, rolling his tongue like a dog when he drinks and he says, sailing away [85] . . . he wrings his neck . . . the ones who do not even know alpha . . . [90] to sell with a knuckle, . . . a cloak . . . alone he chose the Muses . . . munching green figs . . . laughable . . . [95] Do not be persuaded. For even . . . of Charon[22] . . . the hour to sail back . . . in the ass.

[21] Corcyrean, here a term of invective (Strabo 14.1.32).

[22] Ferryman who transported dead souls to Hades (Verg. *Aen.* 6.298–301).

191a *Diegeseis*

Listen to Hipponax! For I have come

He presents the dead Hipponax calling together the philosophers[1] into the temple of Serapis known as that of Parmenio. He exhorts those, who have assembled troop by troop, not to be envious [5] of each other, telling how the

[1] The papyrus of the *Diegeseis* VI.3 reads *philosophoi* corrected by a copyist to *philologoi*. This has been accepted by Pfeiffer and most scholars, but a reference to Euhemerus in the crowd (*Ia.* 195.10–11) shows that philosophers were included as well. On the possibility that Hipponax was addressing a group of statues that included both poets and philosophers, see Rees 1961 and Clayman 2014, 162.

---

[1] φιλοσόφους pap.: φιλολόγους Pf.

νεῖν ἀλλήλοις, λέγων ὡς Βαθυκλῆς Ἀρκὰς τελευτῶν
τήν τε ἄλλην οὐσίαν διέθετο καὶ δὴ χρυσοῦν ἔκπωμα
τῷ μέσῳ τῶν υἱῶν Ἀμφάλκῃ ἐνεχείρισεν, ὅπως δῷ τῷ
ἀρίστῳ [10] τῶν ἑπτὰ σοφῶν. ὁ δὲ ἐλθὼν εἰς Μίλητον
ἐδίδου τοῦτο Θάλητι ὡς διαφέρ[ο]ντι τῶν ἄλλων, ὁ δὲ
ἀπέπεμψε πρὸς Βίαντα τὸν Πριηνέα, ὁ δὲ πρὸς Περί-
ανδρον τὸν Κορίνθιον, ὁ δὲ ὡς Σόλωνα τὸν Ἀθηναῖον,
ὁ [δ]ὲ πρὸ[ς] Χίλωνα τὸν [15] Λ[α]κεδαι[μό]νιον, ὁ δὲ
πρὸς Π[ιτ]τακὸν τὸν Μιτυλη[ναῖον, ὁ δ]ὲ πρὸς [Κ]λεύ[-
βο]υλ[ο]ν τὸν Λί[νδι[ο]ν. [τὸ δὲ ἔκπωμα] ὑπὸ τούτου
[π]εμφθὲν [ἦλθε πάλιν εἰς Θάλητα· ὁ] δὲ ἀνατίθη[σι]
τῷ [Δ]ιδυμ[εῖ Ἀ]πόλ[λωνι δὶς λαβ]ὼν ἀριστε[ῖο]ν. τοι-
γαρ[οῦν] [20] ἔφη [............]αιο [........] ἀλλήλων
κρ τ[..........]ιοιστ[.....] ἐ]ρίζεσθε.

191b Schol. Flor. *PSI* 1094 fr. a, 1–9; fr. b, 10–42

191.1–6

] ρου[α]λλου παραινε[ ]ειαιεικνω η.[
]δὲ κέπφος ἐπ[ ]γαειπω [ ]ν κέπφο[τα .[
]υναλλ[ ]ειονς[

191.26–27

] ὦνδρε ς, ὡς παρ' αἰπόλῳ μυῖαι ἢ σφῆκες

Arcadian Bathycles, when he was dying, distributed the rest of his property and gave a golden cup to Amphalces, his middle son, so that he could give it to the best of the Seven Wise Men. [10] His son went to Miletus and gave it to Thales on the grounds that he surpassed the others, and he sent it to Bias of Priene, who sent it to Periander of Corinth, and he to Solon the Athenian, and he to Chilon the Lacedaemonian, [15] and he to Pittacus of Mytilene and he to Cleobulus of Lindos. And the cup which had been sent by this one came again to Thales. He dedicated it to Apollo at Didyma, after twice receiving it as a prize of honor. Therefore he said . . . of one another [20] . . . do [not] quarrel.

191b Florentine Scholia

191.1–6

. . . he exhorts . . . from another place
kepphos: . . . speaking of a stormy petrel

191.26–27

the men, like flies around a goatherd or wasps

ταῦτα [π]α[ρὰ τὰ τοῦ ποιητοῦ·] ͵"μνιάων͵ ἀδινάω͵ν
ἔθνεα πολλά" καὶ "σφήκ͵εσσ͵ι͵ν ἐοικότες ͵ἐξεχέοντο
εἰνοδίοις" ἢ ἀ͵πὸ θύματος Δελφ͵οί. [τοῦτο καθ᾽ ὑπερ]
βολήν· ἥττους γὰρ [οἱ Δελφοί εἰσι τῶν] μνιῶν καὶ
σφηκῶν. ἡ [δὲ ἱστορία τοιαύτη ἐστίν· τὰ [ἐ]πιθυ[—ἱε]
ρείων δ͵[͵͵]α͵ι͵ο[͵͵] ͵νο[—τούτου ἐπὶ τὸ π[λ]έον ως[—]
καὶ σκωφθῆν[αι] ὑπὸ Αἰσ[ώπου—] τα͵ γ᾽ ἐν Δελφοῖ[ς]
π͵ο͵τε κ[αὶ αἰσθόμενον τὴν] μάχαιραν εἰπεῖν· "Δελφοί,
τ͵ο͵[—] ὑμῶν, ἃ κ[ρύ]φ͵α φέρει·" τοὺς [δ᾽ ἀγανα] κτή-
σαντας τοῦτον κατακρ[ημνίσαι,] οἱ δὲ λιθόλευστον
ποιῆσαί [φασιν.

191.28

ὦ Ἑκάτη πλήθευς· εὖ τὸ τῆς Ἑ[κάτης] ὄνομα ἐπιμνη-
σθῆναι τὸν Ἱ[ππώνα]κτα φθιτὸν ὄντα· χθονία γὰρ ἡ
[Ἑκάτη.]

191b.29

ψιλοκόρσης· ψιλόκουρος. [—

191.30

φυσέων· κακῶς διεῖλεν· οὐ γάρ ἐ[στι πρώ]της συζυ-
γίας τὸ φυσῶ ῥῆμα. [—
ὅκως μὴ τὸν τρίβωνα γυμνώσῃ. [ὅπως] μὴ γυμνώσῃ
αὑτὸν τοῦ τρίβων[ος.

These words are from the poet:[1] "many tribes of swarming flies" (*Il.* 2.469), and "They poured out like wasps from the wayside" (*Il.* 16.259) or like Delphians from a sacrifice. This is hyperbole. The Delphians are fewer than flies and wasps. This is the story: the sacrifices of victims . . . surpassing this . . . and the goings on at Delphi were scorned by Aesop and that perceiving the knife he said "Delphians, the . . . of yours, which he carries off in secret."[2] And they in anger threw him down a precipice, but the poets say he was stoned.

[1] Homer.   [2] A reference to the greed of the priests at Delphi, who cut off pieces of the sacrificial meat for themselves (Ath. 4.173c–d).

191.28

"O Hecate, the crowd!": It is appropriate that Hipponax mentions Hecate since he is dead and Hecate is a chthonic deity.

191.29

psilokorsēs: smooth shaven.

191.30

phuseōn (puffing): he analyzes wrongly, for the word is not of the first conjugation.
⟨h⟩*okōs mē ton tribōna gumnōsēi*: that the man may not be stripped of his cloak.

191.32–36

ἀͺνὴρ Βαθυκλῆς Ἀρκͺὰςͺ· τὸ ἐξ[ῆς· τῶν] πάλαι τις
εὐδαίμωͺν, ἐγένετο· τ[ὰ δὲ λοιπ(ὰ) διὰ [μέ]σου.

191.33

λῶστε· βέλτιστ[ε]
μͺὴ σίμαιͺνε· μὴ σιμοποίειͺ͵[

191.34–35

ͺμέσον Ἀχέͺροντος· ἐν τῷ Ἀχέρον[τι μέσῳ[—]ον:

191.37

λευκὰς ἡμέρͺα[ς—

191.39

——οͺς ἔζωσε· ενλ[—]συνηθ[—]ͺχαραͺς[

191.32–36

Bathycles, an Arcadian man: then, one of the fortunate ones born long ago, and the rest comes in between.

191.33

lōiste: best of men
mē simaine: don't be an ape.

191.34–35

the middle of Acheron: in the midst of the river Acheron

191.37

lucky days

191.39

who lived: . . . of joy

IAMBUS II (192–192a)

192 1–3, Clem. Alex. *Strom.* 5.14.100; 4–17, *P.Oxy.* 1011 fol. 4 verso, 160–73

Ἦν κεῖνος οὑνιαυτός, ᾧ τό τε πτηνόν
καὶ τοὐν θαλάσσῃ καὶ τὸ τετράπουν αὕτως[1]
ἐφθέγγεθ' ὡς ὁ πηλὸς ὁ Προμήθειος[2]
. . . .
τἀπὶ Κρόνου τε καὶ ἔτι τὰ πρὸ τη[
5   λ. ουσα και κως [.]υ σ[.]νημεναις.[
δίκαιος ὁ [Ζε]ύς, οὐ δίκαι[α] δ'αἰσυμνέων
τῶν ἑρπετῶν [μ]ὲν ἐξέκοψε τὸ φθέ[γμα,
γένος δὲ τ.υτ.[.] ρον—ὥσπερ οὐ κάρ[τος
ἡμέων ἐχόντων χἠτέροις ἀπάρξασθαι—
10   …]ψ ἐς ἀνδρῶν· καὶ κ.υ.νὸς [μ]ὲ[ν] .Εὔ.δημος,
ὄ.νο.υ δὲ Φίλτων, ψιττακοῦ δε[
οἱ δὲ τραγῳδοὶ τῶν θάλασσαν οἰ[κεύντων[3]
ἔχο[υ]σι φωνήν· οἱ δὲ πάντες [ἄνθρωποι
καὶ πουλύμυθοι καὶ λάλοι πεφ[ύκασιν
15   ἐκεῖθεν, ὠνδρόνικε· ταῦτα δ' Α.ἴσω.πος
ὁ Σαρδιηνὸς εἶπεν, ὅντιν' οἱ Δελφοί
ᾄδοντα μῦθον οὐ καλῶς ἐδέξαντο.

[1] αὕτως Pf.: αὐτῷ Clem. Alex.: οὕτως Euseb. *Praep. evang.* 13.13.23
[2] Προμήθειος Blomfield: Προμηθέως Clem. Alex.
[3] οἰ[κεύντων suppl. Wilamowitz

IAMB 2 (192–192a)

192 Clement of Alexandria, *Stromata*; Oxyrhynchus papyrus

It was that time when the winged ones, the ones in the sea, and the four-footed ones[1] still spoke like Promethean clay.[2] . . . in the time of Cronus[3] and even earlier [5] . . . saying even how . . . Zeus is just but was not ruling justly when he deprived the animals of their speech, a race . . . as if we did not have enough to pass around to others—. . . [10] to the race of men. And Eudemus[4] has the voice of a dog, Philton, of an ass, ... of a parrot and the tragedians have the voice of those living in the sea. Hence, Andronicus, all men have become verbose and chatterers. [15] These things Aesop of Sardis said, whom the Delphians received ungraciously when he was singing a tale.[5]

[1] For the classification of animals by locomotion, see Arist. *HA* 488a.   [2] In an Aesopic fable (240 Perry), Prometheus molds humans and animals. Then Zeus, noting that there were too many irrational animals, ordered him to remake some of the beasts as humans. The result was humans with the souls of animals.

[3] Titan, father of Zeus and the other Olympians, whose reign was proverbially just and peaceful (Hes. *Op*. 109–20).

[4] Neither Eudemus, Philton, nor Andronicus can be indentified securely with a known individual.   [5] An understatement (cf. *Ia*. 191b, where it is reported that the Delphians stoned Aesop or threw him over a cliff).

CALLIMACHUS

192a *Dieg.* 6.22–32

ἦν κε‚ῖν‚ος ο‚ὑ‚νιαυτός, ᾧ τό τε ‚πτ‚ηνόν

Τἄλλ‚[α] ζῷα ὡμοφώνει ἀν‚[θ]ρώποις, μέχρι κατὰ λύ-
σιν γήρως ἐπ[ρέ]σβευσεν ὁ [25] κύκνος πρὸς τοὺς
θεοὺς καὶ ἀλώπηξ τὸν Δία ἐτόλμησεν μὴ δικαίως ἄρ-
χειν φάναι. ἔκτοτε δὲ εἰς ἀνθρώπους μετήνεγκεν
αὐτῶν τὴν φωνήν, καὶ λάλοι ἐγένοντο· Εὔδημος δέ,
φησίν, τὴν κυνὸς [30] ἔσχε, Φίλτων δὲ ὄνου, παρεπι-
κόπτων τούτους, ἴσως δὲ καὶ Σαρδιανὸν εἶπε τὸν Αἴ-
σωπον.

IAMBUS III (193–193a)

193 1–13, *P.Oxy.* 1011 fol. 4 verso, 174–86; 5–24 (fin.),
P.Oxy. 2215 fr. 1.1–20; 24–39, *P.Oxy.* 1011 fol. 4 recto,
190–205

Ε‚ἴ‚θ᾿ ἦν, ἄ‚ναξ‚ ὤπολλον, ἡνίκ᾿ οὐκ ἦα
    ]αι· καὶ σὺ κάρτ᾿ ε[‚.]‚μᾶσθε
    ]ῖ[   ].[   ].ζεν·
[   ]
5   ].[   ].‚υτης
         ].‚ις αὐτ᾿ ἐποίησεν
        ]νερθε δεῖ κεῖσθαι
        ]λιστι δ᾿ οἰκεῦμεν
       ] ζόη μετέστραπται
10   ]α Φοῖβε, ληκῆσαι

454

IAMB 3

192a *Diegeseis*

It was that time when the winged

The other animals spoke in the same voice as men, until
the swan made an embassy to the gods [to request] release
from old age and the fox dared to say that Zeus did not
rule justly. And from that time he transferred their voice
to men who became chatterboxes. Eudemus, he says sar-
castically, had the voice of a dog, Philton of an ass. And
likewise he spoke about Aesop of Sardis.

IAMB 3 (193–193a)

193 Oxyrhynchus papyrus

I wish I had lived, Lord Apollo, before my time . . . even
you, truly . . . [6] he did the same things . . . should lie
under . . . we live . . . life is upside down . . . [10] Phoebus,

]ον· οὐντραφεὶς δ' ὑμῖν
] ἐκεῖνος ὤνθρωπος
α]ἰ κακαὶ ψῆφοι
]ονοιτ' ἀνάσσ[ο]ντε[ς
15   ]ε δεξιῇ τρώγειν
]λέγουσι τὰ πρῶτα·
]ας με· φεῦ· τὸν ἄκληρο[ν
ἐ]πείπερ ἥμαρτες
]δε λαστ..ρεξ.[
20   ]. πολλάκις......[
]ρ...[.].[.].ς
]τη..ο...
].οσεν[ ]...
.....]ς, ὥσ[π]ερ Εὐθύδημον ἡ μήτηρ
25   ....].ανα νυν οὐδὲ πῦρ ἐναύουσιν
...] χαῖρ' ἔφησα.[.].ιν λῷ [σ]υναντήσας
..]δεξιὴν ἔδωκε κ.πα..σπλάγχνα
[..]ν ἐν ἱραῖς εἶπεν [ἡμέ]ραις ἥκειν
καὶ γαμβρὸν...ω...α[.] φίλον θέσθαι
30   .. υ[.].. χε.[.]ν κρηγύως ἐπαιδεύθην
..[ἐ]φρόνησα τὠγαθὸν βλέψαι
]τε καὶ θεοὺς ἀπρηγεῦντας
]..μόχθηρος ἐξεκνήμωσ.[
].ν μοι τοῦτ' ἂν ἦν ὀνήϊσ[το]ν
35   .]υ[.].[.] Κ[υβή]βῃ τὴν κόμην ἀναρρίπτειν
Φρύγ[α] πρ[ὸς] αὐλὸν ἢ ποδήρες ἕλκοντα
Ἄδω[ν]ιν αἰαῖ, τῆς θεοῦ τὸν ἄνθρωπον,

to bawl ... the one trained with you ... that man ... evil
votes ... the rulers ... [15] to munch with the right hand
... they speak first ... me, alas, without an allotment,
since you failed ... [20] often ... just as his mother ...
Euthydemus[1] ... [25] now they do not even kindle fire ...
I said "Greetings," when I met him ... he gave his right
hand ... over the sacrificial entrails ... he said he had
come on the holy days ... and to hold his suitor dear ...
[30] I was educated rightly ... I thought I saw the good
... and the gods inactive ... a loser I ruined ... for
me this would have been best [35] to toss my hair for
Cybele[2] to the Phrygian flute or trailing my robe to cry
ai ai for Adonis,[3] the Goddess' man. But as it is, madman

---

[1] Probably an archetype of a youthful lover on the Socratic
model (Xen. *Mem.* 1.2.29, 4.2.1–6).

[2] Phrygian mother goddess, worshipped with ecstatic rites;
her priests, the Galli or Gallae, self-castrated (Catull. 63).

[3] A youthful lover of Aphrodite (Theoc. *Id.* 15.100–144)
whose death was mourned annually at the Adonia in Athens
(Ar. *Lys.* 387–90; Plut. *Alcib.* 18.2).

ἰηλεμίζειν· νῦν δ᾽ ὁ μάργος ἐς Μούσας
ἔνευσα· τοίγα[ρ] ἦν ἔμαξα δει[πν]ήσω.[1]

[1] δει[πν]ήσω Kerkhecker, 80n95

193a *Dieg.* 6.33–40

Εἴθ᾽ ἦν, ἄναξ ὤπολλον, ἡνίκ᾽ οὐκ ἦα

Καταμέμφεται τὸν καιρὸν ὡς πλούτου [35] μᾶλλον ἢ
ἀρετῆς ὄντα, τὸν δὲ πρὸ αὐτοῦ ἀποδέχεται ὃς τῆς
ἐναντίας ἦν τούτων γνώμης· παρεπικόπτει δὲ καὶ Εὐ-
θύδημόν τινα, ὡς κεχρημένον τῇ ὥρᾳ πορισμῷ, ὑπὸ
[40] τῆς μητρὸς πλουσίῳ συσταθέντα.

IAMBUS IV (194–194a)

194 1–12, *P.Oxy.* 1011 fol. 4 recto, 206–17; 14–21, *P.Oxy.*
2215 fr. 2.1–8; 22–64, *P.Oxy.* 1011 fol. 5 verso, 218–60;
65–106, *P.Oxy.* 1011 fol. 5 recto, 261–302; 107–17, *PSI*
1216 col. I, 1–11; 115–17 (init.), *P.Ryl.* 485.1–3

Ε̣ἷ̣ς—ο̣ὐ̣ γάρ;—ἡμέων, παῖ Χαριτά̣δεω, καὶ σύ
.[....]ϣίκ[.].[....]᾽[
[   ]
παρ[.....].[
5 ἡ μὲν .[.]ηνέκ[
ἄκου̣ε̣, δὴ τὸν αἶνον· ἔν κοτε Τμώλῳ
δάφνην ἐλαίη νεῖ̣κος οἱ πάλαι Λυδοί
λέγουσι θέσθαι καὶ γα[

458

that I am, I have inclined to the Muses, and I will eat what I have kneaded.

193a *Diegeseis*

I wish I had lived, Lord Apollo, when I did not

He finds fault with the time as valuing wealth rather than virtue and he prefers the previous era which had mores opposite to these. And he ridicules a certain Euthydemus who was introduced to a rich man by his mother and used the bloom of his youth for profit.

IAMB 4 (194–194a)

194 Oxyrhynchus papyri; papyrus fragment; Rylands papyrus

One—is it not so?—of us, son of Charitades,[1] even you [5] . . . do listen to the tale. Once on Tmolus[2] the ancient Lydians say a laurel began a quarrel with an olive . . . a

---

[1] Literally, "Son of the Charites," and so a poet or a musician. [2] Mountain in Lydia, site of musical contests between Apollo and Pan, as well as Apollo and Marsyas (Ov. *Met.* 11.146–71, 6.382–400).

καλόν τε δένδρε[ον
10 σείσασ[α] τοὺς ὄρπηκ[ας
ο.[..]συμη.ηφη[
.]...[.].ε..[.]ελουσιν[¹

†ἐγὼ φαύλη πάντων τῶν δένδρων εἰμί†²

].·[

15 τάλαινα[
ἐμεῦ πα[
τῆ δ᾽ αὐτι[ς
"ὤφρων ἐ[λαίη
ἐγὼ δεμ.[
20 ὁ Δῆλον ο[ἰκέων
καί μευ τ[

ὠριστερὸς μὲν λευκὸς ὡς ὕδρου γαστήρ,
ὁ δ᾽ ἡλιοπλὴξ ὃς τὰ [π]ολλὰ γυμνοῦται.
τίς δ᾽ οἶκος οὗπερ [ο]ὐκ ἐγὼ παρὰ φλιῆ;
25 τίς δ᾽ οὔ με μάντις ἢ τίς οὐ θύτης ἕλκει;
καὶ Πυθίη γὰρ ἐν δάφνη μὲν ἵδρυται,
δάφνην δ᾽ ἀείδει καὶ δάφνην ὑπέστρωται.
ὤφρων ἐλαίη, τοὺς δὲ παῖδας οὐ Βράγχος
τοὺς τῶν Ἰώνων, οἷς ὁ Φοῖβος ὠ[ργίσθη,
30 δάφνη τε κρούων κῆπος οὐ τομ[ὸν λαοῖ]ς³
δὶς ἢ τρὶς ε[ἰ]πὼν ἀρτεμέας ἐποίη[σε;
κ]ἠγὼ μὲν ἢ 'πὶ δαῖτας ἢ 'ς χορὸν φ[οι]τέω

460

beautiful tree . . . [10] after she shook her branches[3] . . .
"I am inferior to all trees[4] . . . [15] wretched . . . my . . . to
her again . . ." "Foolish Olive . . . I . . . [20] the one [inhab-
iting] Delos . . . and my . . . Your left side is white like the
belly of a water snake; the other, which often is left ex-
posed, is sunburned. Is there any house where I am not
beside the doorpost? [25] Is there any seer or sacrificer
who does not carry me? In fact the Pythia[5] sits on the
laurel; she sings the laurel, and laurel is strewn beneath
her. Foolish Olive, did not Branchus[6] cure the sons of
the Ionians who had angered Phoebus [30] striking them
with a laurel and repeating his spell two or three times?
I too frequent the Pythian feasts and dances, and I am

---

[3] The shaking of the laurel, indicating Apollo's presence (Ar.
Plut. 212–13; Call. *Hymn* 2.1).   [4] The olive speaks ironically
([Trypho], *Peri tropōn* 24; Spengel, *Rhet.* 3.206.15).

[5] Priestess who delivered oracles in Apollo's shrine at Delphi,
perhaps named for Python, the snake Apollo killed when he ap-
propriated the site (Strabo 9.3.5).   [6] Branchus is also fea-
tured in Callimachus' fourth lyric poem (*Mel.* 229).

---

[1] Fere 9 versus desunt.

[2] [Trypho], Περὶ τρόπων 24

[3] Suppl. Pf.

τὸν Πυθαϊστήν· γίνομαι δὲ κἄεθλον·
οἱ Δωριῆς δὲ Τεμπόθεν με τέμνουσιν
35 ὀρέων ἀπ' ἄκρων καὶ φέρουσιν ἐς Δελφούς,
ἐπὴν τὰ τὠπόλλωνος ἴρ' ἀγινῆται.[4]
ἱρὴ γάρ εἰμι·[5] πῆμα δ' οὐχὶ γινώσκω
οὐδ' οἶδ' ὁκ[οίη]ν οὐλαφηφόρος κάμπτει,
ἁ‚γν‚ὴ γάρ εἰμι, κού πατεῦσί μ' ἄνθρωποι,
40 ὤφρων ἐλαίη,[6] σοὶ δὲ χὠπότ' ἂν νεκρόν
μέλλωσι καίειν ἢ [τά]φ[ῳ] περιστέλλει[ν,
αὐτοί τ' ἀνεστέψ[αντο χ]ὑπὸ τὰ πλευρά
τοῦ μὴ πνέοντ[ος ...]παξ ὑπ[έ]στ[ρωσαν."
ἡ μὲν τά‚δ', οὐκέτ' ἄλλα· τὴν δ' ἀπήλ[λαξε
45 μάλ' ἀτρεμαίως ἡ τεκοῦσα τὸ χρῖμ[α·
"ὦ πάντα κα‚λή, τῶν ἐμῶν τὸ κ[άλλιστον
ἐν τῇ τελευτῇ κύκνος [ὡς Ἀπόλλωνος[7]
ἤεισας· οὕτω μὴ κάμοιμ[ι ποιεῦσα
ἐγὼ μὲν ἄνδρας, οὓς Ἄρη[ς ἀπόλλυσι
50 συνέκ τε πέμπω χὑ[πὸ
.‚] ων ἀριστέων, οἳ κα......[...].[..].,
ἐγὼ] δὲ λευκὴν ἡνίκ' ἐς τάφον Τηθύν
φέρο[υσι] παῖδες ἢ γέροντα Τιθωνόν,
αὐτή [θ' ὁ]μαρτέω κἠπὶ τὴν ὁδὸν κεῖμαι·
55 γηθέω δὲ πλεῖον ἢ σὺ τοῖς ἀγινεῦσιν
ἐκ τῶν σε Τεμπέων. ἀλλ' ἐπεὶ γὰρ ἐμνήσθης
καὶ τοῦτο· κῶς ἄεθλον οὐκ ἐγὼ κρέσσων
σεῦ; καὶ γὰρ ὠγὼν ο‚ὖν Ὀλυμπίῃ μέζων
ἢ 'ν τοῖσι Δελφοῖς· ἀλλ' ἄριστον ἡ σωπή.

[4] ἴρ' ἀγινῆται Maas, Pf.: ιρὰ γίνηται P   [5] Trans. ex 40

the prize. The Dorians cut me on the peaks of Tempe,[7] [35] and bring me into Delphi whenever the holy rites of Apollo are celebrated. For I am holy; I do not know pain. Nor do I know where the undertaker bends his knee. For I am holy and people do not trample me. [40] But with you, foolish Olive, whenever they are about to cremate a corpse or to lay it out in the grave, they wreathe themselves and strew you by the sides of the one who is no longer breathing." This much she said and nothing more.

[45] But the begetter of the oil replied calmly, "O lovely in every way, you sang of my best aspects at the end, like the swan of Apollo.[8] May I never tire of doing that. For I accompany below the men whom Ares has killed [50] and . . . of the noblest who . . . and whenever children carry to the grave a white-haired Tethys or an aged Tithonus[9] I accompany them and lie strewn along the path. [55] And I rejoice more in this than you in those who bring you from Tempe. But since you mention this too, how am I not an even greater prize than you? For the contest at Olympia is greater than the one at Delphi.

[7] In Thessaly, a gorge between Mts. Olympus and Ossa, where Apollo purified himself after killing Python (Ael. *VH* 3.1).

[8] The swan, which was thought to sing its most beautiful song at its death, is associated with Apollo in Callimachus' *Hymn to Delos* (*Hymn* 4.249) and in Plato (*Phd.* 84e–85b). [9] Archetypes of elderly men and women. Tethys was a Titan, mother of gods and rivers (Hes. *Theog.* 337–70; Hom. *Il.* 14.200–205); Tithonus, lover of Eos, was given immortality but not eternal youth (*Hymn. Hom. Aph.* 5.218–38).

---

sugg. Maas, Pf. add. et corr. (vol. 1, 505).   [6] Trans. ex 37
sugg. Maas, Pf. add. et corr. (vol. 1, 505).   [7] Suppl. Pf.

60 ἐγὼ μὲν οὔτε χρηστὸν οὔτε σε γρύζω
ἀπηνὲς οὐδέν· ἀλλά μοι δύ᾽ ὄρνιθες
ἐν τοῖσι φύλλοις ταῦτα τινθυρίζουσαι
πάλαι κάθηνται· κωτίλον δὲ τὸ ζεῦγος.
τίς δ᾽ εὗρε δάφνην; γῆ τε καὶ κα[. . .]σ[
65 ὡς πρῖνον, ὡς δρῦν, ὡς κύπειρον, ὡς πεύκην.
τίς δ᾽ εὗρ᾽ ἐλαίην; Παλλάς, ἦμος [ἤρ]ιζ[ε
τῷ φυκιοίκῳ κἠδίκαζεν ἀρχαίοις
ἀνὴρ ὄφις τὰ νέρθεν ἀμφὶ τῆς Ἀκτῆς.
ἐν ᾗ δάφνη πέπτωκε. τῶν δ᾽ ἀειζώων
70 τίς τὴν ἐλαίην, τίς δὲ [τ]ὴν δάφνην τιμᾷ;
δάφνην Ἀπόλλων, ἡ δὲ Παλλὰς ἣν εὗρε.
ξυνὸν τόδ᾽ αὐταῖς, θεοὺς γὰρ οὐ διακρίνω.
τί τῆς δάφνης ὁ καρπός; ἐς τί χρήσωμαι;
μήτ᾽ ἔσθε μήτε πῖνε μήτ᾽ ἐπιχρίσῃ.
75 ὁ τῆς δ᾽ ἐλαίης ἐν μὲν †αλιτιτωτ†[8] μάσταξ
ὃ στ[έμφυλο]ν[9] καλεῦσιν, ἐν δὲ τὸ χρῖμα,
ἐν [δ᾽ ἡ κολ]υμβὰς ἣν ἔπωνε χὠ Θησεύς·
τ[ὸ δ]εύ[τερ]ον τίθημι τῇ δάφνῃ πτῶμα.
τεῦ γὰρ [τὸ] φύλλον οἱ ἱκέται προτείνουσι;
80 τὸ τῆς ἐλαίης· τὰ τρί᾽ ἡ δάφνη κεῖται.
(φεῦ τῶν ἀτρύτων, οἷα κωτιλίζουσι·
λαιδρὴ κορώνη, κῶς τὸ χεῖλος οὐκ ἀλγεῖς;)
τεῦ γ]ὰρ τὸ πρέμνον Δήλιοι φυλάσσουσι;
τὸ τ]ῆς ἐλαίης ᾗ ἀν[έπαυσε] τὴν Λητώ.

[8] ὁ ἁλιέως Lloyd-Jones   [9] Suppl. Diels

But silence is best. [60] For about you I murmur nothing kind or cruel. But two birds have been sitting for a long time in my leaves chirping these things, a chattering pair.[10] 'Who discovered the laurel?' 'The earth and . . . [65] like the ilex, like the oak, like the galingale, like the pine.' 'Who discovered the olive?' 'Pallas, when among the ancients around Acte[11] she competed with the one who lives in seaweed, and a man who is a snake below the waist adjudicated.' 'One fall for the laurel. [70] And of the immortals, who honors the olive, who the laurel?' 'Apollo, the laurel and Athena, the one she discovered. 'That is a tie, for I do not distinguish between the gods.' 'What is the fruit of the laurel? For what do I use it?' 'Do not eat it, do not drink it, do not use it for anointing. [75] The flesh of the olive yields what they call an olive cake and also oil, as well as the pickled olive that Theseus drank.'[12] 'I reckon that's a second fall for the laurel. Whose leaf do suppliants offer?' [80] 'The olive's.' 'The laurel is down for the third time.'

(Oh my, they never tire! How they keep tweeting. Impudent crow, how is your lip not sore?) 'Whose trunk do the Delians preserve? That of the olive, which gave rest to

---

[10] Speaking birds also appear in Callimachus' *Hecale* (*Hec.* 70–77); see Hollis, 231–32.   [11] Athena and Poseidon contested for Athens, and Cecrops, the first king of Attica, who was a man above the waist and a snake below, served as judge (Call. *Hec.* 70.9–11). Acte was the ancient port of Athens that preceded the Piraeus and here stands for the primordial city.

[12] A reference to Theseus' famous meal of olives (cf. *Hec.* 36–37); see Hollis, 173–74.

85 .....]οι πολῖται κ[   ]τι τῷ δήμῳ
      ].τανουν ἔστεφέν μιν ἡ δάφνη
      ]α θαλλῷ καλλίνικος ἡλαίη
      ]υφανητε κἠπὶ τὴν ὄγχνην
      ].τερην τιν᾽ αἰνεῖται
90   ].κουτεκοι μάντεις
       ]ν οὔτ᾽ ἐπὶ φλιῆς
[.]   φ]ημι τὴν δάφνην."
ὣς εἶπε· τῇ δ᾽ ὁ θυμὸς ἀμφὶ τῇ ῥήσει
ἤλγησε, μέζων δ᾽ ἢ τὸ πρόσθεν ἠγέ[ρ]θη
95 τ]ὰ δεύτερ᾽ ἐς τὸ νεῖκος, ἔστε τιν.[
βάτος τὸ τρηχὺ τειχέων π..δ.[.]να
ἔλεξεν (ἦν γὰρ οὐκ ἄπωθε τῶν δενδρέων)·
"οὐκ ὦ τάλαιναι παυσόμεσθα, μὴ χαρταὶ
γενώμεθ᾽ ἐχθροῖς, μηδ᾽ ἐροῦμεν ἀλλήλας
100 ἄνολβ᾽ ἀναιδέως, ἀλλὰ ταῦτά γ᾽.β..μ.;"
τὴν δ᾽ ἄρ᾽ ὑποδρὰξ οἷα ταῦρος ἡ δάφνη
ἔβλεψε καὶ τάδ᾽ εἶπεν· "ὦ κακὴ λώβη,
ὡς δὴ μί᾽ ἡμέων καὶ σύ; μή με ποιῆσαι
Ζεὺς τοῦτο· καὶ γὰρ γειτονεῦσ᾽ ἀποπνίγεις
105   ].ς οὐ μὰ Φοῖβον, οὐ μὰ δέσποιναν,
τῇ κ]ύμβαλοι ψοθεῦσιν, οὐ μὰ Πακτ[ωλόν
. . . . 10
              ]ας ἀλλήλους
              ] δρήστης
              ]. ἔστηκεν
110   ]ἥδιστος·
              πε]ποιήσθω·

466

Leto.[13] [85] Citizens . . . for the people . . . the laurel crowned . . . the victorious olive [with] her branch . . . even to the pear tree . . . she praises someone [90] . . . seers . . . not by the doorpost . . . I say the laurel."

So she spoke, but the heart of the other grieved at this speech. And more than before she collected herself [95] for a second contest, until a rough bramble [under] the walls spoke (for she was not far from the trees), "O wretched ones, will we not stop, so that we do not give cheer to our enemies, or shamelessly say [100] ill-omened things to each other, but these . . ." The laurel gave her a look from under her brows like a bull and said, "O evil disgrace, how are you one of us? I mean you. Don't do this to me, Zeus! You choke me, being my neighbor. . . . [105] no by Phoebus, no by the goddess for whom cymbals crash,[14] no by Pactolus.[15] . . . one another . . . a worker . . .

[13] In Callimachus' *Hymn to Delos* (*Hymn* 4.209–11), Leto leans on the trunk of a palm tree when she gives birth to Apollo.

[14] Cybele, Phrygian mother goddess worshipped with ecstatic rites and music (Dem. *De cor.* 259–60).   [15] River in Lydia rising on Mt. Tmolus (Hdt. 5.101).

[10] Versus desunt inter 106 et 107.

]μη χείρων
]ολπηι·
. . . .].

115 .ηρ.[   ].
     τοδ.[   ]ν·
     ἔχει[   ]

194a *Dieg.* 7.1–18

Εἷς—οὐ γάρ;—ἡμέων παῖ Χαριτάδεω καὶ σύ

Διεφέρετο ὁ ποιητὴς πρός τινα τῶν ἐφαμίλλων· Σῖμος δέ τις παρατυχὼν παρυπέκρουεν ἄμφω παρενδεικνύμενος ἴσος εἶναι. [5] Θρᾷκα δέ φησιν αὐτὸν καθεστάναι ⟨—⟩ παιδοκλέπτης ἐστί. καὶ γὰρ τὸν αἶνον παρατίθεται ἀκόλουθον, ὡς ἐν Τμώλῳ ⟨δάφνη καὶ⟩ ἐλαία διεφέροντο ὑπὲρ πρωτείων (παρεπεφύκεσαν δ᾽ ἀλλήλαις), διεξῄεσαν [10] δὲ τὰ προσόντα ἑαυταῖς χρήσιμα. ἐπὶ πλεῖον δὲ διαφερομένων ὑποτυχοῦσα βάτος παλαιά· "πέπαυθε πρὶν εἰ μὴ ἐ[π]ίχαρτοι ⟨τοῖ⟩ς δυσ-[μ]ενέσι γενώμεθα" (π[αρ]επεφύκ[ει δ᾽ αὐ]ταῖς). [15] [πρ]ὸς ἦν ἀποβλέψασα [.........] ἡ δά[φν]η "ὦ κακὴ λώβη," φη[σίν], "ὡς δὴ μ῾ἴ ἡμέ῾ων καὶ σ῾ύ;...]σεικο[......]συε..]ινητ[...]ατωδρα[......]εισεις

he set up . . . [110] the sweetest . . . may it have been made
. . . not worse . . . [115] . . .

194a *Diegeseis*

One—oh no—of us, son of Charitades,[1] even you

The poet disputes with one of his rivals. A certain Simus,[2]
happening by, interrupted both of them to show that he
was their equal. [5] He writes that he is a Thracian[3] and a
trafficker of boys and he adds the following story, how on
Tmolus a laurel and an olive disputed about priority (for
they grew beside one another). They were going through
[10] their own attributes. An ancient bramble happening
by them as they argued even more said, "Stop before we
gratify our enemies," (for it grew beside them) . . . [15]
The laurel looked down at her and said "O evil disgrace,
how are you one of us?"

[1] Literally, "Son of the Charites," and so a poet or a musi-
cian.   [2] Literally, "snub-nosed," so an ape or a lecher (cf. *Ia*.
191.33 above, where Hipponax abuses a heckler using this term).

[3] The Thracian poet Orpheus was said to have invented ped-
erasty (Ov. *Met*. 10.7–85).

IAMBUS V (195–195a)

195 1–7, *P.Ryl.* 485.4–10; 1–34, *PSI* 1216 col. I, 12–14 et
14a–44; 35–68, *PSI* 1216 col. II, 45–78; 54–63, *P.Oxy.*
2171 fr. 2 col. I, 1–10; inter 35 et 53, *P.Oxy.* 2171 fr. 1.1–9
(195a Pf.)

᾽Ω ξεῖνε—συμβουλὴ ˌγὰρ ἔν τι τῶν ἱρῶν—
　　ἄκουε τἀπὸ καρδ[ίης,　　　　]
ἐπεὶ σε δαίμων ἄλφα βῆτ[α　　　]
　　οὐχ ὡς ὀνήϊστον ̣[　　　　　]
5　ἀλλ᾽ οἷον ἄνδρ[α] συ[　].ˌων...πων
　　καὶ σ ̣[　　　　　　　].
ἔ]δ ̣ωκε[　　　　　　].ε ̣η μᾶζα·
　.　.　.　.　　　　　].a
　　　　　　　　　].ιλεοχρη..
10　　　　　]ε. ἐργάτην·
　　　　]μνειν κἠξ ὄρευς ἄγειν ὕλην
　　　　]..ιμαινε.πάϊς·
　　　　].στηρ ἐς θάλασσαν ἐμβαίνειν
　　　　]λλα φρονέων
15　　　　].[.]...[.].[.]ων ἐπαυρήσεις
　　　　].ˌπαθευμεν...
　　　　]ν ἀλγέων μηδὲ γούνατα κλ ̣ί ̣ν ̣ω ̣ν ̣
　　　　]ν ἄσσα τοι λ[έγ]ω·
　　　　]..βουν·....νατω ποδὶ τρ ̣έ ̣ψη
20　　　]κεραυνώσῃ[..]...
　　　　].ον μαστὸ[ν]...[.]κεινωθη

IAMB 5 (195–195a)

195 Rylands papyrus; papyrus fragment; Oxyrhynchus papyrus

O stranger—for good counsel is something sacred—listen from the heart . . . since fortune has made you [a teacher of] the alphabet[1] . . . not best . . . [5] but such a man . . . and . . . he gave . . . bread . . . [10] a worker . . . and to carry wood from the mountain . . . boy. To go to sea . . . thinking . . . [15] you will enjoy . . . neither grieving nor bending the knee . . . whatsoever I say to you . . . an ox . . . may you turn with your foot . . . [20] may you be thunder-

---

[1] Being called a schoolteacher is a common insult attested in comedy and the poetry of abuse, and also in oratory. Epicurus is insulted in this way by Timon of Phlius in his *Silloi* (Clayman 2009, 90–91). It is likely that Callimachus himself suffered the same fate, since the *Suda* says he was a schoolteacher in Eleusis before becoming a poet (cf. Cameron 1995, 5–7).

ὥς, δ᾽ ἄν σε θωϊὴ λάβοι·
τὸ πῦρ δὲ τώνέκαυσας, ἄχρις οὐ πολλῇ
   πρόσω κεχώρηκεν φλογί,
25 ἀλλ᾽ ἀτρεμίζει κἠπὶ τὴν τέφρην οἰ[χ]νεῖ,
   κοίμησον. ἴσχε δὲ δρόμου
μαργῶντας ἵππους μηδὲ δευτέρη̣ν̣ κάμψῃς,
   μή τοι περὶ νύσσῃ δίφρ̣ον
ἄξωσιν, ἐκ δὲ κύμβαχ̣ος κυβισ̣τήσῃς.
30   ἆ, μή με ποιήσῃ γέ[λω.
ἐγὼ Βάκις τοι καὶ Σίβυλλα [καὶ] δάφνη
   καὶ φηγός. ἀλλὰ συμβαλεῦ
τὧνιγμα, καὶ μὴ Πιτθέως ἔχε χρείην·
   ....]τι καὶ κωφεῖ λόγος.
35 ἐγὼ [
   τὸν πα̣[
μη̣ οιακα.[
   συμπαιζ[   ]̣αι̣ετας[
και̣ ̣νε̣[   ]̣ ̣ι̣·
40   ὡς μητ̣[   ]δυτοκαιμον[
δέλτοι γὰρ [   ]
   εἰ δ᾽, ὦνα...[   ]̣ ̣[̣.]ε̣η̣[
καί τοι δοκέω.[   ]
   ἐπαντι...[   ]...προκη..[
45 ἄθυμος οὐδ[   ]ταλαν
   εμευμενες[   ]π̣ρήκουσα[
τῶν εἴ τι π̣[.   .   .   .
   μηδ᾽ ὅσσον̣[
οὔτ᾽ εἶδον· ου̣[

472

struck . . . breast . . . emptied . . . in this way would you be punished. . . . The fire that you kindled, as long as it has not advanced onward with much flame, [25] but keeps quiet and runs among the ashes, put it to bed, and hold back your mad horses from the race nor guide them on the second lap round the turning post,[2] lest they wreck your chariot and you tumble out headfirst. [30] Ah, don't make me a laughingstock. I am your Bacis, your Sibyl, the laurel and oak.[3] But solve this riddle and do not have need for Pittheus[4] . . . speech for a deaf man.

[35] I . . . not . . . play with . . . and . . . [40] how not . . . for writing tablets . . . if . . . and indeed I seem . . . [45] fainthearted nor . . . if something of these . . . not as much

---

[2] Racers drove their chariots out to a turning post then back again to the finish (e.g., Hom. *Il*. 23.309).   [3] A list of oracles: Bacis, in Boeotia (Hdt. 8.20, 9.43); Sibyl, in various locations (Ver. *Aen*. 3.441–52); laurel, the oracle of Apollo at Delphi (*Hymn. Hom. Ap*.); oak, the oracle of Zeus at Dodona (Hom. *Il*. 16.233–38; Hdt. 2:55).   [4] One of the Seven Wise Men and a traditional interpreter of oracles (Eur. *Med*. 683–86; cf. Pittacus in Call. *Epig*. 1).

50   ὀθνεῖα γειν.[
     ὄψεαί με δυσ[
      ποιεῦντα το[
    θ...ων...[.   .   .   .   .
      ἔλαυνε· μη.[   ].[
55 οὐδ' οὑμὸσ.[   ]λ[
      λιπησαδυ.[   ]
    πέμπουσιν[   ]μη[.]ονεινεπασ[.]να[ ]
      φεῦ ταῦτα [   ]ς·
    ἔμπης ..[   ].αιχα...μ.σεων
60   ...ευφ[   ]
    ....[   ].πολ.[.]σ..[ ]
     ψήφ...[...]ί..[   ].[
   ..ε.[.]ση.....[   ].α[
      ἔκφα.[.   .   .   .
65 ησητο..[
     ηδεσμ.[
    καὶ φιμὸν[
     ωγησε..[

195a *Dieg.* 7.19–24

   Ὦ ξεῖνε—συμβουλὴ γ[ὰ]ρ ἔν τι τῶν ἱρῶν—]

Γραμματο[δ]ιδάσκαλ[ο]ν, ὄνομα Ἀπολλώνιον, [20] οἱ
δὲ Κλέωνά τινα, ἰαμβίζει ὡς τοὺς ἰδίους μαθητὰς
καταισχύνοντα, ἐν ἤθει εὐνοίας ἀπαγ[ο]ρεύων τούτῳ
δρᾶν, μὴ ἁλῷ.

. . . I did not see . . . [50] foreign . . . you will see me . . .
doing . . . drive on! Nor . . . [55] nor my . . . they send . . .
alas these things . . . all the same [60] . . . [66] restraints
and a gag

195a *Diegeseis*

O stranger—for good counsel is something sacred—

In the appearance of goodwill, he writes iambic verse
against a schoolteacher, Apollonius[1] by name, but others
call him a certain Cleon, on the grounds that he is abusing
his own students, dissuading him from doing it, so he will
not be caught.

[1] Callimachus clearly did not mention the name of his target
in his poem. Apollonius and Cleon are conjectures of later com-
mentators.

IAMBUS VI (196–196a)

196 1–21, *PSI* 1216 col. II, 79–99; 22–49, *P.Oxy.* 2171 fr. 2 col. II, 1–28; 22–37, *P.Oxy.* 2171 fr. 4 col. I, 1–16; 22f, *P.Oxy.* 2171 fr. 5.2f; 58–62, *P.Oxy.* 2171 fr. 3.1–5

Ἀ‚λεῖος ὁ Ζε‚ύς, ἁ τέχνα δὲ Φειδία
   ..ωχ`....[
η.[.]...το.[
   ..[
5 ..[
   αυτ[
αν..[
   τῶ.[
ουκ[
10   .α..[`].⌢.`[
.ανδιφ....[
   Πῖσαν ω...[
παχ`.τιμ[
   εκδε..[
15 ..[
. . . . ¹

.ς λαγὸς χελύναν,
καὶ τὠπίβαθρον τῶ θρόν[ω] τὸ χρύ[σι]ον
   .].εν ἐπλάτυνται.
25 ..].δ[.]ειρὰν πέντε τε[τ]ρ[άκι]ν [πο]δῶν
   ...]τ[.]δ᾽ ἐς ἰθύ,
...].. τετράδωρα ταν[   ].[

476

IAMB 6 (196–196a)

196 Papyrus fragment; Oxyrhynchus papyrus

Zeus of Elis,[1] the work of Phidias,[2] [9] . . . not . . . [12] Pisa
. . . [22] hare . . . a tortoise, and the gold base of the throne
. . . they widen out. . . . [25] four times five feet . . . straight
. . . four palms long . . . palms . . . of Lydian[3] craftsmanship

[1] Town in the Peloponnese near ancient Olympia that admin-
istered the games (Strabo 8.3.30).

[2] Athenian sculptor who also designed the statue of Athena
Parthenos on the Acropolis. He was later accused of stealing
some of the gold that was purchased for the statue (Plut. *Per.*
31).   [3] Lydia in western Anatolia was a source of luxury tex-
tiles (*Aet.* 80.6; Sappho 98a.11 Voigt), but here perhaps the refer-
ence is to gold.

---

[1] vv. 16–21 vestigia primae litterae aliquorum versus.

```
        ....]αι παλασταί.
     .]Λυδιεργὲς δ' ὦ 'πι θώγιον βρ[έ]τα[ς
30     ..]άνω κάθηται
     ..]ι̣ μὲν τρὶς ἐς τὸ μακρὸν ιδ[.].[...] δέκα
       ]ίκατιν δ' ἐς εὖρος
     .......]υν[......]εσ[...]μ[
     .......]δετοιμ[
35   ....].ακ[..]τα̣ῖος ε[.].ίκοιτ['].̣.[
     .]αχυ..κ' ἐλο.[.].σ̣.
     αὐτὸς δ' ὁ δαίμων πέντ[ε] τ[ᾶ]ς ἐφεδρ[ί]δος
       παχέεσσι μάσσων·
     .]ι̣τεῖ δὲ Νίκα χη̣.ε δὶς δυ.[
40   ....].[.]ει τελει..[
     ....]η.εκηπ['.].̣.[.]αταιδ[
       παρθένοι γὰρ Ὧραι
     τᾶν ὀργυιαᾶν ὅσσον οὐδὲ πάσ[σα]λο[ν
       φαντὶ μειονεκτεῖν.
45   τ[ὸ] δ' ὦν ἀναισίμωμα—λίχνος ἐσσὶ [γάρ
       καὶ, τό μευ πυθέσθαι—
     ....]̣ι̣[.]. μὲν [ο]ὐ̣ [λ]ογιστὸν οὐδ.[.]ε[
     .....] ἔς τε χρυσό[ν
     ......].̣[....].[.].̣[
     . . . . . . . . . . ²
                             ]
            ]ωθεδησ' ὁ Φειδ[ίας
60           ]Ἀθανα[
      ].[.].[..]. δ' ὁ Φειδία πατ[ήρ
      .......] ἀπέρχευ.
```

on which the sacred image [30] sits . . . three times in
length . . . ten . . . twenty in breadth . . . [38] the god him-
self is five-cubits taller than the throne . . . a Nike[4] twice
. . . ends . . . and the virgin Horae[5] say that they are not as
much as a pin smaller than the women who are a fathom
high.[6] [45] The expense of these, for you are curious to
learn this from me . . . not to be calculated . . . the gold
. . . Phidias . . . Athena[7] . . . the father of Phidias . . . depart!

---

[4] Winged statues personifying victory, a suitable adornment
for Olympian Zeus.   [5] The Seasons (Hes. *Theog.* 901–3;
Hymn. Hom. Aph. 6.2–13).   [6] The Charites (Graces), who
were also represented on the back of the throne (*Hymn. Hom.
Aph.* 5.60–63).   [7] Or Athens.

---

[2] vv. 50–57 desunt.

196a *Dieg.* 7.25–31

Ἀλεῖος ὁ Ζεύς, ἁ τέχνα δὲ Φειδία

Γνωρίμῳ αὐτοῦ ἀποπλέοντι κατὰ θέαν τοῦ Ὀλυμπίου
Διὸς εἰς Ἦλιν διηγεῖται μῆκος ὕψος πλάτος βάσεως
θρόνου ὑποποδίου αὐτοῦ τοῦ θεοῦ καὶ ὅση ἡ [30] δα-
πάνη, δημιουργὸν δὲ Φειδίαν Χαρμίδου Ἀθηναῖον.

IAMBUS VII (197–197a)

197 1–14, *P.Oxy.* 2171 fr. 3.6–14 et 14a–18; 11–25, *P.Oxy.*
661 col. I, 1–15; 21–25, *P.Oxy.* 2171 fr. 4 col. II, 1–5; 39–
51, *P.Oxy.* 661 col. II, 16–28

Ἑρμᾶς ὁ Π.ερφεραῖος, Αἰνίων θεός,
    ἔμμι τῶ φ.υγαίχμα
......] πάρεργον ἱπποτέκτον[ος·
......] γὰρ [ὤ]νὴρ
5 ......σ]κέπαρνον αιδ.[
            ].πται·
        ]οἱ βα[.].ά....[
        ]..[
        ]   [
10   ]   [
        ].ῆντο κἀποτη.[
        ].μα..τα·   [
        ]ο Σκάμα[ν]δρος ἀγριωμένος
            ]ξαέρρας

196a *Diegeseis*

Zeus of Elis, the work of Phidias,

For his acquaintance who is sailing to Elis to see [the statue of] Olympian Zeus he describes the length, the height and the breadth of the base, the throne, the pedestal and of the god himself and how great was the cost, and the sculptor, Phidias the Athenian, the son of Charmides.

IAMB 7 (197–197a)

197 Oxyrhynchus papyri

Hermes Perpheraeus, god of the Aeneans,[1] I am . . . the minor work of the deserter who built the horse,[2] . . . for the man . . . [5] an adze . . . [13] the raging Scamander,[3]

---

[1] Aenus, city in Thrace (Strabo 7.51).

[2] The mythological Epeius, who built the Trojan Horse (Hom. *Od.* 11.523–24).

[3] Scamander, river near Troy battled by Achilles (Hom. *Il.* 20.70–74, 21.211–341).

15   ]ν κατὰ ῥρόον
        ]
        ]ι με δικτύοις
        ]
        ]ον, ὦ Παλαίμονες
20 . . .   ]
 .[   ]το θηρίον·
  ο̣[   ]
 [   ]ον, ὦ Παλαίμονες
  ω[   ]
25 ο̣[   ] ἄπωθε τὸν φθόρον
  . . . . ¹

 ποτ' ἀστέρας βλ[επ
40 καὶ τύχαμπυριξ.[
 ἔληγ' ὁ μῦθος· κα[
  πυρδάνω 'πὺ λεπ[τῶ·
 κἠγὼ 'π' ἐκείναν [
  ταῖς ἐμαῖς ἐπῳδα[ῖς·
45 οἱ δ' εἶπαν [...]ν̣ε̣[
  μὴ τύ γ' αὖτις ἔνθ[ῃς."
 ἦ, καί με πόντον [
  ἦνθε σαυνιαστά[ς.
 ἔρριψαν, αὖθι δ' ἐξ ἁλὸ[ς
50 π[.]ρβαλον κατάγρ[
 ἐ[κ] τᾶς θαλάσσας τ[

   ¹ vv. 26–38 desunt.

. . . lifted [15] downstream . . . me with nets . . . O Palae-
mones[4] [20] . . . the beast . . . O Palaemones . . . tossed
[25] into the sea from afar . . . [39] look at the stars . . . and
propitiously set aflame . . . the story concluded. . . . and
from slender kindling . . . and I against that . . . with my
enchantments. [45] They said . . . do not come back again,
you." He said and me into the sea . . . a fish spearer came
. . . they threw [me], and again from the sea [50] . . . they
cast . . . from the sea

[4] Palaemones, marine divinities associated with Melicertes
and his mother, Ino, who leaped into the sea to avoid the mad
attack of his father (Eur. *IT* 270–71).

CALLIMACHUS

197a *Dieg.* 7.32–8.20

Ἑρμᾶς ὁ Περφεραῖος Αἰνίων θεός

Περφεραῖος Ἑρμῆς ἐν Αἴνῳ τῇ πόλει τῆς Θρᾴκης τι-
μᾶται ἐντεῦθεν· Ἐπειὸς πρὸ τοῦ δουρείου ἵππου ἐδη-
μιούργησεν Ἑρμᾶν, ὃν ὁ Σκάμανδρος πολὺς ἐνεχθεὶς
κατέσυρεν· ὁ δ᾽ ἐντεῦθεν προσηνέχθη εἰς τὴν πρὸς
Αἴνῳ θάλασσαν, ἀφ᾽ ἧς [5] ἁλιευόμενοί τινες ἀνείλκυ-
σαν αὐτὸν τῇ σαγήνῃ. ὅτε ἐθεάσαντο αὐτόν, κατα-
μεμψάμενοι τὸν βόλον πρὸς ἀλέαν σχίζειν τε αὐτὸν
καὶ παρακαίειν αὐτοῖς ἐπεχείρουν, οὐδὲν δὲ ἧττον[1]
ἔφθασαν ἢ τὸν ὦμον [10] παίσαντες τραύματος τύπον
ἐργάσασθαι, διαμπερὲς δὲ ἠσθένησαν· καὶ ὅλον
αὐτὸν καίειν ἐπεχείρουν, τὸ δὲ πῦρ αὐτῷ περιέρρει·
ἀπειπόντες κατέρριψαν αὐτὸν εἰς τὴν θάλασσαν. ἐπεὶ
δὲ αὖτις ἐδικτυούλκησαν, θεὸν νομίσαντες [15] εἶναι ἢ
θεῷ προσήκοντα καθιδρύσαντο ἐπὶ τοῦ αἰγιαλοῦ
ἱερὸν αὐτοῦ, ἀπήρξαντό τε τῆς ἄγρας ἄλλος παρ᾽ ἄλ-
λου αὐτὸν πε[ριφέρω]ν.[2] τοῦ δὲ Ἀπόλλωνος χρήσαν-
τος εἱ[σεδέξαν]το[3] τῇ πόλει καὶ [π]αραπλησίως [20]
τ[οῖς θεοῖς] ἐτίμων.

---

[1] ἧττον Π: πλέον Wifstrand: del. Herzog   [2] Suppl.
Herzog, Pf. (vol. 1,193)   [3] Suppl. Norsa-Vitelli

197a *Diegeseis*

Hermes Perpheraeus, god of the Aenians

Hermes Perpheraeus is honored in Aenus, a city of Thrace, from this: Epeius, before [he built] the wooden horse, made a Herm which the swollen Scamander carried off and swept away. And from there it was carried into the sea opposite Aenus, from which [5] some fishermen dragged it in their net. When they saw it, disparaging their catch, they tried to cut it up for heat and to kindle a fire for themselves, but after striking the shoulder [10] they achieved no more than to make the impression of a wound and were exhausted through and through. Then they tried to burn it whole, but the fire crept around it. And giving up they threw it into the sea. When they netted it again, thinking [15] that it was a god or something close to a god they established a shrine for it on the beach and they offered the firstfruits of their catch, carrying him around from one to the other. Following Apollo's oracle they received it in the city and honored it [20] equally to the gods.

CALLIMACHUS

IAMBUS VIII (198–198a)

198 *Dieg.* 8.21

Ἀργώ κοτ' ἐμπνέοντος ἤκαλον νότου

198a *Dieg.* 8.21–32

Ἀ˳ργώ κοτ' ἐμ˳π˳ν˳ε˳οντος ἤκαλον νότου

Ἐπίνικος Πολυκλεῖ Αἰγινήτῃ νικήσαντι διαύλῳ Ἀμ-
φορίτῃ ἐν τῇ πατρίδι. τὸ δ' ἀγώνισμα τοῦτο· πρὸς τῷ
τέρματι τοῦ σταδίου κεῖται ἀμφορεὺς πλήρης [25]
ὕδατος, ἐφ' ὃν δραμὼν κενὸς ὁ ἀγωνιζόμενος ἀναλα-
βὼν τὸν ἀμφορέα ἀνακάμπτει, προφθάσας δὲ νικᾷ.
κατήχθησαν δὲ ἐντεῦθεν οἱ Ἀργοναῦται ἐπιβάντες
τῆς Αἰγίνης, ἡμίλλησαν δὲ ἀλλήλοις [30] ὑδρευόμενοι
ὑπὲρ τοῦ θᾶττον· ὁ δ' ἀγὼν Ὑδροφόρια καλεῖται.

IAMBUS IX (199–199a)

199 1–2, *P.Oxy.* 2221 col. II, 4–6

Ἑρμᾶ, τί τοι τὸ ν˳εῦρον, ὦ Γενειόλα,
ποττὰν ὑπήναν κοὐ ποτ' ἴχνι[ον

486

IAMB 8 (198–198a)

198 *Diegeseis*

Once the Argo, when the south wind was blowing
peacefully

198a *Diegeseis*

Once the Argo, when the south wind was blowing
peacefully

An epinician for Polycles of Aegina[1] who was victorious in
his fatherland in the diaulos[2] Amphorita. This was the
contest: An amphora full of water lies at the end of the
stadium, [25] and the contestant runs to it empty-handed,
and taking up the amphora comes back; whoever gets
there first wins. It originated from this: When the Argo-
nauts disembarked at Aegina they competed with one an-
other [30] carrying water as swiftly as possible. The con-
test is called the Hydrophoria.[3]

[1] Polycles is unknown. Aegina is an island off the coast of
Attica, strategically important to Athens (Thuc. 2.27, 4.57).
[2] A footrace double the length of the stadium, or about 400
meters (Pind. *Pyth*. 11, *Nem*. 8).   [3] The origin of the
Hydrophoria is also told in Ap. Rhod. 4.1765–72.

IAMB 9 (199–199a)

199 Oxyrhynchus papyrus

Hermes, why, O bearded one, does your penis [point] to
your beard and not your feet?

199a *Dieg.* 8.33–40

Ἑρμᾶ τί τοι τὸ νεῦρον, ὦ Γενειόλα

Φιλητάδου παιδὸς εὐπρεποῦς ἐραστὴς ἰδὼν [35] Ἑρ-
μοῦ ἄγαλμα ἐν παλαιστριδίῳ ἐντεταμένον, πυνθάνε-
ται μὴ διὰ τὸν Φιλητάδαν. ὁ δέ φησιν ἄνωθεν εἶναι
Τυρσηνὸς καὶ κατὰ μυστικὸν λόγον ἐντετάσθαι, ἐπὶ
κακῷ δὲ αὐτὸν φιλεῖν τὸν [40] Φιλητάδαν

IAMBUS X (200a–200c)

200a *Dieg.* 8.41

Τὰς Ἀφροδίτας—ἡ θεὸς γὰρ οὐ μία—[1]

[1] ἡ Καστνιῆτις τῷ φρονεῖν ὑπερφέρει πάσας,
ὅτι μόνη παραδέχεται τὴν τῶν ὑῶν θυσίαν
(fr. 200a.2–4 suppl. Pf. ex Strab. 9.5.17)

200b Schol. V, ΓΓΡ ad Ar. *Av.* 873

τὴν ὠγαμέμνων, ὡς ὁ μῦθος, εἴσατο,
τῇ καὶ λίπουρα καὶ μονῶπα θύεται

---

[1] The scholion explains the etymology of the epithet of Arte-
mis Kolainis, which it connects to Agamemnon's sacrifice of *kola*,

IAMB 10

199a *Dieg.* 8.33–40

Hermes, why, O bearded one, does your penis [point]

A lover of the handsome boy Philetadus,[1] when he sees
[35] an ithyphallic statue of Hermes in a small Palaestra,[2]
asks whether his erection is not on account of Philetadus.
He replies that he is originally Tyrrhenian,[3] that his condi-
tion is in accordance with a mystic account, and that the
speaker loves [40] Philetadus for immoral ends.

[1] Literally, "son of a dear one."   [2] A wrestling school.
[3] On the Athenians adopting images of ithyphallic Hermes
from the Pelasgians, see Hdt. 2.51; on the identification of the
Pelasgians with the Tyrrhenians (or Tyrsenians), see Hdt. 1.57.

IAMB 10 (200a–200c)

200a *Diegeseis*

Aphrodite—for the goddess is not a single one—. . .[1]

[1] Pf. creates three additional verses (*Ia.* 200a.2–4; see note
opposite) from a somewhat metrical paraphrase in Strabo (9.5.17):
"The one from Mt. Castnia exceeds the rest in intelligence / be-
cause she alone accepts the sacrifice of swine." See Kerkhecker,
208–9; D'Alessio 2007, vol. 2, 632n125.

200b Scholia to Aristophanes, *Birds*[1]

. . . whose effigy,[2] as the story goes, Agamemnon dedi-
cated, and to whom even tailless and one-eyed animals are
sacrificed.

animals without horns.   [2] Artemis of Eretria, according to
the *Diegeseis* (cf. *Ia.* 200c below).

200c *Dieg.* 8.41–9.11

Τὰς Ἀφροδίτας—ἡ θεὸς γὰρ οὐ μία—

Ἐν Ἀσπένδῳ τῆς Παμφυλίας τῇ Καστνίῃ Ἀφροδίτῃ
ὗς ἱερουργεῖται ἐντεῦθεν· Μόψος ἀρχηγὸς τῶν Παμ-
φυλίων ἐπὶ θήραν ἐξιὼν εὔξατο αὐτῇ εὐβολήσας ὃ ἂν
λάβοι [5] πρῶτον καλλιερήσειν. καὶ δὴ θηράσας κά-
προν ἐτέλεσε τὴν ἐπαγγελίαν. ἀφ' οὗ καὶ Παμφύλιοι
μέχρι νῦν τοῦτο ποιοῦσιν· εἰ μὴ γὰρ ᾔδετο ἡ θεός,
οὐκ ἂν ὁ Μόψος ἐκυνήγησεν τοῦτο. ἐπαινεῖ δὲ καὶ
[10] τὴν Ἐρετριέων Ἄρτεμιν, ὅτι πᾶν τὸ θυόμενον οὐκ
ἀποσείεται.

IAMBUS XI (201–201a)

201 *Dieg.* 9.12

ἀλλ' οὐ τὸν Ὑψᾶν, ὃς τὸ σᾶμά μευ

201a *Dieg.* 9.12–24

ἀλλ' οὐ τὸν Ὑψᾶν, ὃς τὸ σᾶμά μευ

Διημαρτημένως λέγεται παροιμία "ἅρπαγα τὰ Κον-
νάρου·" "Κοννίδα" γὰρ χρὴ λέγειν. [15] ἐντεῦθεν γὰρ
παρῆλθεν· Κοννίδας μέτοικος ἐν Σελινοῦντι πλουτή-

200c *Diegeseis*

Aphrodite—for the goddess is not a single one—

At Aspendus[1] in Pamphylia a boar is sacrificed to Aphrodite Castnia. Mopsus,[2] a leader of the Pamphylians, when setting out on a hunt promised her that, if he aimed well, [5] he would sacrifice whatever he caught first. And so, when he caught a boar, he fulfilled his promise. From then until now the Pamphylians do this. For, if the goddess had not been pleased, Mopsus would not have captured this [beast]. The poet also praises [10] Artemis of Eretria[3] because she rejects nothing that is sacrificed to her.

[1] A city in Asia Minor near the river Eurymedon.
[2] An Argonaut from Thessaly who was a seer and augurer (Ap. Rhod. 1.65–66, 4.1502–36).   [3] City in Euboea opposite Attica, which sent ships to the Trojan War (Hom. *Il.* 2.536–37) and was a major force in Greek colonization and history from the fifth century BC onward.

IAMB 11 (201–201a)

201 *Diegeseis*

but no, by the Hypsa,[1] which [flows by] my tomb . . .

[1] A river near Selinus on the southwest corner of Sicily.

201a *Diegeseis*

but no, by the Hypsa, which [flows by] my tomb

The proverb "The goods of Connarus are there for the taking" is incorrectly stated. One should say "Connidas." [15] The proverb comes from this: Connidas, a resident

σας ἐκ πορνοβοσκίας παρὰ μὲν τὸν ἄλλον χρόνον ‚εν
ἐφήμιζεν, ὡς τὴν αἰσίαν[1] τῇ τε Ἀφροδίτῃ καὶ τοῖς
φίλοις διανεμεῖν. [20] τελευτήσαντος δὲ αὐτοῦ ἡ δια-
θήκη εὑρέθη περιέχουσα "ἁρπαγὰ τὰ Κοννίδα"· ὅθεν
ὁ δῆμος ἐξελθὼν τοῦ θεάτρου ἥρπασεν τὰ Κοννίδα.
Σελινοῦς δὲ πόλις Σικελίας.

[1] αἰσίαν P., Kerkhecker, 213: οὐσίαν Norsa-Vitelli, Pf.

IAMBUS XII (202–202a)

202 1–6, *P.Oxy.* 2218 fr. 1–6; 7–45, *P.Oxy.* 1011 fol. 7
recto, 369–407; 46–86, *P.Oxy.* 1011 fol. 7 verso, 408–48;
57–70, *P.Mich.* inv. 4967

Ἄρτε‚μι Κρηταῖον Ἀμνισοῦ πέδον
ἤ τε Δικτ[
τιμίη‚ [
ἤ σε του‚[
5 ἱ]στίη λ‚[
‚‚]‚‚[

‚‚‚‚‚‚].γὰρ[‚‚‚].αινοι πόλεις
‚‚‚‚‚]κου μο[‚‚]‚‚ οὔρεα βλέπει
καὶ ὔ]μμες[1] ὢ κά[λ]λιστα νήθουσαι μυ[
10 ‚‚‚‚]ουρειησι‚ [‚‚‚]‚‚χθονός
‚‚]θετ᾽ οὐχ υμειν[2] ἀ[
καὶ θέμιν καὶ πα[
τῶνδ᾽ ἄναξ ‚νδ᾽ οι[‚‚‚]‚‚[‚]ους[

alien in Selinus, became wealthy as a brothel keeper and often in the past used to say that he would divide his property between Aphrodite and his friends. [20] But, when he died, his will was found to say: "The goods of Connidas are there for the taking." Consequently the people left the theater and snatched up the property of Connidas. Selinus is a city of Sicily.

IAMB 12 (202–202a)

202 Oxyrhynchus papyri; Michigan papyrus

To Artemis who . . . [ranges over] the Cretan ground of Amnisus and Mt. Dicte[1] . . . honored . . . who . . . you . . . [5] hearth . . . for . . . cities . . . sees the mountains . . . and you, O spinning very beautifully . . . [10] the earth . . . not Hymen[2] . . . both lawful and . . . lord of these . . . lowly . . .

---

[1] River and mountain in Crete associated with Artemis (Call. *Hymn* 3.15–17, 162–65, 193–200; Ap. Rhod. 3.876–83; Strabo 10.4.12).　　[2] God of marriage, whose name is invoked in the wedding hymn (e.g., Eur. *Tro.* 310–14).

---

[1] Suppl. Barber (Pf. vol. 2, 118)　　[2] υμειν Parsons

φαυλ...β.[.]ι.ναποι..[.].[..].ους
15 ἔστιν οἰκ[....].ι... ἀψευδέα λέγων
καὶ τάφο[ν τὸ]ν Κ[ρ]ῆτα γινώσκειν κενόν
φησὶ καὶ πατρῷ[ο]ν οὐ κτείνει ὄφιν·³
τοὔνεκ' ἀντήσ[αιτε], πρηεῖαι θεαί,
τῆσδ' ἐτῆς εὐχῆ[σι.] ἀεισομαι
20 Μοῦσα τῇ μικκῇ τι τε..ηναι μελ[
ἠνίκ' αἰ[....]ν[.]α τὴν γενεθλίην
ἑβδόμην Ἥρ[η] θ[υγ]ατρὸς ἡμέρην
η[..]ν οἱ δ' Ὄλυμπον ητ.σ.....οι
η[...].[.]τις παι.[.καλ]λίστῃ δόσει
25 π.[..]α τιμήσει τ[...].....ερο.[
Ζεὺς πατὴρ οὐ φαυ...[......]..[
πολλὰ τεχνήεντα ποικ[ίλ]α γλ[υφῇ
παίχν[ια] Τριτωνὶς ἤνεικεν κόρ[
πολλὰ δ'⁴.....ίου πυλωρὸς αὐχένο[ς
30 ἔκ τε τῆς ....[.].[.].....[.]ης ἁλός
καὶ τὸ Τυρσην.[.].....[.]....[
σ[.]πνι.χ'.....ς ἐκβάλλ.[
παίχνια χρυσοῖο τιμήεσ[τ]ερ[α
μυρίην λ...ωδε ρη.[.].[
35 ῥηδίως λ[.]..αι γὰρ ηλ.[
πολλὰ κα.α..[...]ρος α[
ἤγαγον μύθοισ[ι......].ψ[.]λ..
ο[ῖ]σι τῆς μουνη[......].ιγεν δάκρυ
παιδὸς η.[........]ληιστῆς[
40 ἵππος αστι[....]δ[..]ην[.].κην κρο.[.].
ἦλθε χὼ τακ[....].......

494

[15] there is . . . not speaking falsehoods and he says that he knows the Cretan tomb is empty and did not kill the ancestral snake.[3] And therefore, gentle goddesses, may you accept these earnest prayers . . . I will sing, [20] Muse, something for the little girl . . .

when Hera . . . the . . . for the seventh day after the birth of her daughter . . . the ones on Olympus . . . [25] who will honor the child with the loveliest gift. Father Zeus not modest . . . and the Tritonian maiden[4] brought many multicolored toys made by carving, and many presents . . . the guardian of the isthmus [30] and from . . . of the sea the Tyrrhenian[5] . . . threw away . . . and toys more honored than gold . . . numberless . . . [35] easily . . . many . . . they brought with words . . . among whom only . . . with a tear . . . of the child . . . booty . . . [40] a horse . . . and . . . he came . . . leading all . . . the workman . . . with

---

[3] Zeus' alleged death in Crete is related in Callimachus' *Hymn to Zeus* (*Hymn* 1.7–9). On his metamorphosis into a snake, see Schol. ad Arat. *Phaen.* 46.   [4] Athena (Hom. *Od.* 3.378). The epithet may derive from lake Tritonis in Libya, near which she was supposedly born (Eur. *Ion* 872 ; Call. *Aet.* 37; Ap. Rhod. 4.1308–11).   [5] The Tyrrhenians, or Etruscans, are associated with the invention of toys and games (Hdt. 1.94); see Kerkhecker, 234n101).

---

[3] Δία· Rea, Coles: obscurum an de Iove serpente Pf.
[4] Suppl. Coles

πάντα κα[.].[....].[.......] ψ' ἄ[γ]ων
ἐργάτης .[.] λιστος οἷσι κυ[..] ν
τασ[...]η στέψει σε σιγησ....[...].
45 οἱ δ' ι.[..γ]λυκεῖαν ἀλλήλοις ἔριν
θ]έντες ἠμ[ι]λλῶντο δω[τί]νη[ς πέρι.
Δ]ήλι' ὤπολλον, σὺ δ' εσκλ[..] ευμ..[
ὅσσα] τοι Πυθῶνος ἀρχα[ίης ἔ]σω
κτη]μάτων ἔκειτο [..] ιπον ρυ[
50   ].ιπεσ.[ ].. [ ]ερουτισοι
                    ].ἤυτει τρίπους
                 ].οι δ' ὑπώροφοι
  .]τατο.[....].ε. ἐφ[θέγ]ξω τ[ά]δε·
  '.]χεισθ[.].[.]οισ[.].[.].οισιν α τε[....]ιρια
55 .εσθ', ἐγὼ δ' ἄλλην τιν' ο[.].ησ[ω...]ιν.
χρεὼ σοφῆς ὦ Φοῖβε π.[..].σθ..τέχνης,
ἥτις Ἡφαίστεια νικήσει καλά.
 αὐτίκα χρυσὸν μὲν Ἰνδικοὶ κύνες
βυσσόθεν μύρμηκες ο[ἴσου]σι πτεροῖς·
60 πολλάκις καὶ φαῦλον οἰκήσει δόμον
χρυσός, ἀρχαίους δ' ἀτιμήσει [......]s.
καὶ Δίκην[5] καὶ Ζῆνα καὶ [..]ου.α.ας
ὑπτίῳ παίσαντες ἄνθρωποι ποδί
χρυσὸν αἰνήσουσ[ι κάλ]λιστον[6] κακόν[.[7]
65 τὴν Ἀθηναίης δὲ καὶ ἑτέρων δόσιν,
καίπερ εὖ σμίλῃσιν ἠκριβωμένην,
ὁ πρόσω φοιτέων ἀμαυρώσει χρ[ό]νος·
ἡ δ' ἐμὴ τῇ παιδὶ καλλίστη δόσις,
ἔστ' ἐμὸν γένειον ἁγνεύῃ τριχός

which . . . he will crown you . . . [45] and they vied with
one another in happy competition over the gift giving.

But, Delian Apollo, you, however many of your posses-
sions lie within ancient Pytho . . . [50] . . . the tripod was
crying out . . . under the eaves . . . you pronounced
these [words] [55] . . . but I . . . something else . . .
Now, o Phoebus, you need wise skill that will surpass
Hephaestus' showpieces. Now then, the Indian dogs, the
ants,[6] will bring gold on their wings gold from the depths.
[60] And often gold will dwell in an inferior home, and
will disregard the ancient . . . and humanity, kicking aside
both Dike and Zeus, will praise gold, a most lovely bane,
[65] the gift of Athena and of the others, though perfectly
well carved, time going forward will obscure. My loveliest
gift for the child, as long as my chin is pure of hair

---

6 Indian ants, which are said to bring up gold, as Greek ants
bring up sand (Hdt. 3.102.2; cf. Theoc. *Id*. 17.106–7). On the
equivocal value of gold, see also Callimachus' *Victory of Sosibius*
(*Carm. Var.* 384.14–15).

---

5 Δίκην *P.Mich.* inv. 4967:]εμιν *P.Oxy.* 1011: Θ]έμιν Lobel
6 κάλλιστον *P.Oxy.* 1011: τίμιον ss κάλλιστον *P.Mich.* inv.
4967   7 κακόν Lobel

70   καὶ ἐρίφοις χαίρωσιν ἄρπαγ[ες λ]ύκ[ο]ι
     ....]τεων..[.]..[.]..[.].ιος πόδας
     .....].. τον.μπλ..[.]ς μόλις
     .[ ].[.] ν σε νύμφα...[.]...ς
     .[..]δ[   ].σ. οισιν ἤεισα..σο..
75   οἱ δ᾽ ι[   ]η π[αι]δὶ νικάτω τα[.]
     ων.[   ]ηραμοι....[
     τ....[   ]ι μιμεισθ.[.]σον
     τέξ[ο]μαι[   ]...[.]...φ.ολος
     εἶκ᾽ ἄναξ ηπ[......ού]κ ἀλλοτρίη
80   ἀλλά μοι μητ[........]ζει..νος
     ὧν χάριν...πλ[........].τροφε
     Κρήσιον κλ....τεφ[.....]αι πέρι
     θη...[.].[..].[....].[....]αι καλόν
     χρὴ καλω[...]ωδε πρ.[.].θα...ιει.
85   τοῦτον..[...]ιππον [ο]ὺχ ν..ρ..[.].ι
     ὠγαθή, .οιρεων τις ο[ὐ]χ ε.ωτιδ[

202a *Dieg.* 9.25–31

Ἄρτεμι Κρηταῖον Ἀμνίσου πέδον

Τοῦτο γέγραπται εἰς ἔβδομα θυγατρίου γεννηθέντος
Λέοντι γνωρίμῳ τοῦ ποιητοῦ, ἐν ᾧ φησιν διενεγκεῖν
τῶν †δεμυνηθεντων[1] τῇ Ἥβῃ ὑπὸ [30] τῶν ἄλλων θεῶν
τὸν ἀσθέντα ὑπὸ τοῦ Ἀπόλλωνος ὕμνον.

[1] δωρηθέντων sugg. Rostagni

[70] and rapacious wolves take pleasure in kids, . . . feet
. . . scarcely . . . a bride[7] . . . I sang . . . [75] and they . . .
for the child let it prevail . . . represent . . . I will bring
forth . . . the king did not yield to another's . . . [80] but
for me . . . for the sake of which . . . nurturer . . . around
the Cretan . . . lovely . . . it is necessary . . . [85] this . . .
not . . . My good woman . . . someone not

[7] Or a nymph.

202a *Diegeseis*

To Artemis, who . . . [ranges over] the Cretan ground
    of Amnisus

This was written for the seventh day [celebration] of the
birth of a daughter to the poet's acquaintance Leon[1] in
which he says that the hymn sung by Apollo was superior
to the gifts for Hebe[2] [30] by the other gods.

[1] Unknown.　　[2] Hebe, daughter of Zeus and Hera (Apol-
lod. *Bibl.* 1.3.1) and cupbearer of the gods (Hom. *Il.* 4.1–3).

IAMBUS XIII (203–203a)

203 1, *Dieg.* 9.32; 2–33, *P.Oxy.* 1011 fol. 6 recto, 336–86;
34–66, *P.Oxy.* 1011 fol. 6 verso, 303–35

Μοῦσαι καλαὶ κἄπολλον, οἷς ἐγὼ σπένδω

. . . .

      ]...[

      ].....[

      ].σα......[

5   ]ς διέπλευσα

      ].αλευσινηρδ.[

      ]τριτη . ὁ Μίμν[ερμος

       ]δ...χ.ουκα.[

        ]ωτεσαπλ.ις[

10   ]..[   ]τ[.]ν ποδαβρε.[

ἐκ γὰρ ......[.οὔτ'] Ἴωσι συμμείξας

οὔτ' Ἔφεσον ἐλθών, ἥτις ἐστι .αμ.[

Ἔφεσον, ὅθεν περ οἱ τὰ μέτρα μέλ.λοντες

τὰ χωλὰ τίκτειν μὴ ἀμαθῶς ἐναύ.ονται·

15 ἀλλ' εἴ τι θυμὸν ἢ 'πὶ γαστέρα πνευσ.[

εἴτ' οὖν ἐπ...ἀρχαῖον εἴτ' ἀπαι.[..].[,

τοῦτ' ἐμπ[έ]πλεκται καὶ λαλευσ[...].[

Ἰαστὶ καὶ Δωριστὶ καὶ τὸ σύμμεικτον[.

τ[ε]ῦ μέχρι τολμᾷς; οἱ φίλοι σε δήσ[ουσι,

20 κ[ἢ]ν νοῦν ἔχωσιν, ἐγχέουσι τὴν[κρᾶσιν

ὡς ὑγιείης οὐδὲ τώινυχι ψαύεις·

ην δητοσωσυπιπε[...]...αι Μοῦσαι."

IAMB 13 (203–203a)

203 *Diegeseis*; Oxyrhynchus papyrus

Lovely Muses and Apollo, to whom I pour [a libation] . . . [5] I sailed across . . . [11] for from . . . not after associating with the Ionians nor having visited Ephesus,[1] which is . . . Ephesus, where those who are about to give birth to choliambs[2] are learnedly inspired. [15] But if something appeals . . . the heart or the stomach, whether ancient or . . . this is woven in and chattering . . . in Ionic and Doric and mixed [dialects] . . . how far do you dare? Friends will bind you [20] and, if they have sense, will toast . . . since you do not touch sanity even with your finger tip . . . the Muses."

---

[1] Ionian city on the coast of modern Turkey and homeland of Hipponax, Callimachus' literary model for choliambic poetry. See Introduction.

[2] The so-called "limping iamb." See Introduction.

οὕτως...ται κα[..].[.]ν[..].ην[.].μ.·
"ὦ λῷστ', ἐρῆμος[　].ρ ἡ ῥῆσις
25　ἀκου....οικε[.]..[...]ην..πέπλ[ον
 οὐ πολλὰ [....].. λ..ν.ε τὰς Μούσας
ὥσπερ λ....ε..ἀπεμπολῇ κόψας
ἐν τωδεδο..ρ.ολ[..]ιν εὑρίσκειν
καλὰς ἀοιδ[ὰσ].........αιρεῦνται
30　τίς εἶπεν αυτ[....]λε..ρ.[....].
σὺ πεντάμετρα συντίθει, σὺ δ' ἡ[ρῴο]ν,
σὺ δὲ τραγῳδε[ῖν] ἐκ θεῶν ἐκληρώσω;
δοκέω μὲν οὐδείς, ἀλλὰ καὶ το.δ..κεψαι
　　　　　　　　　　　　　　1
. . . .

].[.].[
35　].φει[.].δ.[
]φρα καὶ τράπ[
]υνον ἐμβεβ..[
]..καὶ σὺ χωσε[
].ε κην τομηκ[
40　τὰ νῦ.ν δὲ πολλὴν τυ.φεδῶνα λεσχαίνεις
]ὁ τεθμὸς οὗτος[
]ν[..]ν κα..ε.[
]οὐχὶ μοῦνον εξ.[
ο]υς τραγῳδοὺς ἀλλὰ κα[.....].ν
45　π]εντάμετρον οὐχ ἅπαξ.[.έ]κρουσε
]σερω...φαυλα....ουσι
Λυδὸν] πρὸς αὐλὸν λ......καὶ χορδάς
]ην γὰρ ἐντελές τε τὸ χρῆμα
..].[.]ραγεινον καὶ λ....ἀνεπλάσθη

502

In this way . . . "My good man, bereft . . . the speech [25] . . . listen . . . the robe not many . . . the Muses . . . just as . . . in the sale you struck . . . in this . . . to discover lovely songs . . . [30] who said . . . you compose pentameters, you an epic, you are allotted by the gods to write tragedy? No one, I think, but even this . . . and you . . . [40] but as it is, you chatter much nonsense about all this. This custom . . . not alone . . . tragedians, but . . . pentameter not once . . . he struck [45] . . . poor things . . . by the Lydian flute . . . and strings . . . for a perfect thing . . . was

---

1 9 vel 10 versus desunt inter vv. 33 et 34.

50 .]μ.[..]περημεν αἱ θεαὶ γὰρ ο[..]κείνους
.]ι..νηας ἠγάπησαν αἱ τα..αυτη
.].. ναοιδὸς ἐς κέρας τεθύμωται
κοτέω]ν ἀοιδῷ κἠμὲ δει.ταπραχ...[
].δ[ύ]ρηται τὴν γενὴν ἀνακρίνει
55 κα[ὶ] δοῦλον εἶναί φησι καὶ παλίμπρητον
καὶ τοῦ πρ......ου τὸν βραχίονα στίζει,
ὥστ᾽ οὐκ αικε[.....]υσιν α.λ..υσαι
φαύλοις ὁμι[λ]εῖ[ν....].ν παρέπτησαν
καὐταὶ τρομεῦσαι μὴ κακῶς ἀκούσωσι·
60 τοῦδ᾽ οὕνεκ᾽ οὐδὲν πῖον, ἀ[λλὰ] λιμηρὰ
ἕκαστος ἄκροις δακτύλοις ἀποκνίζει,
ὡς τῆς ἐλαίης, ἢ ἀνέπαυσε τὴν Λητώ.
μηθ.[..].............ν ἀείδω
οὔτ᾽ Ἔφεσο.ν ἐλ.θὼ.ν οὔτ᾽ .Ἴω.σι συμμείξας,
65 Ἔφεσον, ὅθεν περ οἱ τὰ μέτρα μέλλοντες
τὰ χωλὰ τίκτειν μὴ ἀμαθῶς ἐναύονται.

203a *Dieg.* 9.32–38

Μοῦσαι καλαὶ κἄπολλον, οἷς ἐγὼ σπένδω

Ἐν τούτῳ πρὸς τοὺς καταμεμφομένους αὐτὸν ἐπὶ τῇ
πολυειδείᾳ ὧν γράφει ποιημάτων ἁπάντων φησὶν ὅτι
[35] Ἴωνα μιμεῖται τὸν τραγικόν· ἀλλ᾽ οὐδὲ τὸν τέ-
κτονά τις μέμφεται πολυειδῆ σκεύη τεκταινόμενον.

504

molded [50] . . . the goddesses . . . those . . . they loved
who . . . they rage horn against horn . . . angry at the singer
and me . . . and [as] he is able he questions his birth [55]
and says that I am a slave, sold and resold . . . and brands
his arm . . . to socialize with commoners . . . they too flew
past him, lest they lose their reputations. [60] Therefore
each one scrapes off with his fingertips nothing rich but
only what staves off famine, just like those who (pick at)
the olive that Leto rested on[3] . . . I sing, though I have not
been to Ephesus nor spent time with the Ionians; [65]
Ephesus, where whoever is about to give birth to choli-
ambs is learnedly inspired.

[3] In *Iamb* 4, Leto rests on the trunk of an olive during Apollo's
birth (*Ia.* 194.84), but in the *Hymn to Delos*, on the trunk of a
palm tree (*Hymn* 4.209–11); later, sailors bite the trunk of the
sacred olive with their hands tied behind their backs (*Hymn*
4.318–24).

203a *Diegeseis*

Lovely Muses and Apollo, to whom I pour [a libation]

In this poem against those blaming him for the variety of
all the poems he writes he says that he imitates [35] Ion[1]
the tragedian. But no one blames a craftsman for making
objects of various kinds.

[1] Ion of Chios (5th c. BC), author of dramas and poems in a
variety of genres. Fragments in Alosius Leurini, ed., *Ionis Chii
testimonia et fragmenta* (Hakkert: Amsterdam, 1992).

IAMBORUM FRAGMENTA INCERTAE
SEDIS (204–25)

204 *P.Oxy.* 1011 fr. 1 recto, 1–5

]ναι..[
].. . ε[
] [ ] ˙κ[
⠀⠀⠀]. [
5⠀⠀⠀⠀]. [
. ⠀ . ⠀ . ⠀ .

204a P.Oxy. 1011 fr. 1 verso, 1–5

⠀⠀] σαιπολ[
⠀⠀] καὶ λε[
⠀⠀]εις βου.[
⠀⠀]λε[
5⠀⠀⠀]φ[
. ⠀ . ⠀ . ⠀ .

205 1–2, *P.Oxy.* 1011 fr. 8 recto, 1–2

. ⠀ . ⠀ . ⠀ .
].ισ.[
].[
. ⠀ . ⠀ . ⠀ .

UNPLACED IAMBIC FRAGMENTS
(204–25)

204 Oxyrhynchus papyrus

. . .

204a Oxyrhynchus papyrus

. . . and

205 Oxyrhynchus papyrus

. . .

205a 1–2, *P.Oxy.* 1011 fr. 8 verso, 1–2

.   .   .

  ].̣.̣[
  ].̣[

.   .   .   .

206 *P.Oxy.* 1011 fr. 15 recto, 1–4

.   .   .

  ]ειϲα̣.̣εν̣.[
  ]αν ἐμὸϲ θ̣.[
  ]ϲ μὲν ἱκ̣.[
  ].̣.̣νουϲ ν[

.   .   .

206a *P.Oxy.* 1011 fr. 15 verso, 1–4

.   .   .   .

  ].̣.̣.̣εν[
  ].̣ϲτον̣.[
  ]ηϲ ν.̣.[
  λ]αβϵ[ῑ]ν̣.[

.   .   .   .

207 *P.Oxy.* 1011 fr. 18 recto

.   .   .

  ].̣.̣[

.   .   .

205a Oxyrhynchus papyrus

. . .

206 Oxyrhynchus papyrus

. . . my

206a Oxyrhynchus papyrus

. . . to seize

207 Oxyrhynchus papyrus

. . .

207a *P.Oxy.* 1011 fr. 18 verso

```
 .      .    .
 ]ιξ[
 .    .    .    .
```

208 *P.Oxy.* 1011 fr. 19 recto

```
 .      .    .
 ]χ.[
 .    .    .    .
```

208a *P.Oxy.* 1011 fr. 19 verso

```
 .    .    .    .
 ]ιη[
 .    .    .    .
```

209 *P.Oxy.* 2171 fr. 6

```
 .    .    .
 ]ασατο· [
 .    .    .
```

207a Oxyrhynchus papyrus

. . .

208 Oxyrhynchus papyrus

. . .

208a Oxyrhynchus papyrus

. . .

209 Oxyrhynchus papyrus

. . .

210 *P.Oxy.* 2171 fr. 7.1–11

```
        .    .    .
        ....[
        καιτ[
        ].θαν[
        ελλα[
    5   ηδυ[
        παιδ[
        φη.[
        ϊε.[
        δ΄λ[
   10   σευχ[
        ..].μ[
        .    .    .
```

211 *P.Oxy.* 2171 fr. 8.1–7

```
        .    .    .
        ].[
        μητ.[
        πολλα.[
        πολλα[
    5   πλεις[
        καιμε[
        ...ε.κ[
        .    .    .
```

210 Oxyrhynchus papyrus
and yet . . . sweet . . . child

211 Oxyrhynchus papyrus
nor . . . many . . . many . . . the most . . . and

212 *P.Oxy.* 2171 fr. 9.1–6

. . . .
```
    ].ω[
  ...]ϊκῶ[
  εινὲμη[
  ]λεγξε[.].[.]..[
5 Ναξίᾳ .[΄]..[
  .]ηγωπροτασ.[
```
. . . .

213 *P.Oxy.* 2171 fr. 10.1–12

. . .
```
   ]π[
   ]   [
  ]οιπυλα[
  ']ανοὺ.[
5 ]θαλα.[
    ].[
  ]κεινη[
  ].υλη[
  ]αιφα[
10 ]ωιδ.[
    ]ηνδ[
    ]..[
```
. . . .

212 Oxyrhynchus papyrus
[5] . . . Naxia

213 Oxyrhynchus papyrus
[7] . . . that

214 *P.Oxy.* 2171 fr. 11

```
 .   .   .   .   .
        ]
    ]ν δέκα χ[
        ισο[
 .   .   .   .   .
```

215 Choerob. *Schol. in Hephaest.* (p. 230.20 Consbruch) s.v. ληκύθιον

ληκύθιον· ἰστέον δὲ ὅτι τοὺς τραγικοὺς ληκύθους ἐκά-
λουν, ὅθεν καὶ Καλλίμαχός φησιν,

   ἥτις τραγῳδὸς μοῦσα ληκυθίζουσα

216 *Et. Gen.* AB s.v. ἀλίβας

ἀλίβας· ὁ νεκρός παρὰ τὸ μὴ ἔχειν λιβάδα μήτε θερ-
μότητα, ὅ ἐστιν ὑγρότητα. οἱ γὰρ ζῶντες ὑγροί. ση-
μαίνει δὲ καὶ ὄξος ὡς παρὰ Καλλιμάχῳ,

   ἔβηξαν οἷον[1] ἀλίβαντα πίνοντες

   [1] οἷον *Et. Gen, Et. Mag.*: ἔβηξαν οἶνον *Et. M.* cod. Dorv.

217 *Et. Gen.* AB s.v. Κεραίτης

Κεραίτης· τόπος Μιλήτου ἀπὸ τοῦ τὸν Ἀπόλλωνα
κέρατα τοῦ ἄρρενος τράγου ἀμελγομένου ὑπ᾽ αὐτοῦ
πῆξαι ἐκεῖ, ὡς Καλλίμαχος ἐν Ἰάμβοις.

214 Oxyrhynchus papyrus

. . . ten

215 Choeroboscus on Hephaestion

lēkythion: one should understand that they called oil flasks tragic, from this Callimachus says,

> whatever tragic Muse speaking as if into an oil flask[1]

[1] Of hollow or bombastic speech (cf. Ar. *Ran.* 1208–48, where oil flasks are associated comically with the style of Euripides' prologues).

216 *Etymologicum Genuinum*

alibas (dead wine): a corpse has neither dampness nor heat which is moist; the living are wet. It means vinegar as in Callimachus,

> they coughed like vinegar drinkers[1]

[1] Also found in Hipponax (134 W.).

217 *Etymologicum Genuinum*

Ceraites: a place in Miletus, from Apollo's driving in the horns of a goat that he attempted to milk. So Callimachus in the *Iambi*.

CALLIMACHUS

218 *Et. Gen.* B s.v. ὄβδην

ὄβδην· ἐπίρρημά ἐστι μεσότητος ἀπὸ τοῦ ὦμμαι
ὄβδην, ὡς ἀπὸ τοῦ ἔστηκα στάδην. συνέστειλε τὸ ω
εἰς ο.

Μούσῃ γὰρ ἦλθον εἰς ὄβδην

219 Schol. V ad Ar. *Av.* 129

πρῴ ἴσον τῷ ἐν ὥρᾳ. τοῦ πρωΐ συναίρεσίς ἐστι τὸ
πρῴ. διὸ ὀξύνεται· τὸ δὲ πρῶν περισπᾶται, Καλλίμα-
χος,

οὐ πρῶν μὲν ἡμῖν ὁ τραγῳδὸς ἤγειρε

220 *Et. Gen.* AB s.v. κόχλος

κόχλος· ὡς παρὰ τὸ ἱερὸς γίνεται ἱέραξ καὶ νέος νέαξ,
ὡς παρὰ Καλλιμάχῳ,

καὶ τῶν νεήκων εὐθὺς οἱ τομώτατοι

221 *Et. Gen.* B s.v. ὦ τᾶν

ὦ τᾶν· σὺ ἑταῖρε· λέγεται καὶ ἐπ' εἰρωνείας· ὡς παρὰ
τὸ μέγιστος μεγιστᾶν καὶ Ἑρμῆς Ἑρμᾶν καὶ Ἑρμᾶν
ἀτρεκέως· καὶ Καλλίμαχος,

αἰτοῦμεν εὐμάθειαν Ἑρμᾶνος δόσιν

218 *Etymologicum Genuinum*

obdēn is an adverb, from the middle perfect *ōmmai* like *stadēn* from [the perfect] *estēka*. The omega shortens to omicron.

> For they came into the Muses' sight.

219 Scholia to Aristophanes, *Birds*

prōi: the same as *en (h)ōra*. It is a contraction of *to prōi*. Therefore it has an acute accent. *To prōin* has a circumflex, as in Callimachus,

> not early for us did tragedy arise

220 *Etymologicum Genuinum*

kochlos (mussel): like *(h)ierax* comes from *(h)ieros*, *neax* comes from *neos*, as in Callimachus,

> At once the sharpest of the youth . . .

221 *Etymologicum Genuinum*

Ō tān: O you comrade; it is meant ironically, like *megistān* from *megistos* and *(H)ermān* from *(H)ermes*, and Callimachus,

> We ask from Hermes the gift of easy learning.[1]

[1] Cf. Call. *Epig.* 48, where a similar request is made to the Muses by Simus the son of Miccus.

519

222 Schol. BD ad Pind. *Isth*. 2.9

οὐδ' ἐργάτις, ὅ ἐστιν αἰτοῦσα μισθὸν ἐφ' οἷς ἔπρατ-
τεν· ἔνθεν καὶ Καλλίμαχός φησιν,

οὐ γὰρ ἐργάτιν τρέφω
τὴν Μοῦσαν, ὡς ὁ Κεῖος Ὑλίχου νέπους

223 Steph. Byz. α 356 Billerbeck s.v. Ἀπέσας

Ἀπέσας· ὄρος τῆς Νεμέας . . . ἀφ' οὗ Ζεὺς Ἀπεσά-
ντιος. Καλλίμαχος δὲ ἐν τοῖς Ἰάμβοις τὸ ἐθνικὸν
Ἀπέσας φησί,

κοὐχ ὧδ' Ἀρίων τὠπέσαντι πὰρ Διί
ἔθυσεν Ἀρκὰς ἵππος

224 Eust. ad *Od*. 9.246 (fr. 53, p. 206 Nauck)

ὁ Καλλίμαχος ἔφη γράψας, τῷ . . . δόκῳ, ἤγουν τῇ
ἐμῇ δοκήσει.

τῷ γ' ἐμῷ δόκῳ

225 *Et. Gen*. B s.v. Εὐκολίνη

Εὐκολίνη· ἡ Ἑκάτη λέγεται παρὰ Καλλ. κατ' ἀντί-
φρασιν, οἰονεὶ ἡ μὴ οὖσα εὐχέρής·

χαῖρ' Εὐκολίνη

222 Scholia to Pindar, *Isthmian Odes*

Not a worker [Muse] who is asking pay for what he has made. From this even Callimachus says,

> I do not nourish a worker-muse like the Cean child of Hylichus.[1]

[1] That is, Simonides (cf. Schol. BD ad Pind. *Isth*. 2.9; Schol. ad Ar. *Av*. 697c–e; Xenoph. 21 W.).

223 Stephanus of Byzantium

Apesas:[1] a mountain of Nemea . . . from which comes the epithet Zeus Apesantius. Callimachus mentions the ethnic Apesas in the *Iambi*,

> Not in this way did Arion,[2] the swift horse, offer sacrifice to Zeus Apesantius

[1] Cf. Paus. 2.15.3. Here Apesas alludes to a horserace held to celebrate the death of Opheltes and the founding of the Nemean games.   [2] The horse of Adrastus (Hom. *Il*. 23.346–48).

224 Eustathius on Homer, *Odyssey*

Callimachus said in his writings, *tōi . . . dokōi*, that is to say, in my opinion.

> in my opinion

225 *Etymologicum Genuinum*

Eucoline (Contented One): Hecate is called this by Callimachus euphemistically, as if she were not dangerous:

> hail, Contented One

LYRIC POEMS

INTRODUCTION

GENERAL FEATURES

Following the *Iambi*, the *Diegeseis* include brief summaries of four poems in lyric meters (*Mel.* 226–29). No title for the group is indicated there or in any quotations from ancient sources, so Pfeiffer suggested that they are the *Melē* (i.e., *Lyric Poems*), a title that he found in a list of Callimachus' works in the *Suda*.[1] Two of these lyrics are cited individually by title in ancient sources: *Pannychis* (*Mel.* 227, "All-night Festival"; Ath. 15.668c) and *Branchus* (*Mel.* 229; Hephaest. p. 30 Consbruch). Pfeiffer supplied the other two with individual titles from the *Diegeseis*: *Pros tous horaious* (*Mel.* 226, "To Young Men")[2] and *Ektheosis Arsinoes* (*Mel.* 228, "The Apotheosis of Arsinoe"). All four have apparently stichic meters, including phalaecean (*Mel.* 226); euripidean, i.e., iambic dimeter + ithyphallic (*Mel.* 227); archebulean (*Mel.* 228); and catalectic choriambic pentameter (*Mel.* 229). The contents are equally varied: *Mel.* 226 is an admonition to enjoy youth, citing the fate of ancient Lemnos as an example of

[1] Cf. T 1.
[2] On the unlikelihood that this is an ancient title, see D'Alessio 2007, vol. 2, 656n2.

what can go wrong; *Mel.* 227 is a choral evocation of a festival or a symposium with erotic overtones; *Mel.* 228 is a lament for the death of Queen Arsinoe II; and *Mel.* 229 celebrates both the founder and the foundation of Apollo's oracular shrine at Didyma. Although the extant verses are few and the *Diegeseis'* summaries are brief, it is possible to find some thematic connections among these four lyric poems and links to some of Callimachus' other works.[3]

RELATIONSHIP WITH THE *IAMBI*

Seventeen poems separate the *Aetia* and the *Hecale* in the *Diegeseis*, marking the end of the *Aetia* (6a/b) with a *sub-scriptio*, but this provides no title for the *Iambi* that follow.[4] Nor is there a *subscriptio* after *Iamb* 13 (*Ia.* 203–203a) to mark the conclusion of the *Iambi*, though a new column begins at this point (*Dieg.* 10.1). Since the author of the *Diegeseis* has not clearly marked the endpoint of the *Iambi*, it is possible that all seventeen poems were included under this rubric, as some have argued.[5]

   Evidence to the contrary includes meter, contents, and editorial factors. The meters of *Mel.* 226–29, especially 228 and 229, are lyrical and have no parallels in the *Iambi*,

---

   [3] For example, Acosta-Hughes (2003, 482–84) argues that the four *Melē* recall the four books of the *Aetia*.

   [4] Though no title is provided, the *Diegeseis* (6.1) start a new column at the beginning of the *Iambi*. Unlike *P.Oxy.* 1011, which provides titles for the *Aetia* and the *Iambi*, the *Diegeseis* include a title only for the *Hecale*.

   [5] For example, Gallavotti 1946; Cameron 1995, 163–73; Lelli 2005, 1–27.

despite their metrical variety. The contents, too, are not at home among iambic poems, which by definition are eristic in character. It is hard, for example, to imagine *The Apotheosis of Arsinoe*, who was an important Ptolemaic queen and patron of the poet, in an iambic context, especially since the poem includes the *aition* of her royal cult.[6] There is also the matter of titles: individual *Iambi* are cited by ancient scholars by their collective title,[7] but *Mel.* 227 and 229 are each cited by an individual title. The third and most powerful argument for thirteen *Iambi* plus four other poems is provided by the *Iambi* themselves. They are a tightly organized ensemble of poems with careful orchestration of meter, dialect, and form, featuring a programmatic beginning that summons Hipponax, a literary predecessor, in his signature choliambic meter (*Ia.* 191) and a similarly programmatic conclusion in the same meter referring to the same predecessor (*Ia.* 203). While these arguments are strong, there is no way to determine the poet's intention on the available evidence. Nonetheless, Acosta-Hughes is surely correct that whatever the poet called these poems, their placement following the *Iambi* associates the seventeen poems closely, and affects how they are read.[8]

[6] Similarly, Cameron (1995, 171–72) suggests that *Mel.* 229 celebrates the Ptolemaic refoundation of Apollo's shrine at Didyma, hardly a subject for *iambi*.

[7] *Iambi* 1, 4, 5, 6, 8, 10, 11, and 13 are all cited in this way: "Callimachus in the *Iambi* (or *Choliambi*)."

[8] Acosta-Hughes 2003, 488–89. That Horace's *Epodes* contain seventeen poems suggests that the Roman poet, at least, regarded the thirteen *Iambi* and four *Melē* as a unit; see Introduction to *Iambi*.

CONSTITUTION OF THE TEXT

The *Melē* are preserved in a few quotations from ancient sources and in three badly fragmented papyri. The only text of *Mel.* 226 is the lemma provided by the *Diegeseis* (*Dieg.* 10.1–5). Seven fragmentary lines of *Mel.* 227 were published in 1912 (*P.Berol.* 13417b, with scholia) by Wilamowitz, who also edited *P.Berol.* 13417a with seventy-five partial verses of *Mel.* 228. Later, twenty-four fragmentary lines of *Mel.* 229 were published by Lobel as *P.Oxy.* 2172 in 1941. Pfeiffer put together the first modern critical text, followed by D'Alessio (1996; 4th ed. 2007), Asper (2004), and Lelli (2005).

CATALOG OF PAPYRI

The list of relevant papyri below follows the numbering and order of Mertens-Pack[3], the online database of the Centre de documentation de papyrologie littéraire (CEDOPAL) at the Université de Liège, which provides additional information and bibliography.[9] Each entry begins with the inventory number assigned by Mertens-Pack[3], followed by the series name in standard abbreviations, the number in Pfeiffer, its estimated date, and the verses in the *Melē* that it supplies.

00201.000: *P.Oxy.* 2168 (+ *P.Berol.* inv. 16629a–b + *P.Berol.* inv. 13417a–b + *PSI* 122). Pap. 32 Pf. 3rd c. AD. *Mel.* 227, 228.

[9] Additional information about the papyri can also be found in Pf. vol. 2, ix–xxvi; *SH*, pp. 89–122; Lelli 2005; Lehnus 2011, 23–38; Asper, 537–39.

00211.000: *P.Mil.Vogl.* inv. 1006 (+ *P.Mil.Vogl.* 1.18 + *P.Mil.Vogl.* inv. 28b). Pap. 8 Pf. 1st–2nd c. AD. *Dieg.* in *Mel.* 226–29.

00222.000: *PSI* 1216 (+ *P.Oxy.* 2171 + *P.Oxy.* 2172). Pap. 7 Pf. 1st–2nd c. AD. *Mel.* 229.

BIBLIOGRAPHY

Acosta-Hughes, Benjamin. "Aesthetics and Recall: Callimachus frs. 226–9 Pf. Reconsidered." *Classical Quarterly* 53 (2003): 478–89.

Acosta-Hughes, Benjamin, and S. Stephens. "Callimachean 'Lyric.'" *Trends in Classics* 9 (2017): 226–47.

Barber, Eric A., and Paul Maas. "Callimachea." *Classical Quarterly* 44 (1950): 96 and 168.

Lelli, Immanuel, ed. *Callimachi: Iambi XIV–XVII.* Rome: In aedibus Athenaei, 2005.

[ΜΕΛΗ?]

[ΠΡΟΣ ΤΟΥΣ ΩΡΑΙΟΥΣ?]

226 (14 Lelli) *Dieg.* 10.1

ἡ Λῆμνος τὸ παλαιόν, εἴ τις ἄλλη

226a *Dieg.* 10.1–5

ἡ Λῆμνος τὸ παλαιόν, εἴ τις ἄλλη

Πρὸς τοὺς ὡραίους φησίν· ἡ Λῆμνος πάλαι ποτὲ
εὐδαίμων γενομένη ἐκακοδαιμόνησε, ἐπιθεμένων τῶν
θηλειῶν τοῖς ἄρρεσιν· διόπερ καὶ ὑμεῖς [5] εἰς τὸ μέλ-
λον ἀποβλέπετε.

[LYRIC POEMS?]

This title Pfeiffer took from a list of Callimachus' works in the *Suda* (T 1).

[TO YOUNG MEN (?)]

This title Pfeiffer took from the *Diegeseis* (226a).

226 *Diegeseis*

Ancient Lemnos,[1] if any other

[1] An island in the northern Aegean off the coast of Thrace, associated in myth with Hephaestus (see below), Philoctetes, and the episode referred to here, when the Lemnian women murdered their husbands who had rejected them for the women of Thrace. The story is told by Apollonius (Ap. Rhod. 1.609–632).

226a *Diegeseis*

Ancient Lemnos, if any other

He says to the youths: Lemnos in antiquity was once fortunate, but suffered misfortune when the women inflicted punishment on the men. Therefore even you should look to the future.

ΠΑΝΝΥΧΙΣ

227 (15 Lelli) Inscr. ap. Ath. 15.668c; 1, *Dieg.* 10.6; 3–9,
P.Berol. 13417b, 1–13

Ἔνεστ᾽ Ἀπόλλων τῷ χορῷ· τῆς λύρης ἀκούω·
καὶ τῶν Ἐρώτων ᾐσθόμην· ἔστι κἀφροδίτη.

.   .   .   .   .   .   ]την[. . .]λ[

θυμηδίην τ[   ]δεῦτε παννυχ[

5 ὁ δ᾽ ἀγρυπνήσας [συνεχὲς]¹ μέχρι τῆς κο[ρώνης
τὸν πυραμοῦντα λήψεται, καὶ τὰ κοττ᾽άβεια
καὶ τῶν παρ᾽ουσῶν ἣν θέλει, χὧν θέλει ᾽φιλήσει.²
ὦ Κάστορ [   ] καὶ σὺ Πωλύδ[ευκες
καὶ τῶν ἀο[   ] καὶ ξενω.[

¹ Suppl. Pfeiffer   ² 6–7 suppl. Wilamowitz ex Ath. 15.668c

227a *Dieg.* 10.6–9

Ἔνεστ᾽ Ἀπόλλων τῷ χορῷ

Παροίνιον εἰς τοὺς Διοσκούρους· καὶ Ἑλένην ὑμνεῖ,
καὶ παρακλεῖ τὴν θυσίαν δέξασθαι· καὶ προτροπὴ
τοῖς συμπόταις εἰς τὸ ἀγρυπνεῖν.

ALL-NIGHT FESTIVAL

227 Athenaeus, *The Learned Banqueters* (attribution); *Diegeseis*; Berlin papyrus

Apollo is in the chorus. I hear the lyre. And I sense the Erotes,[1] and Aphrodite is here.

. . . .[2]

Come here to the all-night festival that pleases the heart! [5] The one who has stayed up continually until the "crow"[3] will take up the sweet cake and the prize for the cottabus,[4] and he will kiss whichever girl he wishes and whichever boy he wishes of those present. O Castor . . . and you Polydeuces[5] . . . and of the guests

[1] Winged love gods associated with Aphrodite (Eur. *Bacch.* 402–5). [2] A gap of uncertain length. [3] A metaphor for something that curves back, that is, the conclusion of something (Lucian, *De mort. Per.* 33). In this case the all-night festival concludes with the dawn (D'Alessio 2007, vol. 2, 658n6).

[4] A game with many variations played at symposia (Ath. 15.665d–68f). [5] Castor and Polydeuces are the Dioscuri (Gemini), sons of Zeus (or Tyndareus) and Leda, and brothers of Helen. They were key members of the Ptolemaic pantheon (Theoc. *Id.* 22).

227a *Diegeseis*

Apollo is in the chorus

He sings a prologue to the Dioscuri and Helen, and he asks them to accept the sacrifice. And there is encouragement to the revelers to stay up all night.

[ΕΚΘΕΩΣΙΣ ΑΡΣΙΝΟΗΣ]

228 (16 Lelli) Inscr. *Dieg.* 10.10–11; 1–38, *P.Berol.*
13417a recto, 1–38; 39–75, *P.Berol.* 13417a verso, 39–75

Ἀγέτω θεός, οὐ γὰρ ἐγὼ δίχ‚α τῶνδ' ἀείδειν
        π]ροποδεῖν Ἀπόλλων
        ]κεν δυναίμαν
        κατ]ὰ χεῖρα βᾶσαι.
5 ‚νύμφα, σὺ μὲν ἀστερίαν ὑ‚π' ἄμαξαν ἤδη
    κλεπτομέν]α[1] παρέθεις σελάνᾳ
        ] ἀτενεῖς ὀδυρμοί
        ] μία τοῦτο φωνά
    ἀμετέρα][2] βασίλεια φροῦδα
10   τ]ί παθὼν ἀπέσβη;
    ἁ δ]ὲ χύδαν ἐδίδασκε λύπα
        ] ‚μέγας γαμέτας ὁμεύνῳ
        ]αν πρόθεσιν πῦρ' αἴθειν
        ] λεπτὸν ὕδωρ
15   Θέτ]ιδος τὰ πέραια βωμῶν
        ]‚[‚‚]ωδε Θήβα .
                ]. ας
σὺ δὲ καὶ]   ]η·
                ]φερτα
20   ]. θη·
            τ]όλμας
                ]α·
            ]ρειδης·

[THE APOTHEOSIS OF ARSINOE]

Pfeiffer took this title from the *Diegeseis* (228a). The subject is Arsinoe II, wife and sister of Ptolemy II Philadelphus, both patrons of Callimachus. The date of her death is uncertain, likely July 268 or 270 BC (Carney 2013, 104).

228 *Diegeseis*; Berlin papyrus

Let the god lead, for I [do not wish] to sing apart from them . . . Apollo to lead the dance . . . May I be able . . . to step [as he gestures with] his hand.[1] [5] Bride, snatched away already under the starry wagon[2] you speed beside the moon . . . strained laments . . . one voice said this . . . our queen is gone . . . [10] suffering what? . . . she has perished . . . overflowing grief taught . . . the great husband for his wife . . . to kindle fire as an offering . . . a little water . . . [15] before the altars of Thetis[3] . . . Thebes . . .

---

[1] Apollo is apparently conducting the dancing chorus.

[2] The constellation Ursa Major (*Ia.* 1.54–55; Arat. *Phaen.* 27), very near the location of the Coma Berenices.   [3] A sea nymph, mother of Achilles, who leads a chorus of Nereids in mourning for Patroclus (Hom *Il.* 18.35–64) and so is a suitable participant in a dirge for Arsinoe, who became a minor sea deity herself. Thetis cared for Hephaestus when Hera threw him out of Olympus (Hom. *Il.* 18.395–409).

---

[1] Suppl. Wilamowitz ex Schol.   [2] Suppl. Pfeiffer

```
                                  ν]ύμφας
25                                ]πλοις
                                  ]αι
                                  ]ει·
        στόματ᾽ οἷς               ]ου
                                  ]
30                                ]ας
                                  ]αντῶν
                                  ]βας
                                  ]μον·
                       ] πόλις ἄλλ[α] τευξεῖ·
35                     ]φέρει θάλα[σσ]αν
                       ]ᾶ παναγὴς ε.[...]ς·
                       ]ν τὰ τάλαντα [....]η·
                       ]ων τὰ καλὰ πτ[....]ᾶ
    Πρωτῆϊ μὲν ὧδ᾽ ἐτύμοι κατάγο[ντο φᾶμαι.
40  σαμάντριαν ἃ δὲ πυρᾶς ἐνόησ᾽ ἰ[ωάν,
    ἃν οὖλα κυλινδομέναν ἐδίωκ[ον αὖραι
    ⟨. . . . . . . .⟩
    ἠδ᾽ ἂμ μέσα Θρηϊκίου κατὰ νῶτα [πόντου
    Φιλωτέρα· ἄρτι γάρ οἱ Σικελὰ μὲν Ἔνν‿α
    κατελείπετο, Λαμνιακοὶ δ᾽ ἐπατεῦ[ντο³
45  Δηοῦς ἄπο νεισομένα· σέο δ᾽ ἦν ἄπ[υστος
    ὦ δαίμοσιν ἁρπαγίμα, φάτο δ᾽ ἡμιδ[
    "ἕζευ Χάρι τὰν ὑπά[τ]αν ἐπ᾽ Ἄθω κολώ[ναν,
    ἀπὸ δ᾽ αὔγασαι, ἐκ πεδίου τὰ πύρ᾽ αἱ σαπ[
    τ]ίς ἀπώλετο, τίς πολίων ὁλόκαυτος α[ἴθει.
50  ἔνι μοι φόβος· ἀλλὰ ποτεῦ· νότος αὐ[
```

and you . . . [21] audacity . . . [24] brides . . . [28] mouths with which . . . the city will build other things . . . [35] carries . . . the sea . . . all-hallowed . . . the scales . . . lovely things . . .

In this way true reports were brought down to Proteus.[4] [40] Philotera[5] noticed the blast, the sign of fire, which the breezes chased as it rolled around in a spiral . . .

and against the mid-back of the Thracian Sea . . . For just now she had left Sicilian Enna,[6] and was hiking in the Lemnian Hills [45] coming from Deo.[7] And she was uninformed about you, O snatched by the gods, and said, "Charis,[8] sit on the height of Mt. Athos[9] and see if the fire is coming from the plain . . . Which city has perished? Which city glows completely burned? [50] I am afraid. But

---

[4] Prophetic old man of the sea who lived on the island of Pharos, off the coast of Alexandria (Hom. *Od.* 4.384–93).

[5] Sister of Ptolemy Philadelphus and Arsinoe II, who never married and predeceased them both. This poem is evidence of her deification.

[6] A site sacred to Demeter (*Hymn* 6.30).

[7] Demeter (*Hymn* 6.17, 132).

[8] Charis, wife of Hephaestus (Hom. *Il.* 18.382–83).

[9] Mountain in northeastern Greece (Hom. *Il.* 14.229).

---

3 βουνοί suppl. Wilamowitz

νότος αἴθριος· ἦρά τι μοι Λιβύα κα[κοῦται;"
τάδ' ἔφα· θεός ἀλλ' ὁπότε σκοπιὰν ἐπ[έπτα
χιονώδεα, τὰν ἀπέχειν ἐλάχιστ[ον ἄρκτου⁴
ἧκει λόγος, ἐς δὲ Φάρου περίσαμο[ν ἀκτάν
55 ἐσκέψατο, θυμολιπὴς ἐβόα[σε
"ναὶ ναὶ μέγα δή τ̣[ι
ἁ λίγνυς ἀφ' ὑμετ[έρας⁵
ἃ δ' ἤνεπε ταῦτα [
τάν μοι πόλιν ᾇ με[
60 κείρουσιν· ὃ δ' ἐς φιλι[
πόσις ᾤχετο πενθερ[
ἄκουσά τε Μακροβίω[ν
ὄφρα δύσποδας ὥς ἑ π[
θ]εὸς ἔδραμεν· αὐτίκ[α
65 ἡξεῖ δόμον." ἁ μὲν [
οὐκ ἤδεε· τᾷ δὲ Χάρ[ις⁶
"μή μοι χθονός—οὐχὶ [⁷
περικλαίεο· μηδέ τ̣ι[
ἄλλα μέ τις οὐκ ἀγαθ[ὰ⁸
70 θρῆνοι πόλιν ὑμετέρ[αν
οὐχ ὡς ἐπὶ δαμοτ[έρων
χθών· ἀλλά τι τῶ[ν] μεγάλων ἐ̣[,
τάν τοι μίαν οἰχομ[ένα]ν ὁμόδελφυν [αὐτάν
κλαίοντι· τὰ δ' ᾇ[κεν ἴ]δῃς, μέλαν [ἀμφίεσται
75 χθονὸς ἄστεα· ν̣[ωϊτ]έρων τὸ κρᾳτ[

---

⁴ Suppl. Wilamowitz
⁵ πόλιος φορεῖται." suppl. Wilamowitz

fly off. The south wind . . . the airy south wind. But is my Libya[10] being harmed in some way?" The goddess spoke. And when she had flown onto the snow-covered peak which word has it is nearest to the polestar, she surveyed the famous coast of Pharos, [55] and faint-of-heart she cried, "Yes, yes. Something [terrible] . . . thick smoke is coming from your [city]," she said these things . . . the city where [60] they cut [their hair in mourning]. And her spouse[11] went to his dear mother-in-law[12] . . . and hearing . . . from the Ethiopians[13] so that . . . slow of foot as . . . the god ran. And at once [65] he will reach home."

She did not know. But Charis said this heavy word to her, "Not by my land—nor . . . should you weep. Not any . . . nor does any good . . . [70] laments [fill] your city nor does the land . . . as if it were for someone of lower rank. But weeping for someone of the great ones, your only sister coming from the same womb, and the [75] cities of the land whichever you see are swathed in black. Our strength

---

[10] Here standing for the whole coast of North Africa, including Alexandria. [11] Hephaestus, the husband of Charis.
[12] Eurynome, the mother of Charis, who assisted Thetis in the rescue of Hephaestus (Hom. *Il.* 18.395–409).
[13] The "long-lived" (e.g., Hdt. 3.23; see Lelli 2005, 191).

---

6 βαρὺν εἶπε μῦθον·, suppl. Wilamowitz
7 τεὰ Φάρος ἀθάλωται—, suppl. Wilamowitz
8 φάτις οὔαθ᾽ ἥκει., suppl. Wilamowitz

228a *Dieg.* 10.10–13

Ἀγέτω θεός, οὐ γὰρ ἐγὼ δίχα τῶνδ' ἀείδειν

Ἐκθέωσις Ἀρσινόης· φησὶν δὲ αὐτὴν ἀνηρπάσθαι
ὑπὸ τῶν Διοσκούρων καὶ βωμὸν καὶ τέμενος αὐτῆς
καθιδρῦσθαι πρὸς τῷ Ἐμπορίῳ.

ΒΡΑΓΧΟΣ

229 (17 Lelli) Inscr. ap. Hephaest. (p. 30 Consbruch); 1,
Dieg. 10.14; 2–23, *P.Oxy.* 2172, fr. 1–22

Δαίμονες εὐυμνότατοι, Φοῖβέ τε καὶ Ζεῦ, Διδύμων γε-
νάρχα

     .   .   .   .   .   .

   τετρ]απ͙οδων[1] λοιμὸς ἐπέλθῃ κατάρατος ἄρπαξ,
   ]ωτρίσεμο χ μεν[ ]λείτας ἀπό κεν τράποιτο
μῆλα δ' ὑπ' εὐ]ηπε[λ]ιης π[ε]ίονα χλωρὴν βοτάνην
   νέμοιτο
5   ] ι [ ] ἑτέρ[ῳ] τῆσδε μελέσθω· [σὺ] δὲ καὶ
                         προπάππων
   ]οδ κ[ ]υσλ [ ]θιν ὁμαρτεῖν· ἐτ[εὸ]ν γάρ ἐστιν
   ]σοι πατρόθεν τῶν ἀπὸ Δαίτε[ω], τὸ δὲ πρὸς
                         τεκούσης

----

[1] τετρα- Lobel, Trypanis: εἰλ[ι]- Barber, Maas

228a *Diegeseis*

Let the god lead, for I [do not wish] to sing apart
from them

The Apotheosis of Arsinoe. He says that she was snatched
by the Dioscuri and that her altar and sacred precinct
were established near the Emporion.[1]

[1] Philadelphus also built her a mortuary temple with a mag-
netized roof and an iron statue of her that appeared to be sus-
pended in midair (Plin. *HN* 34.148).

BRANCHUS

229 Hephaestion (attribution); *Diegeseis*; Oxyrhynchus
papyrus

Gods best-hymned, Phoebus and Zeus, founders of
Didyma[1]

.   .   .   .

Let the accursed, rapacious plague not come upon the
livestock . . . oh three times [beloved] by me, and may it
be turned away . . . and may the flock fattened by prosper-
ity graze on green pasture . . . [5] and may this be the care
of another. And you, from your great-grandfathers . . . to
accompany. For it is true that you are well-born, from your
father [you are descended] from Daites[2] and from your

[1] Didyma, near Miletus, was the site of an oracle and temple
of Apollo. It was destroyed by the Persians in 494 BC and rebuilt
by Seleucus I (Strabo 14.1.5). Bathycles' son finds Thales there
in *Iamb* 1 (*Ia.* 191.51–52)   [2] The son of Machaereus, a
priest of Apollo at Delphi, who killed Neoptolemus, the son of
Achilles (Strabo 9.3.9).

].Λαπίθην α[...].δ.κειομ.[.] εὐγένει[α]ν.[2]
Φοῖβε, σὺ μὲν] το[ιά]δ᾿ ἔφη[ς· το]ῦ δ᾿ἐπὶ δώ[ροις][3]
 ἀνέπαλτ[ο θ]υμός·
10 αὐτίκα δή τοι τέμ[ε]ν[ο]ς [κα]λὸν[4] ἐν ὕλη, τόθι
  πρῶτον ὤφθης,
 κρην]έων δ[ιδύ]μων ἐγγύθι δάφνης κατὰ κλῶνα
  πήξας.
 χαῖρε δὲ [5]Δελφ]ίνι᾿ ἄ[ν]αξ, οὔν[ο]μα γά[ρ] τοι τόδ᾿
  ἐγὼ κατάρχω,
 εἵνεκεν Οἰκούσ]ιον[6] εἰς ἄ[σ]τυ σε δελφὶς ἀπ᾿
  ἔβησε Δήλου,
 ].[.].[.].[.......]α τιμᾷ, μετὰ δ᾿ ἂψ [ἐ]ς ἄλλον
15]υμω[ ]ον Ὀλύμπ[ο]υ θυόεν[τα] νηόν
 ]ουσο.[φ]ιλήτωρ .[.].εξε Φο[ῖ]βο[ς
    ]ατ᾿ ἀνάκτων ἱερὴν γενέθλην
       ]ρις ἕξει
       ]αστηρ
20   ]αρησμ.·
       ]π.·
       ].αοιδη[
       ]ναι.

[2] εὐγένειαν Barber, Maas: εὐγένειον Lobel, Pfeiffer
[3] Suppl. Barber, Maas [4] Suppl. Lobel [5] χαῖρε δὲ
Pfeiffer: ἴλαθι δὲ Lobel: εἴλαθι Barber, Maas [6] εἵνεκεν
Οἰκούσ]ιο Pfeiffer: οὔνεκα Μιλήσ]ιον Lobel

mother, Lapithes.[3] [Phoebus, you said such things.] And
his heart leapt at the gifts . . . [10] at once a lovely precinct
in the woods, where first you[4] were seen near the double
fountains after inserting the branch of the laurel. Delphin-
ian Lord, I begin with this name for you, for a dolphin
went with you from Delos into the city [of Oecus][5] . . .
honor, then again to another . . . [15] the fragrant temple
of Olympus . . . lover . . . Phoebus . . . the holy race of kings
. . . he will have . . . song

[3] Son of Apollo and Stilbe (Diod. Sic. 4.69.1).
[4] Apollo at Delphi.
[5] Miletus, if the supplement is correct.

229a *Dieg.* 10.14–17

Δαίμονες εὐυμνότατοι, Φοῖβέ τε καὶ Ζεῦ,
Διδύμω[ν] γενάρχα

Ἀπ[ό]λλων ἐκ Δήλου ἀφικνεῖται εἰς τὸ Μιλήτου χω-
ρίον ὃ καλεῖται ἱερὰ ὕλη, ἵνα Βράγχος.

229a *Diegeseis*

Gods best-hymned, Phoebus and Zeus, founders of
Didyma

Apollo arrives from Delos in the area of Miletus which is
called the Sacred Wood, where Branchus was.[1]

[1] A shepherd with whom Apollo falls in love and gives the gift
of prophecy along with a shoot of his own laurel tree (Conon,
Narr. 33; *BNJ* 26 F 1). He also healed the Ionians by shaking the
sacred laurel at them and saying some mystic words in *Iamb* 4 (*Ia.*
194.28–31).